Language Invention in Linguistics Pedagogy

"Linguists consider their object of study as part of the natural world. But language is also something we can create. The contributions in this book show how an emphasis on the artificial rather than the natural can help create enthusiasm about linguistics and insight into language, among school children and university students alike."

Marc van Oostendorp, Royal Netherlands
Academy of Arts and Sciences and Radboud University Nijmegen

"This lively volume from well-respected conlangers, teachers, and linguists convincingly makes the case that invented languages can be used as a creative pedagogical tool to introduce students to linguistics. The chapters argue that conlanging in the classroom will allow us to reach a broader student population and better train budding linguists."

Eric Potsdam, University of Florida

Language Invention in Linguistics Pedagogy

Edited by
JEFFREY PUNSKE, NATHAN SANDERS,
AND AMY V. FOUNTAIN

OXFORD
UNIVERSITY PRESS

OXFORD
UNIVERSITY PRESS

Great Clarendon Street, Oxford, OX2 6DP,
United Kingdom

Oxford University Press is a department of the University of Oxford.
It furthers the University's objective of excellence in research, scholarship,
and education by publishing worldwide. Oxford is a registered trade mark of
Oxford University Press in the UK and in certain other countries

© editorial matter and organization Jeffrey Punske,
Nathan Sanders, and Amy V. Fountain 2020
© the chapters their several authors 2020

The moral rights of the authors have been asserted

First Edition published in 2020

Impression: 1

Published in the United States of America by Oxford University Press
198 Madison Avenue, New York, NY 10016, United States of America

British Library Cataloguing in Publication Data
Data available

Library of Congress Control Number: 2020932171

ISBN 978–0–19–882987–4 (hbk.)
ISBN 978–0–19–882988–1 (pbk.)

Printed and bound by
CPI Group (UK) Ltd, Croydon, CR0 4YY

Contents

List of Figures

List of Tables

List of Abbreviations

[±ant]	[±anterior] feature
[±cont]	[±continuant] feature
[±cor]	[±coronal] feature
[±lab]	[±labial] feature
1	first-person
2	second-person
3	third-person
A	subject of transitive verb
ABS	absolutive
ACC	accusative
ADESS	adessive
Adj	adjective
ALM	Audiolingual Method
alv	alveolar
AP	antipassive
AUX	auxiliary
AY	academic year
BCI	Blissymbolics Communication International
bilab	bilabial
C	consonant
CCH	Cross-Category Harmony
CGI	computer-generated imagery
CLPE	Centre for Literacy in Primary Education
DAT	dative
DEF	definite
DEM	demonstrative
dent	dental
DP	determiner phrase
DU	dual
ERG	ergative
ET	extraterrestrial
F1	first vowel formant
F2	second vowel formant
FCP	*Far Cry Primal* (video game)
FUT	future tense
GEN	genitive

Gk.	Ancient Greek
glot	glottal
GTA	Graduate Teaching Assistant
Hitt.	Hittite
IE	Indo-European
IES	Indo-European Studies
INDEF	indefinite
INF	infinitive
IPA	International Phonetic Alphabet
lab-dent	labiodental
Lat.	Latin
LBH	Light Before Heavy
LCC	Language Creation Conference
LOC	locative
MA	Master of Arts degree
N	noun
NEG	negation
NOM	nominative
NONPAST	non-past tense
NP	noun phrase
OBJ	object
OE	Old English
OLat.	Old Latin
OSV	object-subject-verb word order
OT	Optimality Theory
OV	object-verb word order
OVS	object-verb-subject word order
P	1. object of transitive verb 2. preposition
pal	palatal
pers. comm.	personal communication
PFV	perfective aspect
PIE	Proto-Indo-European
PL	plural
POSS	possessive
Poss	possessed noun
post-alv	post-alveolar
Postp	postpositional language
PP	prepositional phrase
Prep	prepositional language
PRES	present tense
PROG	progressive aspect
PST	past tense
REL	relativizer

Rel	relative clause
retr	retroflex
S	subject of intransitive verb
S_A	agentive subject of intransitive verb
SEQs	Student Evaluation Questionnaires
SETI	Search for Extraterrestrial Intelligence
SG	singular
Skt.	Sanskrit
SOV	subject-object-verb word order
S_P	patientive subject of intransitive verb
split-S	S_A marked like A and S_P marked like P
SUB	subject
SVO	subject-verb-object
TOP	topic
TPR	Total Physical Response
TRANS	transitive
uvu	uvular
UWSP	University of Wisconsin–Stevens Point
V	vowel
VC	vowel-consonant sequence
vel	velar
VO	verb-object word order
VOS	verb-object-subject word order
VP	verb phrase
VS	verb-subject word order
VSO	verb-subject-object word order
WALS	World Atlas of Language Structures

The Contributors

David Adger is a Professor of Linguistics at Queen Mary University of London, with many publications in syntax and its connections with morphology, prosody, semantics, and sociolinguistics. Creator of the Warig and Mere languages for the ITV series *Beowulf*, with a lifelong (almost literally) interest in constructed languages.

Skye J. Anderson is a doctoral candidate in Linguistics at the University of Arizona. She earned a BS in Linguistics from Tulane University in 2014 and an MA in Linguistics from the University of Arizona in 2016. Her research interests center on experimental and corpus phonology, speech perception, and visual and auditory word recognition. Her dissertation research focuses on the influence of syllable structure and phonological variation on phoneme processing and auditory word recognition.

James A. Berry is an Assistant Professor of English and Linguistics at the University of Wisconsin–Stevens Point. He has a BA from the University of Florida, and an MA and PhD from Arizona State University. His research interests include generative syntax, language change, sociolinguistics, and pragmatics. His current research is primarily centered on generative approaches to grammaticalization and lexicalization, with a particular focus on the rise of sentence adverbs in the history of English, and the use of certain adverbs as secondary predicates with pragmatic meaning. At UWSP, James regularly teaches several linguistics classes, in addition to freshman and sophomore English. These include Introduction to Linguistics, English Grammars, Sociolinguistics, History of the English Language, and Invented Languages.

Shannon T. Bischoff is a Professor of Linguistics in the Department of English and Linguistics at Purdue University Fort Wayne. He is the Director of the Institute of Research and Innovation. He is also the Interim Chair of Anthropology and Sociology. His work focuses on language documentation, language preservation, community-based research, and language policy. He has worked with Indigenous and minority language communities in the US and in Myanmar. In 2019 he and his colleagues were awarded the Society for the Study of Indigenous Languages of America's Ken Hale Prize. His research has been funded by the National Science Foundation, the National Endowment for the Humanities, the Japanese Society for the Promotion of Science, as well as other organizations. He is the author/co-author of eight books and twenty-seven papers. His most recent publications have been for UNESCO and the British Council, focusing on Indigenous and minority languages and the UN Sustainable Development Goals.

Andrew Miles Byrd is an Assistant Professor of Linguistics at the University of Kentucky. Author of multiple academic articles and books on Proto-Indo-European

(PIE), he spends much of his time investigating problems in historical linguistics that have been difficult (and sometimes impossible) to solve using traditional methodologies. He is particularly passionate about educating the public about historical linguistics. He recently finished work on Ubisoft's *Far Cry Primal*, a first-person shooter set in the Stone Age, for which he led a team of linguists to create two languages based on PIE, and is currently at work on Proto-Indo-European Online, an online resource that teaches PIE as a spoken language.

Brenna Reinhart Byrd is an Assistant Professor of German in the Modern and Classical Languages, Literatures and Cultures Department at the University of Kentucky. She received her PhD in Germanic Linguistics from UCLA in 2010 and has been working at the University of Kentucky since then as Director of Beginning German, overseeing the curriculum and training of instructors for the first three semesters of German. Her research interests include SLA literacy, sociolinguistics, Turkish-German identity, Hip Hop studies, computer-mediated communication, constructed languages, and historical linguistics. She also created a language based on Proto-Indo-European with her husband and fellow linguist, Andrew Byrd, for an internationally successful video game, *Far Cry Primal*. She recently received the 2016 Southern Conference on Language Teaching (SCOLT) Teacher of the Year Award.

Angela C. Carpenter is an Associate Professor of Cognitive and Linguistic Sciences at Wellesley College. Much of her research has focused on the phonological acquisition of language, both child language and adult second-language acquisition. Working in an artificial language-learning paradigm, she has worked on the acquisition of stressed syllables and function words by children learning their first language, and with adults she has studied factors that affect acquisition of stress in a second language. More recently, she has turned her attention to the phonology of creoles. She is exploring questions of dialect loss and dialect shift among native speakers of Jamaican Creole who live in the United States and other English-speaking countries.

Jessica Coon is an Associate Professor of Linguistics at McGill University and holds a Canada Research Chair in Syntax and Indigenous Languages. She finished her PhD at MIT in 2010. She has worked on topics including ergativity, split ergativity, verb-initial word order, and agreement, with a special focus on Mayan languages. Her book *Aspects of Split Ergativity* was published by Oxford University Press in 2013. In 2015, she was the scientific adviser for the linguistics in the major-motion picture, *Arrival*, which stars a theoretical linguist tasked with deciphering an alien language through linguistic fieldwork. In 2019 she was awarded the 'Linguistics, Language, and The Public' award by the Linguistic Society of America for her public outreach relating to the film *Arrival*.

Edward Delmonico holds a BA in Linguistics and a Certificate in Teaching English to Speakers of Other Languages from Barrett, the Honors College at Arizona State University. He is an English teacher at Matsue Kita High School in Japan. As a Language Creation Society member since 2017 and owner of Kyber Consulting for conlangs, Spencer Morrell travels to various comic conventions to discuss the importance of conlangs and overall language representation in books, movies, and television. His purpose is to show writers and language enthusiasts the importance of the linguistics field and the need for its continued support. He also works with businesses in presenting open-forum discussions around sociolinguistic challenges that businesses must address in order to align with communication trends for LGBTQIA+ intersections in the workplace.

Amy V. Fountain is an Associate Professor, Career Track, of Linguistics at the University of Arizona. She earned a Joint PhD in Anthropology and Linguistics from the University of Arizona in 1998, and has been teaching with language invention in large freshmen general education courses since 2006. She teaches a variety of courses in linguistics, primarily for undergraduates, and has research interests in community-based linguistics with Indigenous communities in North America.

Carrie Gillon is an editor, writing coach, and co-host of *Vocal Fries*, the podcast about linguistic discrimination. In a previous life, she researched the syntax and semantics of understudied languages, mainly Indigenous languages of Canada. She wrote *The Semantics of Determiners: Domain Restriction in Skwxwú7mesh*, co-authored *Nominal Contact in Michif*, co-edited the Skwxwú7mesh-English bilingual dictionary, wrote or co-authored eight articles and four book chapters, and co-edited three volumes of UBCWPL, a special edition of the *Canadian Journal of Linguistics* on noun phrases, and the *Routledge Handbook of North American Languages*.

Grant Goodall is a Professor of Linguistics at the University of California, San Diego, where he directs the Linguistics Language Program and the Experimental Syntax Lab. His primary research area is natural language syntax, with a special interest in using experimental techniques to explore syntactic dependencies, including the interplay between grammar and working memory, and the acquisition of syntax. He has spoken Esperanto since early adolescence and is vice-president of the Esperantic Studies Foundation and a member of the Akademio de Esperanto.

Randi Martinez is working on a PhD in Linguistics at Yale University, currently focusing on linguistic variation and grammatical diversity within North American English. Her broader research interests include morphology, syntax, and the interface between syntax and pragmatics. She also enjoys being creative, a trait which she combined with her Linguistics interests by constructing a language for fictional feral goblins for her BA honors thesis. She has also done research on Wangkatja (a Wati language of the Pama-Nyungan language family, spoken in Australia), and she has taught English to speakers of other languages with her TESOL certification.

Spencer Morrell is a former student of Carrie Gillon's with a passion for language and science fiction. After comprehensive research into the fictional history of the Sith species from Star Wars, he created a language (Sith'ari) for the ancient Sith, which was complete with three polysynthetic class-variations, a counting system, and orthography. He later presented on Sith'ari at the LibCon of Chandler on the Xenolinguistics and Languages in Star Wars panels. Today, he is collaborating with Tempe Police to create material for increasing intercultural communicative competence in officers when interacting with speakers of other languages. He is also an instructor in ESL for immigrants and refugees at Gateway Community College.

Arika Okrent is a journalist with a PhD in Linguistics from the University of Chicago. She is the author of *In the Land of Invented Languages* and the 2016 recipient of the Linguistic Journalism Award from the Linguistic Society of America.

Matt Pearson received his PhD in Linguistics from UCLA, and currently serves as Professor of Linguistics at Reed College (Portland, Oregon), where he teaches courses in general linguistics, syntax, typology, morphology, semantics, and field methods. His research on word order and clause structure in Malagasy has appeared in *Natural Language and Linguistic Theory*, an edited volume from John Benjamins, and other publications. In 1996–7 Matt created the alien language for the NBC science fiction series *Dark Skies*. His other constructed language projects have earned mentions in both Peterson (2015) and Okrent (2010).

David J. Peterson studied linguistics at UC Berkeley (BA 2003) and UC San Diego (MA 2005). He served as an adjunct faculty member in the English department at Fullerton College from 2006 to 2008, and then began working on HBO's *Game of Thrones* as a language creator in 2009. In 2011 he began to work as a professional language creator on numerous television shows and movies, including, among others, the CW's *The 100*, Marvel's *Doctor Strange*, Legendary's *Dune*, and Syfy's *Defiance*. In 2017, he taught a summer course on language creation at UC Berkeley in the linguistics department.

Jeffrey Punske is an Assistant Professor of Linguistics at Southern Illinois University in Carbondale specializing in morphosyntax. He earned his PhD at the University of Arizona in 2012. He works on topics including compounding, nominalization, non-compositional language, and incorporation. He has presented work related to xeno-linguistics at a workshop hosted by Messaging Extra-Terrestrial Intelligence (METI) in 2018 and language change during long-distance space travel for a workshop hosted by the Advanced Concepts Team of the European Space Agency in 2019. He was the recipient of the 2018 College of Liberal Arts Early Career Excellence Award at SIU.

Nathan Sanders earned his PhD in linguistics from the University of California, Santa Cruz, in 2003, and is the first Assistant Professor in the Teaching Stream in the Department of Linguistics at the University of Toronto. He has taught across the curriculum in linguistics and is a principal investigator on two pedagogical grants, one with Peter Jurgec for creating an online tool for generating constructed phonology data sets, and one with Keren Rice and Naomi Nagy for developing classroom materials and teaching methods concerning linguistic equity, diversity, and inclusion. His linguistic research centers on how the human body and the physical world around it play a role in shaping language, with a particular focus on biomechanics and perception, for both speech and sign languages. He also works on phonological theory, computational and statistical models of linguistic phenomena, language change, and linguistic typology.

Christine Schreyer is an Associate Professor of Anthropology at the University of British Columbia, Okanagan Campus, where she teaches a range of courses in linguistic anthropology. Her research focuses on language revitalization and documentation, in Canada and in Papua New Guinea, as well as the relationship between endangered language communities and created language communities. She has conducted research with the Na'vi speech community (from the movie *Avatar*), and she is the creator of the Kryptonian language from *Man of Steel* (2013), Eltarian from *Power Rangers* (2017), and Beama from *Alpha* (2018). Recently, she was co-producer of the documentary film *Kala Language Project: Kala Walo Nuā* about her community-based work with Kala speakers. She was also an executive producer for the 2017 documentary film *Conlanging: The Art of Crafting Tongues.*

Kimberly Spallinger is a Teaching Professor at Bowling Green State University in Bowling Green, Ohio. She regularly teaches ESOL, TESOL, linguistics, and Rhetoric and Writing courses, and her main interests relate to pedagogy and teacher training.

Coppe van Urk is a Lecturer in Linguistics at Queen Mary University of London. He received his PhD from MIT in 2015. His research is in syntax, with a particular emphasis on the structure of lesser-studied languages, such as Dinka, Fijian, and Imere.

Sheri Wells-Jensen is an Associate Professor specializing in linguistics at Bowling Green State University, in Bowling Green, Ohio. Her research interests include language construction, astrobiology, disability studies, xenolinguistics, and braille. She is on the board of both Messaging Extraterrestrial Intelligence International (METI) and the Society for Conceptual Studies in Astrobiology (SSOCIA).

1

Introduction

Jeffrey Punske, Nathan Sanders, and Amy V. Fountain

1.1 Bringing language invention into the classroom

At one point in his essay on language construction, "A Secret Vice," J. R. R. Tolkien entertains the notion that he "may be like an opium smoker seeking a moral or medical or artistic defence for his habit" (1997: 206). Ultimately though, he rejects this idea, embracing the true value of the contemplation and practice of constructing languages (or *conlanging*).

However, Tolkien's brief rumination is based on the understandable reality that conlanging has long been viewed as beyond the proper bounds of the academic study of language: the resulting conlangs are consciously and intentionally designed, unlike the natural languages usually of interest in linguistics. The time spent on conlangs and conlanging is thus time not spent on studying "real" languages, so the conlanger is consequently viewed as Tolkien's opium smoker, someone with a vice outside of the acceptable.

However, conlangs have been sources of broad public interest for many years. Aside from the countless individuals who have engaged in conlanging as a hobby, conlangs have also held importance in the sociopolitical arena (as with L. L. Zamenhof's Esperanto) and in the world of literature and science fiction media (for example, Tolkien's Quenya and Sindarin, Marc Okrand's Klingon, and David J. Peterson's Dothraki). Since Tolkien's time, linguists (including many contributors to this volume) have increasingly been called into service as language creators or linguistic advisers for film and television, and many have brought the lessons from their experiences back to the classroom and out into the larger community.

Other linguists, too, have come to recognize the academic value of conlangs and conlanging. In January 2017, a group of linguists gathered at the annual meeting of the Linguistic Society of America in Austin, Texas, for an organized session of presentations on the topic "Teaching Linguistics with Invented Languages." Many of the panelists had independently discovered the benefits

Jeffrey Punske, Nathan Sanders, and Amy V. Fountain, *Introduction* In: *Language Invention in Linguistics Pedagogy.*
First edition. Edited by: Jeffrey Punske, Nathan Sanders, and Amy V. Fountain, Oxford University Press (2020).
© Jeffrey Punske, Nathan Sanders, and Amy V. Fountain.
DOI: 10.1093/oso/9780198829874.003.0001

of using conlangs in the classroom (some had been doing so for over a decade), and this panel represented an important culmination of the sharing of experiences and resources among these disparate instructors. Though not strictly a proceedings collection, this volume grew directly out of that panel and the connections and collaborations it facilitated.

This volume comes at a critical point of development in the field of linguistics as a whole, with a new and renewed focus on pedagogical methods and outreach. In 2013, the flagship journal of the Linguistics Society of America, *Language*, introduced a new section focused on pedagogical practices in linguistics. Similarly, other panels and workshops focused on different approaches to teaching linguistics content have emerged at various conferences around the world. More recently yet, Kazuko Hiramatsu and Michal Temkin Martinez were awarded a 2019 National Science Foundation grant on the Scholarship of Teaching and Learning in Linguistics. Outreach, too, has gained greater prominence in the field, with increased presence of linguists on social media, in podcasts, and in the public eye at large.

Our goal with this volume is to explore the various ways that this secret vice can elevate linguistics pedagogy and outreach, by tapping into increased public interest, promoting increased student engagement with the course material, providing a deeper understanding of the interconnectedness of the different areas of language, drawing upon and strengthening interdisciplinary knowledge, and broadening the use of creative thinking skills. The contributors in this volume examine the multiple aspects of language invention and how it relates to linguistics pedagogy and to outreach, in both academic and non-academic contexts.

This volume is necessarily limited in its scope, and our hope is that it is the beginning of a larger conversation around the academic and pedagogical role of conlangs. For example, questions about socio-cultural factors in designing a language are largely unexplored here. Like any creative act, language construction is not a neutral act; a conlang carries with it the cultural expectations, context, and baggage of its creator. How and why a conlanger chooses to include or exclude any particular linguistic feature when constructing a language open clear academic and pedagogical avenues. We hope that these and other such topics continue to be explored with significantly more depth.

1.2 Breakdown of contributions

Within its scope, this volume is intended as a general guide and toolkit for the pedagogical use of conlangs through a variety of perspectives and contexts, from elementary education through advanced undergraduate studies, as well as beyond the walls of formal education into the world at large. The first two chapters set the larger context for this volume. **Nathan Sanders** opens with a tour through the history and nature of language manipulation in general and conlangs specifically, providing a reference point for the remainder of the volume, while also situating the present discussion in the overall flow of history and language.

Arika Okrent follows with discussion of the types of people who tend to undertake Tolkien's secret vice, and thus, the types of students who are likely to enroll in the relevant courses described in subsequent chapters. Okrent's contribution can be seen as somewhat of a long-form mission statement of this volume: who are we teaching and what do they want to learn?

The next ten chapters provide discussion about what can be learned about language through the use of conlangs, with many chapters offering case studies of specific assignments, projects, activities, and outlines from relevant courses and outreach experiences. **Jessica Coon** was the linguistic consultant for the major motion picture *Arrival* (2016), and in her contribution, she elaborates on the valuable—and sometimes surprising—interplay between the worlds of science fiction, linguistic analysis, and linguistic fieldwork. Language invention in *Arrival* takes on a very different complexion from other media-driven invention projects, and it serves as an engaging entry point for teaching students and society about what linguistics is, what linguists do, and how language might really work.

David Adger and Coppe van Urk describe the application of aspects of language invention to teaching linguistics in contexts beginning with young children at summer camp and continuing through university education. The techniques used in their teaching were inspired and informed by Adger's practical experience in designing the Warig and Mere languages for the television program *Beowulf: Return to the Shieldlands* (2016).

In three case studies, **Grant Goodall** discusses a university course that focuses on invented languages both as objects of study and as artefacts that students design themselves. He shows how such an undergraduate course invites students to interrogate and understand the nature and ontology of the design features of human language.

Matt Pearson discusses language invention as a means for teaching linguistic typology. Pearson's project utilizes observed patterns of incidence of various linguistic features as attested in sources such as the World Atlas of Language Structures Online (http://wals.info) to stochastically constrain grammatical choices made by student teams. The methods described in this contribution can scale to a few workshop assignments in a course or a larger project designed to span an academic term.

Angela Carpenter's contribution focuses on language invention in a capstone course for undergraduate students, as a way in which students can bring to bear their overall mastery of the core concepts and methods of linguistics such that they are encouraged to connect these ideas directly to notions of the cultural and social underpinnings of language use. Carpenter walks the reader through the implementation of a language invention project with an advanced undergraduate audience and details ways in which the exercise generates discussion and analysis of the complex interplay of language, culture, and thought.

James Berry discusses the use of a language invention project in an introductory undergraduate course for English majors at a small university, in an institutional environment of scarcity of resources. The potential of such projects to engage and attract students across disciplines is explored in this contribution.

Carrie Gillon, Edward Delmonico, Randi Martinez, and Spencer Morrell describe how a language invention project in a university classroom can then permeate through the institutional boundaries to take an active role in a local comic convention. This contribution is jointly authored by the students who undertook the work and share their creations here, and thus, it provides a crucial and direct report on the experiences of students who grapple with language invention as part of their university education.

Nathan Sanders and Christine Schreyer describe how language invention is intimately connected to the creation of imaginary worlds in projects undertaken by students in linguistics and anthropology. The examples presented in this contribution show how students are involved in designing languages for non-human species and how language invention sheds light on the intrinsic relationships that language has with biology, physics, and culture.

Brenna and Andrew Byrd use language invention as a strategy for exploring historical linguistics, in particular Proto-Indo-European. As they did for many other contributors in this volume, the pedagogical concepts developed out of a relationship with the mass media, here, the video game *Far Cry Primal*. Many, if not most, linguistic programs have a course on historical linguistics, and the study of Proto-Indo-European extends well into other fields. This chapter offers an innovative and new approach to this well-trodden area of study.

Sheri Wells-Jensen and Kimberly Spallinger describe a set of exercises in which students are invited to engage with an "alien" language and undertake xenolinguistic analysis using information-theoretic principles to decode a set of prepared "transmissions." The exercises can be adapted for use by students in linguistic courses at all levels and could be extended profitably to courses introducing computation, information theory, and even some basic mathematics.

The volume ends with a contribution by **David J. Peterson**, whose work in media projects such as the television program *Game of Thrones* (2011) has been a key driver in students' interest in language invention in recent years. Peterson discusses the complex relationships between academics and the conlang community and describes the roles of aesthetics and authority as they play out in various contexts. As a major and long-term player in both worlds, Peterson brings a unique and crucial perspective to the volume. Readers will benefit from his analysis of the interplay and tension between the pedagogical goals of the instructor and the artistic goals of the student as language creator. As methods like those presented in this volume continue to develop and spread, it becomes even more critical that academics working with conlangs take Peterson's words to heart and build and maintain partnerships with the conlang community, to properly meet the needs of all involved.

1.3 Concluding thoughts

With this volume, we aim to show that bringing conlangs and language invention into the classroom allows us to reach a broader student population and develop in these students the fundamental core skills of linguistics and language analysis. Using language invention as a pedagogical tool is an innovative way to capitalize on the effectiveness of many modern educational approaches, such as problem-based learning, collaborative learning, and active learning, especially for a diverse cohort of learners. The methods and materials presented in this volume help cultivate students' understanding of language, linguistic diversity, linguistic analysis, and the power of creativity.

2

A primer on constructed languages

Nathan Sanders

2.1 Introduction

This chapter provides a tour through the nature and history of *constructed languages*, or *conlangs* for short. Conlangs, such as Esperanto and Klingon, are languages or partial languages that have been intentionally created by the conscious effort of individual humans, unlike languages such as Estonian or Korean, which arose naturally and effortlessly among entire populations from the general subconscious human capacity for language. I begin, in Section 2.2, by highlighting the most ancient notions of consciously controlling and creating language. Then, in Section 2.3, I continue with discussion of the first true conlangs from the Middle Ages up through the Renaissance and Enlightenment, when language creation was guided largely by religious and philosophical concerns, though more creative uses began to appear in this time as well. In Section 2.4, I explore more recent history, when conlangs were believed to have practical purposes as lingua francas to bridge linguistic divides between communities. This period also saw the further development of conlanging as an art form, most notably by J. R. R. Tolkien, setting the stage for the current era of conlanging, discussed in Section 2.5, where conlanging's status as art and even as a profession has been solidified. In Section 2.6, I discuss the role of conlanging as a tool for language revitalization. I conclude in Section 2.7 with a summary of important terms and concepts useful for understanding this primer and the other chapters in this volume. Much of the content in this chapter owes a great debt to various scholarly works with extensive discussion of conlangs and the history of conlanging, especially Knowlson 1975, Eco 1993, Okrent 2010, Adams 2011a, and Stria 2016, as well as Jörg Rhiemeier's (2007–2010) useful online overview of conlang history.

Nathan Sanders, *A primer on constructed languages* In: *Language Invention in Linguistics Pedagogy.*
First edition. Edited by: Jeffrey Punske, Nathan Sanders, and Amy V. Fountain, Oxford University Press (2020).
© Nathan Sanders.
DOI: 10.1093/oso/9780198829874.003.0002

2.2 Ancient notions of language construction

The languages we ordinarily encounter in our daily lives are the result of hundreds of thousands of years of natural, unintentional evolution from the prelinguistic vocalisms and gestures that our Paleolithic ancestors likely used to convey basic information (Danesi 2004). Their rudimentary communications slowly evolved into increasingly complex systems, ultimately becoming true languages capable of expressing the full range of everyday human experience. These so-called *natural languages*, or *natlangs* for short, are intimately tied in with who we are, not just as individual speakers or members of linguistic communities, but more deeply as human beings. The capacity for language is perhaps the single most distinctive property of our species. It is thus no surprise that we have sought to control and manipulate language beyond its natural evolution, as it allows us to exert control over our very identity.

Poetry is one way in which we impose our will on language, intentionally shaping it with structural patterns not typical of everyday use. The earliest recorded poetry dates back more than 4,000 years, to the Pyramid Texts (Old Egyptian hymns, prayers, and spells carved into the burial chambers of the Saqqara pyramids circa 2400 BC; Erman 2012: 1), not long after the invention of writing during the previous millennium. Joking, another kind of linguistic manipulation, seems to be nearly as ancient. One of the earliest recorded jokes is the Sumerian witticism in (1), from a set of 202 proverbs known as Collection 1 or SP 1 (Alster 1997: 9; see also Gordon 1954: 83, Lambert 1960: 260, Gelb et al. 1962: 107, ETCSL 2003–2007, Woods 2013: 509, and Nemet-Nejat 2014: 83 for variations in form and translation), attested as early as 1900–1800 BC from tablets discovered in Nippur in modern-day Iraq (Fant and Reddish 2008: 241–2):

(1) *níg u$_4$-bi-ta la-ba-gál-la*
     ki-sikil-tur úr dam-ma-na-ka še$_{10}$ nu-ub-dúr-re
     'Something which has never occurred since time immemorial:
         Didn't the young girl fart in her husband's lap?'

These kinds of linguistic manipulation, both sacred and playful, eventually expanded beyond the confines of natlangs. We learned to bypass the slow, effortless evolution of natlangs to invent new languages that we could control in every respect, intentionally and actively using our individual imaginations to create something with which we had a fundamentally different relationship than with natlangs. These deliberate linguistic creations have been called by a variety of names (see Section 2.7), but by the 1990s, the term *conlang* (a blend of *constructed language*, coined by Danish linguist Otto Jespersen when he debuted his own conlang Novial in 1928) had gained currency among the conlang community through online discussions and the founding of the popular Conlang email list in 1991 (Peterson 2015: 11). For simplicity of discussion, I use *conlang* (to refer to one of these invented languages) and its derived forms *conlanging* (the practice of language construction) and *conlanger* (someone who engages in conlanging).

Given the human predilection for manipulating language, some form of conlanging has surely existed as long as language itself. The concept of conlanging is perhaps first explicitly mentioned in writing by Athenaeus of Naucratis in his *Deipnosophistae* (*c.* AD 230).

Although the examples he gives are not full languages with detailed grammars, they do represent a rudimentary type of conlang known as a *naming language*: a set of neologisms that can be used as replacement vocabulary or to refer to things that otherwise have no suitable name. Athenaeus writes of people who had created their own naming languages, such as Dionysus of Sicily, who Athenaeus reports had invented words like μένανδρος (*ménandros*) 'wait-man' to be used in place of παρθένος (*parthénos*) 'virgin' and μενεκράτης (*menekrátēs*) 'strong-stay' for στῦλος (*stûlos*) 'pillar' (*Deipnosophistae* Book III.54).

A few centuries later, the first apparent discussion of a full conlang appears in Irish myths about the origin of Gaelic, as described in Longarad's grammar of Old Irish, *Auraicept na n-Éces* (presumed to be from the seventh century). According to legend, King Fénius Farsaid of Scythia journeyed to Mesopotamia in the aftermath of the Biblical "confusion of tongues," in which God fragmented human language (believed to have originally been a single homogenous language) to prevent humans from completing the Tower of Babel and reaching Heaven (Genesis 11: 1–9). In some versions of the story, Fénius was already present in Babel, perhaps having even been one of the tower's builders (van Hamel 1915, Carey 1990). With the help of an army of scholars, Fénius studied the post-confusion languages, and he (or by some accounts, his grandson Goídel Glas; MacKillop 2005) combined the best parts of these languages into a new more perfect language, Goídelc (Gaelic), the original Irish language (Williams 2016). This story seems to be the first written record of the very concept of a human being creating a full language, an ability formerly attributed solely to deities. The Tower of Babel story itself relies on this divine power, and this basic theme dates back at least to the Sumerian epic "Enmerkar and the Lord of Aratta" from the twenty-first century BC, in which the god Enki similarly imposed linguistic diversity on humans (Kramer 1968). Crucially, what distinguishes the Goídelc myth from these earlier stories is that the language in question was supposedly created by a mere mortal, an indication that humans had begun to believe that they could have access to what had previously been exclusively a godly ability.

2.3 Conlangs from the Middle Ages through the Enlightenment

2.3.1 Linguistic mysticism

The belief in the connection between language creation and divinity shaped many early conlangs. If gods created languages, what would it mean for a human to dabble in this enterprise? A common thread in this view was that language could reveal deeper insights into human thought and the nature of the universe itself, so designing a perfect language could reveal truths obscured by the "corruptions" of natlangs (Wilkins 1668: 6), perhaps even getting us closer to knowing the first language handed down to mortals by the gods, if not the gods' own divine language itself. In this section, I provide an overview of these early conlangs, with discussion of a few notable examples; see Knowlson 1975 and Eco 1993 for more information on conlanging in this time period.

Half a millennium after the first record of the notion that a mortal could create a full language in the legendary origins of Goídelc, German abbess and polymath Hildegard of Bingen (1098–1179) created Lingua Ignota 'unknown language', which is popularly credited as the first true conlang. However, Lingua Ignota is not much more than a partial *relexification* (or *relex* for short) of Latin. A relex is a type of naming language used in conjunction with an existing language's grammar, replacing the words or morphemes but keeping the underlying structure. In this case, Lingua Ignota had over 1,000 neologisms to replace Latin words, such as *loifol* 'people' replacing *populus*, but otherwise, it did not appear to have its own grammar separate from Latin, and it retained Latin words where no equivalent in Lingua Ignota existed. In addition to the language, Hildegard also created Litteræ Ignotæ 'unknown letters', a constructed writing system or *neography*, which she used to represent Lingua Ignota (Figure 2.1).

Despite the comparative lack of grammatical depth in Lingua Ignota from the perspective of modern conlangs, Hildegard is revered as a key figure in the

Figure 2.1 Litteræ Ignotæ

Adapted from folio 464v of RheinMain University's digitization of the Riesencodex, http://hlbrm.digitale-sammlungen.hebis.de/handschriften-hlbrm/content/pageview/450562, accessed August 18, 2018

history of conlanging, as the first genuine conlanger. Fitting its name, the true purpose of Lingua Ignota is unknown, though it is likely that it was some sort of sacred language, perhaps used to create solidarity among Hildegard and her fellow nuns. Hildegard's extensive writings, including a record of Lingua Ignota, are collected in the Riesencodex (also called the Wiesbaden Codex after its long-time home in Museum Wiesbaden), an enormous tome compiled shortly after her death. See Higley 2007 for fuller discussion of Hildegard of Bingen and Lingua Ignota.

Though Lingua Ignota almost certainly had some sort of sacred purpose, there is no indication that Hildegard believed she had uncovered a language actually spoken by divine beings. The first attempt at such a discovery seems to have been by mathematician John Dee and occultist Edward Kelley in the 1580s, who claimed that angels revealed their language to them (this language is popularly referred to as Enochian). Adding to the verisimilitude of their "discovery" was the neography they invented for Enochian (Figure 2.2). Its complex organization and ornate glyphs gave the language an otherworldly feel that suited its supposedly angelic speakers, helping this language capture the imagination of believers and skeptics alike for centuries. See Laycock 1978 for more information about the history and structure of Enochian.

The decline in importance of Latin by the 1600s left the scholarly world feeling the need for a suitable replacement universal language (Stria 2016: 50–1); the local natlangs that had supplanted Latin were deemed too unruly for this purpose (see Wilkins 1688: 1ff for a typical scathing view of the "defects and imperfections" in natlangs). This search became the primary

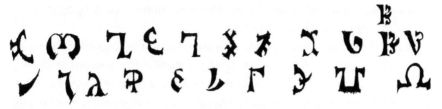

Figure 2.2 Enochian neography
Adapted from Laycock (1978: 37)

focus of conlanging in the seventeenth century, with the resulting conlangs often referred to as *philosophical languages*. These philosophical languages were intended to be perfect languages that would give precision and clarity to reasoned expression and thus, presumably, to thought itself. This belief in a deep causal relationship from language to thought remains a common folk belief to this day, though there is little evidence that there is any significant effect of language on thought (Gleitman and Papafragou 2005).

The earliest of these philosophical languages is likely Jean Douet's "escriture universelle" (1627), and many more followed, including Francis Lodwick's "common writing" (1647, 1652), Sir Thomas Urquhart's Logopandecteision (1652, 1653), Cave Beck's Universal Character (1657), and Philippe Labbé's Lingua Universalis (1663). The most important of these philosophical languages is arguably George Dalgarno's Ars Signorum (1661). Its system of categorizing semantic concepts was developed further into a complex hierarchy by John Wilkins (1668), whose work in turn helped inspire Peter Mark Roget's now ubiquitous thesaurus (Roget 1853: xxiv-v). This style of conlanging continued through the seventeenth century but was all but abandoned in the next century, with only scattered examples in the 1700s (Knowlson 1975).

2.3.2 Early artistic languages

This era also saw the beginnings of the use of *artistic languages*, or *artlangs* for short. Unlike the mystical and philosophical languages that seek to uncover deeper connections to the universe and the human mind, artlangs serve a very different purpose. They are designed to suit some creative goal, usually as flavorful adornment in a work of fiction. These early artlangs were usually little more than rudimentary naming languages, so that characters, places, and important items or concepts in a novel could have realistically foreign names. Although little linguistic creativity was required at the time, these early artlangs represented the first step in the evolution of conlanging into the serious art form it has become today.

One of the earliest artlangs is the language used in the country of Utopia in Sir Thomas More's 1516 *De optimo reipublicæ statu, deque nova insula Utopia, libellus vere aureus, nec minus salutaris quam festivus clarissimi disertissimique viri Thomæ Mori inclutæ civitatis Londinensis civis & vicecomitis*, more popularly simplified as *Utopia*, itself an invented word meaning 'nowhere', coined by More from the Greek οὐ (*ou*) 'not' and τόπος (*tópos*) 'place'. The Utopian language was more than a naming language, though still only a relex of Latin. The language appears only as a few isolated words in the main text (such as *Buthrescas* for a type of religious fanatic and *Cynemernes* for the first day of a month) and as a four-line poem in the addendum written by More's friend Peter Giles (né Pieter Gillis).

Other notable examples of early artlangs were sparse naming languages invented by François Rabelais and Francis Godwin. Rabelais's languages were included in his five-novel series (beginning around 1532) about two giants named Gargantua and Pantagruel, while Godwin included his conlang Lunar in the 1638 novel *The Man in the Moone: or A Discourse of a Voyage thither by Domingo Gonsales the speedy Messenger* (which is further notable for being the first known example of science fiction published in English). Jonathan Swift went beyond mere naming languages for his 1726 novel *Travels into Several Remote Nations of the World. In Four Parts. By Lemuel Gulliver, First a Surgeon, and then a Captain of several Ships* (a.k.a. *Gulliver's Travels*), which featured dialogue from multiple conlangs (Brobdingnagian, Laputan, and Houyhnhnm).

2.3.3 Linguistic deception

Other relexes abounded in the Middle Ages and the Renaissance, though typically with no uniquely identifiable creators or starting point (giving them an intermediate status between true conlang and specialized evolution of a natlang) and with no concern for holy or artistic purposes, as this was also the era of *cryptolects*, secret argots used by certain subcultures who sought to disguise discussion of their activities (thieves, homosexuals, and others who engaged in behavior that conflicted with law and/or social norms). These argots were partial relexes, with various, often incriminating, words and phrases replaced with other words, foreign borrowings, and neologisms. For example, *black-box* 'lawyer' and *rum-dubber* 'experienced lockpicker' are expressions in Pedlar's French, a thieves' cant used in England (documented in B. E. 1698). Despite the desired secrecy, these cryptolects were often well-known enough to feature in public discourse, literature, and dictionaries, with many words transitioning from secretive use to popular slang; for example, modern English *fence* 'recipient of stolen goods' originated in Pedlar's French. Prominent examples of these cryptolects include the jargon of the Coquillards in France (exemplified by Villon 1489), Rotwelsche in Germany (documented in Hütlin 1509), and forbesco in Italy (documented in Brocardo 1545).

Conlangs have been used to deceive in other ways. One of the most notorious and elaborate linguistic hoaxes in history was perpetuated in England in the early 1700s, by a (possible) Frenchman operating under the pseudonym George Psalmanazar, who pretended to be a Formosan (an aboriginal native of Taiwan). He became a minor celebrity with his lectures and 1704 book *An Historical and Geographical Description of Formosa*, regaling the public and academics alike with detailed, horrifying tales of his supposed homeland and his path from savagery to Christianity (Keevak 2004). A crucial part of Psalmanazar's charade was a conlang he used as his "native" language, which convinced potential skeptics, as they found it to be "so regular and grammatical, as well as different from all others they knew, both with respect to the words and idiom, that they gave it as their opinion that it must be a real language" (Psalmanazar 1764: 180–1). However, Psalmanazar's "Formosan" conlang had no actual relationship to any real Formosan languages of the Austronesian family, such as Atayal or Bunun. People were convinced by Psalmanazar because England at the time had little knowledge of East Asia at all, let alone the Formosan people or their languages. In essence, Formosa could be whatever Psalmanazar said it was, and he was safe from challenge. Later in life, his conscience weighed heavily upon him, and Psalmanzar came to regret his "wretched youthful years" (1764: 5). As an apology to the world, he laid out many details of his early life and his Formosan hoax in his memoirs (published posthumously in 1764), though he characteristically took the secret of his birthplace and real name to his grave.

2.3.4 Early conlanging beyond Europe

The record of non-European conlangs during this time is sparse. The most well-documented early conlang from outside of Europe is the sixteenth-century religious conlang Bâleybelen (a.k.a. Balaibalan), created by Turkish dervish Muḥyī Gülşenī (1528–1606) (Koç 2005, Emre 2017). Unlike languages like

Lingua Ignota and the European cryptolects, Bâleybelen is not just a relex, since it has its own constructed morphology and syntax, though it is still heavily inspired by Turkish, Persian, and Arabic (Bausani 1970). There are also some notable non-European conlangs invented or first recorded in the twentieth century, such as Damin in Australia (Hale 1992), Eskayan in the Philippines (P. Kelly 2012), and Medefaidrin in Nigeria (Gibbon et al. 2010), which have many structural and functional parallels with Bâleybelen and the European conlangs of this era, so while they may not belong together in time, they surely belong in spirit.

2.4 Early modern conlangs

2.4.1 Connecting the world through language

A main focus of conlanging efforts after the decline of interest in philosophical languages was finding an ideal *auxiliary language*, or *auxlang* for short, which could be used as a practical lingua franca for people with different linguistic backgrounds. Most auxlangs of this period were intended for international or even worldwide use; an auxlang with such a large scope is sometimes referred to as an *international auxiliary language*. The most famous and successful of these is Ludwik Lejzer Zamenhof's Esperanto (1887), but many notable auxlangs came before it. One such example, highlighting the inventiveness of conlanging, is François Sudre's Solresol (created and publicized beginning in 1827 but not published until 1866, by his widow after his death), in which the syllables can be mapped to musical notes, colors, numbers, abstract lines, gestures, etc. (Figure 2.3), allowing the language to be communicated in different modalities (speech, music, art, etc.; Rose 2013). For example, the name of Solresol itself can be communicated as the spoken or written word *solresol*; the musical tune G-D-G; a color block made up of light blue, then orange, then light blue; the number string 525; pointing to the tip of the ring finger, then to the pinky knuckle, then back to the tip of the ring finger; etc. Any set of seven distinct atomic units of any type can be used, giving Solresol incredible flexibility in how it is expressed.

Other auxlangs of this period include Joseph Schipfer's Communications-sprache (1839), a simplified version of French; Jean Pirro's Universalglot (1868), one of the first fully developed auxlangs to integrate linguistic features from multiple languages; and Johann Martin Schleyer's Volapük (1880), which was the most successful auxlang until Esperanto supplanted it. The particular

Elle est PARLÉE, lorsqu'on prononce les notes :

do, ré, mi, fa, sol, la, si.

Elle est ÉCRITE, lorsque ces mêmes notes sont tracées sur le papier, comme ci-après :

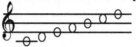

Elle est MUETTE, lorsque les notes sont indiquées sur les doigts, comme il suit :

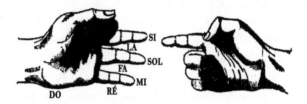

Figure 2.3 Some syllable correspondences in Solresol
Adapted from Sudre 1866: xxxii

successes of Volapük and Esperanto spurred the creation of many other auxlangs, especially by those who sought to improve upon previous auxlangs. The first offshoot of Esperanto was Jacob Braakman's Mundolinco (1888), but the most successful was Ido, the result of a battle among Esperanto enthusiasts over whether Esperanto should be, or could even be allowed to be, improved. Presumably created by Louis Couturat and Louis de Beaufront (né Chevreaux), Ido was submitted anonymously in 1907 to the Délégation pour l'Adoption d'une Langue Auxiliaire Internationale, an organization founded by Couturat and Léopold Leau and including in its membership the famed linguists Jan Baudouin de Courtenay and Otto Jespersen (who went on to publish his own conlang, Novial, in 1928). The Délégation's support for Ido's reforms, such as eliminating accent marks and case-marking, triggered a significant split in the Esperanto community (Forster 1982).

Attempts at auxlangs continued for much of the twentieth century, though none managed to match Esperanto's success, and Esperanto itself fell far short of Zamenhof's intentions. A fascinating example is Charles Bliss's sophisticated system of visual elements called Blissymbolics, developed beginning in 1942 and first published in 1949.[1] Blissymbolics uses an intricate system of simplified iconic glyphs, notational conventions, and compositionality to allow for representation of a wide range of concepts. For example, 'teacher'

---

[1] The Blissymbolics system was originally copyrighted © C. K. Bliss 1949, with copyright transferred to Blissymbolics Communication International (BCI) in 1975. Bliss-characters and Bliss-words appearing herein are used with permission and conform to the BCI Authorized Vocabulary as published by BCI.

Figure 2.4 Sample Bliss-words in Blissymbolics

Adapted from the website for the Blissymbolics Communication Institute—Canada, http://blissymbolics.ca/, accessed June 7, 2018. © C. K. Bliss 1949. Blissymbolics Communication International 1975, 1982, 2010

and 'student' are each represented as a string of symbols, one for 'person', then one for either 'give' or 'get' as appropriate (they differ iconically by the reversal of the direction of the arrow), and finally one for 'knowledge', which is itself a blend of the symbols for 'house' and 'mind' (Figure 2.4).

Blissymbolics failed to become the international auxlang Bliss had hoped it would be, but some organizations around the world have successfully adopted it as a communication method for people with speech disorders.

2.4.2 Rising artistry in conlangs

This period also saw authors taking more care in developing artlangs for their fictional universes. Like their earlier counterparts, artlangs in this period were largely naming languages, focused on vocabulary rather than syntax or morphology, a sharp counterpoint to the contemporaneous auxlangs. However, the quantity and quality of the constructed vocabulary of this time were noticeably improved over earlier artlangs, presaging an increasing level of rigor that conlangers would eventually embrace as standard practice. Notable examples include Frederick Spencer Oliver's Poseid for his 1894 novel *A Dweller on Two Planets: Or, The Dividing of the Way*; Edgar Rice Burroughs's Barsoomian for his John Carter of Mars stories, beginning with a 1912 magazine serial eventually re-published as the 1917 novel *A Princess of Mars* (Barsoomian was later expanded by Paul Frommer for the 2012 film *John Carter*); George Orwell's Newspeak for his 1949 novel *1984*; Anthony Burgess's Nadsat for his 1962 novel *A Clockwork Orange*; Frank Herbert's Fremen for his Dune series of novels, beginning in 1965 with *Dune*; and Richard Adams's Lapine for his 1972 novel *Watership Down*.

2.4.3 J. R. R. Tolkien

Among those who created artlangs in this time, John Ronald Reuel Tolkien was an aberration. The effort typically spent on a conlang by his contemporaries was proportional to its intended practical use: artlangs were minimalist dashes of flavor added to a larger work of fiction, while auxlangs were intricate machines designed to support the full range of human communication. Tolkien bridged the gap between these two extremes by creating fully formed languages and giving serious, dedicated focus to every aspect of his languages, but without any larger functionality or purpose beyond the sheer intellectual joy of doing so. However, he believed that his "secret vice" would not be taken seriously on its own, so he wrote his Middle-earth novels as a way to showcase them. Thus, while other writers created conlangs for their fiction, Tolkien created fiction for his conlangs (Tolkien 1981: 219). As a scholar of philology and practitioner of multiple languages, Tolkien drew heavily from his extensive linguistic knowledge in building his conlangs, setting a high standard in rigor and verisimilitude that would not be reached again until the closing decades of the twentieth century. Tolkien did not just impact the art form of modern conlanging; he essentially defined it.

Tolkien showcased multiple conlangs in his Middle-earth novels, from *The Hobbit* in 1937 to his posthumous *The Silmarillion* in 1977: three languages for elves (Quenya, Sindarin, Terelin); three for humans (Adûnaic, with fragments of Rohirric and Westron); one each for dwarves (Khuzdûl), spirits (Valarin), and ents (Old Entish, though only the single word *a-lalla-lalla-rumba-kamanda-lindor-burúme* 'hill' appears in Tolkien's novels); plus the Black Speech, the language used for the One Ring's inscription (2).

(2)   Ash nazg durbatulûk, ash nazg gimbatul,
          ash nazg thrakatulûk agh burzum-ishi krimpatul.
      'One Ring to rule them all, One Ring to find them,
          One Ring to bring them all and in the darkness bind them.'
                                                      (Tolkien 1954: 247)

Interestingly, within the lore of the Middle-earth stories, the Black Speech was created by Sauron to unite his servants in Mordor, making it one of the most notable examples of a conlang designed to be understood within its associated fictional setting as an actual conlang, rather than as a natlang.

2.5 Increasing sophistication and community in modern conlanging

Tolkien did not live to see the true impact that his work would have on the evolution of conlanging. In 1974, a year after Tolkien's death, the television series *Land of the Lost* premiered, and it featured the conlang Paku (sometimes called Pakuni), created by renowned UCLA linguistics professor Victoria Fromkin. Since she was paid to create the conlang for someone else's purposes rather than her own, Fromkin is likely the first professional conlanger (*Bucks County Courier Times* 1974, Erickson 1998: 114–15, Peterson 2015: 11, Fimi and Higgins 2017: 26). Though Paku is not as extensive as some of Tolkien's more robust conlangs, Fromkin imbued it with her expertise in linguistics, giving it realistic structure and substance inspired by languages of West Africa, further leading the art of conlanging down the path started by Tolkien. Though inexpert conlangs would continue to be built, Tolkien, Fromkin, and those who followed in their footsteps were establishing a new normal, and in the ensuing decades, it became standard and expected for conlangs to be based on systematic principles and typological facts discovered by the blossoming science of linguistics.

A decade after Fromkin created Paku, linguist and science-fiction author Suzette Haden Elgin created Láadan for her *Native Tongue* series of novels (beginning with *Native Tongue* in 1984). Like Fromkin, Elgin was a linguistics professor, and she similarly used her knowledge of linguistics to give Láadan naturalistic structure. Láadan also holds a deeper purpose as an *engineered language*, or *engelang* for short: a conlang designed to explore one or more specific linguistic properties. In this case, Elgin constructed Láadan to be a feminist language that directly encodes issues and perspectives relevant to women (Elgin 1988: 3–6). In the same year, *Star Trek III: The Search for Spock* showcased the alien language Klingon, which went on to become one of the most celebrated conlangs of all time. A few words of Klingon were first created by actor James Doohan (who portrayed the character Lt. Commander Montgomery Scott, better known as Scotty) for 1979's *Star Trek: The Motion Picture*. Marc Okrand (who, like Fromkin and Elgin, has a PhD in linguistics) was later tasked by Paramount to create a full language compatible with Doohan's original words (Okrand et al. 2011, Marc Okrand pers. comm. December 2016). The massive success of Klingon marks an important turning point in the history of conlanging, bringing the path taken by Tolkien, Fromkin, and Elgin to a new level of prominence and respectability, with Okrand's thoughtful, informed design setting a high bar for future conlangs.

This bar has been reached many times since by conlangers, especially those with training in linguistics. Syntactician Matt Pearson created Hivespeak (Thhtmaa) for the 1996 television series *Dark Skies* while working on his PhD in linguistics (Matt Pearson pers. comm. September 2018); Paku creator Victoria Fromkin also created the vampire language for the 1998 film *Blade*

(Conley and Cain 2006: 21); Klingon creator Marc Okrand also created Atlantean for the 2001 film *Atlantis: The Lost Empire* (J. Kelly 2001, Marc Okrand pers. comm. December 2016); Said el-Gheithy, director of London's Centre for African Language Learning, created Ku (Chi'itoboku) for the 2005 film *The Interpreter* (King 2005, Conley and Cain 2006: 95); Paul Frommer (a communications professor with a PhD in linguistics) created Na'vi for the 2009 film *Avatar* and Barsoomian for the 2012 film *John Carter* (building upon Burroughs's original work) (Ekman 2012, Fimi and Higgins 2017: 26, Paul Frommer pers. comm. July 2017); linguistic anthropologist Christine Schreyer created Kryptonian for the 2013 film *Man of Steel*, Eltarian for the 2017 film *Power Rangers*, and Beama (Cro-Magnon) for the 2018 film *Alpha* (Christine Schreyer pers. comm. August 2018, Sanders and Schreyer 2020 (this volume, Chapter 11)); linguist Nick Farmer created the Belter creole for the 2015 television series adaptation of James S. A. Corey's *The Expanse* series of novels and related stories (beginning with *Leviathan Wakes* in 2011) (LeVine 2016, Dreyfusss 2017); syntactician David Adger created Warig and Mere for the 2016 television series *Beowulf: Return to the Shieldlands* (Adger and van Urk 2020 (this volume, Chapter 5)); and linguist Alison Long created Illitan for the 2018 miniseries adaptation of China Miéville's 2009 novel *The City & the City* (Long 2018).

In most of these cases, the conlangers in question have worked on only one or two conlangs as side projects from their regular careers. However, at least one conlanger has managed to shift this pursuit from a side project to full-fledged career. David J. Peterson (who studied linguistics as an undergraduate and for his masters) has long been an avid conlanger and active participant in the conlanging community, helping found the Language Creation Society in 2007. The creators of the 2011 *Game of Thrones* television series (based on George R. R. Martin's *A Song of Ice and Fire* novel series, beginning with *A Game of Thrones* in 1996) wanted to have elaborated versions of the various languages used in Martin's fictional world, so that extended dialogue in these languages could be spoken on screen. The creators turned to Arika Okrent, who directed them to the Language Creation Society. The Language Creation Society in turn collected and filtered a number of proposals from its member-ship and passed them along to the producers, who ultimately selected Peterson's work. He rose to prominence for his versions of Dothraki and Valyrian and has built a prolific career as a conlanger, with a long list of projects, including work for the 2013 television series *Defiance*; the 2013 film *Thor: The Dark World*; the 2014 television series *Dominion*, *Penny Dreadful*, *Star-Crossed*, and *The 100*; the 2016 television series *The Shannara Chronicles*;

the 2016 films *Doctor Strange* and *Warcraft*; the 2017 television series *Emerald City*; and the 2017 film *Bright* (David Peterson pers. comm. August 2018).

With so many high-profile conlangs being built by conlangers trained in linguistics, conlanging is increasingly considered a serious activity requiring specialized knowledge, artistic skill, and hard work. It is now rarely sufficient for modern works of fiction to use impoverished conlangs on the antiquated model of haphazardly combining sounds and letters without an underlying structure. A notorious exception is the *Star Wars* franchise, which has generally avoided the kind of sophisticated conlangs used in the franchises listed above. Instead, the conlangs of the *Star Wars* universe are typically superficial impressionistic babbling used to approximate alien languages (Zimmer 2009), which can lead to odd results, such as in 2015's *Star Wars: The Force Awakens*, when the character Tasu Leech says something sounding like *ʃi-dʒi-ga-ni-ga-ma-di-ja* twice in the same conversation, once subtitled as 'it's over for you' and the second time as 'twice'. While the pronunciation is slightly different each time (especially the tone on the second syllable *dʒi*, which is lower in the second occurrence), this would still be a unusual situation in a natlang (and thus, in a naturalistic conlang), though unsurprising given the origin of Leech's speech, which is bits of Indonesian, Sundanese, and other Asian languages cobbled together by Sara Maria Forsberg (a Finnish singer who rose to fame on YouTube with her 2014 video "What Languages Sound Like to Foreigners", in which she fluidly uses mostly spontaneous gibberish to mimic the sound of 20 natlangs; Zimmer 2016).

Though professional conlanging receives the most public attention owing to the popularity of the franchises that feature conlangs, conlanging is increasingly being seen as a valid artistic pursuit with its own merits and purposes, aided in part by publication of conlang grammars, such as Okrand 1985/1992 and Okrand 1997 (for Klingon) and Peterson 2014 (for Dothraki). One of the earliest notable conlangs of this newly empowered generation of personal artlangs is Brithenig, created in 1996 by Andrew Smith as a linguistic thought experiment, to see what kind of Romance language would result if Latin had displaced Celtic in the British Isles and had undergone Celtic linguistic change (Okrent 2010: 286, Stria 2016: 86).

Aided by the expansion of the Internet in the 1990s, and especially the creation of the Conlang email list in 1991, modern conlangers have developed a robust community for exchanging ideas, critiques, and tools, allowing them to develop increasingly sophisticated and experimental conlangs. Many of these are catalogued and archived on various websites, including Linguifex (http://www.linguifex.com/) and the Conlang Wikia (http://conlang.wikia.com/), and many are discussed in the 2017 documentary film *Conlanging: The Art of Crafting Tongues* (http://conlangingfilm.com), directed by Britton Watkins. The Language Creation Society publishes an online journal, *Fiat Lingua* (http://fiatlingua.org/), and hosts the biennial Language Creation Conference (LCC). There are also countless conlang resources on the Internet and in print, including important works such as Rosenfelder 2010 and Peterson 2015. Long viewed as a fruitless pastime by linguists, conlanging has more recently even been the subject of serious academic study within linguistics itself, especially as a pedagogical tool (for example, Gobbo 2013, Weltman 2015, and Sanders 2016; various articles in *Fiat Lingua*, such as Schreyer et al. 2013, Garrett 2016, Anderson et al. 2017, and Pearson 2017; a dedicated panel discussion entitled "Where do Conlangs Belong in the Academy?" at LCC 7, held in 2017; and the Teaching Linguistics with Invented Languages organized session at the ninety-first annual meeting of the Linguistic Society of America in 2017, from which the contributions to this volume are largely derived).

2.6 Applications for language revitalization

Conlanging also has a practical role to play in efforts to revitalize endangered and even extinct languages. Once a generation of children does not acquire a language, its ordinary evolution via native acquisition is broken, which is a devastating blow that languages normally cannot recover from. As the remaining generations of native speakers age and die, their knowledge of the linguistic structure is lost. Languages can be documented, of course, but no matter how robust a corpus, grammar, or dictionary may be, even collectively, they are not a complete substitute for access to natively acquired grammatical competence. Even for English, perhaps the most documented and rigorously analyzed language on earth, linguists are still discovering new facts and new data, so it is not hard to imagine how much information must be lost in typical cases of language documentation of an endangered language, with vastly less material written in or about the language, often filtered through only a handful of speakers and linguists.

Although the natural development of a language may be irrevocably broken by the lack of intergenerational transmission, a sufficiently documented language may yet still be revitalized in some form, so that a version of the language may continue to be spoken and perhaps someday even be natively acquired again. Language revitalization is difficult, requiring not only extensive documentation and massive resources and time, but most importantly, motivation within the community. As Schreyer (2011) notes, language revitalization can take cues from conlanging to aid its success, by drawing upon some of the same technology and by tapping into the same "coolness factor" to build prestige and a stronger sense of identity.

Indeed, even the actual act of conlanging itself can be a part of language revitalization. A particularly fascinating case (reminiscent of the well-known creation of Modern Hebrew as a partly constructed revitalization of Biblical Hebrew; Spolsky and Cooper 1991) is that of Patxohã, a constructed form of Pataxó, an extinct Maxakalían language of the Macro-Jê family, formerly spoken by the Pataxó people in the southern part of the Brazilian state of Bahia. Anari Braz Bomfim, a member of the Pataxó community and scholar of Pataxó culture and language, provides extensive information on the Pataxó people and their construction of Patxohã (Bomfim 2012, 2017), which I briefly summarize here. As part of a larger interest in preserving their cultural heritage, members of the Pataxó community began serious work on revitalizing Pataxó in the 1990s. They collected whatever records they could find, including the oldest known record of Pataxó, a list of ninety lexical items compiled by German Prince Maximilian of Wied-Neuwied in his famed 1815–17 expedition to Brazil, documented in two volumes published in 1820 and 1821. By 1999, interest in revitalizing Pataxó reached a critical point, with increased interest from younger members of the community and the formation of the Projeto de Pesquisa e Documentação da Cultura e Língua Pataxó [Project for Research and Documentation of Pataxó Culture and Language].

The Patxohã revitalization effort is ongoing, and pieces of Pataxó have been collected from written records, songs, elders' memories, related languages, and even remnants lurking in the Portuguese spoken by the Pataxó today. Patxohã now has over 2,000 carefully cultivated words and is being taught in schools. Crucially, this revitalization effort would not have worked without the strong motivation of the community and their willingness to engage in a bit of conlanging, by creating native-like neologisms (as seen in the constructed name *Patxohã* itself, which is a clever blend of *Pataxó*, *atxohã* 'language', and *xôhã* 'warrior') and by repurposing conflicting or redundant lexical items, so that every traceable word in the language could still retain value rather than being discarded. For example, both *miãga* and *txiäng* are documented as having the meaning 'water', but *txiäng* has been repurposed with the narrower meaning 'rainwater'. There are essentially no records of Pataxó grammar, so that has to be constructed as well, and the Pataxó researchers are basing Patxohã's constructed grammar largely on Portuguese, because that is the current native language of the community, with some inspiration from the related language Maxakalí. Although the end result of this process will not be the original Pataxó (a fact explicitly recognized by the researchers in giving Patxohã a distinct name), it will still be a truly Pataxó construction, built by the Pataxó, for the Pataxó.

From religion and philosophy, to art and entertainment, to education and language revitalization, the human drive to build languages has a range of purposes, both fanciful and practical, and the various ways these disparate purposes connect to one another is worth cultivating and exploring.

2.7 Terminology summary

The following is intended to serve as a convenient reference for the reader of this volume, a catalog of definitions of some of the most crucial terms related to conlanging that are used in typical discussions about conlanging. A *natlang* (natural language) is an ordinary language that evolved naturally without conscious planning, such as English, Finnish, Mandarin, Quechua, and Arabic. This stands in contrast to a *conlang* (constructed language), which is deliberately designed by one or more *conlangers*, the real humans whose imagination and hard work a conlang is derived from, such as Hildegard of Bingen, J. R. R. Tolkien, Marc Okrand, David J. Peterson, and the Pataxó community building Patxohã. A conlang may sometimes also be referred to as an *artificial language, imaginary language, invented language, model language,* or *planned language*, though these expressions may carry different connotations or even denotations for some people (van Oostendorp 2019). The English-speaking conlang community has largely accepted *conlang* as the preferred generic term, though the other terms do appear in some sources, especially prior to the online coalescence of the community in the 1990s. Some languages, such as sign languages like American Sign Language and revitalized languages like Modern Hebrew, blur the line between natlangs and conlangs, because they have communities of native speakers like a natlang, despite having some amount of intentional design. Even an originally pure conlang like Esperanto has come to be natively acquired or nearly so by hundreds of speakers (Versteegh 1993, Corsetti 1996, Bergen 2001), allowing it to transition into having properties of a true natlang.

Conlangs can be classified most basically according to whether or not they are modeled in large part on some existing language. An *a posteriori* conlang is primarily modeled on one or more specific existing languages, which may be natlangs or conlangs (for example, Herbert's Fremen is based on Arabic, and

Ido is based on the conlang Esperanto), while an *a priori* conlang such as Klingon is created from scratch, with no direct connection to any particular existing languages. Note that Klingon does have features in common with existing languages, such as the object-verb-subject word order it shares with Hixkaryana (Derbyshire 1977), but crucially, Klingon is not directly derived from Hixkaryana itself. The line between a posteriori and a priori is usually more obvious in the lexicon. With morphological and syntactic structure, the distinction is not as strict, because most conlangs use some grammatical features found in existing languages, if not directly borrowed, at least through inspiration or necessity. For example, all six of the possible orderings of subject, verb, and object are found in the world's natlangs (Dryer 2013a), so any conlang with some ordering of those three units is necessarily duplicating the order from some natlang, whether intended or not. There is no objective turning point at which this kind of linguistic borrowing causes an a priori conlang to be classified as a posteriori instead, so the distinction is more of a gradient scale than a categorical contrast (van Oostendorp 2019).

In addition to its basic linguistic foundation or inspiration, a conlang may also be classified by its creator's motivation. There are three major categories for reasons why someone might want to create a conlang. Nowadays, the most popular type of conlang is almost certainly an *artlang* (artistic language), which is created for some predominately creative purpose, such as use in a work of fiction (for example, Klingon, Elvish, and Kryptonian) or to stand on its own as a work of art, perhaps even just for its creator's own personal satisfaction. The creator of an artlang may also design or draw inspiration from a corresponding *conworld* (constructed world) and/or *conculture* (constructed culture) for the beings the conlang is intended for.

An *auxlang* (auxiliary language) is a conlang created for practical communication among groups of people with different languages; an auxlang intended for international or even world-wide use is sometimes referred to as an *international auxlang*. Experienced conlangers familiar with the history of conlanging are aware of the seemingly insurmountable obstacles preventing an auxlang from fulfilling its purpose, even on a relatively local scale, so they tend to eschew creating pure auxlangs. Indeed, the typically contentious ideological discussions surrounding auxlangs are among the primary sources of tension within the conlang community; for example, the original Conlang email list eventually split in 1996 into two lists, Conlang and Auxlang, to keep the discussions separate (Peterson 2015: 12).

An *engelang* (engineered language) is a conlang created to have some specific structural properties, such as a restricted grammar and/or lexicon (as in Newspeak), using a modality other than speech or sign (e.g. musical notes, colors, or textures), or violating certain linguistic universals (as in Sylvia Sotomayor's (1980–2019) Kēlen). A prominent type of engelang is a *loglang* (logical language), which is created with some sort of overarching logical criteria, usually with the primary goal of having no ambiguity. The most notable well-developed examples of loglangs are James Cooke Brown's Loglan (1960) and its derivative Lojban, which was developed between 1987 and 1997 by the Logical Language Group (Cowan 1997).

These three categories, artlang, auxlang, and engelang, are not mutually exclusive, so a conlang may fall into more than one, as with Elgin's Láadan, which was featured in her *Native Tongue* series of novels, and thus, is an artlang, but which was also designed with particular structural constraints in mind (having a distinctly female worldview), making it an engelang as well.

A *naming language* is a special type of minimal utilitarian conlang, usually an artlang for works of fiction, created primarily to account for a relatively small number of words and phrases, especially proper names and common nouns (as with Lapine). Despite the lack of explicit grammar, naming languages may still have an underlying set of implicit phonotactic and/or morphological rules governing what makes a well-formed word, though they may be somewhat more haphazard and fluid than in a fully specified conlang.

A *relex* (relexification) is an a posteriori conlang in which the lexicon of the source language is replaced (in whole or in part), while its syntax is retained. If the replacement vocabulary also comes from an existing language (making the relex doubly a posteriori), the language providing the replacement vocabulary is called the *lexifier*. Modern relexes are often disdained in the conlang community for being perceived as unimaginative and lazy (though older relexes, especially those marking notable milestones in the history of conlanging, such as Lingua Ignota, are treated somewhat more generously).

A *cryptolect* is a special way of speaking used to disguise a language, often in the form of a relex, with a variety of obscure slang, borrowings, and neologisms replacing important words. A cryptolect is arguably not so much a conlang as it is a specific register, though there is a certain amount of conscious intentionality to a cryptolect that distinguishes it from how registers normally evolve. A particular type of cryptolect is a *ludling*, which involves regular phonological, rather than lexical, manipulation of an existing language, so that the original language is disguised but recoverable by someone knowledgeable in the rules of the ludling (Laycock 1972). Some phonological manipulations found in ludlings include: moving phonemes, as with the baliktád ludling in Tagalog, in which *salá:mat* 'thanks' becomes *tamá:las* by reversing all of the phonemes (Conklin 1956); inserting phonemes, as with Jerigonza in Peruvian Spanish, in which *maestro* becomes *cha-ma-cha-es-cha-tro* by insertion of *cha-* before every syllable (Piñeros 1988); and combining both movement and insertion, as with Utrovački in Serbian, in which *grad* 'town' becomes *ud za granje* by reversing the order of *gra-* and *-d* and then inserting *u-* at the beginning, *za* in the middle, and *-nje* at the end (Rizzolo 2006).

Though not a conlang in and of itself, a ***neography*** (literally 'new-writing') or ***conscript*** (constructed script) is a related concept, an invented writing system. A special kind of neography is a ***pasigraphy***, which is designed as a written representation of meaning only, without connection to any particular language or pronunciation (such as Blissymbolics). Neographies are often created to represent a conlang (such as Tolkien's Tengwar scripts for Elvish), though neographies for natlangs also exist (such as Sequoyah's syllabary for Cherokee and Sejong the Great's hangul for Korean). The distinction between a neography and a truly natural writing system can be difficult to define, since natural writing systems typically have much more intentionality behind them than natlangs do, but known natural writing systems like the Greek alphabet and the Chinese logosyllabary evolved in a largely organic and gradual way, rather than being intentionally designed as a complete writing system in a short period of time.

Acknowledgments

Many thanks to Paul Frommer, Khadija Jagani, Piers Kelly, Suzi Lima, Marc Okrand, Arika Okrent, Matt Pearson, David Peterson, Christine Schreyer, and Ida Stria for conversations and feedback which have helped improve this work in its depth, breadth, clarity, and accuracy.

3

Budding linguists and how to find them

Arika Okrent

Most fields of study begin with love. A noticing, an obsession, a feeling of centrality and importance about how the universe works. The budding geologist inspects the lines in a rock and senses the history of earth being formed, layer by layer, in her hand. The future physicist bounces a wet tennis ball and intuits an explanatory beauty in the pattern the drops make on the pavement. The future historian participates in a time-capsule opening at school, and he marvels at the sense that people from the past had such similar yet different lives. The kind of love that leads to further study is not just fondness or affection, but also a form of wonderment that sparks a desire for deeper understanding.

There are many ways to love language, but not all of them lead to linguistics. On the contrary, it seems that most of them don't. The origin stories of many poets, writers, and students of literature include an obsession with words, seeking out new ones, listing them, feeling them roll off their tongues. There are paeans to the rhythm and musicality of perfect phrases and tender descriptions of the evocative power of perfect metaphors. In most accounts of language love, there is an appeal to a mysterious quality and a kind of magic. Words are things, but more importantly, they *do* things; they do things to us. The desire for understanding that this kind of love inspires asks questions like: Why is this beautiful? Why does this work? Why does this affect me the way that it does?

These are not the questions that the field of linguistics seeks to answer, and often, the lover of language experiences an introduction to the field as a brutal draining away of the magic. They are not wrong to feel this way. Linguistics wants to explain the explainable, not appreciate the magical. That drive can seem cold and clinical to some lovers of language, but it too is motivated by love. It's just a different and very particular kind of love. And there's a certain type of kid that will be drawn to it. You know the type.

You can get some insight into the nature of this type at The Linguist List, an online resource for announcements and information about linguistics, which

Arika Okrent, *Budding linguists and how to find them* In: *Language Invention in Linguistics Pedagogy*. First edition. Edited by: Jeffrey Punske, Nathan Sanders, and Amy V. Fountain, Oxford University Press (2020). © Arika Okrent. DOI: 10.1093/oso/9780198829874.003.0003 includes a collection of autobiographical accounts by famous linguists under the heading "How They Became Linguists"[1] and in the "Featured Linguist" series.[2] If the literary language lover experiences linguistics as a cold departure from the type of understanding they seek, many linguists' stories go in the opposite direction. They describe an early draw toward language but an inability to maintain interest in what seems to be the only place available in which to indulge that interest, a literature program.

For example, Barbara Partee loved studying different languages and especially loved Russian, but she discovered in college that "you couldn't major in Russian grammar, and that all the language majors regarded grammar as something you had to do to get to the literature. I was scared of literature classes (I had no idea how to tell right answers from wrong ones.)"[3] Sarah Thomason decided to major in German and wrote a beautiful, well-argued term paper that her professor loved, but "I didn't believe any of it; it was just an exercise in inventiveness. I thought it was the best work I could do in literature, and I didn't think it was worth the effort." Then she found a linguistics class that "gave me a glimpse of an exciting academic world, a world that had the advantage of dealing with facts about languages rather than with slippery literary constructs that didn't lend themselves to testable hypotheses."[4] Larry Hyman landed in a French department and struggled with the literary aspects of the courses to the point of dread. He perfectly sums up the natural linguist's stance toward the situation in an anecdote he likes to tell (that he admits is apocryphal) about a course he took on Stendhal's *Le Rouge et Le Noir*:

> The teacher asks, "Why do you think Julien Sorel took the hand of Madame Renal?" and then calls on ME! I wouldn't have dared then, but in the story I answer in [colloquial] French: "J'sais pas, moi. Mais ce que, moi, je veux savoir, c'est pourquoi est-ce qu'il a utilisé le subjonctif?" ('I have no idea. But what *I* want to know is why he used the subjunctive?')[5]

That's the perfect anecdote with the perfect laugh line for an audience of linguists, summing up the familiar feeling of being that strange, annoying kid, ignoring the magic for the machinery. At the same time, it conveys

---

[1] https://linguistlist.org/studentportal/linguists/, accessed May 16, 2018.
[2] https://blog.linguistlist.org/tag/featured-linguist/, accessed May 16, 2018.
[3] https://linguistlist.org/studentportal/linguists/partee.cfm, accessed May 16, 2018.
[4] https://linguistlist.org/studentportal/linguists/SarahThomason.cfm, accessed May 16, 2018.
[5] https://linguistlist.org/studentportal/linguists/hyman.cfm, accessed May 16, 2018.

pride in having special ability to see that the machinery itself has its own kind of beauty.

Linguists experience themselves as different from their peers in this way. Brian Joseph remembers taking Latin and "reveling in the declensional and conjugational regularities, admiring the structure, and thoroughly enjoying the whole experience (in contrast to many of my classmates, for whom high school Latin was torture!)."[6] The very aspect of the machinery that the budding linguist finds beautiful—the structure and systematicity—is the least inspiring part for everyone else.

The draw toward systematicity is another recurring theme in linguists' stories. Monica Macaulay took a linguistics course because she thought it might help her with her crossword-puzzle obsession and realized "I had finally found the place where I could combine my love of words and my love of organizing things into systems."[7] Angelika Kratzer "discovered modern linguistics when I tried to find a way to combine my love for the shape of languages and mathematics."[8] Anthony Woodbury remembered learning sentence diagramming in fourth or fifth grade and suddenly had the thought: "This stuff is at least as complicated as the math we're doing, yet we learned it in less than a day. It must be that we really knew grammar all along, and only needed the names. Nice trick!"[9] Most language lovers don't go into their studies excited to find a way to incorporate more math into their passion.

Of course, a literary love of language is not incompatible with a linguist's love. C.-T. James Huang ran his own literary magazine as a high-school student and was so dedicated to it that he failed all his classes and had to return home. He went on to win an English proficiency competition, special admission to university, and a Fulbright fellowship to study linguistics at MIT.[10] My own origin story is heavily tilted toward literature. I always loved a good, messy symbolism hunt. But I also noticed things in a way that I now look back on as particularly linguistic noticing. I remember reading *Les Misérables* at a pretty young age, somewhere around 11 or 12, and picking out the unfamiliar words *serene* and *serenity*. (A quick text search of a popular English translation shows they occur over 40 times in the book.) I intuited what they meant from the context, and I somehow knew how they were

[6] https://linguistlist.org/studentportal/linguists/joseph.cfm, accessed May 16, 2018.
[7] https://blog.linguistlist.org/uncategorized/featured-linguist-monica-macaulay/, accessed May 16, 2018.
[8] https://linguistlist.org/studentportal/linguists/kratzer.cfm, accessed May 16, 2018.
[9] https://linguistlist.org/studentportal/linguists/woodbury.cfm, accessed May 16, 2018.
[10] https://linguistlist.org/studentportal/linguists/huang.cfm, accessed May 16, 2018.

pronounced, because I would repeat them over and over in my head as a pair "serene serenity, serene serenity", feeling that second vowel switch back and forth. This led to the dawning realization that the root of *clarity* was *clear*. "Serene serenity. Clear clarity." I took it no further at the time, but I remember the satisfying feeling of having uncovered a hidden systematicity.

In some cases, this love of system generates a creative impulse to design a system. Pius ten Hacken not only loved Latin paradigms "but also invented phonological and morphological systems for a range of imaginary languages during my school days."[11] Christian DiCanio drafted a new alphabetic system for English.[12] Hana Filip thought "that the grammar rules in my textbooks 'could have been formulated better'. So I tried to come up with various ways of improving on them, 'putting them in a better order', according to what, to me at least, were underlying regularities and relationships among them."[13]

Ironically, this analytical bent toward the machinery of language and away from the layers of meaning, the stories, the allusions, can lead right back around to its own form of creativity, one that puts the magic back in a different way.

J. R. R. Tolkien had both a literary and a linguistic love of language. He luxuriated in symbolism and aesthetics, but he noted that a valuable "freshness of perceptions of the word-form" was gained from working with an unfamiliar language, or better yet, a dead one (Tolkien 1997: 206). Removed from a context of full understanding, a language was sound and structure and could be contemplated as such. The magic stripped away to reveal the bones. Even better still, the raw materials of sound and structure could then be put into service for an act of language invention, a "fitting of notion to oral symbol, and pleasure in contemplating the new relation established" (Tolkien 1997: 206). Tolkien's pursuit of that pleasure through language invention, what he called the "secret vice," was a way of putting his own personal creative vision onto the bones of language.

After I published a book on the history of language invention (Okrent 2010), I received dozens of messages from people who had been that type as kids. Some had their passion sparked by Latin paradigms or sentence diagrams and moved on to drawing up secret languages to use with friends, but they left language behind by the end of high school and went on to other arenas to indulge their feeling for systematicity. Others had never thought about

[11] https://linguistlist.org/studentportal/linguists/hacken.cfm, accessed May 16, 2018.
[12] https://blog.linguistlist.org/fund-drive/featured-linguist-christian-di-canio/, accessed May 16, 2018.
[13] https://blog.linguistlist.org/fund-drive/featured-linguist-hana-filip/, accessed May 16, 2018.

language until encountering a fictional one. They were drawn in by Tolkien's magic and stayed to look more closely at the bones underneath. Or they started looking at Klingon through fandom, and it led them to want to learn Russian or Turkish because they got a kick out of structural features that were alien to English.

David Adger explains how he came to linguistics through the idea of a fictional language, how one can move from "this is cool!" to "how does this work?" to "how does language work?":

> When I was about 11 or so, I grew fascinated with language, mainly from reading Ursula Le Guin's *A Wizard of Earthsea*, a book I still completely love. Le Guin envisaged a world where the words actually created the reality, and every single piece of existence had its own particular name. Fascinated by this idea, and already developing my inner language geek, I started making up languages to explore whether they could work like that. To do this, I had to learn how real languages actually worked.[14]

This type is everywhere: the kid who has an eye and an affinity for abstract systems and comes to notice and appreciate that quality in language. The appreciation may deepen into a kind of love. It may lead to linguistics or simply to a lifetime of enjoyment of that love. If these kids manage to find their way to this love through Latin paradigms and sentence diagrams, how many more might find it through an act of creation, of thinking through problems by making something?

---

[14] https://blog.linguistlist.org/fund-drive/featured-linguist-david-adger/, accessed May 16, 2018.

4

The linguistics of *Arrival*

Heptapods, field linguistics, and Universal Grammar

Jessica Coon

4.1 "Story of Your Life"

I first read the short science-fiction work "Story of Your Life" by Ted Chiang—
on which the film *Arrival* is based—in the summer of 1999, just after it came
out. It was the year after I had graduated from high school and before I started
college. While I now can't be sure whether it was really the first time I had
heard the word *linguist*, I am confident it was the first time I encountered *field
linguistics*. The story came to me seemingly by accident, one chapter away
from a friend's mother's story in a *Year's Best Sci-fi* volume that happened to
be lying on a coffee table in their living room, one summer afternoon in rural
Oregon. From a Heptapod's point of view, though, I think it is safe to say that
nothing should be considered truly an accident.

*   *   *

Two years later, just after finishing my sophomore year in college, I arrived in
Mexico for my first summer of linguistic fieldwork. I flew to Mexico City and
took a bus twenty hours south to the beautiful mountain town of San Cristóbal
de las Casas. Once there, I was to meet up with my undergraduate linguistics
professor, a renowned fieldworker, anthropological linguist, and Mayan languages expert named John Haviland. Haviland gave me a tour of town,
installed me in a guest room in his house, and after a few days instructed me
to repack my bags. The next morning, before dawn, we started out in his truck
down winding mountain roads into the hot jungle lowlands, into Ch'ol
country. With us that morning was a young Ch'ol-speaking woman who
was working on a linguistics MA thesis there in San Cristóbal, along with
her two small nieces, all returning home.

Jessica Coon, *The linguistics of* Arrival: *Heptapods, field linguistics, and Universal Grammar* In: *Language Invention in
Linguistics Pedagogy.* First edition. Edited by: Jeffrey Punske, Nathan Sanders, and Amy V. Fountain,
Oxford University Press (2020). © Jessica Coon.
DOI: 10.1093/oso/9780198829874.003.0004

It is clear to me in retrospect that during that seven- or eight-hour trip I should have been asking more questions: What did I need to know about Ch'ol culture? Were there things I should definitely do? Or definitely not do? What should my goals be for that summer? How did one get started doing fieldwork? And importantly: how should I get back to San Cristóbal? Instead, I spent much of my time staring out the window silently, in a combination of awe at the beautiful scenery—pine forests giving way to thick jungle, cornfields perched on cliffs, people of all ages carrying impossibly large bundles of firewood and corn on their backs along the highway—and panic at the realization of what I had signed myself up for. My silence may also have been due in part to my recognition of just how poor my Spanish really was, as Haviland and his student chatted incomprehensibly, and perhaps a concerted focus on my part to not get carsick.

We arrived sometime in the midafternoon heat at a Ch'ol-speaking Mayan village. Children were sent to find adults, and eventually we were ushered into a small home with a thatched roof, a packed-earth floor, and wood still smoldering next to the comal in the elevated cooking fire (I remember Haviland remarked that, back up in the highlands, the cooking fires are always directly on the ground to help heat the house; here in the jungle the extra heat would be unwelcome). My surprised host family-to-be included the MA student's brother, his wife, and four children: the girls from the truck ride and their two brothers.

It is possible that they had not been warned about our arrival because it simply is not easy to get messages into this village, which at the time had a single satellite phone that rarely worked. Or perhaps they were not alerted on purpose, because it would be easier to say no to this strange request without me standing in their home, looking bewildered and (maybe, slightly) pitiful. Whatever was the case, after a negotiation I mostly didn't understand, Haviland got ready to drive back to the city. Overwhelmed, with no Ch'ol to speak of, a handful of introductory linguistics courses on my transcript, and my courage quickly slipping away, I asked my professor to remind me again what exactly I was supposed to be doing there that summer. "Make some friends," he said casually, "learn some Ch'ol." Then he got back in his truck and drove away.

4.2 *Arrival*

I have to imagine that Dr. Louise Banks, the fictional field linguist and protagonist of the 2016 motion picture *Arrival*, knows the feeling (for more on this feeling, and some tips on how to lessen it, see Monica Macaulay's excellent 2004 article, 'Training Linguistics Students for the Realities of Fieldwork'). A similar mixture of panic, excitement, and self-doubt must have begun to settle in as she was rushed by military helicopter from her comfortable university office to the site of an enormous alien spaceship. Once there, she is tasked with deciphering the language of the recently-arrived Heptapods—a task daunting enough to shake anyone's confidence.

Though the *Arrival* filmmakers consulted me on many aspects of the linguistics in the film, the comparison between Dr. Banks' situation and my own that summer in Mexico is, in truth, hardly fair. For one thing, my job in Chiapas was to learn about the grammar of Ch'ol, a language spoken by around 200,000 Indigenous Maya people in southern Mexico. Today there are about thirty different languages belonging to the Mayan family in Mesoamerica (the exact number depends on what counts as a dialect, and what as a separate language). Taken all together, speakers of Mayan languages total more than six million today. This group of languages is called a "family" because the modern languages are descended from a common ancestral language, Proto-Mayan, partially reconstructed by historical linguists and proposed to have been spoken roughly four thousand years ago. Though there was relatively little work on Ch'ol itself when I started out, the Mayan language family as a whole is one of the best documented language families in the Americas (Aissen et al. 2017).

Dr. Banks' job, on the other hand, was to decipher Heptapod, a language spoken by at least two giant aliens from somewhere deep in outer space (or maybe at least twenty-four giant aliens if one counts the twelve different spaceships that landed around Earth, and assumes that each ship is staffed by two creatures). Whereas I had a body of research on related Mayan languages to read up on, a recent MA thesis by a native speaker of Ch'ol, and even an old Ch'ol–Spanish dictionary produced by missionaries, there is of course no *Learn Heptapod* book for Dr. Banks, no work on related languages (that we know of), and even the best language-learning apps or translation software won't help with Heptapod.

Our work environments were very different too. While I still had a lot to learn about Ch'ol culture, I also had a very welcoming and patient host family to live and work with. They quickly integrated me into the family as something like a useless older sister. I was barely able to sleep in a hammock, open coconuts with a machete, or get my clothes clean in the river—skills which any competent eight-year-old should have mastered. My tortillas never turned out very well, but I discovered that grinding corn was a good arm workout, requiring endurance but not much skill, and I could help out by grabbing groceries on my way back from my weekly trips to Salto de Agua, the nearest town with payphones and an Internet café. I learned that "going for a walk" was not something that women were expected to do alone, but I could volunteer to trek to the river to carry back water from the spring (though while my young host sisters could carry large buckets up and down over the hills without spilling a drop, I required containers that sealed shut in order to avoid an extra bath). Exactly what I was doing learning Ch'ol was not immediately clear to anyone, but everyone rose to the challenge of teaching me their language, patiently answering my requests for translations, judgments, and slow repetitions.

Dr. Banks, on the other hand, had a military tent, a cot, and two giant, seven-limbed aliens in a spaceship. There were other important differences as well. Whereas I had a knowledgeable undergraduate research supervisor in a not-so-distant city (which I eventually did learn how to travel back to), she had military generals yelling at her to hurry up. While my undergraduate honors thesis felt like a very daunting task at the time, Dr. Banks faced impending world war if she didn't get things right. I also had one more significant advantage, though it was not obvious to me at the time: I had Universal Grammar on my side.

4.3 "Universal" Grammar

Here on Earth, language sets humans apart from all other species. Human babies—remarkably bad at basic tasks like feeding themselves, tying their shoes, and adding sums of numbers—effortlessly learn any language (or languages) to which they get sufficient exposure. While children make mistakes along the path of acquisition, even these mistakes follow certain patterns and developmental trends. By the age of five, nearly every child has mastered a complex system of grammar that organizes sounds into words and words into sentences. Beginning from a very early age, kids can produce and comprehend an infinite number of novel utterances—a feat that anyone who has tried to learn a new language as an adult can appreciate.

What linguists call Universal Grammar is the innate human capacity for language: core principles that all human languages share. Though languages show an apparently high degree of variation—the grammar of English is different from the grammar of Japanese, which is different from the grammar of Inuktitut—linguists have discovered that languages vary in limited and constrained ways. In fact, languages tend to follow certain recipes in their grammars (see Mark Baker's *The Atoms of Language* for an accessible introduction to some of these recipes). The syntax of Japanese, for instance, looks in many important ways like the syntax of Quechua, an unrelated language indigenous to the Andes Mountains in South America. Both languages show a basic subject–object–verb (SOV) word order, and in both, direct objects are marked with accusative case, as shown by the sentences in (1) and (2).

(1) Mariya   papa-**ta**   ranti-chka-n.   (Quechua)
     Maria   potato-ACC   buy-PROG-3SG
     'Maria is buying potatoes.'

(2) Maria-**wa**   zyagaimo-**o**   ka-ttei-ru.   (Japanese)
     Maria-TOP   potato-ACC   buy-PROG-NONPAST
     'Maria is buying potatoes.'

Just as the order of verbs and objects is the reverse of what we find in English, "adpositions"—little words like *in*, *on*, and *at*—in both Japanese and Quechua also follow the nouns with which they combine. In English we call them prepositions, while in Japanese and Quechua they are postpositions, as shown by the examples in (3) and (4).

(3) wasi-kuna-**pi**   (Quechua)
     house-PL-in
     'in the houses'

(4) ie-**ni**   (Japanese)
     house-in
     'in a house'

Overwhelmingly, these properties tend to cluster together across human languages: if the verb precedes the object, the language will have prepositions; if the verb follows the object, the language will have postpositions. This is known as Greenberg's Universal #4—one of a list of language "universals" (or in many cases, tendencies), documented by the linguist Joseph Greenberg. These patterns lead linguists to hypothesize that variation among human languages is constrained to certain parameters. Children acquiring language have a head start because their brains are hard-wired with at least some of the basic building blocks of language. Given sufficient exposure to a particular language, these parameters get fixed one way or another: once a kid learns that the verb precedes the object, that kid can then be reasonably confident that an adposition will precede its noun.

In another example, Niuean, a Polynesian language spoken on the island of Niue, shares a number of grammatical properties with Q'anjob'al, a Mayan language related to Ch'ol spoken in the highlands across the border in Guatemala. Both Niuean and Q'anjob'al have a relatively rare basic order of verb–subject–object (VSO), found in fewer than 10% of the world's languages (and following Greenberg's Universal #3, these and other VSO languages are languages with prepositions). Both languages also show what is known as an ergative-absolutive pattern of alignment, in which transitive subjects pattern differently from intransitive subjects; this pattern is found in roughly one quarter of the world's languages (Dixon 1979; Coon et al. 2017). In Niuean in (5), the transitive subject appears with *he* (not found on intransitive subjects), while in Q'anjob'al in (6) the transitive subject triggers a special prefix *s-* on the verb, also not found with intransitive subjects.

(5)　Ne　kai [$_s$　**he**　pusi][$_o$　ia　e　moa].　　　(Niuean)
　　　PST　eat　　ERG　cat　　　that　ABS　bird
　　　'The cat ate the bird.'

(6)　Max　s-tzok'　　　[$_s$　naq　winaq][$_o$　te'　si'　　]. (Q'anjob'al)
　　　PFV　3ERG-chop　　　the　man　　　the　wood
　　　'The man chopped the wood.'

Interestingly, both languages also sometimes permit objects to appear without articles (in indefinite nonspecific contexts). When this happens, the ergative marking disappears, and the order changes to VOS, as shown in (7) and (8).

(7)　Ne　inu　　[$_o$　kofo　kono　] [$_s$　e　Mele　].　　　(Niuean)
　　　PST　drink　　　bitter　coffee　　　ABS　Mary
　　　'Mary drank bitter coffee.'

(8)　Max　tsok'-wi　[$_o$　si'　　] [$_s$　naq　winaq　].　　　(Q'anjob'al)
　　　PFV　chop-AP　　wood　　　the　man
　　　'The man chopped wood.'

Do these three characteristics—VSO order, ergative marking, and VOS order with article-less objects—pattern together for a reason? Or is this an accident? If it's not an accident, why should these relatively unique properties go together? These are the kinds of research questions that linguists are interested in.

Linguists working on understudied human languages benefit in different ways from the same head start that human babies have. A linguist who learns that a subject of a transitive sentence in Ch'ol triggers a special prefix on the verb is not surprised to also learn that possessors trigger an identical prefix on a possessed noun—because exactly this pattern (specifically, a syncretism between ergative and possessive morphology) is found in unrelated languages around the world. A linguist working on a VSO language such as Q'anjob'al expects that question words such as 'what' and 'who' must appear at the beginning of a sentence, as in English, while a linguist working on an SOV language like Japanese is unsurprised to learn that question words may remain in their base positions.

But when it comes to describing the grammar of the newly arrived Heptapods, even the most seemingly basic human language distinction, like the difference between "nouns" and "verbs," or between a statement and a question, is no longer a given. Linguists who coined the term "Universal Grammar" had only the universe of human beings—not Heptapods—in mind. They weren't thinking that far ahead.

4.4 Heptapod A and Heptapod B

In *Arrival*, following the plot of Chiang's "Story of Your Life", the seven-limbed Heptapods have two different languages: a spoken language (dubbed "Heptapod A" in the story) and a written language ("Heptapod B"). Heptapod A, as we learn in more detail in the short story, does not exactly follow the patterns of human languages. But as Dr. Banks notes, it is also not wildly different:

> It didn't follow the pattern of human languages, as expected, but it was comprehensible so far: free word order, even to the extent that there was no preferred order for the clauses in a conditional statement, in defiance of a human language "universal." It also appeared that the heptapods had no objection to many levels of center-embedding of clauses, something that quickly defeated humans. Peculiar, but not impenetrable.
>
> Dr. Banks, in Ted Chiang, "Story of Your Life"

Having flexible word order is not uncommon in languages of the world—but even given word-order variation and flexibility, human languages nonetheless maintain certain consistencies. As the quote from Dr. Banks notes, one such property (Greenberg's Universal #14) is that the antecedent of a conditional (the if-clause) will always precede its consequent (the result). Despite the fact that English and Japanese have reverse orders when it comes to verbs and their objects and adpositions and their nouns, the order of clauses in a conditional is identical:

(9) Ame-ga   fut-ta-ra,   watasi-wa   ie-ni   i-ru.   (Japanese)
     rain-NOM   fall-SUB-if   I-TOP   house-in   stay-NONPAST
     'If it rains, I'll stay home.'

Heptapod A also apparently permits rampant center-embedding, another feature that human languages universally tend to avoid. Consider the sentences in (10). The sentence in (10b) adds a relative clause modifying the subject, *the cat*, to the basic sentence in (10a)—embedding a clause in the middle of another clause. However, if we try to add another instance of embedding, as in (10c), things become dramatically worse, and (10d) is basically word salad (indicated in linguistics by a *).

(10)   a. The cat fell.
      b. The cat [that the dog chased] fell.
      c. ??The cat [that the dog [that the mouse scared] chased] fell.
      d. *The cat [that the dog [that the mouse [that the bird saw] scared]
         chased] fell.

The interesting thing about the degraded nature of English (10c) and (10d) is that this can't be easily pinned to a rule of the syntax specifically; as (10b) illustrates, embedding a clause inside another is not in and of itself a problem. Instead, the problem has been claimed to be one of processing. Our human short-term memory has a difficult time storing up the subjects and then later matching them to their disjoint predicates. In (10d), for example, one has to wade through three other clauses before *the cat* can be associated with its predicate, *fell*. Heptapods are apparently unfazed by this extra tax on memory load—perhaps unsurprisingly, given what we learn about their general cognitive capacities.

Indeed, the devout *Arrival* fan will also not find it surprising that the order of conditional clauses may be reversible in Heptapod. Chiang has clearly done his homework here. While Heptapod A violates human language norms, it does so in an expected way based on what we know of the Hetapods' special cognitive abilities. Chomsky's (1993) Strong Minimalist Hypothesis, formulated for human language, is that language is an optimal solution to interface conditions—that is, to human conceptual and articulatory or sensory-motor needs. Though linguists are still working to understand exactly what these needs are, and what an optimal solution to them would be, if it eventually turns out that all we need to do to predict properties of Heptapod is to modulate our theories appropriately for Hetapods' particular conceptual and articulatory abilities, then perhaps the term "Universal Grammar" may not be so far off the mark after all.

While Dr. Banks makes progress with the spoken Heptapod A, her real focus turns to Heptapod B. For one thing, unlike aliens in many sci-fi films, Heptapods do not have humanoid vocal tracts, and the sounds they make—created in the film by splicing together various animal calls with the help of my phonetician colleague Morgan Sonderegger, and described in the story as sounding "vaguely like that of a wet dog shaking the water out of its fur"—are not reproducible by humans. Indeed, as Dr. Banks notes, we can't even be sure our human ears would be able to pick out which sounds are meaningful. Heptapod B is also preferred over Heptapod A, because Dr. Banks recognizes the importance of being able to interact directly with her language consultants. Colonel Weber initially approaches Banks to do the translation work by simply listening to audio recordings. In the story, she is having none of it:

> But the only way to learn an unknown language is to interact with a native speaker, and by that I mean asking questions, holding a conversation, that sort of thing. Without that, it's simply not possible. So if you want to learn the aliens' language, someone with training in field linguistics—whether it's me or someone else—will have to talk with an alien. Recordings alone aren't sufficient.   Dr. Banks, in Ted Chiang, "Story of Your Life"

Once inside the shell, her attempts to reproduce the alien sounds with her human vocal tract predictably fail. While she is able to make recordings and play them back, she has much more luck working with the writing system.

The written Heptapod B is described by Chiang as being "semasiographic"—a symbolic way of communicating information without a direct tie to phonetic speech. While human writing systems differ from one another in important ways, they are all based in some way on the spoken language. Some human writing systems are alphabetic, with symbols representing individual sounds, while others are syllabic, languages in which symbols represent entire syllables. Still others are logographic—in them a symbol may represent an entire word or concept. Many languages of the world do not have writing systems at all; writing is a useful tool, but not a central part of the innate human cognitive capacity for language. What all human writing systems do have in common is that the writing system is based on the spoken language (or perhaps, on an earlier version of it, as English spelling demonstrates).

We learn that Heptapod B, on the other hand, has no connection at all to Heptapod A. In the film, the Heptapod "semagrams" are beautiful circular swirly symbols; they look something like stains made by a coffee mug, but appear to move like smoke through the air, constantly changing. In the story, they are described by Chiang as resembling "fanciful praying mantids drawn in a cursive style, all clinging to each other to form an Escheresque lattice, each slightly different in stance."

Why have two separate languages in the first place? As the linguist–physicist duo speculate in both story and film, the Heptapods would similarly wonder why we humans aren't taking better advantage of these two distinct media. While spoken languages are constrained in time, written languages need not be. Dr. Banks muses:

> For them, speech was a bottleneck because it required that one word follow another sequentially. With writing, on the other hand, every mark on a page was visible simultaneously. Why constrain writing with a glottographic straitjacket, demanding that it be just as sequential as speech? It would never occur to them. Semasiographic writing naturally took advantage of the page's two-dimensionality; instead of doling out morphemes one at a time, it offered an entire page full of them all at once.
>
> Dr. Banks, in Ted Chiang, "Story of Your Life"

While some people are disappointed to learn that I did not create the language for *Arrival*, often they are even unhappier to learn that it is not really a language at all. Instead, the symbols in the movie are based on the beautiful paintings of Montreal-based artist Martine Bertrand. While the filmmakers went to great lengths to achieve consistency across different scenes, and even created a small manual of roughly one hundred symbols used in different parts of the film, one cannot learn Heptapod B the way one can learn Klingon or Na'vi. (Nor can one sell merchandise promising to translate any English phrase into Heptapod, as one vendor hoped to solicit my expertise for.) And given the consequences of learning Heptapod B, as Dr. Banks does in the story, creating such a language would be no small feat.

Indeed, both the film and Chiang's original work are short on details of the grammar of Heptapod B. We do learn in the story that some elements of Heptapod B are "uniquely two-dimensional"—the curvature and thickness of a line, the manner of undulation, the relative sizes, distances, and orientations of the meaningful elements all play important roles in the grammar. But neither Chiang nor the filmmakers can really be blamed for a lack of detail here. In fact, it isn't clear that even Dr. Banks could fully articulate how she has come to learn this language. Movie viewers watch a montage in the movie of her staying up late nights, furiously decoding semagrams, the wall plastered with symbols and scribbles (my scribbles, at the request of the set designers); concern is expressed for her mental and physical well-being as she begins to learn the language. In the short story, Dr. Banks notes that "the semagrams seemed to be something more than language; they were almost like mandalas. I found myself in a meditative state, contemplating the way in which premises and conclusions were interchangeable." In both the short story and the film, the language-learning experience takes on a surreal quality.

4.5 Linguistic Relativity

It is the uncertainty about how an alien language might differ from human language—and whether and how we humans might be able to learn such a language—that makes the premise of "Story of Your Life" and *Arrival* so thought-provoking. The plot draws heavily on the Sapir-Whorf Hypothesis (left implicit in the short story, but discussed explicitly in the screen adaptation), also known as Linguistic Relativity. Most famously attributed to Benjamin Lee Whorf, Linguistic Relativity is the hypothesis that the language we speak directly affects how we view the world. According to Whorf, speakers of different languages have correspondingly different thoughts.

Whorf was a chemical engineer who studied linguistics with Edward Sapir at Yale University during the 1930s, while still keeping his day job at the Hartford Fire Insurance Company. During this time, he also began his controversial work on the Uto-Aztecan language Hopi, which would come to play a big role in his promotion of Linguistic Relativity. He wrote:

> I find it gratuitous to assume that a Hopi who knows only the Hopi language
> and the cultural ideas of his own society has the same notions, often supposed
> to be intuitions, of time and space that we have, and that are generally

assumed to be universal. In particular, he has no general notion or intuition of time as a smooth flowing continuum in which everything in the universe proceeds at an equal rate, out of a future, through a present, into a past...

Benjamin Lee Whorf, "An American Indian Model of the Universe"

According to Whorf, the Hopi people viewed time differently from English speakers, and this was a direct result of the nature of their language; Whorf claimed that the Hopi language had no way to directly refer to the present, past, or future—or to the passing of time at all. Whorf also famously spread the idea that Alaskan Yupik people's apparently expanded vocabulary for different types of snow meant that they must also think more precisely about snow than the average English speaker (Whorf 1940).

Whorf's linguistic claims about the Hopi language have since been discredited (e.g. Malotki 1983), and in his 1991 essay "The Great Eskimo Vocabulary Hoax," Geoffrey Pullum, citing work by Laura Martin, notes that any English-speaking skier has as many words for snow as speakers of Yupik are claimed to have (think *snow, slush, sleet, powder, blizzard*...). Indeed, Pullum argues that the disputed size of the Yupik lexicon for snow is no more interesting than the fact that professional typesetters know more names of fonts than the lay typist; a fact that is barely noteworthy, and certainly not headline news. Among human languages—which appear to follow the same underlying principles, and differ in interesting but ultimately constrained ways—the strong version of the Sapir-Whorf Hypothesis, Linguistic Determinism, has been argued to be not only wrong, but also dangerous. As Whorf's quote above illustrates, it provides an easy rationale for exoticizing people who speak different languages.

This is not to say that all people view the world in the same way, just that our view of the world is not strictly determined by the language we speak. In his 2014 book *The Language Hoax: Why the World Looks the Same in Any Language*, John H. McWhorter offers an accessible look into some of the debunked myths surrounding Linguistic Relativity, as well as a survey of the more recent and interesting scientific work on subtle correlations between language and thought. In the end, however, McWhorter concludes that language is not the best place to look for differences among humans:

If you want to learn about how humans differ, study cultures. However, if you want insight as to what makes all humans worldwide the same, beyond genetics, there are few better places to start than how language works.

John H. McWhorter, (2016) *The Language Hoax: Why the World Looks the Same in Any Language*, Oxford University Press, p. 29

Indeed, based on the deep commonalities among human languages, Noam Chomsky has famously stated that a visiting Martian (or perhaps Heptapods) would view all human speech as essentially dialects of the same language.

While some linguists have complained about the spotlight given to the Sapir-Whorf hypothesis in the film, in the end, we have to remember that it is science fiction—"fiction" being the operative word—and like all good science fiction, it does make one think: how could an alien's linguistic system differ from our own? What correlations might there be between their language and their cognitive system? And if their language were so different as to change our way of thinking... would we be able to learn it at all?

Personally, though I enjoyed my time working with the filmmakers, I think there are bigger things for Louise Banks and the rest of us linguists to complain about. Take Colonel Weber's attempt at flattery early in the film, when he tells Dr. Banks that she is at the top of everyone's list when it came to translation (groan), the physicist Dr. Donnely's attempt at flattery when he tells her that she really thinks like a scientist (duh), or Banks' opening-scene lecture about how Portuguese is different from other Romance languages (huh?). Though I marked these in red in multiple versions of the script, and offered to write Dr. Banks a more engaging introductory linguistics lecture for the spaceships to interrupt, the filmmakers gently explained to me that in the end linguists are not Hollywood's main audience.

My interactions with the filmmakers did also force me to think: how would we get to work deciphering an alien language when the time comes? How hard would this be? While our knowledge of human language will only get us so far, the tools we have developed for linguistic fieldwork and analysis will be critical. At least I hope this is true, because if aliens have just showed up and someone at the FBI is googling "alien linguistics," my name comes up pretty high on the list.

4.6 Linguistic fieldwork and language diversity

In the movie *Arrival*, Dr. Banks recognizes that the constraints and patterns linguists know to be found in human languages may be of no help in her new fieldwork situation. She nonetheless approaches the daunting task of deciphering the Heptapod language as any good fieldworker would. Inside the Heptapod shell, she is the first to take off her protective spacesuit and approach the glass divide. While theoretical linguists are interested in the abstract properties of language—the formal system that allows us to put sounds together to make words, and words together to make sentences—access to that system is not direct, but must be accomplished by careful work with native speakers of the language in question. As Dr. Banks knows, establishing a positive working relationship is the first step in any successful data-gathering activity.

Louise Banks also knows that progress doesn't happen overnight. Despite the urgent orders of military generals to get to the point—why are they here?— Dr. Banks insists that she must start with the basics. Even seemingly benign concepts, like asking a question or grounding an event in space or time, may have no direct correlate in Heptapod. But if there is hope of deciphering Heptapod at all, it should at least be compositional: that more complex concepts are formed in systematic ways from smaller units of meaning, as they are in human languages. Jumping straight to an exciting complex sentence before understanding the smaller parts from which it is constructed is a first-order error learned in any linguistic field-methods class (and then often learned again the hard way when one is actually in the field).

Finally, Banks recognizes that misunderstandings are virtually guaranteed, and that one can't be too careful drawing conclusions from freshly collected data from an unfamiliar language. My first summer in Chiapas, I was especially interested in Ch'ol's VOS word order—a basic order found in 3% or fewer of the world's languages. Interestingly, Ch'ol is like Q'anjob'al insofar as VOS order is found when the object has no article, and VSO occurs when it has one. But unlike Q'anjob'al, it is not uncommon to find articleless nouns in Ch'ol; articles in Ch'ol are not strictly required for definite interpretations, the way they are in English or Q'anjob'al. Also unlike Q'anjob'al, the ergative marking does not disappear in a Ch'ol VOS sentence, as shown in (11). The Q'anjob'al VOS sentence from above is repeated in (12) for comparison.

(11) Tyi   i-kuchu   [$_O$ si'   ] [$_S$ jiñi x'ixik   ].   (Ch'ol)
      PFV   3ERG-carry   wood   the   woman
      'The woman carried wood.'

(12) Max   tsok'-wi   [$_O$ si'   ] [$_S$ naq winaq].   (Q'anjob'al)
      PFV   chop-AP   wood   the man
      'The man chopped wood.'

A number of other factors have been claimed to interact with word-order alternations in Mayan: animacy, definiteness, and specificity, as well as the relative ranking of the subject and object with respect to some combinations of these properties. In my first summer of linguistic fieldwork, I naively thought

I would jump in by trying to systematically isolate these factors, asking my host family for judgments on the sentences I created.

—Can I say *tyi ikuchu jiñi si' x'ixik*? What about *tyi ikuchu si' x'ixik*? And could I say *tyi ikuchu jiñi si' jiñi x'ixik*?

The answer to every question, over and over again, to my great puzzlement, was "yes." At some point, after a few sessions of this, it occurred to me to rephrase my question.

—Wait...can *you* say *tyi ikuchu jiñi si' x'ixik*?
—No! I would definitely not say that, that's not Ch'ol. But you sound pretty good when you say it—you're getting much better!

Not only is establishing rapport and a clear mutual understanding good for collecting data, it is also a moral imperative. In recent decades, linguists have begun to recognize that earlier colonialist models of linguistic fieldwork— arrive in a community, interview speakers, and extract language data to be published years later in arcane journals—are neither sustainable nor ethical, especially when it comes to the world's many threatened minority languages. On the other hand, active collaboration between linguists and language communities has the potential to lead to benefits on both sides. While the task of language maintenance and revitalization, along with the expertise and knowledge on how to approach it in any given community, ultimately lies with the language community itself, linguists may be able to help with everything, from the creation of descriptive grammars or dictionaries, organizing and archiving material, to navigating the bureaucracy of grant-writing and reporting for language programming. Long-term collaboration with a community in turn will almost certainly provide linguists with a more complete and accurate picture of the language as it is truly spoken and used (see e.g. Hinton et al. 2018, Hinton & Hale 2001, and works cited there).

The above paragraph may suggest that linguists and language communities are distinct entities, though this is not necessarily or even ideally the case. The Mayan language family is perhaps the most impressive example of the importance and impact that native-speaker linguists can have on the health and understanding of languages (England 2007). Maya-speaking linguists have not only produced a wealth of documentary and theoretical work, but also had an important impact on curriculum development, education, and language policy—areas that are more difficult for outsider linguists to affect. This work has led to both increased support for the languages, and a deeper understanding of their fascinating grammars.

In order to fully understand the human capacity for language it is essential that we develop a better understanding of the world's understudied languages. The scientific study of human language is relatively new, and many theories about the principles and parameters of human language were developed on the basis of better-studied languages such as English and French. Though huge leaps in understanding have been made in recent decades, it is crucial that linguists continue to develop and test theories on a typologically and genetically diverse set of languages. The theory of human language must account for the fact that children can acquire any language with ease—Niuean and Ch'ol as well as Russian and Spanish.

This study is also urgent. Today there are around six thousand languages spoken in the world—but 96% of these languages are spoken by just 3% of the world's population (UNESCO 2003). According to some estimates, more than half of the world's currently spoken languages will no longer have living speakers by the end of this century, unless major steps are taken to reduce current trends of language loss (Hale et al. 1992). Modern-day language loss is occurring at a rate never before seen in human history. As Ken Hale writes in the introduction to the special 1992 *Language* volume on language endangerment:

> It is part of a much larger process of loss of cultural and intellectual diversity in which politically dominant languages and cultures simply overwhelm indigenous local languages and cultures, placing them in a condition which can only be described as embattled.
>
> Ken Hale, "On Endangered Languages and the Safeguarding of Diversity"

In addition to contributing to our scientific understanding of the range and limits of possible language variation, a growing body of research has shown that the health of a community's language is a good predictor of other human health and wellness factors (e.g. Walsh 2018). For communities worldwide working to maintain and revitalize their languages, language reclamation has helped lead to a strengthened cultural identity and sense of community empowerment. Also, language revitalization and economic participation are not a zero sum game: maintaining and promoting Indigenous languages does not necessarily come at the expense of the economic opportunities generally associated with speaking the regional majority language. The benefits of multilingualism for both kids and adults have been well documented, and hold true regardless of whether the languages learned are English and Spanish, or Spanish and Ch'ol.

*   *   *

I did eventually find my way back from the village that first summer, and have continued working on Ch'ol and other Mayan languages in the years since. While learning Ch'ol did not alter my perception of reality the way that learning Heptapod did for Dr. Banks, some of my work on the grammar of Ch'ol has helped to shape linguistic theory. More than a decade later, for example, I think I finally have a better handle on VOS~VSO word order variation in Ch'ol (Clemens and Coon 2018). In the years since that summer I have dropped my own students off in fieldwork situations, and now that I understand the true wisdom of Haviland's simple instructions—make some friends, learn some Ch'ol—I haven't left them with much more than this.

That first summer in Chiapas, I did make friends, lifelong ones, along with a handful of godchildren. One of my goddaughters is graduating from college during the month that I am writing this article. She is already a vocal advocate for the Ch'ol language, and the pride she has in speaking her language is a model for her peers and younger family members. She has been actively involved in Ch'ol language research with me for the past few years and is now considering graduate programs in linguistics. I have encouraged her along the way because—whatever one thinks of Linguistic Relativity, Heptapod center-embedding, and our possibilities for extraterrestrial communication—one thing *Arrival* clearly gets right is that language is a powerful tool.

Acknowledgments

This is an expanded version of a piece I wrote for *The Museum of the Moving Image* (www. scienceandfilm.org), edited by Sonia Epstein and developed further here with permission. Thank you to Masashi Harada for Japanese examples and to Pedro Mateo Pedro for Q'anjob'al examples; Quechua examples are from Sánchez 2010, and Niuean examples are from Massam 2001. Special thanks to the editors and reviewers for valuable feedback, and to the many colleagues who encouraged my work with the film.

5

Three conlang projects at three educational levels

David Adger and Coppe van Urk

5.1 Introduction

Over the last few years, we have been working on a project to use constructed languages as a new way to teach linguistic knowledge to three different educational groups, each with a different set of educational aims. The first group is younger children (between 5 and 10) who are learning to read and who are developing an explicit knowledge of core aspects of English grammar. In a summer school at Queen Mary, we have also been using constructed languages to introduce teenage children (about 14 or 15 years old) to linguistics, at a time when they are considering university choices and embarking on foreign language and English language examinations. Finally, constructing a language is at the heart of an undergraduate course aimed at final-year undergraduates who have done an appreciable amount of linguistics in their degree programs, and helps them consolidate this knowledge while also providing an example of how their academic skills could be put to use in a potential career.

The project is focused on educational goals that are, in some ways, particular to the United Kingdom (indeed, English) educational system, but the techniques and ideas have, we believe, broader applicability. The particular educational aims we sought to target are the following: (i) helping younger students with aspects of language (skills in reading, writing, speaking, and explicit knowledge of grammar); (ii) introducing students to concepts that, given the absence of linguistics at school, they otherwise don't have a chance to encounter (especially linguistic typology); (iii) helping students who have been learning about linguistics at university understand what kinds of broad skills the subject gives them and how to deploy them creatively.

Why use constructed languages for this purpose? The answer is that constructed languages involve discipline and knowledge, mixed with creativity

David Adger and Coppe van Urk, *Three conlang projects at three educational levels* In: *Language Invention in Linguistics Pedagogy*. First edition. Edited by: Jeffrey Punske, Nathan Sanders, and Amy V. Fountain, Oxford University Press (2020).
© David Adger and Coppe van Urk.
DOI: 10.1093/oso/9780198829874.003.0005

and play. Constructed languages have a long history, going back in the West to Hildegard von Bingen's *Lingua Ignota*, and are found across cultures (for example the Damin taboo language of the Lardil tribe in Australia has been argued to be a constructed language (Hale and Nash 1997)), but they have come to particular prominence lately through the growth of world creation in entertainment (films, books, games, etc.). This makes them particularly apt as a means of leveraging interests many students already have in the interests of educational goals.

The idea of using constructed languages as part of a linguistics education started from Adger's involvement with a television series (*Beowulf: Return to the Shieldlands*) for which he constructed two languages. *Beowulf* was produced by ITV Studios, one of the major players in broadcasting in the UK; it aired in the UK in early 2016 and ran for twelve episodes. It attracted about 2.5 million viewers but was not recommissioned for a second series. Adger worked with the production company to develop two languages: one spoken by a tribe of semi-human creatures called the Warig, and the other by a human group called the Mere. Though much of the language translation work was ultimately not used, three of the episodes involved the languages.

The experience of working with the production team, which involved developing a detailed understanding of the brief given by the producers, explaining to the producers how a language would work, and developing the languages, was the initial seed of the idea that these would be good skills for final-year undergraduate students to have in their careers. Further, the enjoyment of creating the languages and the way that it allowed the combination of linguistic knowledge from Adger's core research with a creative project led Adger to propose and develop a course entitled "Constructing a Language," aimed at final-year undergraduate students.

Following on from the success of this module, Adger and Van Urk set up a week-long summer school to work with high-school students from schools local to the Queen Mary University of London area. The idea here was to provide a fast but in-depth introduction to some ideas from linguistic typology for school students. Over the course of the week, the students learned some basic concepts about language that they would have not met, or only touched on superficially, in foreign language or English classes. We taught them some core concepts in linguistics (morphotactics, aspects of writing systems, word order, case, agreement) as well as practical skills (some non-English phonetics, interlinear glossing of examples, etc.) and gave them a series of worksheets where they had to make typological choices about their language each day. This culminated in a poster competition where the students composed a piece of creative writing in their constructed language.

The most recent initiative is a new project set up with the Centre for Literacy in Primary Education. This is a charity whose aims are to improve literacy and the love of reading amongst primary school children (ages 5–12). Adger and Van Urk are working with the Centre to train teachers to create materials that they can then use with their classes.

Overall, these three projects exemplify a number of techniques that teachers can use to make learning about language and linguistics both fun and useful. They show the ways that constructed languages can be used as a means of enhancing students' understanding of language at each educational level.

5.2 Primary education

5.2.1 Educational partners

The Centre for Literacy in Primary Education is a national charity based in London whose aim is to help primary school children engage with books, and to engender a life-long love of reading in them. Recently, the UK government has established what amounts to a National Curriculum for primary schools, requiring teachers to engage with some quite complex linguistic concepts, and to use these in their teaching. The two most important areas are the use of a roughly phonological approach to reading called phonics, and the use of a set of grammatical terms for older children to use in analyzing English. Teachers, who have usually had very little linguistics in their training, struggle with both of these, and need help and guidance in embedding them in their teaching. We have been working with the CLPE to develop materials around these two areas to help teachers engage with the core concepts in a way that allows them to directly import the ideas into their teaching while covering the requirements of the National Curriculum.

5.2.2 Synthetic phonics

The phonics approach to reading involves the development of phonemic awareness in children and then a fairly explicit understanding of the rather complex relationships between the phonemes of English and their graphemic representations.

The most common approach to using phonics in primary school teaching in the UK is the synthetic phonics approach. This involves helping children to become aware of the likely phonemic values of individual graphemes or collocations of graphemes, and then how they can be blended together to give the sounds of whole words so that children can read them. This approach can also be used for writing, where children use the same phoneme-to-grapheme correspondences to segment the pronunciation of words into phonemes and thereby to work out the probable corresponding graphemes. After explicit teaching, these various tasks become routinized in the children's suite of cognitive skills.

The way that reading is tested in the UK involves the children's being examined on the "pure" synthetic phonics skills. That is, children are asked to read words with no context, or surrounding text. They are also asked to read made-up words, using the grapheme-to-phoneme correspondences they have learned. A substantial number of teachers, and of children, find this testing stressful (Cook et al. 2007). Part of the task we set ourselves is to work out a way of relieving some of this stress by engaging with synthetic phonics through constructed languages, which, given the prevalence of made-up words in the phonics tests, involves closely related skills. The core idea here is to inject fun and creativity into the learning for both the teachers and the pupils, while reinforcing some of the core concepts and ideas that are needed for the tests.

The model we have developed with the Centre for Literacy in Primary Education follows a broad pattern that the charity has used previously for changing practice amongst teachers. We provide workshops for groups of teachers (about twenty at a time over a day) and they then use what they have learned in their own teaching practice, reflect on this, and then feed it into improved training. We provide lesson plans, ideas, guidelines for activities, as well as the method of using constructed languages to teach the core concepts.

5.2.3 Sounds

Constructed languages are an ideal way to teach some of the concepts behind phonics. A constructed language has its own phonology, but it also has what is usually described as a romanization: that is, a mapping of the phonemes into graphemes and collocations of graphemes. These are typically highly systematic. Constructed languages can also have their own writing systems, which may have single symbols for what are expressed as digraphs in the romanization. Finally, since the phonics test involves made-up words, constructed languages are an ideal way to inject creativity into this otherwise seemingly meaningless process.

The lesson plans follow a careful structure, starting with examining published books to teach certain important concepts, and then expanding to using the students' own imagination and creativity to develop their own linguistic systems.

For example, to teach the conventionality of graphemes, we developed a plan for lessons that first involved the teacher exploring, with the students, the way that the runes in Tolkien's *The Hobbit* are used, or the coded symbols in Eoin Colfer's *Artemis Fowl* books. These are simple systems that transliterate English spelling into unfamiliar symbols. Once the students have learned how these work, they practice them by using them to write coded messages to one another. This teaches the students that the notion of a grapheme is something purely conventional. It also engages their natural fascination with codes and secrets.

At the next level, the students are told that they are going to create a language, and the teacher invites them to pick a subset of English phonemes for this language, working initially with just the sounds. With these in place, the students are then each asked to create a random syllable using the sounds they like best, but these syllables can't be English words. The result of this exercise is that the class together has a collection of syllables made out of English phonemes. The teacher then helps the students put their syllables together to create words (with the condition that their words are not allowed to be extant English words). All of this is done purely using spoken sounds. Finally, the teacher asks the students how these non-English words would be spelled in English. This allows teachers to highlight the difference between a single sound and its spelling as a monograph or digraph. It also allows the students to use some of the spelling rules they have learned looking just at English.

Another lesson plan extends this approach and teaches the students the difference between phonemes and graphemes. In this lesson, the students are asked to draw objects which are signified by the words that the class has made up. For example, if one of the words that has been developed is *gragoo*, then one of the children will be asked to draw some object that *gragoo* denotes (say a special kind of tree, or a monster, or an animal). The teacher then collects the drawings and connects each drawing to a sound in the word (usually the initial sound). In our example, the sound *g* from *gragoo* could be connected with a drawing of a tree. The students then simplify their drawings to turn each into a kind of letter. The teacher can talk about the ways that the letters can be made (via scratches on stone, or brushes and ink, or paper and pen) and the children can be given different materials to make their letters with. Finally, the class will end up with a kind of alphabet where each sound has a symbol. This is a subtle way to help children see the difference between a phoneme (the initial sound) and a graphemic representation of that phoneme. The children can then use the alphabet they have created to send coded notes to one another, in English, or even in a mix of English and the language they have created. They can critically interrogate which system works better (for example, they might have a single symbol for something English represents as a digraph, or they might have a single symbol for something English represents with a complex spelling rule).

This idea can be extended in many ways. For example, it is possible to teach conventions of capitalization by getting the children to explore changing their writing systems so as to make certain letters special: the first in a sentence, the first in a word, the last in a sentence, the last in a word, etc. This can be made to connect with art education by the use of decorative illuminated letters from real manuscripts. Students can develop a project on drawing a word in their writing systems using their special letter conventions. The purpose of this kind of work is to establish in students' minds the idea that there are clear, if arbitrary, conventions governing when capital and non-capital letters are used.

The same system can also be used to teach the core idea of the conventions of English punctuation. For example, when the children are sending coded messages to one another, are they using English punctuation in their writing systems? Teachers can encourage them to change this, for example by using interpuncts instead of spaces; by changing the order of the writing system from left to right to right to left, or top down, or boustrophedon; by changing the punctuation for commas; by introducing special punctuation for questions and orders. Teachers can then bring this back to English by writing English sentences using the students' new punctuation (writing right to left, or top to down, using interpuncts, etc.). This can be played with in poetry (using, for example, concrete poetry).

The same basic set of resources, developed by the children themselves, can now be used to teach other conventions too, as well as to raise phonemic awareness. For example, teachers can teach the children the simple distinction of vowels versus consonants and ask them to organize their writing system by vowel versus consonant. There can then be a critical discussion on why the English system is organized as it is. More advanced levels can teach the children further aspects of phonemic awareness, such as simple places of articulation, asking them to organize their writing system in that way.

Recall that an important part of the synthetic phonics approach involves the twin notions of blending (i.e. taking graphemes that have some phonemic value and combining them) and segmentation (i.e. working out what the phonemes associated with graphemes are, and what their likely value is in a word). The writing-system approach can be used to teach skills of blending and segmentation via a lesson where children pair up and work on writing each other's names in their writing systems, developing their ability to do segmentation. The children then make badges in their writing system, which they decorate.

The next stage of teaching blending and segmentation involves using a picture book of an alien planet with strange objects and actions. In this lesson the students are asked to make up words for these, using the phonemes of English, and they use their writing system to spell out the words for the objects and actions. The children then use their writing system to annotate the picture books, enhancing their skills of segmentation. This can be taken further by asking children to draw a map of an imaginary world, with seas, mountains, forests, etc., which they give names to, which are then used to annotate the map, again using their writing system, plus an effective romanization.

A further lesson plan is to develop a project for the children where they write a poem using some of the words made up for the imaginary objects or place names, with a rhythm and a rhyme. They are asked to write this in the writing system and decorate it, with an initial illuminated letter.

All of these lesson plans use the students' creativity to make up words, to design a writing system, and to use what they have created. Working on this requires the same set of skills that is core to the phonics approach, also the skills that are tested in the phonics test. However, because the students get to play with this material, and develop the words themselves, they come to own the skills, and this is intended to make the whole process less stressful.

5.2.4 Grammar

The National Curriculum for primary school children in the UK requires the children to be able to deploy quite a rich set of grammatical terms correctly. Much like phonics, this is a skill that many teachers will not have gained during their training. The grammatical concepts go beyond the terminology, ranging from fairly simple ideas such as grammatical number, tense, and syntactic categories, to more complex ideas about word order used for emphasis, agentive nominalizations, allomorphy, etc. The selected set of terms to use in describing these concepts has been stipulated for the National Curriculum (passive, modal verb, relative clause, determiner, subordinate clause, etc.); these must be used by the teachers and learned by the students. This approach has been controversial, attracting much negative comment in the press and from teachers (Mansell 2017), and the surrounding discourse has led to much negativity, as the teaching of formal aspects of grammar has led to criticisms that creativity is stifled, and that the skills learned are not helpful to students in their reading or writing (Rosen 2015). What is needed is a way to re-engage teachers, and hence students, with the idea that using formal aspects of grammar can be purposeful and can, in fact, be a way to develop disciplined creativity in the children, and to enhance their imaginative capacity.

Again, constructed languages open up an opportunity to explore issues of word order, category, the grammatical forms associated with speech act, and many other grammatical concepts in a way that can be fun and creative as well as enlightening, giving motivation to the acquisition of the terminology and a practical task to help embed the concepts. There are also a number of children's books that can be more or less directly used as ways of approaching various grammatical issues through constructed languages, most notably Carson Ellis's *Du is tak?* and Jon Scieszka's *Baloney (Henry P.)*.

The work on grammar builds on the work that the students have already done in developing a writing system and a vocabulary of words in a constructed language. The materials developed for teachers are intended to address some core concepts in grammar (these are at what is called in England, Key Stage 1, covering the first two years of primary school, ages 5–7).

One important concept that children need to learn is the different functions that words and grammar have. A simple way of doing this is to begin by taking a picture book and asking the children to write a story about what is happening in the book, mainly in English, but substituting in words from their constructed language wherever they can. This is already a technique that has been used by Jon Scieszka in his *Baloney (Henry P.)*, and it can be used easily in the initial lesson plan that starts this series of classes off.

The next set of lessons all depend on the children creating a world with places, creatures, objects, things the creatures can do, etc. The first lesson involves the students working in groups. The teacher asks the students to draw the creatures in their world, what kind of dwellings they live in, any special tools they use, what food they eat and how they catch it, and to make a map of the country the creatures live in. With this all created, the creatures will need a language to communicate in.

This world can now be used to teach all sorts of grammatical ideas. The concepts of singular and plural (and associated terminology) can be taught by asking the students to create words in their language for the various objects they have drawn and then ask them how to signify two or more of these objects. The technique the teachers use is to teach the idea of suffixes and prefixes in English, and then give the students a choice (effectively a design choice for their language) about whether they use suffixes or prefixes to mark singular and plural. There's a fair amount of National Curriculum-mandated terminology here (singular, plural, noun, suffix, prefixes), but it is all in service of some creative act that the students are engaged in, so it has meaning for them. This same technique can then easily be extended to teach other core concepts of the curriculum.

For example, to teach the concept of adjectives, teachers continue the same exercise but modify the nouns. How do the students want to say *big tree* or *happy monster*, etc.? Is there a rule for where the noun and the adjective go (word-order conventions)? How do the creatures say that something is the biggest, or happiest? Teachers can use the terminology of the National Curriculum with examples from English, and then offer the students a design choice for their own language (e.g. adjective before or after the noun; super- lative marker as a separate word or as an affix). The students then vote on these choices in their groups. Prepositions can be taught in the same lesson by modifying the nouns with locative prepositional phrases. How do the students want to say *tree in the forest* or *happy monster under the tree*, etc.?

In the following lesson, teachers can continue the same exercise but now ask what the creatures are doing. This allows them to introduce different verb types (transitive and intransitive), as well as past and present tenses, continuous aspect, and modifiers of verb phrases. Each case involves teaching a very simple aspect of English, not for its own sake, but so the students can make a choice for their own language. In this way, the learning of grammatical terminology is made immediately relevant to what the students are doing. The differences can be emphasized by finishing the lesson with a competition about whose language is most different from English. This requires the students to have understood, and been able to explain, aspects of English grammar.

The final set of lessons move up from teaching about grammatical categor- ies to teaching about the grammar of sentences. The teacher asks students to draw a very small comic strip using the world they have made up. They then need to create sentences to explain what is going on in the comic strip. To do this, they need to decide what the order of subject, verb, and object is. The creatures need to say things to each other, so the students need to be able to make decisions about whether the grammar of statements is the same as the grammar of questions and commands. They can even write the dialogue in their own script, deciding on how to use punctuation to differentiate these different types of speech act.

The final and most complex lesson plan involves grammatical subordination. For this, the teacher provides the children with some simple examples of subordination in English, pointing out the connection between verbs and clauses. The teacher then creates a dialogue a few sentences long for students to translate. This dialogue involves some simple verb-complement structures, using *say*, *ask*, *think*, *believe*, and *know* with pronouns in the subordinate clauses and crucially a distinction between direct and indirect speech. Students then translate this dialogue into their language, and the lesson ends by again bringing the topic back to English: how is their language different from English?

These various tasks are intended to allow the students to be creative with language, and to not only teach them the terminology and concepts, but to give them a motivation for learning. A significant advantage of using constructed languages in this context is that it provides a way of making grammatical knowledge purposeful, because students have to understand the concepts discussed in class in order to complete the tasks they have been given and successfully design a language. In addition, one of the main complaints about the grammatical terminology in the National Curriculum, as well as the way that phonics is taught, is that these are divorced from the reality of the students' day-to-day lives. What the constructed language technique does is to provide a bridge between grammatical knowledge and the creatures and worlds that children invent, providing motivation for learning by giving the children a project that stretches their imaginations and engages their creativity.

5.3 Secondary education

In 2016, Adger and Van Urk developed a proposal, as part of Queen Mary University of London's Widening Participation scheme, to run a one-week summer school for high-school children (Year 10 in the English educational system, which is roughly 15-year-olds). The project was called *Creating a Language*. Interest in constructed languages has grown steadily amongst this age group over the past few decades (Okrent 2010). Much of this is due to the commercial success of *The Lord of the Rings* films (featuring Tolkien's constructed languages Quenya and Sindarin), *Avatar* (with the constructed language Na'vi), the rebooted *Star Trek* series (which uses the constructed language Klingon), and most recently, with the huge success of the *Game of Thrones* series, where the constructed languages Dothraki and Valyrian play a central role.

The proposal intended to capitalize on this popularity and to run a summer school on how to "build your own constructed language." The core idea was to use this to teach some basic linguistics to students, partly to show them what a linguistics degree program might involve, and partly to make the ideas and concepts of linguistics more available to school-age children. Linguistics is not taught systematically at secondary level in the English high-school system, though there is some sociolinguistics and language acquisition as part of the English Language curriculum. However, this is very focused on English, and the purpose of the summer school was to introduce an understanding of some of the structural aspects of how languages work in general: issues of the organization of sound systems, morphological typology; morphosyntactic features such as person, number, gender, case, tense, aspect; and ideas from syntax about word order, agreement, and case assignment.

Knowledge of linguistics is crucial for constructing a language, and this workshop was intended to give interested students the basic tools they need, and hopefully to spark a deeper interest in linguistics. Further, the summer school introduced school children from less-advantaged backgrounds to a university level subject that is not taught in school, opening up new opportunities for them in tertiary learning (including an excellent item for personal statements in their university applications). Because the summer school engaged students' creativity, it gave them the experience of not only learning new concepts and putting them to use, but also working with them to achieve their own goals, in their own ways. The excitement of the process, which directly connects to aspects of popular culture that they know well, raised their aspirations about coming to university, and their confidence in working with unfamiliar concepts.

The summer school was run by Adger and Van Urk. Daniel Harbour, an expert in writing systems, gave a guest lecture on that topic, and Francis Nolan from Cambridge, who developed the language *Parseltongue* for the Harry Potter films, gave a seminar on how he did this. In summary, the aims of the summer school were:

- to introduce some basic linguistic ideas to students (there is no part of the high-school curriculum that involves linguistics besides some fairly low-level material in an optional examination on English Language): the way that sounds are organized; how words are structured; basic notions of syntactic structure; and historical relatedness;
- to provide students from less-advantaged backgrounds with university-level teaching in a subject they would otherwise not have access to;

- to highlight the inherent interest of studying the basic building blocks of language and to connect real linguistic research with the commercial entertainment world; and
- to enthuse students to apply to degree courses that include some linguistics and highlight the expertise at Queen Mary University of London in this area.

Summer schools of this sort are a well-established vehicle for engaging school students, and raising their aspirations to attend university. Each day involved two two-hour workshops. The afternoon session discussed constructed languages currently used in books, TV series, and films, and introduced linguistic concepts through these, but also through various languages of the world, drawing on original research work that Adger and Van Urk had done themselves on languages such as Kiowa, Gaelic, Fijian, and Dinka (e.g. Adger et al. 2009; Adger 2010; Van Urk and Richards 2015; Van Urk 2019). This allowed us to show the students what unfamiliar human languages could do in terms of important linguistic concepts such as free word order, verb initiality, possessive syntax, and word formation, while at the same time introducing them to the idea that there are limits to human languages. The morning workshops were dedicated to the students developing and later presenting aspects of the constructed language they had designed.

We engaged two student ambassadors who helped with the summer school. Student ambassadors are undergraduate students at Queen Mary University of London with an interest in working with school-age students who wish to come to university. We ensured that appropriate parental permissions were in place for travel arrangements.

We organized the teaching of concepts around the idea of "design choices." For each topic, we would teach the students some basic linguistic ideas, and present them with choices that they would have to make for their languages. For example, we taught the students that languages differed in how long their words could be, either because they were just long (an extreme example of the latter is Tolkien's Entish language, where the word for 'hill' has fifteen syllables!), or because they were morphemically complex. We introduced the idea of morphemes, of affixes, and then used that to talk about isolating versus agglutinating languages. With that in hand, the students made a design choice about the length of their words, and from that flowed various other implications (how plural, or tense marking worked). We also introduced them to certain categories they might not have experienced before (dual, paucal, remote past) and morphemic mechanisms such as full and partial reduplication. These too were associated with design choices. By the end of the second day, the students had a sketch of the word structures of their language.

Similarly, we introduced students to an intuitive notion of subject and object, and then gave them examples of radically different word-order systems (Klingon with OVS order, Fijian and Gaelic with verb-initial order, and Na'vi and Warlpiri with free word order). We extended this to possessor-noun and adpositional structures, and again asked them to make design choices. We then asked them to develop a dictionary, and to translate some simplified paragraphs from Harry Potter into their language. Finally, they all made posters where they presented the world they had invented, the creatures that inhabited it, and the language these creatures wrote and spoke, together with a poem, myth, song, or other piece of writing in the language, which they glossed. The students produced some excellent work, and Adger wrote a blogpost on this, which attracted a fair amount of attention. Some of the work of the students can also be seen on the blog.[1]

The students' conlangs were extremely impressive given the short timescale of the summer school. For example, one of the languages used partial reduplication for paucal number and full reduplication for plural; another required all syllables to be of VC shape (which the student found hard to keep to, but he creatively solved the problem by introducing certain phonetic rules to explain some of his non-VC cases). There was also a language with circumfixal tense marking and one where the word order varied depending on the gender of the speaker. A couple of the languages used boustrophedon writing systems, which the students matched carefully to the history and technology of the speakers. Overall, the quality of the students' work, and the amount of material they learned in an extremely short timescale, were both impressive, and a testament to the method.

At the close of the summer school, we presented students with a certificate of attendance, and awarded prizes for the final posters they produced. In addition, the students filled in evaluation forms, and the comments were overwhelmingly enthusiastic and positive about their experience. The student ambassadors also took part in the development of a conlang (they were English Literature students with no prior experience of linguistics).

One of the teachers of the students commented, "Our three students reported back that they had an amazing week and felt privileged to be there. Thank you for the wonderful experience you gave them."

---

[1] https://davidadger.org/2017/05/29/inventing-languages-how-to-teach-linguistics-to-school-students/

Overall, this was an excellent way to provide a small group of students with an experience of learning about linguistics in a way that was otherwise completely unavailable to them at school.

5.4 Tertiary education

In 2014, Adger was contacted by a TV production company who were creating a version of the Old English epic *Beowulf* as a TV series for a modern audience. The series had a fantasy aspect, and involved two races for which the plot required languages. Adger worked with the company over a period of a few months to create these two languages. This involved continually reshaping the grammar and sound systems of the languages so as to meet the practical and creative desires of the TV production company, ITV Studios. For example, the company wanted one of the languages to be "harsh" and "guttural," and the other to be maximally different from this. This involved Adger in trying to understand exactly what the producers meant by "guttural" (which they didn't really know themselves). It also involved continually redrafting the language so that it was phonemically simple enough for actors who were working as extras, and also so that the sentences were short enough for the extras to remember. For example, after sending in the translation of the relevant parts of an episode-script, the producers responded with:

> Thanks so much for the work you've done on the Mere language. I love the sound of it. I was wondering if it is possible to simplify the sounds/the number of words. It sounds great, but I think the actors will find the range and nuances quite a challenge. I could listen to this all day, but I fear it may take all day to get these right, it's fine if you can't, but could you have a think, else we'll have to cut the Mere dialogue back.

In the end, much of the two languages ended up on the cutting-room floor, with only three episodes featuring Adger's work. However, the experience was integral in designing a third-year university-level module based on the students creating a language for a fictional TV production company. This course, *Constructing a Language*, has, by 2020, run four times very successfully.

The impetus for designing the course for final-year students is that many students who have taken some linguistics are not immediately able to see what general skills they have learned, beyond the specific knowledge that their previous courses have given them, or how they can be creative by bringing all their skills and knowledge together. Because the course was designed around an interaction with a fictional employer, the students gained experience in a range of important general skills. The course gives the students a chance to bring together the linguistics they have already learned into a single system, incorporating phonetics, phonology, writing systems, morphology, syntax, lexical semantics, and historical linguistics; it gives them the experience of working to a set of guidelines, experience of how such specifications can alter across a project, and how to react to that; it shows them that they can be creative even within the confines of an externally imposed task; it allows them to show their capacity as professional linguists.

The overall structure of the course is that students are working to put together a pitch for an invented language for one of two projects. The pitching process takes place over the semester, and at the same time, the script is being written, so students have a chance to feed in their ideas about the languages and cultures involved.

Students are asked to choose one of two scenarios. The first is a sci-fi film where a crew of human astronauts come across an ancient tomb on a deserted (they think!) planet. One of the team is a linguist who begins to decipher inscriptions and activates a machine which throws her crewmate's mind back in time to when the planet was inhabited, but it also throws the mind of one of the aliens forward into the crewmate's head, so that he is, to all intents and purposes, an alien amongst his own crew. His speech is in the alien language and is to be subtitled.

The second scenario is a fantasy TV series where the invisible veil that separates humankind from the supernatural world is breaking down. Individuals, who to all intents and purposes were as human as anyone else, are revealed as supernatural creatures who feed on human souls: their ability to blend in is being lost, and they even stop being able to speak a human language. One of the first people to find out about this is a London police-woman, whose area is Mile End and Bow, and whose first encounter is seeing one of the muggers she's arrested turn into a strange blurred creature, whose English is replaced by fragments of a strange language.

Students are assigned into one of the two groups, and each week there is a lecture on some aspect of linguistics important to constructed languages. Over the course of the semester, the students design a phonology for their language, a writing system, and they begin to develop a history and culture for the creatures that they are writing about. The breadth of the two scenarios has allowed the course tutor to change the details over the years that the course has run. In the first year the aliens were a kind of jackal-like creature roughly based on Anubis from Ancient Egyptian mythology, while the urban fantasy series involved cat-like demons. In the second year the aliens were moth-like flying creatures, while the urban fantasy involved demonic humanoids. It's important to give the students some specificity so as to guide their creative choices, and these different scenarios have led to some incredibly impressive design choices for the languages, from phonologies mimicking cat communication involving huge numbers of triphthongs (with an associated writing system as a reverse abugida, where the consonants are decorations on the core vowel graphemes) to chittering clicks marking speech-act types for the moth-like aliens.

Students are given a task each second week via Production Directions, which act as briefs that they need to keep to. The production directions are organized so as to extract more and more complexity from the students' languages as the course progresses. For example, the initial directions for scenario A are as follows:

> We urgently need about 30 seconds of monologue. It has to sound really alien and weird. This is just a one off with an extra, so can you record it for us. It doesn't really matter what the monologue says, as we just want to show a scene where a mugger flickers between human and demonic creature, but something that's along the lines of "Let me go. Do not touch me. Pathetic human. I will kill you..." plus some other stuff like that would do. Can you make it sound quite scary – they're meant to be demons. We'll be picking up on this language later, so it'd be good to reuse bits of this down the line. Can you send a romanization and a version in IPA, too?

The directions leave quite a lot of freedom for the different students, but highlight that they need to start being consistent, that a recording is needed, as well as a romanization and a version in IPA. In the class, the students have already been shown how to present the material in glossed form. The directions for the two scenarios are parallel, so as to keep the complexity of the grammars of the class roughly at the same level. In this first set of directions, the translations are kept very brief and simple, as the emphasis is on designing the sound system and initial basic vocabulary.

The second production instructions require the students to have come up with a writing system. In the class, they have been taught about the historical development of writing systems, and they've done an advanced version of the exercise that the elementary-school children do, drawing symbolic representations of lexical items, turning these into letters, allowing for historical changes in the sound systems and the lexis, and deciding on whether their system will be alphabetic, an abjad, an abugida, a syllabary, or involve ideophones. The instructions for scenario B here are as follows:

> Hi, David here again from the production team. We really love the work you're doing, and the language is sounding great. We have a couple of things coming up in the script, that need some more linguistic input. The East End cop, during her investigation, has come across an underground shrine of some sort, and on the floor, in a circle of some kind, there's a text written in the demon language. This is going to end up being a portal into the realm of the night and shadow, and the only way a human can move into that realm is by standing in the circle while the words on it are read. The cop doesn't quite realize what she is doing until she is standing on it, is suddenly held fast by a strange force, and one of the demons steps out from behind the altar and begins to read:

> "Oh circle of the dark realm, hear me and by the names of X and Y obey me. You are the circle that opens the way. Open now for this mortal who I give to you. Take her into the dark realm. Let my spell shake the stars, for I am the claw in the heart. I am the dark shadow by the door. Hear my call. Circle of the night, open!"

> (You can put in X and Y as whatever name you like—they're just meant to be some gods of the demon creatures).

> We need a fragment of the text in the alien language in a writing system to inscribe the circle with, but also one of the actors (a very accomplished actor) will have to read this aloud, so we need it in the romanization you have put together, as well as a recording. Thanks!

Again, scenario B is more or less parallel (involving a special ritual to bring the human mind back from the depths of time). Crucially, both production instructions are designed to elicit certain grammatical structures: in this case vocatives, imperatives (including jussives), equative constructions, subject and object extraction from relative clauses, genitives, etc. Some of the work that the students completed for this was truly impressive. One student developed a computer font for her language and inscribed the whole circle (Figure 5.1), while another designed his script around the kinds of claw marks that putative cat demons would have, and his recording was set to music! (Figure 5.2).

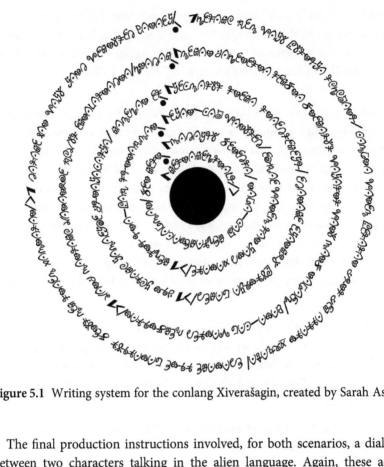

Figure 5.1 Writing system for the conlang Xiverašagin, created by Sarah Asinari

The final production instructions involved, for both scenarios, a dialogue between two characters talking in the alien language. Again, these added syntactic complexity into the system, requiring the students to have made choices about various kinds of wh-question dependencies, modality, evidentiality, purpose clauses, and free relatives.

The final assessment for the module is the write-up of how the students responded to the production instructions, including recordings, plus a grammar of their language, setting it in the context of the created world, discussing in detail aspects of the sound system, the writing system, and the grammar. Again, some of the output work was truly outstanding. The course gave students an ability to develop their linguistic knowledge, to interact with cutting-edge research (much of the material on the typology of languages used to illustrate the range of typological choices, as well as the limits of human languages, was taken directly from research work by Adger and Harbour on Kiowa, from Adger's work on Scottish Gaelic, and from Van Urk's work on Fijian, Imere and Dinka.).

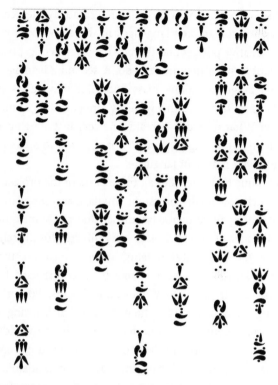

Figure 5.2 Writing system for the conlang Kakhelija, created by Alexandre Etcheheguy

The anonymous student evaluations of the course show that it has met its core objectives. Comments like the following were typical:

A fun course that helps students be creative while they learn specific linguistics notions.

Stimulating and challenging – forces you to look at all areas of linguistics and to explore them in a totally different way than usual. Learning to keep to a brief and be consistent was very useful.

We learn about the limits of human languages, and then are able to break them!

5.5 Conclusion

This chapter has described a three-level project, using constructed languages in teaching different aspects of linguistics, from very young elementary-school

students to those in the final year of their undergraduate degree. The fundamental advantage of constructed languages in these scenarios is that it har-
nesses students' creative powers and thereby makes the concepts and terms of
linguistics relevant to what they want to do. A second advantage is related to
this: constructed languages allow play, and that play raises questions in
students' minds. Is it OK if I do this with my language? Do human languages
work in this way? What rules can I break? The very fact of being able to break
rules in constructing a language (and who doesn't want to break rules?) shows
the crucial rule driven nature of language.

The core technique that underlies all three parts of the project is to use the
project of constructing a single consistent language as a motivation for learning and understanding fundamental linguistic concepts, some quite advanced,
and then using the idea of design choices (very directed for the schoolchildren,
much less so for the university students) to encourage creativity within a
highly disciplined framework. At the same time, constructed languages are
being put to use to target different educational aims. For primary-school
children, creating a language allows them to see that learning grammatical
concepts can be purposeful and connected directly to the worlds and beings
that live in their imaginations. With teenage schoolchildren, constructing a
language provides a way of introducing linguistics as an academic discipline as
well as providing a sense of what university is like, while using a fun set of tasks
that allows them to be creative. For undergraduate students, a course centered
around constructed languages provides an opportunity to consolidate and
review the knowledge they have acquired in previous courses and to show
how these academic skills can be put use in a potential work environment.

We think that the kinds of techniques sketched out here can be adapted to
many other cases where linguistic concepts can be taught. For example, one-
off afternoon workshops for families at Science Fairs, workshops in University
Open Days, outreach activities to schools, or public engagement activities. We
hope that this chapter is useful to those seeking to use constructed languages to
bring linguistic concepts and terminology further into educational and public
discourse.

Acknowledgments

Many thanks to Sarah Asinari and Alexandre Etcheheguy for permission to use their
work, and to the reviewers and editors of this volume for comments which have helped
improve the chapter.

6

The design(ing) of language

Grant Goodall

6.1 Introduction

Linguistics, more than related fields such as anthropology, philosophy, and psychology, faces a problem in attracting the attention of undergraduate students. Students have heard of these other fields and usually even have some idea, however wrong in detail, of what issues they address. With linguistics, however, students are often unaware that such a discipline even exists, and although they can surmise that it relates to language, they often imagine that it focuses on prescriptive grammar or some other relatively unappealing topic. For this reason, attracting students to an "Introduction to Linguistics" course can be difficult when they are able to choose between this and a course in a field which sounds more enticing and in which they have a better sense of what is involved.

There are two obvious strategies that many universities have adopted to try to surmount this problem. One is to promote the field among students so that they know that it exists and have some idea of what it is about. Another is to retitle and repackage the "Introduction to Linguistics" course so that it sounds more attractive to students. "An Introduction to Human Language" and "Languages of the World" are two of the most common titles used for what can be, to a large extent, introductory courses in linguistics that do not advertise themselves as such.

In recent years, courses on the linguistics of invented languages have begun to be taught, often as a kind of gateway course, an introduction to the field. The draw that such courses have for students is obvious: Novels, movies, and television series featuring invented languages have become enormously popular, and students are understandably curious about how this is done, either because they want to know more about a particular invented language or because they want to create their own (or both). The content of these courses, however, often resembles that of a traditional introduction to linguistics, in that learning how to put a language together involves learning some phonetics,

Grant Goodall, *The design(ing) of language* In: *Language Invention in Linguistics Pedagogy.* First edition.
Edited by: Jeffrey Punske, Nathan Sanders, and Amy V. Fountain, Oxford University Press (2020). © Grant Goodall.
DOI: 10.1093/oso/9780198829874.003.0006

phonology, morphology, and syntax, among other things. In fact, a good introductory book on creating languages, such as Peterson (2015), gives students much of the same background that they would get from a textbook for introductory linguistics, but in a way that students find much more intriguing and thought-provoking.

All of this is a good thing. If invented languages are the hook that brings students into linguistics, and this allows them to develop their understanding and appreciation of the human capacity for language more generally, then this is clearly a positive development. In this chapter, though, I want to argue that courses on invented languages can do more than this. They can bring to the forefront certain foundational characteristics of human language that are rarely, if ever, discussed in standard introductory linguistics courses, or even in more advanced courses, but that are nevertheless important if students are to develop a fuller understanding of the nature of language. In short, by learning how to design a language, students learn about the design of language.

To show that courses on invented languages can do this, I will present three case studies from three different components of such a course. All three stem from the idea that when students are learning how to design a language, they inevitably confront questions about what the basic design features of human language are and why they exist. A course on invented languages is an ideal place to address these questions, and doing so allows students (and indeed, linguists in general) to deepen their understanding of how human language works.

The three case studies come from two different parts of the course: one where students learn about languages that have been created by others, and another where they learn how to create their own. These case studies deal with three different aspects of language (the lexicon, phonemic inventories, and inflectional morphology), but the general approach and the lessons learned can be applied much more broadly.

The case studies presented are drawn from my experience teaching a course on "The Linguistics of Invented Languages" at UC San Diego. This is a lower-division course with no prerequisites. Some of the approximately seventy students that enroll are linguistics majors, but most are not. During the ten-week term, there are homework assignments and exams, but students are also required to construct a language and write a simple story or poem in it as their final project. I have handled the language-construction part of the course in two different ways: having each student construct their own or doing it as a class project where all students contribute to a common language. The latter method has been far more successful and is now my standard procedure for this course. With either method, though, we start the language-construction process from the ground up (i.e. starting with the phonemic inventory), and I require that the language be designed to be spoken by humans or some human-like species. This provides a common set of constraints within which students' creativity can flourish (Stokes 2005) and allows them to appreciate the elegance of the design of naturally occurring languages at a much deeper level. Nevertheless, the case studies presented below do not depend on the specifics of the course as I have taught it; many other configurations are possible.

6.2 Saussurean arbitrariness

The first case comes from a part of the course dealing with the history of invented languages. This general topic strikes many students by surprise, since they might understandably imagine that the history only goes as far back as the *Star Trek* movies, but in fact, the history is so long and deep and has influenced so many aspects of students' own daily lives that it merits some treatment (see Large 1985, Okrent 2010, and Sanders's chapter in this volume). In addition, linguists might imagine that this part of the course would have little to do with linguistics itself, and to an extent, this is true, but there are also ways in which this part of the course allows one to address design features of language that won't come up elsewhere.

Here I will show how one fascinating chapter in the history of invented languages, the philosophical language of 1668 of John Wilkins, can help us understand better the concept of Saussurean arbitrariness, an essential element in any discussion of the basic design features of human language. John Wilkins (1614–72) was an English theologian whose great work, *An Essay towards a Real Character and a Philosophical Language*, attempted to create a hierarchical system of semantic categories that could be used to classify any concept in the universe.[1] For example, if we begin with the category 'beasts' (itself a subcategory of several others that are higher in the hierarchy), this can be divided into those that are 'viviparous' and those that are 'oviparous', the viviparous ones can be divided into 'whole-footed', 'cloven-footed', and 'clawed', the clawed ones can be divided into 'non-rapacious' and 'rapacious', and so on. In this manner, a concept such as 'dog' can be seen as a series of choices in a hierarchy of categories, as in (1).

---

[1] Okrent (2010) gives a very detailed yet accessible introduction to Wilkins' work.

(1)   special > creature > distributively > substances > animate > species > sensitive > sanguineous > beasts > viviparous > clawed > rapacious > oblong-headed > European > terrestrial > big > docile

Creating such a system was an enormous undertaking, but Wilkins was motivated by the desire to understand and codify the nature of all objects in the world and the relationships among them, and to create a language which makes all of this fully evident. Such a language would be in sharp contrast to naturally occurring human languages, in which the form of the word typically says nothing about the nature of the thing denoted or about how that thing is related to others. For example, nothing about the phonological form of the word *dog* tells us that it means 'dog', and the fact that dogs and wolves are extremely similar biologically does not mean that the words *dog* and *wolf* need to be similar phonologically (they clearly aren't, in English). These facts about the words *dog* and *wolf* are of course straightforward examples of the core idea of Saussurean arbitrariness: words have meaning, but they are composed of arbitrary combinations of segments that do not have meaning.

Wilkins' language is very clearly designed so that it does not have Saussurean arbitrariness. The form of the word for 'dog', as in (1), is supposed to tell us exactly what a dog is and what it is not. Even when the sequence in (1) is given a phonological form (Wilkins sets up a system for doing this), it is still the case that the form of the word tells us what the word means. The word for 'dog', for instance, is *zita*, because *zi* means the sequence up to the category 'beast', *t* means the sequence from 'beast' to 'oblong-headed', and *a* means the sequence from 'oblong-headed' to 'big'. A speaker of this language would then immediately know what *zita* meant, even if they had never heard the word before. Importantly, they would also immediately understand that dogs and wolves are almost the same simply from hearing the words *zita* and *zitas*, since *zitas* signifies the same sequence of categories as in (1), but the final *s* indicates 'wild' instead of 'docile' (the default).

The very intentionally non-arbitrary nature of Wilkins' language makes it natural to discuss linguistic arbitrariness in general at this point in the course, but more importantly, having an understanding of Wilkins' language first enables students to approach Saussurean arbitrariness in a much more meaningful way. That is, the fact that they are able to see in detail what a language would look like without arbitrariness allows them to appreciate more deeply how naturally occurring human languages are clearly systems with arbitrariness, and they thus confront directly a fundamental design property of human language. This, in turn, can lead to informed and interesting discussions about the advantages and disadvantages of arbitrariness, why the human language capacity might have evolved to have arbitrariness as an essential property (if in fact it has), the extent to which there are non-arbitrary elements in natural language, etc. In short, an exploration of Wilkins' proposed language leads students to a much more meaningful and sustained engagement with Saussure's fundamental concept of *l'arbitraire du signe* than they are likely to get in any other linguistics class.

An engagement with Wilkins' project carries other benefits as well. Wilkins' desire to create a language where the words reflected the true nature of the objects described and of the relationships among them did not arise in isolation. It was a concern of many other thinkers of the period also, most notably Leibniz, and it was part of a broader effort to understand the world in a more rigorous and systematic way. Wilkins' system may seem slightly ridiculous to modern readers, but it is not difficult to see similarities between it and our modern system of binomial nomenclature for organisms, the periodic table of the elements, the Dewey Decimal system, and formal logic and mathematics more generally. In this way, by delving into the details of Wilkins' language, students are able to get a sense for this larger chapter in intellectual history to which they had probably devoted very little thought previously, but which clearly has direct effects on many aspects of their current lives.

We will now turn from the history of invented languages to two aspects of the course that deal with the process of creating a language. In many courses on invented languages, this is where students can try their hand at putting together their own language and it is where they come closest to the nuts and bolts of linguistic analysis that are the core of many other linguistics courses.

6.3 Phonemic inventories

One of the first steps in creating a language is deciding on a phonemic inventory. In a course, this means that students will need to learn some basic articulatory phonetics, and in this sense, an invented languages course is similar to a course in introductory linguistics. Beyond that, however, they differ, and once again, the concerns of designing a language from scratch force one to engage with some basic design principles of language that are very unlikely to be dealt with in other linguistics courses.

One of these basic principles is dispersion, the idea that the phonemes that make up the inventory will be as perceptually distinct from one another as possible (Lindblom and Engstrand 1989; Flemming 2005). As a goal to strive for, maximizing dispersion seems like common sense, even for students with no background other than very basic phonetics. If phonemes are all that distinguish one word from another, then it seems obvious that we would want these phonemes to be maximally distinct. Language is often used in noisy environments, after all, so if the difference between two phonemes was difficult to perceive, the chances of perceiving a different word than what was intended would increase, which hardly seems desirable.

The principle of dispersion is easy for students to grasp, and it is easy for them to put it into practice as well. If tasked with designing a phonemic inventory with seventeen consonants, students have little difficulty seeing that the inventory in Table 6.1, which clearly does not maximize dispersion, would be a very poor solution to the problem.

Table 6.1 Sample consonant inventory with poor dispersion

	labial	dental	alveolar	retroflex	palatal	velar	uvular	glottal
stop	p b	t̪ d̪	t d					
fricative	f v	θ ð	s z					
nasal	m	n̪	n					
glide								
flap			ɾ					
trill								
lateral			l					

Similarly for vowels, students can easily see that an inventory like that in Figure 6.1 would not be a good design for a five-vowel system.

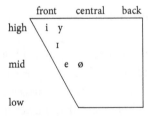

Figure 6.1 Sample vowel inventory with poor dispersion

A second basic design principle that affects phonemic inventories is that to the extent possible, phonemes within the inventory should form natural classes. This is one of the insights behind the theory of distinctive features (Trubetzkoy 1939; Jakobson, Fant, and Halle 1954; Chomsky and Halle 1968), but the thrust of it can be conveyed using the simple phonetic categories in Table 6.1 and Figure 6.1. For example, rather than having just one fricative or one alveolar, a language is more likely to have a series of fricatives or a series of alveolars. Similarly, if it has one pair of sounds that contrast in voicing, it is likely to have others.

The concept of natural classes is somewhat harder for students to grasp, but they can readily see that although the consonant inventory in Table 6.2 has good dispersion, there is nonetheless something odd about it.

Table 6.2 Sample consonant inventory with good dispersion but poor natural classes

	labial	dental	alveolar	retroflex	palatal	velar	uvular	glottal
stop	b		t	ɖ				
fricative	f	ð	s		ç	ɣ	χ	h
nasal		ņ			ɲ		N	
glide						w		
flap								
trill								
lateral					ʎ		R	

There is a series of stops and a series of fricatives, but voicing seems to be random and is never used contrastively. In addition, all of the available places of articulation are used, but retroflex is only used once and most of the others only twice. The seventeen consonants in Table 6.2 clearly achieve better dispersion than those in Table 6.1, but they do a poor job of forming natural classes. Individual consonants seem to have been chosen randomly, with little sense of series or patterns.

A similar contrast for vowels can be seen between Figures 6.1 and 6.2.

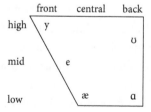

Figure 6.2 Sample vowel inventory with good dispersion but poor natural classes

Both are inventories of five vowels, but although Figure 6.2 is clearly better than Figure 6.1 in terms of dispersion, Figure 6.2 is nonetheless not good in terms of natural classes. There is a series of front vowels, for instance, but they do not match in lip rounding, nor do they correspond straightforwardly to a series of back vowels.

One of the reasons that it is a little harder for students to understand natural classes, as opposed to dispersion, is that poor dispersion is typically very visually perspicuous in the tables of phonemic inventories. It is easy to see at a glance, for instance, that all of the consonants in Table 6.1 and all of the vowels in Figure 6.1 are crowded into one part of the space and that many other parts of the space are underutilized. Seeing the lack of natural classes in Table 6.2 and Figure 6.2, on the other hand, requires examining the table in more detail and understanding what all of the terms and symbols mean.

In addition, if the motivation behind dispersion seems intuitively very clear, the motivation behind natural classes is much less so and requires some explanation. Understanding some of the motivation is not beyond students' reach, however, even if they know very little about phonetics and phonology. Students can intuitively understand the oddness of the inventory in Table 6.2, for instance, where speakers would have to know how to manipulate voicing in obstruents (since some are voiceless and others are voiced) but would never benefit from this by using voicing contrastively. Similarly, they can understand the oddness of learning the gesture required for retroflex consonants (or for front rounded vowels in Figure 6.2), but then only using this gesture for a single consonant (or only using lip rounding for a single front vowel and then, never contrastively). Since being able to produce retroflex consonants in flowing speech requires some practice, as English-speaking students can easily appreciate, it seems intuitively inefficient to profit from this skill with only a single phoneme.

Moreover, students can be told, without going into too much technical detail, that there is abundant evidence that language processes affect natural classes, such as voiceless stops, more than they do individual phonemes, such as /p/, /z/, or /w/ (e.g. Chomsky and Halle 1968). A quick demonstration of aspiration in English, for instance, can show students how this process affects the full series of voiceless stops in the language. This can be seen from the neurolinguistic side as well, where there is evidence for neural selectivity for features such as voicing and manner of articulation, rather than for individual phonemes (Mesgarani et al. 2014).

Ultimately, of course, students need to understand how both principles, dispersion and natural classes, work together in shaping the form that phonemic inventories take. That is, they must be able to see that Table 6.3, though it has the same number of consonants as Tables 6.1 and 6.2, manages to be well dispersed and utilize natural classes at the same time.

Table 6.3 Sample consonant inventory with good dispersion and good natural classes

	labial	ental	alveolar	retroflex	palatal	velar	uvular	glottal
stop	p b		t d			k g		
fricative	f v		s z			x ɣ		
nasal	m		n			ŋ		
glide								
flap			ɾ					
trill								
lateral			l					

Similarly in the case of vowels, Figure 6.3 is better than Figures 6.1 or 6.2.

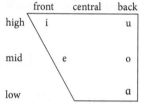

Figure 6.3 Sample vowel inventory with good dispersion and good natural classes

In order to learn how to apply both principles simultaneously, it helps to see that to a large extent, they are in direct conflict. The principle of dispersion, for example, pushes languages to make their phonemes as different from one another as possible, while the principle of natural classes encourages phonemes to be as similar to each other as possible (e.g. all stops, all voiceless, etc.). At a more intuitive, less technical level, then, the two principles could be rephrased for students as "maximize differences" and "maximize similarities." As they create phonemic inventories, the students must thus find a middle way between these two conflicting principles, making sure that the individual phonemes are as distinct from one another as possible, as mandated by "maximize differences," while still making sure that there are common traits within series of sounds, as mandated by "maximize similarities." This is a hard conflict to resolve, but in essence, every existing language is a possible solution to this problem, and if we want to create a language that will sound human-like, we must create a possible solution as well.

The overall picture that emerges is that natural language, or at least this component of it, is a reasonable solution to a problem created by two competing forces. When we get to the level of fine detail, there are many possible solutions, so it is not surprising that there are many languages, but all languages are subject to these same two forces and manage to negotiate a way between them.

In most introductory linguistics courses, and even in many advanced courses, the phonemic inventory for a language is simply a given, a necessary basis on which to do further analysis. In a course on inventing languages, on the other hand, the phonemic inventory begins as a blank slate and students need to learn how to create it. In doing so, they come face to face with the two basic design principles of language that we have been examining here, "maximize differences" (= dispersion) and "maximize similarities" (= natural classes). Importantly, they also see how these principles conflict with each other and how each language, whether naturally occurring or created, is a possible resolution of this conflict. For students who are getting an overview of human language, this is arguably one of the most important lessons of all.

6.4 Inflectional morphology

Let us now turn to the level of morphology. In a traditional introductory course in linguistics, students are typically presented with a set of words in the language and then learn how to break those words into morphemes and do other types of morphological analysis. In a course where students are learning how to create a language, they must decide how much morphological structure to include in their language and what that structure will look like. In the area of inflectional morphology in particular, it is well known that languages vary greatly in terms of how much structure there will be, so there is clearly no single best way to do it. As we saw with phonemic inventories, however, it is possible to identify some competing pressures that can help students conceptualize the problem of deciding how much inflectional morphology to have and what the form of that morphology will be. The concepts needed are within reach even of students with no background in morphology, but once again, learning how to apply these concepts in creating a morphological system gives them important insights into fundamental design principles of natural language.

To begin, let us imagine that we are at a stage where students have created monomorphemic words, but nothing else. For instance, take a possible word as in (2).

(2) mosu 'cow'

Leaving this word uninflected would of course be attractive, from the standpoint of acquisition, at least, but it would also be not very informative. If this was a word in an utterance, one could imagine that it would be very useful for the listener to have some morphology giving us additional information. If the noun was marked for number, definiteness, and case, for instance, we would know immediately, after hearing this single word, whether one cow or many were being referred to, whether the cow had already been mentioned in the discourse or was new, and whether this noun phrase would be the subject or object of the predicate. One can imagine a kind of Gricean sense of informativity applying pressure on languages, then, encouraging languages to use as much inflection as possible so that single words can be as informative as possible.

If informativity were the only pressure exerting itself on languages, then we would expect not to find words like (2), and to find those like (3) instead.

(3) mosu-ta-le-wo
     COW-PL-DEF-NOM
     'the cows'

Just as we can imagine informativity as a factor influencing the morphological design of languages, however, we can also imagine a Gricean avoidance of prolixity applying pressure in the opposite direction, encouraging languages to have words that are as short as possible. As we saw earlier with phonemic inventories, then, here there seem to be two competing pressures that are in clear conflict: informativity (use inflection to make words as informative as possible) and word length (keep words as short as possible). There is no single best compromise between these two pressures, but it is easy for students to see that different languages choose different compromises, and that in creating one's own language, one must navigate a path between the two.

One way to compromise between the need to be informative and the need to keep the word short is to make any inflectional affixes as short as possible, but it is easy to see that this can create problems of its own. If we follow the pattern in (3) but make all of the suffixes single consonants, for example, thus reducing the overall number of syllables in the word from five to two, we get (4).

(4) mosu-t-l-w
     COW-PL-DEF-NOM
     'the cows'

(4) is good in terms of informativity and word length, but it is very likely that it would run afoul of the phonotactics of the language, given that word-final consonant clusters tend to be highly constrained across languages. Phonotactic restrictions are thus another pressure affecting the choice of inflectional morphology in a language. Compared to informativity and word length, the notion of phonotactics is less intuitive and more technical, but at this point in the course, students know enough to be able to work with phonotactics in an informed manner. If they have already created words, then they know about phonemic inventories and about syllable structure, so they know whether the final syllable in (4) would be allowed in their language or not.

One way to get around the phonotactic problem posed by (4), while still maintaining the same level of informativeness and the same length (two syllables), could be to use only one suffix that combines the meanings of the three separate suffixes in (4), as in (5).

(5)   mosu-t

COW-PL.DEF.NOM

'the cows'

(5) is relatively informative and short, and it could plausibly satisfy the phonotactics of the given language, but here too, it creates its own problems that might make it a less than optimal choice. At the most basic level, the suffix -*t* in (11) with the meaning 'PL.DEF.NOM' would lead us to expect that there would be similar suffixes with meanings such as 'PL.DEF.ACC', 'SG.DEF.NOM', 'PL.INDEF.ACC', etc., and it is very likely that we would run out of single consonants that could function as suffixes here while still satisfying the phonotactics. At a larger level, though, (5) seems less than optimal in that a lot of information is crowded into a single segment. If languages obey a general principle of trying to maintain uniform information density (Frank and Jaeger 2008; Pellegrino et al. 2011), then (5) is pushing against that, as the consonant /t/ carries three distinct pieces of information (i.e. plural, definite, and nominative). If information density is an independent pressure shaping the inflectional morphology of a language, then (5) is worse in this regard than (2)-(4), even though it is better than (2) with regard to informativity, better than (3) with regard to length, and better than (4), presumably, with regard to phonotactics.

We have now identified four pressures that plausibly influence the form of inflectional morphology in languages: informativity, length, phonotactics, and information density. All four of these can be usefully understood at an intuitive level by students with very little background (though entering into more formal definitions is of course also possible, if desired). The most technical of these is phonotactics, but students will have already gotten the main background that they need for this when they learned about creating words, where they will have become familiar with phonemic inventories and syllable structure. As we have seen, these four pressures are often in conflict, with the result that any piece of inflectional morphology is a trade-off among them, so an important learning goal for students is to see how the form of individual morphemes can be a reasonable compromise among these competing demands.[2]

As should now be becoming clear, the approach to inflectional morphology that one takes in a course on inventing languages is different than that in a traditional introductory linguistics course. In an introductory course, one typically begins with a set of data, which students then learn to analyze (i.e. identify morphemes, morphological processes, etc.). For example, students might be presented with a list of nouns, both singular and plural, with their task being to identify the plural morpheme, the conditions that govern its various allomorphs, etc. In a course on inventing languages, on the other hand, there is no existing set of data to analyze, as students must instead create the morphology that is needed. They might, for example, be presented with a list of singular nouns and be tasked with finding a way to pluralize them. If they do this by means of a plural affix, they will need to create an affix that is not too long and that will satisfy the phonotactics of the language, taking into account the variety of bare noun forms in the list (assuming that the choice of marking plurality with an affix is inherently a good way to satisfy the demands of informativity and information density). In deciding how much inflectional morphology to have and what form any inflectional morphemes should take,

---

[2] Students can also see that the way that these competing pressures interact can be influenced by areas of grammar beyond morphology. We have already seen the important role that phonotactics plays, with the result that in languages with tightly constrained phonotactics, inflectional morphology is likely to be relatively costly. It is presumably not an accident, for instance, that Mandarin Chinese, with its very limited use of syllable-final consonants, has little inflectional morphology, since any affix would likely be a full syllable and would thus make words significantly longer (though such considerations clearly cannot be the only factors at play, since some languages with similarly constrained phonotactics (e.g. Japanese) nonetheless have rich inflection). In the realm of syntax, there are also many plausible interactions, since inflectional morphology is often implicated in syntactic effects such as freedom of word order, dropping of arguments, etc., that might have their own advantages and disadvantages. A full treatment of the competing pressures involved in choosing the amount and form of inflectional morphology thus ultimately requires examining the grammar as a whole. Whether it is appropriate to explore these topics in a course on inventing languages depends on the amount of time available and the students' background and sophistication in linguistics.

students become intimately acquainted with the four competing pressures we have discussed, and thus intimately acquainted with some important design properties of human language.

It should be emphasized that becoming familiar with these design properties is not just useful in the process of creating languages; it is also very helpful in understanding the structure of existing natural languages, even if the approach taken is different from what might be assumed from traditional courses in linguistics. Take, for instance, the plural morpheme /-s/ in English. Traditionally, the existence of this plural morpheme is a given for students, and the challenge lies mainly in understanding its varied forms and the conditions governing their appearance. From the standpoint of invented languages, however, the question is 'why /-s/?' That is, why should we mark plurality at all, and if we do, why should we do it with an affix, and if we do it with an affix, why should it be /-s/? The factors that we saw above shed some light on why we might want to mark plurality overtly (it increases informativity) and on why we might want to do it with an affix (it keeps information density relatively uniform). As for the exact form of this affix, we can see an immediate advantage in its consisting of a single consonant (it allows us to increase informativity while keeping the number of syllables constant).

The exact identity of this single-consonant affix is largely determined by phonotactics. When one decides between using a prefix or suffix, for instance, a suffix is a far better choice phonotactically. English has very tight restrictions on word-initial consonant clusters, so it would be virtually impossible to have a single-consonant prefix that would be compatible with a wide range of noun roots. Choosing a suffix will be easier, though still not easy, because English allows many more consonant clusters word-finally, so there is a greater likelihood that we will be able to find a consonant that is able to function as a suffix for all (or at least many) noun roots. Simplifying somewhat, there are four consonants in English that are able to appear as final consonant in a large number of word-final consonant clusters. These are the alveolars /t/ and /s/, and their voiced counterparts, so these are all excellent choices for single-consonant suffixes, given the phonotactics of English. It is not a surprise, then, that these are the consonants that are actually used: /-d/ for the past-tense suffix on verbs and /-z/ for the plural suffix on nouns (putting aside well-known morphophonemic complications). Other candidate single-consonant suffixes would work considerably less well, which perhaps explains why English also uses /-z/ as the suffix for third-person-singular agreement on present-tense verbs and for possessives, despite the fact this complication of the form–function mapping likely makes acquisition more difficult (Slobin 1980).

From this perspective, then, English appears to be very well-constructed, at least in the way it marks plurality on nouns. Through this example, we see also that a course on inventing languages can help students understand more deeply not just languages like Klingon and Dothraki, but also natural languages such as English.

Lest students get the impression that English alone among natural languages is particularly well-designed, it can be useful to see that the same four pressures we discussed help shape inflectional morphology in other languages as well. Spanish has an especially rich system of verbal morphology, and many students are familiar with its basic outlines because of prior study in school or exposure to the language at home, so it makes a very good case study. To begin, let us consider the verb root [kant-] 'sing'. This root would violate Spanish phonotactics if it were the entire word (as students can easily verify by trying and failing to find any native words with word-final -nt), but suffixes can "rescue" it, since Spanish finite verbs must be inflected minimally for mood and person/number, as the factor of informativity encourages. If we were creating this language from scratch, we would now have to decide whether mood and person/number should be represented on two distinct suffixes or on just one. One could imagine this going either way, since information density would pressure the language to have two distinct suffixes, while length would pressure it to have just one. Let us say that information density wins in this case and we have two distinct suffixes. Length will still play a role, though, since we now expect the two suffixes to be as short as possible. The first suffix, which we will say will be mood (for reasons that do not concern us here), needs to begin with a vowel in order to resolve the phonotactic problem of [kant-], and ideally, it will consist of only a vowel, in order to satisfy length. What vowel will this be? Spanish only has five vowels, and owing to phonotactic restrictions, only three of them (/a/, /e/, and /o/) can be unstressed in word-final position. Not surprisingly, all three of them are used: /-a/ is the suffix for indicative mood, /-e/ is for subjunctive mood for this class of verbs, and /-o/ combines indicative mood and first-person-singular person/number into a single suffix.

What about the person/number suffixes? Length encourages these, too, to be very short (a single consonant would be ideal) and phonotactics very tightly restricts what this single consonant could be, limiting it to four: /-ð/, /-s/, /-n/, and /-r/. Of these, /-ð/ and /-r/ are already used as verbal suffixes with other meanings, so this leaves /-s/ and /-n/. Not surprisingly, then, these are used for two of the most frequent person/number values (/-s/ for second-person singular and /-n/ for third-person plural). A zero morpheme is also a possibility (a very straightforward way to satisfy length), and this is used for first-person singular and third-person singular. There is more to be said about how the least frequent person/number values are handled (first-person plural and second-person plural), but the basic picture is clear and is one that students can easily grasp: the morphology of verbs in Spanish is a straightforward and reasonable way of satisfying the four pressures on inflectional morphology discussed. As we saw with English plural /-s/ earlier, the structure of the system of verbal morphology in Spanish seems remarkably well-designed. Although this conclusion is the same for both the English and the Spanish examples, it is the Spanish case which is often the most striking to students, since many have a long history of memorizing these forms in language classes. Most students have never asked why verbs in Spanish look the way they do, and they never imagined that there was a possibility of an answer.

We began this section by exploring four basic factors that come into play in choosing the form of inflectional morphology. Students need to learn to navigate among these competing pressures in order to find reasonable compromises when they are creating an inflectional system for a language, assuming that they want their language to be usable by humans and to sound natural and human-like. The surprising thing for students (and perhaps also for instructors!) is that when looked at from this perspective, naturally occurring languages such as English and Spanish also have optimally designed affixes. Morphological properties of these languages that might have seemed random or arbitrary actually appear to be the best possible solutions to the problem of satisfying the conflicting pressures that affect all inflectional systems.

6.5 Conclusion

Introductory courses in linguistics allow students to analyze language(s) in a systematic and rigorous way. For many students, this is the first time they have done this, and the simple fact that it is possible is a revelation. Such courses are very worthy and important, but they differ in interesting ways from the type of course that I have been discussing here. In an introductory course, students learn how to identify the main components of the language (i.e. phonemes, affixes, etc.), while in a course on invented languages, students begin to understand why the language has the components that it does. That is, they begin to see why it has those particular phonemes, those particular affixes, etc. In this way, students see natural language from a perspective that is ordinarily not employed in other linguistics courses, and in doing this, students become deeply engaged with basic design principles that are fundamental to all human languages.

The three case studies that I have presented here are ones that seem to me to be particularly simple to implement in a course, but that have potentially very profound lessons for students. Nonetheless, they are only samples. With regard to the history of invented languages, I have discussed here Wilkins' project of 1668, but there are other historical periods that offer similarly rich terrain for analysis. The international auxiliary languages that were proposed in the late nineteenth and early twentieth centuries, for instance, such as Volapük, Esperanto, and Novial, are especially noteworthy in this regard (see Garvía 2015 for recent discussion focusing on the social and political sides of this). With regard to levels of grammatical analysis, I have focused here on the various pressures constraining phonemic inventories and inflectional morphology, but one can apply the same approach to any other level. In the realm of syntax, for instance, it is not difficult to imagine a small set of factors that constrain basic word order in languages in particular ways, resulting in the overrepresentation of SOV and SVO among the six logical possibilities (see Gibson et al. 2013 for an attempt along these lines). A sketch of such an analysis could be sufficient for class purposes, even if the details or ultimate correctness of the approach still await further research. Similarly, it is easy to conceive of the well-known difference between *wh*-movement and *wh*-in-situ languages as resulting from conflicting pressures toward representing the scope of the *wh*-phrase overtly versus representing the argument position overtly, with different languages resolving this conflict in different ways. Here too, the thrust of the approach is sufficiently clear and appealing to use in class, even if the details are still the topic of much ongoing research.

Regardless of the details of the implementation, it seems clear that courses on the linguistics of invented languages are more than just a novelty and more than just a way to entice students into the field. They can help students see human language in a new way, allowing them to come face to face with fundamental design principles that they are unlikely to encounter anywhere else.

7

Using language invention to teach typology and cross-linguistic universals

Matt Pearson

7.1 Overview

In this chapter, I describe a linguistics class project where students collaborate to create a typologically plausible constructed language (conlang), using a semi-randomized procedure to determine grammatical features such as phoneme inventory, word order, and case alignment. The goal of the project is to investigate linguistic typology in a hands-on, creative way, using language invention to teach students about cross-linguistic variation, implicational universals, and markedness hierarchies (Greenberg 1963; Hawkins 1983; Croft 2002; etc.). By working together to invent a conlang that conforms to known statistical tendencies, students gain exposure to the idea that natural languages do not vary randomly in their grammatical structure but instead follow predictable patterns.

The idea for this project originated with Susan Curtiss as part of a UCLA undergraduate honors course on mental grammar. When I was a graduate student at UCLA in the 1990s, I worked as a teaching assistant for this course and helped to develop the project, following a model established by a previous teaching assistant. This project formed the focus for a series of typology-themed discussion sections which I taught to supplement the main course lectures. In describing the project here, I have further refined our original procedure to reflect the increased availability of numerical data from large language samples, most especially the World Atlas of Language Structures (WALS) online database (Dryer and Haspelmath 2013). In Section 7.2, I lay out the general parameters for the exercise and discuss some of the sources that instructors can use to generate questions and topics related to morpho-syntactic variation. In Section 7.3, I describe how the structural parameters of the conlang are determined using a semi-randomized procedure that

Matt Pearson, *Using language invention to teach typology and cross-linguistic universals* In: *Language Invention in Linguistics Pedagogy*. First edition. Edited by: Jeffrey Punske, Nathan Sanders, and Amy V. Fountain, Oxford University Press (2020). © Matt Pearson.
DOI: 10.1093/oso/9780198829874.003.0007

reproduces the statistical patterns expressed by implicational universals. In Section 7.4, I discuss how students can work to flesh out the language by adding vocabulary and cultural details, and creating their own texts. I also give examples of Nattiki, the conlang we constructed when I led students through this exercise at UCLA.

7.2 Focus of the project

This project may be carried out over several class periods, or even an entire semester. It can form a unit or mini-course within a discussion-based class on the structure of the world's languages, or an activity carried out during the discussion sections in a large lecture course. It can also be adapted for use outside the classroom as part of an extracurricular activity, independent study, or typology workshop.

The project is divided into units, with the number of units depending on the topic of the class and the time available. Each unit focuses on a domain of cross-linguistic variation for which language universals have been proposed. At the beginning of each unit, the instructor and students review data from natural languages to learn about the range of cross-linguistic variation, along with any implicational generalizations which have been proposed to capture patterns of covariation. Some types of generalizations which might be covered, with an example of each, are listed in (1):

(1) a. *Phonological implicational universals*: If a language has voiceless nasals and approximants, it will also have their voiced counterparts—e.g. if a language has /n̥/ it will also have /n/, but the converse does not hold (Maddieson 1984).

   b. *Word order correlations*: If a language has object-verb (OV) order, it is highly likely to have postpositions; if it has verb-object (VO) order, it is highly likely to have prepositions (Greenberg 1963; Hawkins 1983; Dryer 1992).

   c. *Implicational universals related to grammatical categories*: If a language has a grammatical gender category, it will also have a number category. That is, if the nouns in a language are grouped into agreement classes (genders), they will also inflect for singular versus plural (Greenberg 1963).

d. *Markedness asymmetries*: If a language has a paucal number, it will also have a dual number; if a language has a dual number, it will also make a singular/plural distinction. In languages that make morphological number distinctions, plural marking involves at least as much morphology as singular marking, and dual/paucal marking involves at least as much morphology as plural marking. These generalizations implicate a markedness hierarchy for number: PAUCAL > DUAL > PLURAL > SINGULAR (Croft 2002; Corbett 2000).

After learning about the patterns of cross-linguistic variation and markedness found in natural languages, students must then decide which grammatical features their conlang will have. Essentially this involves generating a series of design questions which must be answered—or, in Generative Grammar terms, a series of parameters which must be set for the conlang. In (2), I list some possible topics for units, along with sample design questions for each unit. This list is by no means exhaustive; it is merely meant to suggest the range of decisions that must be made in order to develop a grammatically fleshed-out conlang.

(2)   a. *Phoneme inventory* (Maddieson 1984):
  - Which vowels will the language have and how will they be arranged in the vowel space? e.g., will the language have a three-vowel system, a five-vowel system, etc.?
  - Which places and manners of articulation will be distinguished among the consonants?
  - What other phonetic features will be contrastive for different classes of sounds? For example, will [voice] be a contrastive feature of consonants? Will [nasal] be a contrastive feature for vowels?
  - Will length be a distinctive feature of consonants and/or vowels?
  - Will the language have tones?

  b. *Syllable structure and phonotactic constraints* (Blevins 1995):
  - Will the language permit codas? That is, will the language include both open and closed syllables, or open syllables only?
  - Will the language permit complex onsets? If so, what combinations of consonants will be allowed?
  - If coda consonants are permitted, will there be restrictions on which classes of consonants can occur in coda position (e.g. only coronal codas, only sonorant codas, etc.)? Will the language allow complex codas, and if so, which combinations of consonants will occur?

c. *Morphological types* (Comrie 1989; Baker 1996; Nichols 1986; Velupillai 2012):

- How much bound morphology will the language have? Will it be analytic or synthetic? If it is synthetic, will it include features of polysynthesis such as noun incorporation?
- If the language is synthetic, will it have strictly agglutinating morphology, or will it also include fusional and non-concatenative morphology (e.g. templatic morphology)?
- If the language is synthetic, will it be primarily suffixing, primarily prefixing, or a combination of both?
- Will the language have reduplication? If so, what functions will be associated with reduplication (plurality, imperfective aspect, etc.)?
- To express argument-structure dependencies (subject and object roles), will the language make use of head marking (indexation/agreement), dependent marking (morphological case), both, or neither?

d. *Lexical and functional categories* (Schachter and Shopen 2007; Harley and Ritter 2002):

- Will the language include a category of adjectives, as distinct from nouns and verbs?
- Will the language have a category of adpositions, or will it express relational concepts by other means (such as case marking)?
- What sort of pronominal/phi-feature system will the language have? Which person, number, and gender/animacy distinctions will be made by the pronouns and agreement markers? For example, will the language have distinct pronouns for first-person-plural inclusive and exclusive, or will it use the same pronoun for both?
- Will nouns in the language inflect for number, and if so, will the language have a two-number system (singular/plural), a three-number system (singular/dual/plural), or a four-number system (singular/dual/paucal/plural)?
- Will the language have articles or other grammatical means for expressing definiteness?
- Will the language have a tense category? If so, what kinds of tense distinctions will it make?

e. *Constituent order* (Greenberg 1963; Hawkins 1983; Dryer 1992, 2007):

- Will the language have OV or VO as its unmarked order for verb and object, or will both orders be allowed (non-configurationality)?

- If the language is VO, will the subject precede or follow the verb and its object (SVO, VSO, VOS)?
- If the language has an adposition category, will it have prepositions or postpositions?
- If the language has an adjective category, will attributive adjectives precede the modified noun (Adj-N) or follow the modified noun (N-Adj) within the noun phrase? Or will both orders be allowed?
- Will relative clauses precede the modified noun (Rel-N) or follow the modified noun (N-Rel)?
- In possessive noun phrases, will the possessor precede the possessed noun (Poss-N) or follow the possessed noun (N-Poss)?
- In forming constituent questions, will the language employ wh-movement, wh-in-situ, or both options?
- Will the language have topic- and focus-fronting constructions?

f. Case, agreement, and syntactic dependencies (Comrie 1978; Palmer 1994; Andrews 2007):

- If the language has morphological case and/or agreement for core arguments, will it have an accusative alignment, an ergative alignment, a split-S alignment, or a tripartite marking system? (See Section 7.3)
- If the language is ergative, will it be strictly ergative, split-ergative based on tense/aspect, split-ergative based on a person/animacy hierarchy, etc.?
- Will the language have constructions for changing the valence of the clause by promoting or demoting core arguments: e.g. passive, antipassive, reflexive, causative, applicative?
- If the language has case marking on noun phrases, what non-core cases, if any, will it have (dative, instrumental, locative, etc.)?
- If the language has grammatical number (and gender) categories, will attributive adjectives and other modifiers agree in features with the noun they modify?

There are a number of useful resources for generating topics and design questions and identifying related language universals. The WALS database website (http://wals.info, Dryer and Haspelmath 2013) includes an extensive list of articles on topics related to cross-linguistic variation. More in-depth discussions of some of these topics can be found in typology textbooks and reference works such as Maddieson (1984), Shopen (1985, 2007), Comrie

(1989), Payne (1997), Croft (2002), Velupillai (2012), Moravcsik (2013), and Song (2018). A particularly useful source is the *Lingua Descriptive Studies* questionnaire (Comrie and Smith 1977), which provides a comprehensive list of topics and questions related to grammatical structure. Although this questionnaire is intended as an outline for field linguists writing a reference grammar of a natural language, it can easily be repurposed for determining the grammatical features of a conlang. A similar questionnaire, but more condensed and focused on morphosyntactic topics, is included in Payne (1997). Finally, the University of Konstanz's *Universals Archive* offers an extensive database of possible language universals, with citations of works in which those universals are proposed or discussed. This archive can be accessed at http://typo.uni-konstanz.de/archive/intro/index.php.

7.3 Deciding on the features of the conlang

As the project was originally conceived by Susan Curtiss, the major structural properties of the conlang are decided at random by spinning a wheel. The intention behind this choice was, in part, to introduce a game-like element into the creation of the language. By leaving certain decisions up to chance, students are forced to exercise their creativity within predetermined structural constraints, avoiding any temptation to make their conlang either overly familiar and English-like, or overly alien and exotic. Either of these extremes would defeat the purpose of an exercise focused specifically on learning about natural language typology.

At UCLA, we used a carnival-style wheel built for this purpose by Curtiss's husband. The wheel was mounted vertically on a wooden frame with a flexible pointer attached to the top. When the wheel was spun, the pointer would brush against nails protruding from the circumference of the wheel until it came to rest at a particular point (think of the spinning wheels from the game shows *Wheel of Fortune* and *The Price is Right*). For instructors who lack the resources to build or purchase a carnival wheel of their own, a large spinner from a board game like *Twister* can also be used. Perhaps the easiest and most flexible option is to use an online application such as Wheel Decide (http://wheeldecide.com). Applications of this sort are particularly useful because they allow the user to create new wheels quickly by inputting numerical data. Other random selection methods are also possible, such as rolling a set of multi-sided dice from a role-playing game; here, however, I focus on using a wheel for this purpose.

For each grammatical parameter to be specified, a pie chart is attached to the spinner wheel with slices representing features or settings for the parameter in question. The size of each slice is determined by the rough proportion of the world's languages that have that parameter setting (in combination with other parameter settings, where relevant). When the project was originally developed, these proportions had to be estimated. Now, however, statistics from the WALS database or similar sources may be used for this purpose. For each decision to be made, a student volunteer comes to the front of the room and spins the wheel. Whichever slice of the pie chart the pointer lands on determines the parameter setting that the conlang will have.

For example, suppose that the students are studying case/agreement systems and need to establish which core alignment system their conlang will have. This involves determining how the conlang will distinguish subjects of intransitive clauses (S), subjects of transitive clauses (A), and objects of transitive clauses (P) using case marking, agreement, word order, or some combination of these. Among natural languages, the four most common alignment systems are as follows (see Comrie 1978, Dixon 1994, Palmer 1994, Coon et al. 2017 for discussion):

(3)   a. *Accusative alignment*: A and S are marked the same way (nominative), while P is marked in a different way (accusative).

b. *Ergative alignment*: P and S are marked the same way (absolutive), while A is marked in a different way (ergative).

c. *Tripartite system*: A, S, and P are all marked differently (ergative, nominative, accusative).

d. *Split-S alignment*: S arguments are divided into two classes according to how they are marked. More agentive S arguments (S_A) are marked the same way as A arguments, while more patientive S arguments (S_P) are marked the same way as P arguments.

The relative prevalence of each alignment type among the world's languages is suggested by Table 7.1. The N values in this table are taken from the WALS sample of languages with morphological marking of core case roles (Dryer and Haspelmath 2013). In the third column, these N values have been converted into approximate whole-number percentages. For the sake of simplicity, languages with alignments other than accusative, ergative, tripartite, and split-S are excluded.

Table 7.1 Distribution of alignment types in WALS

	N	%
accusative (A+S vs. P)	52	57
ergative (A vs. S+P)	32	35
tripartite (A vs. S vs. P)	4	4
split-S (A+S_A vs. P+S_P)	4	4
total	92	100

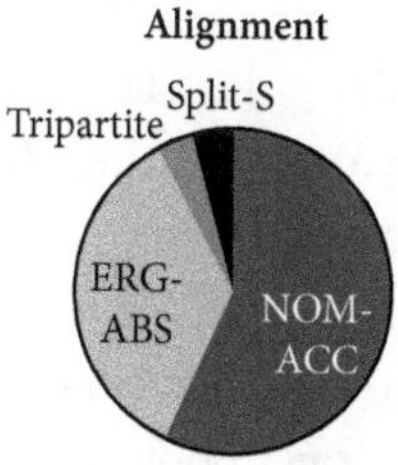

Figure 7.1 Spinner wheel for determining core case alignment

Using the percentages in Table 7.1, we can construct a pie chart where each slice represents a different alignment type, as shown in Figure 7.1. This chart is attached to the wheel, the wheel is spun, and whichever slice of the pie the pointer lands on determines which alignment the conlang will have.

The probability that the conlang will end up with a given feature as a result of a random spin is determined by the relative size of the corresponding pie slice. In the case of the alignment parameter, the wheel in Figure 7.1 ensures that there is a greater likelihood that the pointer will land on the accusative setting (57% chance) as opposed to the ergative setting (35% chance), and a greater likelihood that it will land on the ergative setting as opposed to the tripartite or split-S settings (4% chance each). In this way, the probability that the conlang will end up with a given alignment roughly approximates the probability that a randomly chosen natural language will have that alignment (yielding what Peterson (this volume) calls "weak naturalism").

As each parameter of the conlang is set, the probabilities governing subsequent decisions are adjusted based on known statistical correlations. In other words, each spin of the wheel determines what the pie charts for certain subsequent spins will look like. This provides students with a concrete illustration of the fact that parameter settings in natural languages do not vary randomly, but are instead interdependent.

For example, suppose that previous spins of the wheel have determined that the conlang has a default order for verb and object in basic transitive clauses, either OV or VO, and that it also has an adposition category. Will the conlang have prepositions or postpositions? Dryer (1992) and others have shown that, overwhelmingly, VO languages are prepositional, while OV languages are prepositional. For example, French, which places the verb before its direct object (4a), also places the adposition before its complement (4b); whereas in Malayalam, which places the verb after its direct object (5b), the adposition appears after its complement (5b):

(4) a. [$_{VP}$ **voir**   [$_{DP}$ la   chaise]]   b. [$_{PP}$ **sur**   [$_{DP}$ la   chaise]]
         see.INF   the   chair   on   the   chair
      'see the chair'   'on the chair'

(5) a. [$_{VP}$ [$_{DP}$ oru   pustakam]   **vaayiccu**]   b. [$_{PP}$ [$_{DP}$ ii   peena]   **koṇṭə**]
            one   book   read.PST   this   pen   with
      'read a book'   'with this pen'

Table 7.2 supports the generalization that adposition type strongly correlates with object placement, with *N* values again taken from the WALS language sample (Dryer and Haspelmath 2013).

The number and percentage of OV languages in the WALS database with postpositions (Postp) is vastly larger than the number and percentage of OV languages with prepositions (Prep): 97% and 3%, respectively. Conversely, the proportion of VO languages with prepositions is much larger than the proportion of VO languages with postpositions: 92% versus 8%. The strong statistical correlation between adposition type and the default order of verb

Table 7.2 Distribution of adposition type by object placement in WALS

	N	%
OV and postpositions	472	97
OV and prepositions	14	3
total OV	486	100
VO and postpositions	42	8
VO and prepositions	456	92
total VO	498	100

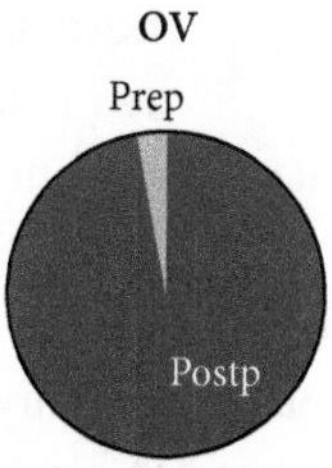

Figure 7.2 Spinner wheel for determining adposition type (language is OV)

OV

Figure 7.3 Spinner wheel for determining adposition type (language is VO)

and object can be expressed as a pair of biconditional universals: OV ↔ Postp and VO ↔ Prep.

As a consequence, the pie chart for determining adposition type in the conlang will look very different depending on how the OV/VO parameter had been set by a previous spin of the wheel. If the conlang has OV order, the pie chart for determining adposition type would look like Figure 7.2 below, resulting in a 97% chance that a random spin of the wheel will yield postpositional order. On the other hand, if the parameter has been set to VO, the pie chart for determining adposition type would look like Figure 7.3. Here, a random spin of the wheel would have a 92% chance of landing on the preposition setting.

A somewhat different kind of word order correlation is exemplified by the relationship between OV/VO order and the position of a relative clause (Rel) with respect to the noun that it modifies (Dryer 1992). Languages with VO order overwhelmingly place the relative clause after the noun (N-Rel). This is illustrated in (6) for the VO language Malagasy. Languages with OV order, on the other hand, show no tendency with regard to the position of the relative clause: instead, they are roughly equally likely to have either N-Rel order or Rel-N order. The former option occurs in the OV language Yaqui, for example (7a); while the latter option occurs in the OV language Basque (7b) (data in (7) taken from Keenan 1985):

(6)   ny   **boky**   [$_{Rel}$ novakin' ny   mpianatra tany   an-tokotany]
        the   book   PST.read the   student   there   LOC-garden
        'the book that the student was reading in the garden'

(7)   a. hu   **kari**   [$_{Rel}$ in   acai-ta   hinu-k-aʔu]
        this   house   my   father-DEF buy-PFV-REL
        'this house which my father bought'

      b. [$_{Rel}$ gizon-a-k   liburu-a   eman   dio-n]   **emakume-a**
         man-the-ERG book-the give   has-REL   woman-the
        'the woman that the man gave the book to'

This partial correlation between OV/VO order and relative clause position is supported by Table 7.3 (*N* values from Dryer and Haspelmath 2013).

In the case of adposition type, the correlation with default order of verb and object is bidirectional. If a language has OV order it is highly likely to have postpositions, and conversely, if it has postpositions it is highly likely to have OV order; likewise for VO order and prepositions. In the case of relative-clause position, however, the correlation with the order of verb and object is not bidirectional. If a language has VO order, it is overwhelmingly likely to have postnominal relatives (N-Rel), whereas no prediction can be made regarding the position of relative clauses in OV languages. On the other hand, if a language has prenominal relatives (Rel-N), it is overwhelmingly likely to also have OV order, while no prediction on the order of verb and object can be made for languages with postnominal relatives. This can be expressed as a pair of unidirectional implicational universals: VO → N-Rel and Rel-N → OV. In each case the converse implication does not hold: N-Rel order does not entail VO order, and OV order does not entail Rel-N order.

Table 7.3 Distribution of relative clause position by object placement in WALS

	N	%
OV and Rel-N	132	54
OV and N-Rel	113	46
total OV	245	100
VO and Rel-N	5	1
VO and N-Rel	416	99
total VO	421	100

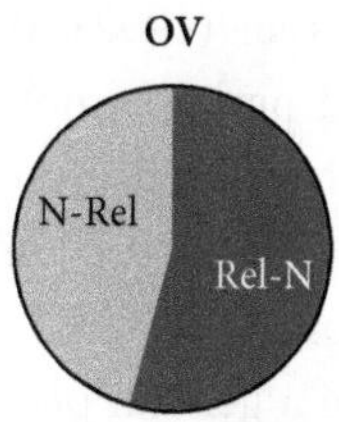

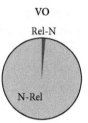

Figure 7.4 Spinner wheel for determining order of noun and relative clause (language is OV)

Figure 7.5 Spinner wheel for determining order of noun and relative clause (language is VO)

Figures 7.4 and 7.5 show the alternative pie charts, derived from the data in Table 7.3, which would be used when spinning the wheel to determine the order of noun and relative clause in the conlang. If the conlang is OV, the chart in Figure 7.4 would be used. Here there is a roughly equal chance that the pointer will land on N-Rel (46%) or on Rel-N (54%). If the conlang is VO, however, the chart in Figure 7.5 would be used, in which case there is an overwhelming probability (99%) that the pointer will land on N-Rel.

This exercise gives students the opportunity to investigate language universals in an original and hands-on manner. Typological research has shown that natural languages do not vary arbitrarily in their structure, but can instead be grouped into types (word-order types, morphological types, etc.) based on shared formal properties. By exploring how the setting of each structural parameter in their "naturalistic" conlang affects subsequent parameter settings—in some cases drastically—students learn how the statistical tendencies described by implicational universals conspire to give a language its overall grammatical shape.

As the conlang takes shape, students can be invited to speculate about *why* certain grammatical features tend to cluster together in natural languages while others do not—whether this reflects external functional constraints on language design, arbitrary properties of Universal Grammar (UG), or other factors. Although there is no consensus on what accounts for language universals, discussion of this issue can be found in

Travis (1989), Dryer (1992), Baker (1996), Newmeyer (2005), Christiansen et al. (2009), and perhaps most notably Hawkins (1983, 1990, 2004, 2014), who proposes that word-order correlations can be explained in terms of constraints on sentence processing (for an overview of Hawkins's work, see chapter 10 of Song 2018).

An example of a general principle which has been proposed to account for certain word-order correlations is Cross-Category Harmony (CCH), which roughly states that languages tend to prefer a consistent ordering of heads and dependents across phrases of different categories (Hawkins 1983 et al.). This principle manifests itself, for instance, in the correlation between adposition type and order of verb and object (OV ↔ Postp, VO ↔ Prep). Verb-object order and prepositional order both instantiate a preference for the head to precede the dependent (see 4 above), while object-verb order and postpositional order both instantiate a preference for placing the dependent before the head (see 5).

As for the partial correlation between order of verb and object and order of noun and relative clause (VO → N-Rel and Rel-N → OV), we might account for this pattern by appealing to the interaction between CCH and other word-order constraints. For example, various authors have noted a cross-linguistic tendency—possibly rooted in sentence-processing preferences—for phonologically light (simple) constituents to precede phonologically heavy (complex) constituents. We might refer to this weight asymmetry as Light-Before-Heavy (LBH). The LBH preference seems especially apparent when the heavy constituent is an embedded clause: for instance, Hawkins (1990) notes that in many OV languages (Farsi, German, Hindi, etc.), complement clauses optionally or obligatorily extrapose after the verb. Somewhat similarly, Malagasy exhibits VOS order when the O is a noun phrase but VSO order when the O is a complement clause. In both of these cases, a clausal dependent occurs further to the right than its non-clausal counterpart. Turning to relative-clause constructions, the LBH principle would favor N-Rel order cross-linguistically. If we were to treat CCH and LBH as ranked word-order constraints, as in Optimality Theory approaches, the distribution in Table 7.3 can be derived. In a language with VO order, N-Rel order is optimal regardless of which constraint is ranked higher: N-Rel order is harmonic with the order of verb and object (head precedes dependent), and is thus favored by CCH; N-Rel is also the order in which the heavy constituent follows, and is thus favored by LBH. However, if a language has OV order, then the position of the relative clause will depend on how the constraints are ranked relative to one another: if CCH outranks LBH, this will favor Rel-N order (the order where the dependent precedes the head); whereas if LBH outranks CCH, this will favor N-Rel order (the order where the light constituent precedes the heavy one). Assuming that both rankings are equally likely to arise, we are led to expect that roughly half of all OV languages will have prenominal relatives while the other half will have postnominal relatives.

7.4 Fleshing out the conlang

A language is more than just a set of categories and parameter settings: it also has a vocabulary, a cultural context, and so on. It is in working together to flesh out these aspects of the conlang that students are able to exercise their individual and collective creativity within the confines laid out in the previous section. When we carried out this project at UCLA, our first step was to determine the phonemes of the language, as well as permissible syllable types and phonotactic constraints. For example, we used successive spins of the wheel to determine that our language would have a five-vowel system with phonemic length, voiced and unvoiced obstruents, a voiceless lateral, coda consonants, a ban on complex onsets and codas, palatalization of coronal stops, and rules prohibiting certain kinds of consonant clusters (e.g. sequences of two plosives with different places of articulation). With these phonological properties established, we were able to give the language a name. One of the students in the class suggested *Naptiki*, but since the [pt] sequence did not conform to the phonotactics we had established, the name was altered to give the final form *Nattiki* [natːiki].

Having named the language, we proceeded to invent some vocabulary. Grammatical morphemes were decided on as a group during class discussions, and lexical roots were coined as needed to allow us to practice the features of the conlang by constructing example sentences. For example, in an early class we determined through successive spins of the wheel that Nattiki would have VOS order and an accusative alignment, with subjects and objects both marked by case suffixes. Once these features had been established, I solicited forms for the nominative and accusative case suffixes from the class. One student suggested *-tem* for the nominative suffix, while another suggested *-op* for the accusative suffix. After these had been accepted by the rest of the class, students took turns proposing noun and verb roots until we had enough vocabulary to construct some simple transitive and intransitive sentences in Nattiki, such as those in (8).[1] Whenever a new morpheme was suggested, we would check to make sure that it conformed to the phonological constraints of the language (e.g. that it used only permissible phonemes and syllable types) before accepting it.

(8)   a. Nesabu   putáka-tem
         sing   hamster-NOM
         'The hamster sings.'
      b. Embalu   didma-op   ké-tem
         hug   dog-ACC   boy-NOM
         'The boy hugs the dog.'

Further grammatical details were added in the same manner. For instance, in one class we determined that Nattiki would mark tense by means of verb prefixes, and discussed as a group what kinds of tense distinctions would be made. Students then took turns proposing forms for the tense morphemes, allowing us to construct verb paradigms (9).

(9)   kima   's/he sees'; '(to) see'   [simple present; nonfinite]
      bob-kima   's/he is seeing'   [present progressive]
      o-kima   's/he saw'   [past]
      šu-kima   's/he will see'   [future]

Likewise, we determined through a spin of the wheel that Nattiki would be a pro-drop language. As a consequence, we decided that Nattiki would have subject agreement encoded by verb prefixes, with third-person-singular agreement being unmarked (10):

(10)   i-šu-čé   'I will run'   fo-šu-čé 'we will run'
       na-šu-čé   'you (SG) will run'   zi-šu-čé 'you (PL) will run'
       šu-čé   's/he will run, it will run'   te-šu-čé 'they will run'

Notice that subject agreement does not distinguish gender or make an inclusive/exclusive distinction in the first-person plural, these features having been arrived at by spins of the wheel to establish the pronoun system. Interestingly,

---

[1] In the transcription system used here, č = [tʃ], š = [ʃ], and ł = [ɬ]. Long vowels are marked with a diacritic (e.g. á). All other symbols have essentially their IPA values, modulo allophonic alternations (e.g. palatalization: /t, d/ → [c, ɟ] / [i]).

another spin of the wheel determined that Nattiki nouns would not encode a number distinction. Hence the agreement on the verb ended up being the only indication of whether the subject is singular or plural (11).

(11) a. Šu-čé   dezét-tem
          FUT-run   child-NOM
          'The child will run.'

      b. Te-šu-čé   dezét-tem
          3PL.SUB-FUT-run   child-NOM
          'The children will run.'

When it was determined by a spin of the wheel that Nattiki would have object markers as well as subject markers, the students devised a set of verb suffixes for encoding the person and number of pronominal objects. We decided to extend these same morphemes to nouns for use in marking the person and number of pronominal possessors (12).

(12) te-čaló-la   'they love me'   didma-la   'my dog(s)'
      te-čaló-oni   'they love you (SG)'   didma-oni   'your (SG) dog(s)'
      te-čaló-weo   'they love him/her/it'   didma-weo   'his/her/its dog(s)'
      te-čaló-ep   'they love us'   didma-ep   'our dog(s)'
      te-čaló-do   'they love you (PL)'   didma-do   'your (PL) dog(s)'
      te-čaló-zet   'they love them'   didma-zet   'their dog(s)'

Subject, object, and possessor agreement (and pro-drop) are further illustrated by the contrast in (13):

(13) a. I-bob-łag   dučču-la-op
          1SG.SUB-PROG-talk.to   boyfriend-1SG.POSS-ACC
          'I am talking to my boyfriend.'

      b. Bob-łag-la   dučču-la-tem
          PROG-talk.to-1SG.OBJ   boyfriend-1SG.POSS-NOM
          'My boyfriend is talking to me.'

Additional grammatical properties of Nattiki are illustrated by the sentences in (14). As these examples show, Nattiki has wh-movement (14d–f) and places attributive adjectives before the noun head (14a,b,d). Note also that the attributive adjective inflects for case in agreement with the noun. In accordance with the word order correlations discussed in Section 7.3,

Nattiki (a VO language) has prepositions rather than postpositions—e.g. *ka* 'to' in (14b,c)—and places the relative clause after the modifying noun (14f). Notice also that prepositions take accusative complements, and that relative clauses are introduced by a wh-element such as *báka* 'who'.

(14) a. Te-o-šóan   ógu-op   méli-op
        3PL.SUB-PST-drink sour-ACC   milk-ACC
        'They drank the sour milk.'

   b. Šu-łomapo gú-op   ka pačé-op   dabet-op   dezét-tem
        FUT-give   book-ACC   to obese-ACC doctor-ACC   child-NOM
        'The child will give the book to the obese doctor.'

   c. I-o-łomapo-zet   ka didma-op
        1SG.SUB-PST-give-3PL.OBJ   to dog-ACC
        'I gave them to the dog.'

   d. Báka-tem   o-embalu   čona-op   didma-op?
        who-NOM   PST-hug   old-ACC   dog-ACC
        'Who hugged the old dog?'

   e. Kej   te-šu-jéta   kúmajalá-tem?
        when   3PL.SUB-FUT-eat.lunch   elephant-NOM
        'When will the elephants eat lunch?'

   f. O-gíšú-la   ké-tem   báka-tem   o-embalu   didma-op
        PST-visit-1SG.OBJ boy-NOM   who-NOM   PST-hug   dog-ACC
        'The boy who hugged the dog visited me.'

As the grammar and inflectional morphology of Nattiki were being developed during class meetings, each student was required to help expand the vocabulary by proposing five new roots per week (with definitions) and submitting these suggestions to me. Since the Internet was still in its infancy when this exercise was developed, we asked students to include a list of proposed Nattiki roots as part of their weekly homework assignments. Nowadays, to avoid students proposing different lexical items for the same concept, vocabulary suggestions could be uploaded to an online platform such as a course website or a wiki. For each round of submissions, proposed roots would be vetted by the instructor, or a designated student, to make sure they conform to the phonological constraints of the language. Approved roots can then be added to an online dictionary updated every week.

As an additional way to expand the lexical resources of the language, instructors can ask students to invent derivational morphemes (or derivational processes such as reduplication and compounding), and practice creating new lexical items from pre-existing roots. Including productive derivation allows the vocabulary to expand quickly by giving students and instructors the means to coin words on the fly without having to invent additional morphemes.

Finally, students can be invited to expand the grammar and cultural background of the conlang through term-paper projects. For example, students may be required to invent and describe some grammatical feature of the conlang which was not specified as part of the group project. The description could take the form of a sample chapter from a hypothetical reference grammar of the language, which explains the feature concisely and illustrates it with glossed example sentences. Alternatively, students could be asked to construct a sample text in the language, such as a folk tale or dialogue, or to translate a text from English. Students in the UCLA course who chose this option for their final project were required to provide the Nattiki text, a free English translation, and interlinear glosses, together with supplemental vocabulary and cultural notes. In many cases the need to write a complete text in the conlang led the student to propose additional grammatical features not covered in class. In (15), I give a sample Nattiki text, *Kunug da Sisíla* 'The Pig and the Oak Tree', adapted from a traditional fable.

(15)   Odé kunug bákatem otóse tus čonaop sisílaop da ołoło bapasisílaop. Bado ołoło zuzop bapasisílaop sašáop opila kada, omíbod limá. Ep očaguweo bóa aóweotem, da omiba diče katłosop.

"Mi nałé dogop!" ozí ka lapop kunugop wudugitem bákatem oludú łi hančaop bap sisílaop. "Zigá tat našudiza katłosop, šumaka łostem."

"Mi išuwiša tat šumaka łostem," ozí kunugtem. "Išupila kada lam bapasisílaop be łíčubop."

Odú atapa čonatem sisílatem: "Men nadé, kunug! Tat tetelo kima hančalaop łononitem sašátem heo tenebé udifaop, nabiš báfa kan teúji łila úmunmutem gibuktem sašáop nałoło ukúli. Zigá nabobluka á, nabobasfó ujošop wáfimonoop."

Interlinear glosses for this text are provided in (16)–(26). These further illustrate the grammatical properties of Nattiki just discussed. Note how the text features the use of compounding to form new lexical items, such as *bapa-sisíla* 'acorn' (lit. 'oak-fruit'), as well as the coining of roots with no single-word translation equivalent in English, such as *míbod* 'sleep soundly' and *bóa* 'after a while'.

(16) O-dé   kunug báka-tem   o-tóse   tus   čona-op
     PST-be   pig   who-NOM   PST-stand   under old-ACC
     sisíla-op   da   o-łoło   bapa-sisíla-op
     oak.tree-ACC   and   PST-eat   fruit-oak.tree-ACC
     'There was a pig which was standing under an old oak tree and eating
     acorns.'

(17) Bado   o-łoło   zuz-op   bapa-sisíla-op   sašá-op   o-pila
     after   PST-eat   all-ACC   fruit-oak.tree-ACC   what-ACC   PST-able
     kada,   o-míbod   limá
     find   PST-sleep.soundly   satisfied
     'After it had eaten all the acorns it could find, it slept soundly, satisfied.'

(18) Ep   o-čagu-weo   bóa   aó-weo-tem,   da
     but   PST-awaken-3SG.OBJ after.a.while   hunger-3SG.POSS-NOM   and
     o-miba   diče   kat-łos-op
     PST-begin   poke/prod   root-tree-ACC
     'But after a while its hunger awakened it, and it began to poke and prod
     at the tree roots.'

(19) Mi   na-łé   dog-op!   o-zí   ka   lap-op   kunug-op
     NEG   2SG.SUB-do   that-ACC PST-say to   that-ACC pig-ACC
     wudugi-tem báka-tem o-ludú łi hanča-op   bap sisíla-op
     bird-NOM   who-NOM   PST-sit on branch-ACC   in   oak.tree-ACC
     'Don't do that! a bird which was sitting on a branch of the oak tree said
     to that pig.'

(20) Zigá   tat na-šu-diza   kat-łos-op,   šu-maka łos-tem
     because   if   2SG.SUB-FUT-damage   root.tree-ACC   FUT-die tree-NOM
     'Because if you damage the tree roots, the tree will die.'

(21) Mi   i-šu-wiša   tat šu-maka łos-tem, o-zí   kunug-tem
     NEG   1SG.SUB-FUT-worry   if   FUT-die tree-NOM PST-say pig-NOM
     'I won't worry if the tree dies, said the pig.'

(22) I-šu-pila   kada lam   bapa-sisíla-op   be   łíčub-op
     1SG.SUB-FUT-able   find always fruit-oak.tree-ACC   for   food-ACC
     'I will always be able to find acorns for food.'

(23) O-dú   atapa   čona-tem   sisíla-tem: Men
     PST-speak all.at.once old-NOM   oak.tree-NOM   stupid
     na-dé,   kunug!
     2SG.SUB-be pig
     'All at once the old oak tree spoke up: You are stupid, pig!'

(24) Tat   te-telo   kima   hanča-la-op
     if   3PL.SUB-could   see   branch-1SG.POSS-ACC
     łon-oni-tem   sašá-tem   heo   te-nebé   udifa-op...
     eye-2SG.POSS-NOM   what-NOM   only   3PL.SUB-look.at   dirt-ACC
     'If your eyes that only look at the dirt could see my branches...'

(25) Na-biš   báfa   kan   te-úji   li-la
     2SG.SUB-would   know   that   3PL.SUB-grow   on-1SG.OBJ
     úmunmu-tem   gibuk-tem   sašá-op   na-łoło   ukúli
     lovely-NOM   morsel-NOM   what-ACC   2SG.SUB-eat   greedy
     'You would know that the lovely morsels that you eat so greedily grow
     on me.'

(26) Zigá   na-bob-luka   á,   na-bob-asfó
     because 2SG.SUB-PROG-act   blind   2SG.SUB-PROG-destroy
     ujoš-op   wáfimono-op!
     future-ACC   feast-ACC
     'Because you are acting blindly, you are destroying (your) future feasts!'

7.5 Summary

I have described a collaborative project where students work together to invent
a typologically plausible language. The major phonological, morphological,
and syntactic features of the language are determined at random by spinning a
wheel to decide among a set of alternatives (for instance, the alternatives for
core argument alignment might be accusative, ergative, tripartite, and split-S).
In each case the alternatives are weighted in accordance with their prevalence
among the world's languages, as extrapolated from numerical data found in
the WALS database and other large language samples. In this way, the
probability that the conlang will end up with a particular grammatical feature
as a result of a random spin approximates the probability that an arbitrarily
chosen natural language will have that feature.

In cases where different grammatical features correlate with one another, the result of a given spin will determine how the alternatives for subsequent spins are weighted. For example, since adposition type correlates with the default order of verb and object, the probability that the conlang will have prepositions (versus postpositions) as a result of a random spin of the wheel is adjusted based on whether the conlang is OV or VO, as determined by a previous spin.

Through this exercise, students are able to study linguistic typology first-hand by seeing how those universals play out in the development of a "naturalistic" conlang grammar, which may lead them to speculate on why certain grammatical features align with one another while others do not. Cross-linguistic word-order correlations and other implicational universals can be highly abstract, and thus their significance can be difficult for beginning students to grasp. By treating these universals as design constraints on a conlang, students gain an understanding of how the universals play out in the grammars of individual languages. Within the parameters defined by these design constraints, students can then exercise their individual creativity by inventing new vocabulary and producing texts and other artifacts, thereby fleshing out the conlang and giving it a distinctive personality and cultural background.

8

Teaching invented languages to the undergraduate major

A capstone course

Angela C. Carpenter

8.1 Introduction

I have designed the course, Invented Languages: From Wilkins' *Real Character* to *Avatar*'s Na'vi, as a capstone for linguistics majors and others interested in linguistics. Since it is a capstone course, majors pull together the various linguistic strands from previous courses and apply them to inventing their own language. Courses we offer in linguistics in addition to the introductory course include syntax, semantics, phonetics/phonology, sociolinguistics, psycholinguistics, and historical linguistics, among others. The capstone course allows students the opportunity to use this prior training to inform their decisions about the grammar of their language.

8.2 Course structure

This course is a seminar for upper-level students with a preliminary requirement that they have taken Introduction to Linguistics and at least one other related intermediate course in linguistics, anthropology, psychology, or philosophy. The majority of students have taken an average of three to four linguistics courses before enrolling in the Invented Language class. The class is limited in size to fifteen students and meets for 2 1/2 hours, once per week, for fourteen weeks. Each class session has two parts. The first half is a discussion of assigned readings on the history, philosophy, sociology, and psychology of invented languages, as well as student presentations of their own research on other invented languages. The second half is conducted as a

Angela C. Carpenter, *Teaching invented languages to the undergraduate major: A capstone course* In: *Language Invention in Linguistics Pedagogy*. First edition. Edited by: Jeffrey Punske, Nathan Sanders, and Amy V. Fountain,
Oxford University Press (2020). © Angela C. Carpenter.
DOI: 10.1093/oso/9780198829874.003.0008

grammar workshop where I present possible grammars that students can adapt for use in their developing language.

8.2.1 Readings and discussions

The readings provide an overview of the history and philosophy of invented languages, ranging from Francis Lodwick's *A Common Writing* (1647) and John Wilkins' *An Essay towards a Real Character and a Philosophical language* (1668) through Arika Okrent's *In the Land of Invented Languages* (2010). Reading Wilkins and Lodwick in 17th-century English challenges students to understand the motivation and rationale behind these early efforts to "improve" language. Other readings include excerpts of Umberto Eco's *The Search for the Perfect Language*, Fellman's *The Revival of a Classical Tongue: Eliezer Ben Yehuda and the Modern Hebrew Language*, and a variety of articles. Our discussions begin with a brief explanation of the language inventor's philosophical background and the context in which the language was invented. These early language inventors expose students to a philosophy of language that was informed by their particular time and place. Reading and deciphering these texts allows students to think about some of the external factors that contribute to the urge to invent a language. Our class discussion touches on issues of ethnocentricity in Western thought, philosophical idealism, and an emerging pragmatism in expansionist Europe as expressed by the authors' desire to have a common language for communicative clarity as well as facilitating commercial exchange. Students quickly come to see that despite the language inventors' efforts, the majority of the populace (Modern Hebrew being the exception) fails to adopt the language. The question then becomes, why such consistently negative results? This question leads to many vigorous discussions about how natural languages develop and evolve, who owns a language, and whether efficiency and exactness in communication are desirable or attainable goals for language.

For example, our discussion of language ownership begins with the observation that language evolution and change occur in natural languages in an organic process that stretches over periods of time. However, when similar processes occur in constructed languages, the reaction from the language inventor and speakers can range from acceptance to extreme displeasure and schisms (e.g. the schism in Volapük between its inventor and learners, Okrent 2010). Examples of disagreements between the language inventor and the speakers raise the questions of ownership: Who owns an invented language, the inventor or the speakers? Does exerting strict control over the language once it goes out into the world help to advance the language or stifle its growth? What is more important to the inventor, maintaining linguistic "purity" of the invention or allowing organic growth and change? Discussions on these and other issues of language growth and change can be brought out of the realm of the purely intellectual by asking students how they would feel if others were to change the language on which they have worked so diligently? Often the answers vary based on the purpose for which the language is being invented. Further, the question of language change is one with which many societies struggle, and have done so over the centuries. Examining language change from the viewpoint of invented languages allows students to extrapolate from individual societies' actions to enforce language retention to come to a greater understanding of the various issues that arise as languages change.

In addition to the assigned readings, each student prepares an oral presentation of an invented language of their choice. The presentation includes the background and goals of the inventor and an overall description of the language with examples of the phonology, morphology, and syntax. Each presentation also includes a lesson in the language so that students have the opportunity to evaluate the learnability of each language. Students are free to choose any invented language that interests them. Even with that open-endedness, some languages, such as Klingon, Na'vi, Quenya, Láaden, and Dothraki are almost always chosen for presentations, for various reasons. The class attracts students who are fans of science fiction, fantasy novels, or both, so many of them are acquainted with Klingon from the *Star Trek* series and Dothraki from the popular *Game of Thrones* television show. Each class usually has at least one big fan of J. R. R. Tolkien's writings, intrigued by the fact that his novels were developed in order to situate his invented languages in a time and place. As Tolkien himself put it, "The invention of languages is the foundation. The 'stories' were made rather to provide a world for the languages than the reverse" (Tolkien 1981: 219). Thus, one or more of Tolkien's languages, often Quenya, is chosen for presentation. Láaden, invented by Suzette Elgin, is of interest because it was "designed as a language to express the perceptions of women" (http://www.sfwa.org/members/elgin/NativeTongue/Laadan_FAQ.html). This woman's viewpoint on language is of interest to our students, who have chosen to attend a women's college.

8.2.2 Language and culture

As students begin to build their language, they are also encouraged to think about the speakers of the language and the culture in which their language resides. Speakers and their culture are entwined and the language is influenced by both. This idea may seem to fly in the face of the generative tradition of linguistics, which has moved far away from the Whorfian notion of linguistic determinism. As Pinker states "...there is no scientific evidence that languages dramatically shape their speakers' ways of thinking" (1994: 48). A language having a specific word that perfectly captures a concept, such as Spanish *sobremesa* (the deliciously languorous feeling generated by good conversation following a lovely meal) or German *Schadenfreude* (enjoyment from knowing of the troubles of others) does not indicate that speakers of another language cannot experience the same feelings. Another language may simply need many words to express the same feeling or experience. So the notion of linguistic determinism, in its strongest form, that language shapes thought, has been debunked. However, the idea of culture influencing language, at least in the lexicon, has been less controversial (Kramsch 1998). Although thought itself does not seem to be determined by language, some cognitive processes may be, such as how a speaker stores an event in memory. For example, speakers of Guugu Yimitthir in Australia and Tzeltal in Mexico primarily use cardinal terms such as north, south, east, and west to describe spatial relationships, and their recollections reflect this cardinality (Levinson 1997a). The cultural norm of expressing directions with non-egocentric words influences how they store spatial relationships in memory (Levinson 1997b). Of course, just as speakers of English can understand cardinal directions, speakers of Guugu Yimithirr and Tzeltal would also be able to understand egocentric directions, but they would not immediately remember them in those terms. The culture affects the language, but the language does not limit their ability to understand concepts that are not prevalent in their language or culture.

Thus, we make a distinction between language shaping thought and language being shaped by culture or cultural norms. For example, languages will coin words, such as Spanish *quinceañera*, that denote a practice that might not exist in another culture. In that sense, students invent a lexicon that is uniquely suited to their culture. Many go to the realm of science fiction or fantasy and create non-human speakers with non-human cultures and thus they feel free to reshape language to more or less suit their constructed world (cf. Sanders and Schreyer 2020, this volume). For example, one student invented an alien, but humanoid, species with a large nasal cavity. She used this facial feature as a basis for an articulatory feature and included a wide range of nasal sounds in the phonemic inventory. Other students have created languages based on cultures described in novels, such as the worlds of Orson Scott Card's *Ender's Game* series and Dr. Seuss' *The Lorax*; television shows, such as *Game of Thrones*; and movies, such as *Trollhunter*. Some languages have been built to illustrate cultures at the moment of creole genesis or intense language evolution, or to reflect speakers whose intelligence is artificial or even alien.

While students incorporate special words unique to their culture into their language, they also take their real or imagined cultural backgrounds into account at every step of their language invention, from phonetics onward. One language where tree-like speakers have to communicate over large distances included many fricatives but few stops in order to increase perceptibility. Culture can also affect morphosyntactic development in the students' invented languages.[1] In a culture where individuals have near-immortality, the past tense can be divided into recent past (up to 100 years ago), distant past (between 100 and 10,000 years ago), and remote past (over 10,000 years ago), all with different morphological affixes. That culture also has several second-person forms, where an individual can be addressed respectfully or not. As the student explains:

> Nouns in Renan Elvhen only mark person and number; gender is not inflected. However, there are eight different forms of person (Table 8.1). The four categories of second-person pronouns are used to demonstrate the relationship between the speaker and their interlocutor. The formal pronoun is used in situations where the interlocutors are just meeting or are in a formal situation such as a ritual, trial, or meeting, or when the person being spoken to is of higher social class than the speaker. The respectful pronoun is derived from the word for 'teacher', harɛn, and is usually used to refer to the speaker's teacher, mentor, or leader... The derogatory pronoun is exactly as it says; its use shows contempt or animosity, and is moderately insulting or condescending to use to another person. The neutral, of course, is neutral...   A.B. 2017

Table 8.1 Sample person and number morphology

	singular	plural
first person	ar	va
second person neutral	ma	na
second person formal	maʔn	naʔn
second person respectful	hɑ	hɑɛ
second person derogatory	maɛ	naɛ
third person neutral	kalɛn	galɛn
third person formal	kalɛ	galɛ
third person derogatory	kal	gal

A.B. 2017

---

[1] In general, most linguists would not credit culture as affecting morphosyntax. However, there are some exceptions to this general belief as seen in works by Wierzbicka (1986, 1985) and Hale (1966).

As would be expected, lexical items are unique to each language, and culture plays a major role in word choices. However, students do have to follow some guidelines in building the lexicon. After introducing a source on language typology (Comrie 1989), I require that their languages include a selection of mass nouns along with appropriate classifiers. This requirement still allows a great deal of creativity, while it forces students to think about the connection between substances and their divisible parts. Using notions of water, fire, and grass as examples, students construct the physical elements of their world and decide how various mass substances should be partitioned. This assignment allows practical application of semantic distinctions that may have been discussed as theory in previous courses, but often not covered with a hands-on approach. The following is a sample of one student's use of classifiers, which she uses as measure words:

> *bexor* 'rock-box' (used to measure water)
> *θasuʃ* 'breath' (used to measure fire)
> *minvallor* 'flame' (used to measure lightning)
> *pidra* 'dragon foot' (used to measure land, grass, etc.)
> *xaʃ* 'hunt' (noun, used to measure skill)   J.P. 2013

8.2.3 Grammar workshop

The second half of the class is centered on a grammar lecture and discussion designed to expose students to the crucial grammatical elements needed to construct their own language. This portion of the course is where the nuts and bolts of language invention are introduced and applied. While some of the lessons serve as reminders of material covered in previous courses, the unique perspective provided by having to create and implement grammatical structures in a new language is quite challenging. Each workshop begins with a presentation of the week's grammatical focus, including an explanation and discussion of the underlying linguistic principle for the week's topic and a typological survey of how different languages express the grammatical feature. Time is provided for students to work in small groups to brainstorm their own ideas on how to express that grammatical feature in their own language. For example, beginning with phonetics, we review the IPA chart and practice producing familiar and unfamiliar sounds. Students then discuss with their peers the kinds of sounds that they would like to have in their language and begin to put together their own consonant and vowel charts. I encourage students to choose a phonemic inventory that includes at least some sounds that are not used in English. Allophonic variation is included in their description of the phonology of the language. Table 8.2 is a representative sample of one student's consonant chart, in which every plosive and nasal has a labialized counterpart:

Table 8.2 Sample consonant chart

	bilabial	dental	alveolar	retroflex	velar
plosive	p pʷ b bʷ	t tʷ d dʷ			k kʷ
nasal	m mʷ		n nʷ		ŋ
trill	ɸ β				
fricative		θ ð			
approximant				ɻ	
lateral approximant			l		

A.B. 2017

Once their phonetic inventories have been created, students make decisions about the phonology, including syllable structure, stress assignment, and phonological rules. Describing phonological rules challenges students to identify the rules they naturally produce in English or their native language and to explicitly describe those rules if they use them when speaking the invented language; otherwise they must change those rules so that the "new" language is not spoken with their native accent. For example, if their language includes nasals, they need to decide if the homorganic nasal rule or a vowel nasalization rule applies. Rules such as alveolar flapping, unstressed vowel reduction, and voiceless stop aspiration are quite unconsciously produced. This exercise allows students the opportunity to reflect on the phonological rules of English or their native language, examine those rules, and then decide whether their invented language should retain them. I encourage students to think carefully about whether or not to reproduce English phonology in their new language, as doing so will affect how the language sounds. I assure them that rules can be added or changed later, but it is important for them to think through these early phonological decisions and understand the notion that their invented grammars must be rule-governed.

Following phonology, we move on to the morphology of verbs and nouns. After a review of the argument structure underlying transitivity, students are presented with a typology of affixation along with pertinent examples of prefixing, suffixing, infixing, circumfixing, and using auxiliary words. Armed with this knowledge, they decide on the types of affixation that are most appropriate

Table 8.3 Sample verb morphology system

	perfective	imperfective
indicative	-f	-ʃ
subjunctive	i-[root]-f	i-[root]-ʃ
conditional	x-[root minus first consonant]-f	θ-[root minus first consonant]-ʃ
imperative[a]	ǀ-[root]-k	ǀ-[root]-k'
interrogative	o-[root]-f	o-[root]-ʃ

[a] Note that [ǀ] is the IPA symbol for a dental click.

M.A.C. 2017

for their language. Again, I encourage them not to merely repeat what English does. But usually at this point students are very excited about being creative in constructing their grammar. Table 8.3 demonstrates how one student uses a combination of suffixes and circumfixes to indicate verb tense and mood.

By approaching morphology through a description of affixing, students are initially encouraged to develop an agglutinative language. The advantage of this approach is that students have to think clearly about tense, mood, and aspect on verbs and person, number, and gender on nouns. Having to think about whether or not to create morphemes for these verbal and nominal features tends to distinguish and clarify the information each feature contributes to verbs and nouns. A disadvantage of this approach is that they come to see that their words tend to be long and sometimes cumbersome. Later, I introduce the class to verb inflection, which then allows them to combine several features into one morpheme, if they so desire. At this point though, they better understand the combinatorial function of the inflecting morpheme. They thus increase their knowledge of grammar in general.

We spend several sessions working on tense, mood, aspect, and verb agreement. Students need to make decisions on how much information their verbs need to communicate and how to express that information, which allows them to really begin to understand the layers of information words and structure convey and how different languages choose to communicate this information. For example, word order is quite crucial in some languages, but not as important in others. But there is usually a trade-off, so students must decide how much information they want individual words to convey. If a student wants few constraints on word order, then she must use a strong case system.

The workshop format continues throughout the semester so that students are progressively immersed in the structure of their languages. They discuss the development of their language with one another along the way, and they incorporate changes and refinements as needed. They also get to practice speaking their language to classmates, an important factor in making the language come alive. A crucial part of the language construction, however, occurs out of the classroom by means of homework assignments.

8.2.4 Homework

Each week students are given a homework assignment that advances the development of their language. Thus, their languages are built step by step as they add necessary grammatical elements, such as syllable structure, morphology, word order, case, and more. For example, after the first week of class, students have to develop the phonemic inventory for their language, and the next week they add syllable structure, stress pattern, phonotactic restrictions, and other phonological rules. By week 4 they have developed the verb system, including tense, mood, and aspect, within a morphological framework (prefixes, suffixes, etc.). From the first week, I introduce the idea that languages dwell within a culture, so from the beginning of the language-building process they also start thinking about and constructing the world in which the language and culture dwell.

In doing the homework, students have to work out the interacting processes that affect their language and solve the unexpected issues that arise. I discourage them from taking the easy way out by saying that an anomaly is "an exception." Rather, they need to add, delete, or change a rule. It is not unusual to receive updates and changes to the phonology and syntax in the ninth and tenth weeks of class as students grapple with using the language in sentences. They can also justify what might seem to be a linguistic anomaly by invoking a historical change, which has to be explained. We spend an entire workshop on language change, and thus they get the opportunity to explore this aspect of their language thoroughly. Language change is discussed in Section 8.2.5.

8.2.5 Language change

An important part of inventing the language is to account for language change within a cultural context. While some of our majors take a course in historical linguistics before enrolling in the Invented Languages capstone, not all students have done so. Therefore, I provide a brief explanation of language change along with some phonetic, phonological, syntactic, and semantic examples from natural languages. Students who have taken the historical linguistics course will usually provide additional examples based on the research they undertook for previous papers. The assignment then is to describe a language change, phonological, morphological, syntactic, or semantic, that the language has undergone, and to provide the historical context in which the change occurred. Below is an excerpt from a student's final paper in which she describes a language change that occurred as a result of a natural phenomenon in the environment.

> Another sound change that occurred in ʃaʃʍeθ is the shift from *fips ('thought') to pifs. This type of change is called a metathesis, where two sounds switch positions. This metathesis in particular stemmed from the common expression 'tsopjofuː tipifs'. Literally it means 'thoughts move on their own', and is used to indicate that someone cannot sleep. Because the cave was frequently uncomfortable for the children, they used this expression often, and fips became pifs to match the order of the 'p' and 'f' sounds in 'tsopjofuː'.   M.S. 2017

In addition to invoking language contact situations, students have described dialect formation based on schisms in a community, semantic changes linked to patterns of migration, diachronic phonetic changes, and more. The experience of having to account for the development of particular aspects of their language brings linguistic theory to life in a way that is particularly meaningful and realistic to the student.

8.3 Other features of the course

8.3.1 Translation

An important assignment for these students is to be able to translate the Tower of Babel story from the Bible book of Genesis into their language, a standard conlang sign of accomplishment. This translation assignment marks a milestone in the development of the language as students have to grapple with creating words for concepts that might not have existed in their language, such as the 'bitumen' and 'mortar' used to build the tower in the Bible account. Translating provides an opportunity for students to see how consistently their grammatical structure works. The translation assignment also allows them to get practice in glossing as well as translation.

8.3.2 Short essay

Midway through the course students are required to write a short 5–7-page paper, with a clear thesis, stating their views on invented languages based on the readings, discussions, and their own outside research. As a general guide for the paper, I invite them to consider the following: We have discussed invented languages from philosophical, historical, and sociological viewpoints and seen that almost all of the languages have failed. Describe the ways in which they have succeeded or failed. Have those languages provided any benefits, in spite of overall failure? Languages designed for entertainment and/or to flesh out virtual worlds have seen a measure of success in recent years. Why might that be? What do these languages provide that previous invented languages have not? How has our society changed that there might be a forum for these types of languages? Should invented languages have a place in society?

8.3.3 Guest speakers

A feature of the course that students really love is the opportunity to meet and learn from members of the conlanging community. We have had class visits by Paul Frommer, Arika Okrent, Britton Watkins, and David Peterson. Each has given a lecture on a linguistic feature they have used in their own conlang, sometimes introducing students to new possibilities in their language invention process. In addition to the class lectures, we include a lecture or event for the entire Wellesley College community and the general public. These lectures and visits provide our students and the general public a glimpse into the burgeoning popularity of invented languages in entertainment and the media. Further, our guest speakers increase the community's interest in invented languages and by extension, linguistics in general. Thus, we have seen a rise in enrollments in the Introduction to Linguistics course over the past several years.

8.4 Pedagogical pillars

From a pedagogical point of view, this course allows me to put into practice pedagogical pillars designed to help students master essential reasoning skills and further their linguistic knowledge. These pillars include peer-to-peer learning, close and critical engagement with original source materials, problem solving, and creativity.

8.4.1 Peer-to-peer learning

Peer-to-peer learning, or specifically "a two-way reciprocal learning activity" (Boud 2001: 3), occurs in several forms: in-class group work, discussions about grammatical features, exchanges of ideas on language development, and active teaching of their language to each other individually and to the group. Time is set aside during each class period for students to discuss their developing language with their peers. These discussions usually center on the grammar focus of the day. For example, after discussing tense, mood, and aspect, students discuss with one another how they will implement those grammatical elements into their verbs. They discuss the pros and cons of having different morphemes for tense, mood, and aspect versus collapsing some of those grammatical functions into a few morphemes. Questions for discussion include: How many tenses will their language have and what kind of affixes will they use to express tense? Will they use a case system, adpositions, or both? Inevitably, some students will have a better understanding or retention of particular grammatical features than others, so they help each other with explanatory details. Of course, I am available to answer questions or to provide guidance as they work together. As students try ideas out with one another, they are encouraged to give constructive feedback to their classmates, while paying attention to how the interaction between language and culture informs the grammatical decisions made. This weekly give-and-take allows students to explore new ways of thinking about language, practice speaking their developing language, and listen critically to other linguistic possibilities.

Students are required to teach an aspect of their language twice during the course. About halfway through the course students give a language lesson to a fellow student and that student in turn has to explain the lesson to the class in general. This sequential teaching opportunity enables the language creator to see how easily the target feature can be learned and also allows both students to see how accurately the feature can be explained. Another teaching opportunity occurs at the end of the course when each student teaches a different aspect of their language to the entire class. To prepare for this, they research language-teaching techniques and then use one of those (or their own) techniques in making up a lesson plan. These teaching lessons allow the student to test out the learnability of their language and also give them an opportunity to have some fun. We have learned how to count by singing a nursery rhyme in an invented language, how to distinguish two different dialects of another invented language through a call-and-response exercise, and how to use six different past tenses as part of an immigration interview.

8.4.2 Close and critical engagement

Close and critical engagement with original source materials provides opportunities for students to explore real-life applications of linguistic theory, grapple with various forms of scholarly exposition, and develop their own informed opinions on current thinking across the many subdisciplines of the field. For example, as previously noted, early in the semester students are required to read a large portion of Wilkins' *An Essay towards a Real Character and a Philosophical Language* (1668) and Lodwick's *A Common Writing* (1647), written in 17th-century prose. These texts not only describe the philosophy behind these invented languages but they introduce readers to 17th-century ideas of a scientific approach to language. Students must translate these ideas into present-day English and compare them to current scientific approaches, which leads to lively discussions and interpretive analyses. Students engage in animated discussions of the pros and cons of individual constructed languages and exchange ideas on why these invented languages have usually failed to reach their goals.

8.4.3 Problem-solving

Problem-solving is a large part of linguistic analysis and it is a key aspect of the courses our majors take through their undergraduate studies. Creating their own language requires students to make countless decisions about the structure of their language, and these decisions all have to tie together to create a more or less logical and cohesive whole. While grappling with the details of building the structure of the language, they also have to keep the bigger language and cultural picture in mind. As each student's language develops she often comes upon unanticipated problems, particularly in interface areas of morphophonology and syntax–semantics. As noted above, they are encouraged to not just take an easy way out ("this is an exception") but to work through a plausible explanation for the conflict. For example, a student might come to realize that the best explanation for an exceptional phonological rule may be diachronic language change, which she then has to incorporate into the grammar as a whole, along with an explanation of the change. Now she has to draw on her knowledge of historical linguistics to give a viable account of this phonological exception. Another typical morphophonological problem arises when morphology interacts with phonology to produce an illicit consonant cluster or vowel hiatus. While there are relatively simple solutions that include epenthesis, deletion, or metathesis, for example, once again students are encouraged to come up with a consistent rule or rationale for their choices that fits into the overall tendencies of the language. Of course, their languages can have anomalies, just as natural languages do; however students need to develop a "back story" that accounts for the anomalies or inconsistencies. Having to come up with a reasonable rationale for linguistic anomalies has provided some of the most creative and satisfying moments in the language-invention process. Students call on their knowledge of historical linguistics, language change, language contact, creole genesis, bilingualism, and language acquisition, gleaned from previous courses in the linguistics curriculum.

8.4.4 Creative engagement

Creative engagement is most evident as a result of the requirement to build a culture within which the invented language exists. Developing the culture is an ongoing process that evolves as the language evolves. There are fits and starts and much revision, but students are thrilled to have the opportunity to let their imaginations run free and to bring their personal interests into the language creation process. While some students build and expand on an already-existing culture, for example, creating a language for the animals in C. S. Lewis's *The Chronicles of Narnia* series, others develop a fantasy world of their own making. As a result of taking a course on creoles, one student created a language for the culture of a group of children who formed a creole of English, French, and Wolof in West Africa, and another student is creating a creole spoken on Mars.

The cultural background is fully explained in the final paper, accompanied by an original story, poem, or song written in the language that provides insight into the culture. Although it is not required, inevitably some students will create a writing system for their language. The writing system brings their creative engagement with the language to another level.

8.5 Assessment

How does one grade the quality of a language that is completely invented? Assessing a student's work is actually not very difficult. At the most basic, students need to complete their weekly assignments, make a minimum of three class presentations (original research on a conlang, teaching an aspect of their language to the class, and the final presentation of their language), write a short, 5–7-page, viewpoint essay based on the readings, and put together the final package. The final package includes a description of the culture and a detailed description of the grammar; an invented language-English and an English-invented language lexicon; the Tower of Babel translation; an original story written in the language; an audio recording of the story; and appendices as needed.

The weekly assignments and presentations are not graded, but are checked to see that they have been completed. I provide feedback with comments and suggestions for each weekly assignment. Students are also required to post discussion questions and comments each week on the class online site. These discussion questions form the basis of our weekly in-class discussions and students' participation grade includes these online postings. The short paper is graded, like any academic paper, for development of a thesis, content, ideas, and grammaticality.

The most enjoyable yet difficult part of the assessment is the final paper. In fact, the biggest drawback for the teacher in a course with this much work for the student is the amount of time it takes to thoroughly read and evaluate the presentation of each invented language. It is a pleasure to read the product of the entire semester's work. Students are proud of their work and I am proud of them. When reading the papers, however, I find it difficult to remember every grammatical detail of every language, so I limit myself to reading no more than two papers in a day in order to wrap my brain around the complexity of each grammar. Even at that, keeping track of all the grammatical details is almost impossible, so I try to evaluate the overall grammar for cohesiveness and consistency. After reading and making notes on the details of the grammar, I move on to the short story written in the language, along with the accompanying gloss and translation to English. After spending a couple of hours with the grammar, I find it easier to spot inconsistencies in its usage in the story. I also listen to their audio recording and compare their pronunciation of the language with their phonological rules. Few students get everything perfectly correct according to their own rules, but some students are much better at speaking their language than are others. Outstanding work and indifferent work are easier to identify and grade than work that has some great ideas, but is inconsistent in the execution. Nonetheless, students are all commended for the amount of work and effort they put into the course.

8.6 Student comments

The following are excerpts of students' comments gathered anonymously through the college's Student Evaluation Questionnaires (SEQs). From the comments one can see that students really appreciate the course and have gained some valuable insight about language from it. The following are five typical comments from students on the SEQs for the Invented Language course:

> I learned so much in this course—the workshop-style set-up was sort of like [Introduction to Linguistics] again but applied to creating a language. I got to review all of the material I have learned over the past four years and put it to use, and it wasn't until this course that all of it sort of came together. I also loved the assigned readings and discussion of the search for a "perfect language," which made me remember why I love language and linguistics (for its diversity, not for an attempt at sameness).

> ...Doing this class has felt like one of the triumphs of my Wellesley career and this semester we have had so many opportunities to connect with the conlang community outside Wellesley.

> The many linguistic topics that were covered were very good for understanding the building blocks of language. This class really helped me to analyze language—everywhere. I can now appreciate the similarities and differences between languages, and 'understand' them to a degree. It's hard to even capture how much I think I've gotten out of this class.

> This course challenged me to recall all of the linguistic knowledge and skills that I have acquired over the past years, and apply [them] to a very large and interesting project. This course challenged me to think about linguistics in a creative way, and it also introduced me to linguistic features that I never knew even existed. It was fascinating, engaging, and challenging all semester long.

> Making my own language forced me to be very detailed and meticulous. I feel that this made me better at linguistics in general. Also having to make

decisions about features of my language and consistently use them made me understand those features better.

8.7 Conclusion

As a capstone, this course has been very successful in having students bring together various strands of linguistics into one complete package, their own invented language. Without a doubt, completing this course entails a lot of work. Students often report that they spend many more hours each week on this course than on others, but that they're willing to spend the time because it is their own creation. The depth of linguistic and cultural detail they include in the final paper speaks to their level of commitment to forming a solid, linguistically sound language.

The inclusion of the design of a historical language-change component is a recent addition to the syllabus. I was very pleased to see how excited students were to rise to that challenge. A few of them even stated that having to include language change helped them to solve some problems they had come upon during the semester. One addition I would like to make to the course would be to have students explicitly add some sociological factors that might induce dialectal variation in their language. This might be a bit ambitious, but a few students over the years have incorporated sociolinguistics into their languages in interesting ways. For example, one student created a culture in which speakers are encouraged to enter an introverted state that encourages active listening to one another. In that state, they speak a different dialect in which voiced stops and fricatives become voiceless and full vowels in unstressed syllables reduce to schwas. The student describes the dialect difference:

In Zeɪva, there are only voiced consonants; when talking in Seɪfə [the introverted dialect] voiced consonants in Zeɪva verbs and nouns become voiceless

In /zeɪva/: /wæt.kʼan/

In /seɪfə/: /wætkʼan/ becomes /ˈʍæt.kən/   S.B. 2013

A sociolinguistic component added by students would be required to be rule-governed, even if the rules have not been observed in human language. The important point is that, as for other grammatical elements in the language, there needs to be a rule-based consistency even in a proposed dialect.

Another student built her language entirely around issues of class, creating two versions of her language. She explains the background for this approach as follows:

> I knew that I was going to take the invented languages class since I first heard about it in my sophomore year. As such, I was already thinking about the possible ideas for my language [while] studying abroad in Denmark. One of the topics that I covered there was the tension of the British Class System as represented in the musical, *Billy Elliot*. As my classmates and I were talking about the immediate judgment people had towards the working class due to their accents, we also talked about some differences among British English speakers, American English speakers, and English speakers in Denmark in their word choices, mostly focusing on the frequency of the word "sorry" and the difference in the directness of their speech. These discussions heavily influence my decisions in forming the culture and the rules of puɹ.he.ʃu.i.jo o.tu.pli.   I.S. 2015

While I would not require students to come up with two complete dialects, bringing in a sociolinguistic component would add a new dimension to their language invention capstone course.

Finally, although this course is a great deal of work for the teacher as well as the students, it is a real pleasure to teach the course; I thoroughly enjoy witnessing and participating in our students' creative efforts and the deepening of their understanding of linguistic principles.

9

Teaching invented languages as an introductory course

Unfamiliar territory

James A. Berry

9.1 Introduction

An invented languages class or unit can be a useful and creative way for faculty and students to bring together their accumulated linguistic knowledge. As a result, many of the authors in this volume have taught invented languages as an advanced or even a capstone (e.g. Carpenter, this volume) course for linguistics majors or minors. However, many linguistics instructors across the United States and elsewhere do not operate within a designated linguistics program. They often work in programs where linguistics plays a support role.

My own faculty experience is of this type. I decided to introduce an invented languages course after hearing about colleagues' success at other universities. With borrowed syllabuses and frequently used texts for inspiration, I sought to translate the invented languages experience to my own, somewhat different, theater of operations—an English department at a smaller state university. The seminal article by Sanders (2016) was published at the beginning of the semester, and I used it as a source of helpful advice as the course moved on. Because of the constraints of the class, I also kept in mind the questions asked by Kuiper (2011: 182) of his introductory classes, boiled down to this: "[W]hat can and should be crammed into a one-semester course?"

In the remainder of this chapter, I discuss the background of the course and some of the parameters I have to work within. These parameters are largely dictated by forces outside my scope of influence. Nevertheless, even with these limitations, I intend to show that the structure inherent in an invented languages course is flexible enough to act as an effective introduction to linguistics.

James A. Berry, *Teaching invented languages as an introductory course: Unfamiliar territory* In: *Language Invention in Linguistics Pedagogy*. First edition. Edited by: Jeffrey Punske, Nathan Sanders, and Amy V. Fountain, Oxford University Press (2020). © James A. Berry.
DOI: 10.1093/oso/9780198829874.003.0009

9.2 Institutional background

The University of Wisconsin–Stevens Point (UWSP) is a comprehensive state university located in Stevens Point, Wisconsin, a city of approximately 28,000 people in the geographical center of the state. The area around Stevens Point is largely farmland, with small towns and areas of wilderness mixed in. Larger metropolitan areas, such as Madison, Milwaukee, and Minneapolis-St. Paul, MN, are a two-plus-hour drive away. This geographic isolation helps to define UWSP, its faculty, and its student body.

As a comprehensive state university, its educational focus is on undergraduates, with a limited number of master's and doctoral programs in a few areas. UWSP has, in its history, seen its fortunes wax and wane with the major shifts in American post-secondary education. Originally a normal school, it became a four-year institution before World War II and part of the Wisconsin State University system afterward. In 1971, the Wisconsin State University system was merged with the flagship University of Wisconsin in Madison, WI, creating the current UW System.

The comprehensive universities in the UW System are often distinguished by their geography and by specialized programs they offer. In the case of UWSP, its location at the southern edge of the great pine forests of Wisconsin have enabled university leaders to develop a unique program in natural resources (e.g. forestry and water management) and a strong program in paper science. Both of these programs have helped to define UWSP as a science-heavy campus. With reduced financial resources directed to state universities, there has been pressure within the state for campuses to define themselves by specialties such as these.

Since the 1980s, there has been limited growth among the comprehensive universities, and UWSP has recently seen enrollment decline by about 20% (to approximately 8,000 students). This has resulted in some well-publicized budget deficits that have affected humanities programs in particular. These budgetary constraints make the acts of introducing or expanding course offerings, particularly in non-STEM (Science/Technology/Engineering/Mathematics) areas, more difficult.

The English Department at UWSP is one of the larger humanities programs. It is home to more than 150 majors, approximately 50 of whom are enrolled in the English Education track. The major focuses on literature; one linguistics course is required of English majors and one of English Education majors. A well-enrolled writing minor and a minor in women's and gender studies are also housed in the department. Freshman and sophomore composition courses are taught by all faculty in addition to their individual specializations.

9.3 Limited growth in linguistics offerings

Despite some of these limitations, there has been potential for growth in linguistics at UWSP. In 2015, after I was hired as a second linguist in the department, efforts were made to broaden the curriculum and to develop a linguistics minor. The first step was to create an Interdisciplinary Certificate in Language Study, incorporating eleven credit hours already required for the BA in English (eight hours of a world language and three hours of a linguistics course) and adding seven hours (two approved linguistics courses from English or another department, plus a one-credit capstone).

This certificate program has indeed attracted student interest and, to date, several students have completed the program. Because of further budgetary insecurity, however, the creation of a linguistics minor has been shelved indefinitely.

Before 2016, there were four linguistics courses offered by the English Department: Introduction to Linguistics, History of the English Language, English Grammars, and English Language for Teachers (specific to the English Education track). The courses added since my hire have included Invented Languages (detailed in this chapter), Sociolinguistics, and Language, Gender, and Sexuality. These classes were added to help broaden both the material covered and the appeal of linguistics in a setting where there were limited opportunities for exposure to the discipline. Another focus is on the inherent interdisciplinarity in linguistic studies (see also Sanders and Schreyer this volume); connections to other fields offer the possibility of creating new networks among faculty and students.

However, because of the limited number of courses and the requirement that English majors only need to take one three-credit course, there is no current course sequence. Students can enroll in any class without prerequisites. This situation ensures that each course must include a fair amount of introductory material and adds a significant pedagogical constraint to course instruction.

9.4 Invented Languages course

In fall 2016, the Invented Languages course was first offered as a special topics course under an omnibus course number. This initial version of the class was conceived as an applied introductory class, where students would encounter various subfields and apply their knowledge to create the basic structure of a new language. The course was split into two main sections.

The first such section asked students to consider the cultural phenomenon of creating languages. We examined both real-world (*auxlang*) and creative (*artlang*) communication needs and considered the ways in which language invention can meet those needs. This initial three-week period allowed us to contextualize the human urge to invent languages and the communities that can arise from this urge.

The remaining twelve weeks of the semester were devoted to building languages. As in many other courses, the students were required to create a semester project that would consist primarily of a descriptive grammar of their invented language. This was approached in stages that coincided with the material being learned at the time, much as in other courses detailed in this volume.

The course that was taught in fall 2016 had a small enrollment, in part because the special topics designation allowed for only limited advertising. However, ten students finished the class. Of those ten, six had taken other linguistics courses, and most had studied other world languages, such as Spanish, French, German, Russian, and Japanese. Two were non-native English speakers, and they brought their native knowledge of Colombian Spanish and Egyptian Arabic to bear on our discussions. I encouraged a seminar style for discussions, with a mixture of lecture and reflective commentary on readings. With such a small group, the students were quite friendly, and they were happy to offer suggestions on one another's projects. They were also excited about the subject material and how they could apply it to their projects, so discussions were enthusiastic and broad-reaching.

9.4.1 Invented languages in culture

The first part of the semester was devoted to reading and discussing. We read Okrent (2010) and selected chapters from Adams (2011a). Both of these texts focus on the reasons for language invention and the different kinds of solutions historically offered among a variety of literary and real-world languages. Starting with these texts reflected some of my own biases: although I have a background in generative syntax, I am currently more focused on sociolinguistics and historical linguistics, both of which are heavily concerned with the ways in which language reflects human needs, concerns, and behaviors.

As a class, we started with the big question "Why?" Why do humans need to create new languages when there are natural languages at nearly everyone's disposal? Adams (2011b: 10–14) offered us five historical motivations:

1. retrieving the lost original human language, as detailed in religious or mythological texts;
2. encouraging world peace through an international auxiliary language;
3. retrieving a lost culture through reviving a dead language (Hebrew, Manx);
4. using a created language as a 'safe space' for the communicative needs of threatened and/or marginalized groups; or
5. creating a new world through a literary language.

These topics engaged the students, and a concern for the language of marginalized peoples became a theme for many of them as they began their semester projects. Such a focus on marginalization drives the class in sociolinguistics, which some of the students had taken, and also a significant amount of the coursework in the English and English Education majors. So our discussions were able to take previous work as scaffolding for the exploration of language invention.

International auxiliary languages were an area of strong interest, and we spent a couple of class periods on Esperanto, as the most successful of these. Our initial discussion covered not only the language but its creator, L. L. Zamenhof, and his goals of bringing people and nations together through a common language, goals made more poignant by the murders of two of his children in Nazi concentration camps.

Again, here the context of the language drove interest in it, and we spent a class period with the grammatical rules of Esperanto and some translation worksheets. Because Esperanto words are largely Romance and Germanic, most students were able to read and understand much of the vocabulary fairly quickly. They also recognized linguistic patterns of syntax and morphology and were able to apply these to new sentences with a dictionary. Several students found this experience exciting and determined to use Esperanto as inspiration for their own languages.

We were able to contrast the designed simplicity of Esperanto with the complexity of Quenya, Dothraki, and particularly Klingon. We looked at nominal morphology and contrasted simpler systems such as Esperanto (and English) with more complex comingling of number, gender, and case. The emphasis in our discussion was not only on some of the details of the complexity but also on the goals of that complexity. The fact that a language like Klingon is technically accessible to all humans but requires a significant cognitive load (particularly for speakers of English) became a starting point for the idea of foreignness or Otherness. A population speaking such a 'strange' language is marked by its differences rather than its similarities. This 'strangeness' can then be used or manipulated by authors, along with other creative devices, to make the speaker population more difficult to know and understand.

At this point, two important guidelines for the remainder of the class were introduced: first, that we would examine ranges of options for the various linguistic elements through lenses of markedness and, more broadly, typology; and secondly, that the extremes of these ranges would encompass a sort of 'smorgasbord' approach to language-building. Typology was initially approached through a lecture and reading from Whaley (1997: 3–29) and through the examination of the Austronesian-Southern Oceanic language Mwotlap (François 2005), spoken in Vanuatu, which has several characteristics that English-speaking students processed as marked. We particularly talked about the complex nominal system. Students were asked to hold on to their readings and notes as they began to work on their languages.

9.4.2 Semester project

Once we had a macro-level understanding of what could be possible in language invention, we began to move from the outside in. Because of the challenges inherent in such a project, I encouraged students to work in pairs but allowed them to work independently, if they desired. Four students formed two pairs; the other six decided to work on their own. For some of those who chose to work independently, they were inventing languages for worlds and populations that had been created already, while others were wary of any sort of group project.

The project consisted of four sections of a linguistic grammar: (i) the world of the language; (ii) the sound system; (iii) the morphosyntax; and (iv) the lexicon, semantics, and pragmatics. Students would prepare these sections as written assignments, each due after we had covered and discussed the relevant topic. During the last week of class, each language would be presented to me and the other students, and the collected grammar (with revisions) would be submitted as a single electronic file, with an accompanying reflection essay, during finals week.

9.4.3 World-building

As the class moved into their projects, the first two or three weeks were spent on world-building. Just as with examining languages as cultural phenomena, the creative act of building a new world was exciting and highly exploratory for students. At least three of the students were creative writing minors, so world-building was a more comfortable exercise for them to engage with. They helped to lead several class discussions and were broadly collaborative with classmates who had not created worlds before.

As this was the aspect of language creation to which I had not been introduced before (I entered this class without conlang experience), it was the perfect opportunity to collaborate with other English Department faculty members. I met a few times with the faculty member who teaches fiction writing, and we were able to put together a brief but comprehensive list of both natural and social elements for the act of world-building. This guidance was very helpful for me.

During our class periods, the students and I examined some of the types of worlds they could develop. In order to accomplish this, we gathered models from a variety of authors, particularly those of science fiction and fantasy literature. As a starting point, I assigned "The Ones Who Walk Away from Omelas," by Ursula K. Le Guin, as a brief and accessible yet highly detailed short story with the description of a society in another world. Aside from the power of the story itself (which is in fact deeply entangled in its social organization), we had a discussion about the culture—the details Le Guin provides, those she leaves out, and those she purposely and often playfully leaves vague. We also looked at other types of worlds: the planets and galaxies of the Star Wars and Star Trek universes; the fantastical semi-terrestrial worlds of Oz (L. Frank Baum and Gregory Maguire) and Middle-earth (J. R. R. Tolkien); and alternate realities, such as Jasper Fforde's Britain.

In the assignment for the world-building project, I asked students to consider drawing a map, laying out the physical constraints of their worlds. We looked at sample maps for inspiration. Whether or not they were comfortable with drawing, I also asked for physical or metaphysical descriptions of their worlds, whether extraterrestrial or earthly. I also asked for brief, initial discussions of the culture(s) of their worlds as expressed through their:

- speakers
- social organization
- customs and traditions
- religion
- arts and literature
- government
- economic system
- technology
- history

These prompts were a spark for several students (many of whom brought experience to the class), although they were intimidating for others. It was, admittedly, a large amount of information to create in a relatively brief period of time.

For those who were concerned about the breadth of information requested, I reminded them that they were working on a draft and acknowledged that I was asking a lot of questions that they might not yet be ready to answer. Because of these limitations, and in order to keep this assignment enjoyable, I asked students to concentrate on providing detailed answers for a few items of their choosing. While doing this, I requested that they sketch out more generalized thoughts about the other categories. If students had more material to submit for the assignment than I required, this was welcome (and I would provide feedback). However, no one was punished for providing the basics.

This assignment became the prototype for the 'smorgasbord' approach I used during the rest of the semester. I set limited, reachable requirements, while allowing more motivated students the ability to move beyond the basics.

The students in our class responded with a great deal of creativity. Most of the speakers in the worlds were human or humanoid, but there were sapient plants, cats, and equines (horses, unicorns, and pegasuses). The created worlds were mostly alternate versions of Earth, although a few were on other planets. Some alternate Earths were post-apocalyptic, and there were two alternate-reality islands in the eastern and western Mediterranean serving as homes to different groups of speakers.

My concept for these first weeks of the semester was to use contextualization (of the history and uses of invented languages, and then of the new worlds in which students' own languages would appear) as a way to prepare students for the next, more conventional sections of an introductory linguistics class. When students work with a creative endeavor, set within a world of their own making (with parameters they control), they expose and make decisions about systems that are assumed as background in the world of the mundane. The goal of linguistics instruction is to explore and make visible, in much the same fashion, the means of communication—highly complex systems that are taken for granted by most users. The rich discussions and creative endeavors of those first weeks served to build enthusiasm, to establish language invention as a discipline, and to help students in the process of recognizing and building patterns. These introductory weeks limited the time we could devote to conventional linguistics instruction but were crucial in setting the tone for the remainder of the semester.

9.4.4 Sound systems

Once the worlds were begun, we began to move into the more typical subfields of linguistics. I prefer to teach introductory classes in the order: phonetics, phonology, morphology, syntax, semantics, and pragmatics/discourse analysis. I followed the same pattern with the invented languages course. At this point, Rosenfelder (2010) became our primary text, supplemented as necessary by handouts. We spent four to five weeks on sound systems.

As with other introductory courses, we used the chart of the International Phonetic Alphabet to understand and classify speech sounds. We examined consonants and vowels, non-pulmonics, tones, suprasegmentals, and syllable structures. This section of the class was, unsurprisingly, a more challenging one for students, and the differences between linguistics novices and those who had had more education in phonetics and phonology became quite apparent. With each topic, our discussions included in-class worksheets, and the first of two quizzes was given at the end of the section, to supplement the project assignment.

At this point, we returned to our earlier discussions of typology and markedness. We examined two natural languages with marked phonemic inventories (Hawaiʻian, with only thirteen phonemes, and East !Xoon, with an extensive number of click and pulmonic consonants and clusters). We also looked at Klingon, with its marked concentration of velar and uvular consonants.

In the project assignment, I provided students with universals and markedness constraints that they could choose to follow or to break with. I asked for sound inventories and a set of phonotactics, along with some explanations for their choices.

More confident students used this opportunity to add some less typical sounds to their inventory, particularly consonants. One student opted to add some clicks; a few included more extensive palatals and velars. The vowel systems, however, were largely timid, with five-vowel inventories being the most common. No one chose to utilize tone systems. Stress and syllable structure were also minimally changed from English.

The lower level of engagement, and the preference for familiar items from the smorgasbord, were not unexpected. Because we were moving from a broader to a more focused examination of language (and in a subfield to which few other courses at UWSP were devoted), students were outside their comfort zones, and the results—in terms of the reduced level of creativity from the first assignment—showed that to be so.

9.4.5 Grammar

After some of the challenges we faced when discussing the sound system, I decided to curtail the section on morphology and syntax. The smorgasbord would still be available, but it was more limited.

At this point, students were beginning to collect words for their languages, and we were able to use those words in the classroom. We began to place words into categories (primarily lexical categories) in order to then discuss morphological patterns. Our focus for morphology was on inflection, with a limited discussion of derivation. The typology of isolating, fusional, agglutinating, and polysynthetic languages was examined, and most students chose fusional and agglutinating languages, with moderately complex morphology.

Several students found inspiration from our earlier discussion of Esperanto (and from English as well) and created inflectional systems for nouns that were fully formed but simplified—in terms of gender and case, in particular. However, one pair of students created an eight-case system for nouns, with dual number and marking for animacy. This may have been inspired by discussions of the Basque case system and by our reading on Mwotlap, which has single, dual, trial, and plural marking for human nouns, and no number specification for non-human nouns (François 2005: 118–23).

Word order was a major part of the project assignment. Students assigned a default argument structure to their language, with its typological associations (particularly in phrase structure/headedness). They created pronoun paradigms. Other topics we covered fairly briefly were questions and negation, and coordination and subordination. As before, the students who were more familiar with these topics were more willing to play with them. Those who were new to linguistic terminology tended to stay with native or native-like patterns.

9.4.6 Lexicon, semantics, and pragmatics

The final project for the course was focused on word lists, semantics, and pragmatics. Some of the students had lost some enthusiasm by this point (there was also a presidential election in the midst of project 3), but they were re-energized by the focus on accessible elements of language study.

For the lexicon, we started with a Swadesh list, but I asked the students to go back to the detailed questions I had asked during the world-building unit so that they could build lists based on the needs of their worlds. The student with the sapient equines, whose enthusiasm was sustained through the semester, created a 500-word list; other students were at the 200-word mark. In addition, they were asked to create some sentences and typical adjacency pairs.

One of our discussions revolved around the concept of semantic fields, and how they could be represented by the sound system. This led to sound symbolism, and we looked at the *gl-* initial cluster in English as an interesting example. We also examined prototype theory: for example, what is understood by the word 'tree' in their world? Cultural metaphors were another way to organize information. Several of the final projects included metaphors based on important real-world concerns for speakers, such as "community is stability."

For pragmatics, many of our discussions revolved around politeness and taboo. Some students had sacred words or curse words. Most of these did not revolve around religious subjects, but more around topics that were of direct threat to the community.

9.5 Results from the course

For their final assignment, students were asked to turn in portfolios of their projects (revised to reflect the feedback they received) along with a reflection essay on their experience during the semester. I reiterated to them that the goals of the course had been to reinforce any previous linguistic exposure they had had and to introduce unfamiliar topics related to each subfield. The responses were generally positive—phonology and syntax were difficult, and everyone wished for more time in the semester, but overall they enjoyed the course.

When I read over the portfolios, I was surprised by the amount of material most students had tackled. Only one student had regularly completed only the minimal amount of work requested; everyone else had sampled freely from the smorgasbord of options. This was evidence to me that these students really responded to the creative challenge and were eager to explore language-building.

The success of the class, even on a small scale, and even with the constraints that had to be observed, did not go unnoticed in the department. My colleague (the senior linguist in the department) has recently retired, and I may not be able to offer the course as often as I had planned. But I plan to teach it again, under its own number and description, and I expect to attract a larger cohort of students.

Was the course a difficult one to teach? Yes. I was only casually familiar with conlangs before preparing to teach this course, and there were other limitations that were challenging (for example, it was scheduled as a fifty-minute Monday/Wednesday/Friday class, which made transitioning from lecture to practice to in-class work on projects more difficult).

Would I teach it again, and would I recommend it to others in a similar situation? Without hesitation, yes.

10

Bringing language construction from the classroom to the community

Carrie Gillon, Edward Delmonico, Randi Martinez,
and Spencer Morrell

10.1 Introduction

This chapter describes a constructed language (conlang) course taught at Arizona State University in Tempe, Arizona, by Carrie Gillon (CG) in Spring 2016. This course was run as an ENG 414: Special Topics in Linguistics course. Edward Delmonico (ED), Randi Martinez (RM), and Spencer Morrell (SM) were enrolled in this course. The (former) student authors were chosen to co-author this chapter because they had participated in one of two convention panels that arose from this course (described in Section 10.4.4). (A fourth student who also participated in a panel did not respond to a request to co-author this chapter.)

CG decided to create this course for four main reasons. First, the course was broader in scope than many of the other linguistics courses available in the English department. This course was intended to help students learn about more types of linguistic features than can be taught in an English-focused course. Second, conlang courses provide students with an opportunity to better understand a subset of linguistic features, as they must work with them in the creation of their language. Third, conlangs are popular, and many people learn Klingon, Na'vi, or Dothraki; CG decided this course would be able to capitalize on their popularity. Finally, the course was intended to market linguistics to undergraduate students who might not otherwise know what linguistics is. Conlangs were a way to appeal to non-majors, who might connect to the material as creative writers, mathematicians, and/or lovers of pop culture.

This chapter provides an overview of this conlang course, how it was structured, and how it could be improved, along with three examples of

Carrie Gillon, Edward Delmonico, Randi Martinez, and Spencer Morrell, *Bringing language construction from the classroom to the community* In: *Language Invention in Linguistics Pedagogy*. First edition. Edited by: Jeffrey Punske, Nathan Sanders, and Amy V. Fountain, Oxford University Press (2020). © Carrie Gillon, Edward Delmonico, Randi Martinez, and Spencer Morrell.
DOI: 10.1093/oso/9780198829874.003.0010

conlangs created in this course. It ends with a discussion of four outcomes of this class: the linguistic knowledge the students gained, the creativity that this class unleashed, the research some of the students undertook as a result of this course, and the participation of the students in two fan convention panels. One of the most important aspects of this course was that it was able to bring linguistics out of the classroom and into the community at large. For example, four students in this course took part in two panels where they were able to talk about their projects and languages and share their love of pop culture, aliens, androids, and/or linguistics.

In this chapter, each participant shares their perspective. We mark individual contributions with the use of the participant's initials; the rest of the chapter is co-written by all participants. This chapter has the following structure. In Section 10.2, we describe the structure of the course, including how each class was structured and the expectations for the student presentations and rough drafts, and we discuss the pros and cons of this particular structure. In Section 10.3, we provide examples of the languages created in the class (including those by the authors). In Section 10.4, we discuss some interesting (and, in some cases, unexpected) outcomes of this course. Section 10.5 concludes.

10.2 Structure of the class

The class was structured in such a way as to allow students maximum time to work on their individual languages. In this section, we describe the class composition, format of the course, presentations and rough drafts, and advantages and disadvantages of this particular structure.

10.2.1 Class composition

This class had a cap of 38 students; a total of 32 students completed the course. This class had one prerequisite: ENG 213: Introduction to the Study of Language, the introductory course for linguistics within the English department. There were a few students who were enrolled without meeting this prerequisite (it is unclear how this happened, but CG did not kick any students out of the course), and most of them stayed despite their lack of background. Approximately half of the students enrolled in the course were linguistics majors and had taken other linguistics courses beyond the introductory class. The rest were students in other majors, including creative writing, computer science, Spanish, among others. Most of the students were juniors or seniors, along with a few sophomores.

10.2.2 Course format

The first lecture of the course was more traditional than the remaining lectures: CG outlined the many different kinds of conlangs and some of the stories behind them. Each subsequent class consisted of 5–10 minutes of lecture followed by 65–70 minutes of "studio" time. During this studio time, students were encouraged to focus on the topic of that class's lecture and to make decisions about which features their languages would have. During this time, CG made herself available to answer questions, and she encouraged the students to talk to each other about their languages, any problems they had with their languages, or the day's topic in general.

On the course, CG covered three main areas. Area 1 comprised phonology and writing systems, Area 2 comprised syntax and morphology, and Area 3 comprised semantics and pragmatics. In each area, CG discussed natural language systems and their typology, as well as existing conlangs and how each one fit (or did not fit) into the relevant typology. CG emphasized that human languages should probably fit into the typology and that alien languages should probably differ from it (as Marc Okrand had done for Klingon; see Okrand et al. 2011; Prisco 2018). However, this was not a requirement; students were encouraged to create a language that made sense to them.

Each area was subdivided into smaller topics. Area 1 covered (i) sounds (consonants and vowels), (ii) phonological typology, (iii) phonological processes, (iv) syllable structures, and (v) writing systems. Area 2 covered (i) syntax, (ii) syntactic typology and word order correlations, (iii) inflectional morphology, (iv) derivational morphology, and (v) morphological typology. Area 3 covered (i) first words, (ii) word meaning, (iii) language and culture connections, and (iv) pragmatics.

At the very beginning of the course, students had to come up with a story for their language before they began working on it. This was so that the students would have a clear idea of what their language was being created for (e.g. magic, mermaids, vampires, medieval people, the underground railroad, etc.), and the kind of structure they might want to use to match their story.

Students were also expected to work together on a group presentation on a chapter from *From Elvish to Klingon: Exploring invented languages* (Adams 2011a). This was intended to give them a broader sense of what conlangs can be like, why their creators decided to create them, and the choices the creators made for their language.

10.2.3 Individual presentations and rough drafts

Students presented on their languages four times throughout the term. These presentations were intended to help students stay on track with their languages and to spark creativity in one another. Students often took ideas from each other to improve their own languages. These presentations were on (i) the sounds in their language (Area 1), (ii) how the language is written (Area 1), (iii) how the language's grammar works (Area 2), and (iv) how the language builds words and groups them semantically (Areas 2 and 3).

After each presentation, students were encouraged to talk about the presentations and to discuss what they appreciated in each set of presentations. CG also provided feedback on their PowerPoint or handout for each presentation, in preparation for their rough drafts. There were three assigned rough drafts: rough draft 1, after presentations 1 and 2 (sounds and writing systems); rough draft 2, after presentation 3 (forming words and constituents); and rough draft 3, after presentation 4 (semantics and pragmatics). These rough drafts put together constituted the final paper, after the incorporation of CG's feedback on each draft.

10.2.4 Reflections on the course structure (CG)

This course was quite large, given the type of course it was, with a total of 128 individual presentations, 96 rough drafts, and 32 final papers. I do not regret having so many students present so many times, because those were the times that students really saw how the other conlangs were coming together and how they could improve their own languages. Grading this class was also far more enjoyable than grading any other course, because in most ways, there were no wrong answers. Instead, I gave constructive feedback (and, of course, corrections if certain features did not make sense or the wrong symbols were used). Although this course involved a lot of work, it was almost entirely enjoyable work. Even the final paper was easy to grade, as I had already seen most of them before; I was mainly looking for improvements based on the comments I had already given them. Most students did well with each individual part and most of them took the final draft seriously, so grading was relatively painless, despite the large load.

The prep time was also minimal in comparison to other courses: I spent a bit of time coming up with the 5–10-minute lecture for each day, leaving most of the time for students to play around with their language. The tradeoff (less prep time, but more grading) worked well for this course. The studio structure seemed to be extremely successful; each student worked hard to make their language the best that it could be. They also used that time to talk with one another about the types of features they were considering using and to ask me for advice as needed. Sometimes their questions led me to add to the next day's lecture or to take a few minutes to re-explain a concept I had introduced earlier that day. The students seemed to appreciate the flexibility of this course, even though it forced them to do a lot more work during class time.

However, if I taught this again, there are a few adjustments I would make. First, I would downplay the writing system, perhaps adding it as a bonus assignment rather than as a regular one. This might help students remember that writing is secondary to speech/sign, to focus on the features of their language, and to practice using the IPA (for spoken languages). Students often focus more on writing than speech or sign, and it can be a distraction from seeing how their language actually works.

Another issue I struggled with was the group presentations. Some of them went on for way too long, even though students were more concise about their own work. In future, I might have the students present one last time on their own languages. The individual presentations were a lot more fun than the group ones, and I think the students got the most out of presenting their languages and the choices they had made. I solicited feedback from the students at the end of each presentation day as to which languages they especially enjoyed or which features they really liked. This led to lively conversation, and I think it sparked even more creativity in the students. Each student had such interesting and clever ideas for making their languages work within their stories. I recommend checking in with the class in this way, to allow the students to reflect even more on their choices, and for them to learn from each other.

10.3 Conlang examples

This course resulted in many different and creative conlangs. We present the three (former) student authors' languages here.

10.3.1 Ryazhyavū (ED)

Ryazhyavū[1] is a language developed by a race of synthetic humans left behind on Earth after humanity transcended their physical bodies. The synthetics, left all alone with no idea where they came from, are forced to explore and understand the technologically advanced cityscape that is their home. In a way, their language developed under the *opposite* conditions from those of our ancestors: the only world the synthetics know is totally artificial, full of human-created structures. Their phonology develops from the sounds made by humanity's advanced technology, as opposed to from what they hear in nature. Their writing system is influenced by circuit-board diagrams, and they write with scavenged cutting lasers. Their basic words revolve around computers and other machines. Eventually, when nature begins taking back over, they are forced to adapt their technology-based language and thinking to natural phenomena, as opposed to the other way around.

I designed Ryazhyavū with two fundamental principles: (i) that their language reflect technological advancement in reverse and (ii) that it be optimized for modularity. I imagine the synthetics to be a people constantly discovering new things in the world around them, with entire civilizations devoted to understanding the technological ecosystem they have inherited. I did my best to make these ideas manifest in many aspects of the language.

10.3.1.1 Phonology

One example of manifesting my ideas about the synthetics and their language was the phonological inventory. My conception of the future involves melody—beeps, whistles, and the raising and lowering of force fields. For this reason, I elected to use consonants that were capable of carrying a pitch, in order to give the language a melodious feel. Initially, I created my consonant inventory by deleting all of the obstruents from those of English, but I did not like the way it sounded. I decided instead to only exclude *voiceless* obstruents, thus giving the consonant inventory a little more variety. I also added in the voiced velar fricative, mostly just for fun. The entire consonant inventory in the IPA is provided in Table 10.1.

---

[1] This is a transliteration into English orthography of /rjæʒjævɔ̃/, where a = /æ/, zh = /ʒ/, and $ō$ = /ɔ̃/, used here for simplicity. The rest of the Ryazhyavū vocabulary is presented in the IPA.

Table 10.1 The consonants of Ryazhyavū

	bilabial	labiodental	dental	alveolar	post-alveolar	palatal	velar
stop	b			d			g
nasal	m			n			ŋ
fricative		v	ð	z	ʒ		ɣ
approximant						j	
trill				r			
tap/flap				ɾ			
lateral approximant				l			

Ryazhyavū has four vowels: /ɪ/, /æ/, /ʊ/, and /ɔ/, chosen for their laxness. They can all be nasalized.

10.3.1.2 Orthography

Another more obvious (or perhaps ostentatious) example of the synthetic aesthetic is in Ryazhyavū's writing system, which can best be described as logophoric with a twist. Writing a sentence requires a grasp of three different forms: (i) lexical characters, (ii) grammatical characters, and (iii) the vowel pathway. Sentences are made using lexical characters linked together with grammatical characters. The vowel pathway is a waveform running through the middle of the line that provides readings of the lexical characters. However, informal communiqués can be written without the pathway to save time (somewhat like Arabic, in that it is only necessary to write the vowels in the Qur'an, where mistakes in understanding might lead to incorrect beliefs). The name of Ryazhyavū in the orthography is given in Figure 10.1.

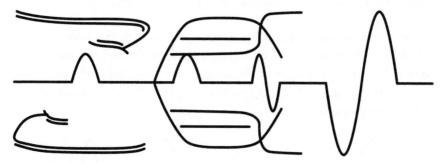

Figure 10.1 Ryazhyavū (written in Ryazhyavū)

Lexical characters are logographs that take up the full height of the line. Each represents a rough category of meanings—for example, one character represents perceiving, discovering, and showing. Phonetically, each character represents a cluster of consonants, not unlike a triliteral root system (again, reminiscent of Arabic). A few examples are provided in Figure 10.2.

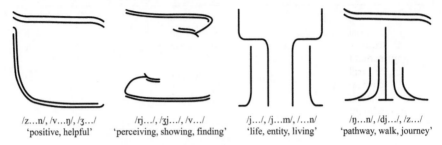

/z...n/, /v...ŋ/, /ʒ.../   /rj.../, /ʒj.../, /v.../   /j.../, /j...m/, /...n/   /ŋ...n/, /dj.../, /z.../
'positive, helpful'   'perceiving, showing, finding'   'life, entity, living'   'pathway, walk, journey'

Figure 10.2 Examples of lexical characters in Ryazhyavū

Most of the grammatical characters function very much like particles in Japanese or Toki Pona, which denote the function of a word within a sentence. Ryazhyavū's grammatical characters are used to mark nominative and accusative case, conjunctions, complement clauses, and negative sentences. Grammatical characters take up the middle third of the line and do not interact with the pathway. A few examples are provided in Figure 10.3.

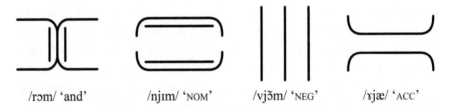

/rɔm/ 'and'   /njɪm/ 'NOM'   /vjɔm/ 'NEG'   /ʁjæ/ 'ACC'

Figure 10.3 Examples of grammatical characters in Ryazhyavū

The vowel system is where Ryazhyavū gets particularly interesting. As mentioned before, the lexical characters do not by themselves *contain* any vowels; they are just clusters of consonants. The vowel path tells you what consonants go where. Each of the four vowels in Ryazhyavū is represented by a different waveform (Figure 10.4).

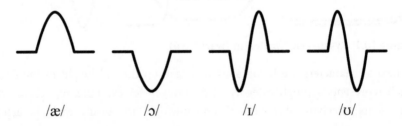

/æ/   /ɔ/   /ɪ/   /ʊ/

Figure 10.4 Ryazhyavū vowel system

These waveforms occur within each lexical character, effectively "slotting" vowels into the consonant root's blank spaces. The average word is around three syllables, which allows for sixty-four different readings. Therefore, creating a new word is as easy as tweaking the vowels within an existing root. This also has the benefit of immediately associating the new word with an already-understood family of words. That makes it very easy to create new words on the fly, with broadly intelligible meanings. This is something I personally plan to have fun with as I try to understand (and evince) my conculture's thought processes—what concepts do they associate closely to each other? What compound words do they create? And when it comes to cataloging nature, how do they make it "gel" with their existing systems of meaning?

An example of a sentence written in Ryazhyavū's system is given in Figure 10.5. The large wave in the pathway at the end represents a period.

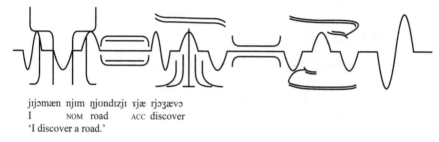

jɹjɔmæn njɪm ŋjʊndɪzjɪ ɹjæ ɹjɔʒævɔ
I   NOM road   ACC discover
'I discover a road.'

Figure 10.5 Example sentence in Ryazhyavū

The aesthetic of the writing system is another attempt to invert the way a primitive language usually develops. When creating orthography for our conlangs, CG encouraged us to think about what tools and media our societies would have available—for example, if our concultures primarily carved things on stone tablets, they would probably eschew curves in favor of easy-to-draw straight lines, whereas with paper, the approach would be quite different. In this vein, I tried to think of a style that would look utterly unlike anything early humans would have made. Eventually, I settled on having the synthetics use small cutting lasers to write, and worked from there. Since the writing instrument does not even touch the surface being written on, there is no resistance or difficulty changing line direction. This would also mean, I figured, that straight lines would actually be *more* difficult to draw. Thus, I ended up with a writing system that features long, curved lines.

10.3.1.3 Derivational morphology
The third major feature of Ryazhyavū is its derivational morphology. Ryazhyavū is analytic, bordering on isolating, which means it uses very little

morphology. The main avenue for making meaning is word compounding, and Ryazhyavū has a few different compounding rules. Typically, when words are compounded, both words only retain the first or first and second syllables. The first word in the compound is always the head. Compounding can be used to make new nouns and verbs, as seen in (1). (In Ryazhyavū, adjective-like and preposition-like words are treated like verbs, and therefore there are only two main lexical categories).

(1)   a.   *noun-verb agentive noun compound*
           æjɔ-rjæ
           person-discover
           'explorer'

      b.   *verb-noun adjectival-like compound*
           zæn-vɪzǽ
           hum-inner.workings
           'to be intelligent'

      c.   *verb-noun prepositional-like compound*
           vær-vɪzǽ
           malfunction-inner.workings
           'to be within and causing problems'

      d.   *verb-noun verb compound*
           ʊʒɪ-vɪ
           rend-inner.workings
           'kill'

This use of compounding is particularly prevalent in words concerning nature: as the synthetics begin to explore the world outside of their technologically advanced cityscape, they are forced to cobble together words for the new things they discover from the "technology" words they are used to, such as the examples in (2).

(2)   a.   væm-rjʊʒjǽ   b.   jæm-zærjɪm   c.   lʊm-vɪʒǽ
           pylon-reaches   entity-network   inert-inner.workings
           'tree'   'flock, herd'   'rock'

Broadly speaking, Ryazhyavū's semantics is characterized by its speakers' exposure to advanced technology well before their exposure to nature. As such, their language evolved to better describe the complex inner workings of machines as opposed to, say, weather or animals. Semantic distance and word meaning, then, are heavily influenced by their interactions with machines. For example, the word ӡæzɪrjǽ 'cut' actually refers specifically to the act of separating objects using a cutting laser. To describe the act of cutting something with a sharp tool, one uses ʊӡɪrjǽ, which is closer in meaning to 'break' or 'rend'.

10.3.1.4 Conclusion

My goal was to create a language spoken by a people whose development was wholly opposite to our own. How would a race suddenly thrust into a world full of advanced alien technology react to it? How would it reflect in their language? What would happen when they discovered nature, having only been exposed to a completely artificial ecosystem? CG's class was a fantastic resource for this—as we learned about different factors to consider in developing a language, such as the effect of the local environment and the potential to evince culture in semantics and pragmatics, I was able to take those ideas and either use or invert them as needed. What I came up with was a language that is as bizarre and messy as it is entertaining. It is still very much a work in progress—I don't want to think about how long it would take to learn, in its present form—but it was a thought experiment with endless room for creativity and speculation. It was also very, very fun to make.

10.3.2 Dǝӡɲæk (RM)

The language I created was designed for a novel in progress titled *MaddConn* by Jon Bendera, for which I was a reader/editor. The novel is based on Irish mythology and is about an enforcer named Connor who has to save his girlfriend Maddi from a hell called Depths-Gate. Dǝӡɲæk was created specifically for goblin creatures whose existence began prior to humanity, but who still reside underneath modern-day Boston, imperceptible to the human eye. If they are "seen" by humans, they are perceived to be humans, but goblins avoid humans and stay underground if they can help it. Goblins are part of a large group of creatures, both good and evil, known as *fae*—or, in Irish lore, as *Sidhe*.[2] They come in a wide variety of groups: elves, orcs, goblins, giants, and demonkind. In particular, the language of the goblins has been unaffected by any language contact because of their isolated existence.

---

[2] This is the word Bendera uses to refer to all fae-like creatures, following Yeats (1899).

There are two types of goblins in the novel—the Feral Goblins and the Market Goblins. The goblin creatures are half demon-kind (called *Fomori*) and half elf (called *Tuatha*), but a change in regime long ago split the goblins, where half were ruled by the Fomori and half by the Tuatha. The goblins ruled by Fomori became the Feral Goblins. Their culture and demeanor are unruly. Feral Goblins are not social creatures and hardly have any social order, except for a queen named Fishbone. Other than Fishbone, the Ferals do not care about anybody and will not let anyone or anything get in their way in their search for food. They are always hungry and are very violent. The Market Goblins (raised by the Tuatha) studied and learned the language of the Ferals in order to gain some control over them and exploit their labor to dig up jewels for trade operations. Their culture and anatomy influenced their language, which is called *dəʒɲæk*, seen in Figure 10.6 in the dəʒɲæk orthography. The name of the language is also the Ferals' word for 'food'. The Market Goblins gave the language this name because it was the word they heard spoken most frequently by the Feral Goblins before they learned the language.

Figure 10.6 'dəʒɲæk' as written in dəʒɲæk

10.3.2.1 Phonology

Physically, goblins are small creatures, and the Feral Goblins are very strong and fast. They are bipedal creatures with small bodies and long limbs. They have large heads and huge mouths. Their mouths are wide and shallow with thin lips, very sharp teeth, and long, thick tongues. The thinness of their lips causes some difficulty in labial manipulation. The farther forward in the mouth, the more space there is, as the opening stretches across almost the entire face. The back of the mouth leads into a human-like throat, with a pharynx, epiglottis, and larynx, except for an extra muscle on the very poster-ior part of the roof of their mouth that helps them to swallow large pieces of

Table 10.2 The consonants of dəzɲæk

	bilabial	labiodental	dental	alveolar	palatal	velar	glottal
stop	p b			t d		k	ʔ
nasal		ɱ			ɲ		
fricative	β	v	ð	s z			ɦ
approximant				ɹ	j		
tap/flap				ɾ			
lateral fricative				ɮ			
lateral approximant				l			

food. They have only three fingers on each hand. Their anatomy played a part in my decision-making regarding the sound and writing systems.

Dəzɲæk has mostly alveolar and coronal consonants. The Feral Goblins have difficulty using both of their lips to articulate, because of their large mouth openings and thin lips. Further, their tongues are so long and large that they have a hard time working with precision in the back of the mouth. The Ferals also have a tendency to voice consonants because of their loud, forceful, and aggressive nature. An exception to this is their use of [k], rather than [g]. The muscle on the posterior roof of the mouth causes difficulty in making voiced velar sounds, because with voicing it involuntarily flexes just enough to reach their tongue and obstruct the sound. The voiced glottal fricative [ɦ] is used often, as it is part of the morpheme that denotes animacy on nouns. Dəzɲæk has nineteen consonants in total. See Table 10.2 for the complete consonant chart.

Dəzɲæk has seven vowels: /i/, /ɪ/, /e/, /ɛ/, /æ/, /ɯ/, and /ɑ/. Feral Goblins avoid rounded vowels, as it is difficult for them to round their thin lips. There are also more front vowels than back vowels (and no central ones). There is more space in the front of their mouths, and they have more difficulty creating sounds with the back of the mouth. There are no diphthongs in the language.

10.3.2.2 Orthography

In class, we discussed various orthographies, which made me consider what type of writing system would make the most sense for the time, place, anatomy, and culture of the goblins. The orthography for the language of the Feral Goblins is an alphabetic writing system. There is one symbol for every sound (and vice versa). It is written from left to right. This writing system arose when the Morrigu, one of the primal forces of this world, taught a runic writing system to the tamer goblins, the Market Goblins, who worked for the Tuatha. They have a need for a writing system, whereas the Feral Goblins do not. The Market Goblins often trade with the Feral Goblins who reside near Depths-Gate, and, for trading purposes, they worked to translate their language and write it down as well. The Market Goblins applied their runic writing system to the language of the Feral Goblins, switching and tweaking some of the symbols as necessary. As goblins have only three fingers on their hands and often carved their writing, the straight lines and simple symbols of the runic system are practical. This is the only writing system that has ever been applied to the language of the Feral Goblins, so it has over time become accepted as the orthography. Each symbol can be seen in Figure 10.7, along with its IPA equivalent.

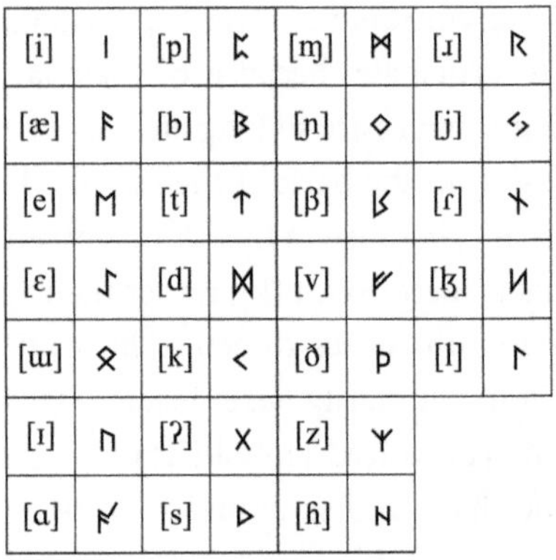

[i]	I	[p]	Ƙ	[m̥]	ᛗ	[ɹ]	R
[æ]	ᚠ	[b]	ᛒ	[n]	◇	[j]	ᛰ
[e]	ᛘ	[t]	↑	[β]	ᛦ	[ɾ]	⅄
[ɛ]	ᛡ	[d]	ᛝ	[v]	ᛕ	[ɮ]	ᚴ
[ɯ]	⚒	[k]	<	[ð]	þ	[l]	ᚱ
[ɪ]	ᚾ	[ʔ]	X	[z]	Y		
[ɑ]	ᚸ	[s]	▷	[ɦ]	ᚻ		

Figure 10.7 Dəʒɲæk orthography

When I thought about the orthography, I considered why orthographies develop. I considered what types of things the goblins might use writing for, and why and how writing would be important. I realized that the Feral Goblins would not have a fraction of a thought about writing, or documenting anything, or conserving their culture or language. I wanted to have a writing system to discuss that still made sense with the Feral Goblins' story, and I figured their neighboring Market Goblins would have a writing system, so I incorporated that into my language project. This section was interesting in that we had to think about the importance of orthographies and how orthographies and the spoken language might affect one another.

10.3.2.3 Morphology

Before I took this class, I did not have much knowledge about morphology. We got an overview of inflectional versus derivational morphology and saw examples of the morphological systems of various languages. Seeing how languages could encode information in so many different ways opened up seemingly thousands of new questions about what could have influenced languages to take such different forms. I wanted my language to have some realistic (in comparison to natural human language) historical patterns of change, so I tried to take into account what a prior language could have been like and what things could have influenced it to change into what it is "now" (which was definitely not necessary for the novel or the class, but was very fun for me). This class was probably the first time I thought critically about diachronic morphological change. The background story of my language allowed me to ignore a lot of possible influences, such as language contact, but I still considered how changes in the goblins' environment, culture, and regime could have affected their language. It was a lot to take in, especially how and why derivational morphology might change, so I decided that morphology would be an area I needed to investigate further in the future, but that for my language I would just add something simple and fun, even if it did not align well with morphological change patterns in natural human languages. For example, I liked the idea of circumfixes and infixes.

I created two new types of affixes: the violentive and shinitive affixes. The circumfix ɯ- -aɹd adds a sense of violence to a word, as in (3). The shinitive prefix zi- denotes shininess or brightness, as in (4). These are only found in the language of the Feral Goblins, as violence is central to their personalities, and they work with jewels, which they see as shiny stones. They are more attracted to shine than the Market Goblins are. As Feral Goblins are usually in the dark, seeing a shine on objects does not happen frequently.

(3) a. ɯ-krejŋ-aɹd
         VIOLENTIVE-talk-VIOLENTIVE
         'to argue'

     b. ɯ-ɦek-aɹd
         VIOLENTIVE-hammer-VIOLENTIVE
         'bec de corbin'

(4) a. zi-blet
         SHINITIVE-stone
         'jewel'

     b. zi-vlʉt
         SHINITIVE-ocean
         'sparkling ocean'

Another way I could exemplify their character was through compounding. The compounds in this language are noun-adjective compounds, where there is an adjective attached to a noun, making one word, as in (5):

(5) a. βap-væʤ   e. ðwɪz-deɪɲlɛp
         blood-wet   fear-hungry
         'bloody'   'unruly'

     b. bɛʔ-βɪt   f. blet-ɲjetdæd
         sleep-weak   stone-hard.to.chew
         'tired'   'not chewable'

     c. bæðpɛt-ɾæɲkbɪð   g. kɹæɲej-βɪt
         fight-sick   sun-weak
         'injured'   'weak from sunlight'

     d. slivæɾ-æzt   h. zip-wʃib
         heat-red/orange   water-blue/green
         'fire'   'ocean'

It was fun to think about what Feral Goblins might focus on enough to have words for, such as an adjective that means something similar to 'hard/difficult to chew', which when compounded with the word for 'stone' means 'impossible to chew' (5f). I thought about what events, characteristics, etc. they might want to have a word for and how they might categorize or conceptualize their world. Then I tried to compound some of their more common words to create such meanings.

Realizing that there were numerous and complicated ways in which the morphosyntax of the language could be related to the culture or anatomy of the Feral Goblins, I came up with questions I knew were better suited for research outside of the conlang. With too many open questions to do anything wild with the language in this respect, I kept it rather simple (for me, a native English speaker), and tried to make it more or less realistic for a natural human language.

10.3.2.4 Semantics

Polysemy in the language was also fun to create. One example is the word βap, which means both 'fruit juice' and 'blood' (animal or human). Other examples of polysemy include zæʤklæd (both 'docile' and 'useless') and kɹuɲt ('map' and 'expedition'). Feral Goblins eat everything and do not differentiate between fruits and animals; they just eat them, and the liquids inside them both are described by the same word, *βap*. They also think of being docile as being useless, so they have the same word, *zæʒklæd*, for both. I found it interesting to consider how the Feral Goblins might conceptualize their world, how they might categorize things, and which similarities and differences between things might stand out more than others.

10.3.2.5 Conclusion

When I began creating the language, I had not yet taken a formal syntax class, and I initially chose rather random word orders. I decided to change the word orders to look more like Celtic languages instead of a non-human language. I modeled other languages for this at first, but it led to my discovering more theoretical literature and reading further into topics such as universals, syntactic structure, scope, and the Mirror Principle, for example. Of course, much of this was just enough of an introduction to make me realize how much there is in linguistics for me to learn about. Thus, not everything I read about was incorporated into the language, as some things were not necessary to implement, and other things opened too many doors for me to choose from. I was introduced to a lot of topics that I could (and did) continue reading more about, and I was always finding new and interesting questions. The morphosyntax was one of my favorite parts of the creation of this language because I found so many new avenues of research that I wanted to explore.

10.3.3 Tho Yor: Ancient Sith (SM)

I can remember the first week of class knowing almost immediately that I would be doing a Star Wars language, but more specifically a language for the ancient Sith species. These are not the Sith as we know them today (e.g. Darth Vader), but these are in fact the original Sith, whose origins date back 25,000 years before the first modern Sith. This language is intended to be a snapshot of the language as it was about 42,000 years before *Star Wars Episode I: The Phantom Menace*, based on the fictitious timeline in Star Wars.

With the vast market that is behind the Star Wars expanded universe material (i.e. all officially licensed spin-off materials beyond the films: novels, comic books, animated television series, etc.), there is already content on the languages and cultures within the Star Wars universe. Research into those existing languages helped me decide what language I wanted to create. I had read a book by Daniel Wallace called *Star Wars: Book of Sith* (2013) where he created a fictional history of the Sith. Wallace briefly talks about the modern

Siths' discovery of the ancient Sith on the planet Korriban. The ancient Sith species vary in gradients of red and have three subspecies that are based on the physiological differences between the nose and the nasal cavity. The Kissai have two large tendrils that are connected to the nasal cavity and hang far past their chin. The Zuguruk have tendrils that are disconnected from the nasal cavity, and the Alassassi lack a nose altogether, and have tendrils attached to their scalp, which fall back as hair does on humans. There is an undisclosed reason, but the three subspecies have a natural class system: the Kissai are at the top, the Zuguruk are in the middle, and the Alassassi are the peons. I decided to use Wallace's book as the main source material because much of the world-building for my language would already be done. From there, I knew almost immediately how I would shape the language. Since there was no indication as to why the class system existed, I decided to outline the class structure based on the very human concept of giving value judgments to certain varieties. So, my goal for the language was to reflect this class-based system due to varietal differences as a part of the physiological factors that separate the three species. The Kissai, with their expanded nasal cavities that are connected to the tendrils and being from the highest class, I imagined an emphasis on the nasality of sounds, setting them apart from the other two subspecies.

When I started the class, I had very little exposure to conlangs. Since the class, my understanding of conlangs and, more importantly, linguistics has expanded exponentially. At the beginning of this course, I had taken the general introductory linguistics class (ENG 213) and an in-depth syntax class (ENG 314: Modern Grammar), but that was the extent of my linguistics experience. In hindsight, this course was an amazing way to dive deeper into what only was covered in a surface-y way during my introductory course.

10.3.3.1 Phonology

One of my great fears of this class was the section surrounding our phonology creation. While I was taking this course, I was simultaneously taking a class in introductory phonology. However, this course gave me a unique way to apply the knowledge that I was gaining in my other coursework. My phonology class exposed me to natural languages and their sound systems, but this class is where I would test out my knowledge and experience my learning in a hands-on way. It was this exceptional learning opportunity that assisted me tremendously in being successful in my phonology class and with the creation of my language's phonology.

Table 10.3 The consonants of Tho Yor

	bilab	lab-dent	dent	alv	post-alv	retr	pal	vel	uvu	glot
stop	b		t d					k	ɢ	ʔ
fricative		f	ð	s	ʃ			x	ʁ	ɦ
nasal	m	ɱ				ɳ	ɲ	N		
approximant			l				j			
lateral fricative				ɮ						

Given the importance of nasality for two of the subspecies, I wanted to set out to ensure that nasals were a large part of my phonetic makeup for the language. I spent time researching languages that utilize nasals and the culmination of that research produced the sound inventory for Tho Yor. There are a lot of nasals to accommodate the language's crucial need for nasality. The rest of the consonants were largely derived from the sound inventory of Arabic, because when I envisioned hearing this language Arabic resonated with me. The rest, which are not a part of the Arabic inventory (/ɢ/, /ɦ/, and /ɮ/), were chosen because I simply enjoyed the sounds. I could also say that the voicing asymmetry found in my inventory, even though it happened mostly by accident, speaks volumes about the stereotypical notion that the dark side is the 'unbalanced' side to the Force, an amazing factor to incorporate into the sound inventory. The consonant system is given in Table 10.3.

The vowel inventory represents the breadth of both the Kissai and Zuguruk varieties, which share the same phonemes. The difference between them is that, with Kissai, the nasality resonates more because the tendrils are connected to the nasal cavity. The Alassassi share the same consonants except for the nasals, as they lack the physiological features to create a nasal sound. Tho Yor has seven base vowels (which can all also be nasalized in Kissai and Zuguruk): /i/, /ø/, /œ/, /ʉ/, /u/, /ɤ/, and /ɒ/.

During my research, I found an interest in Breton, a language that has nasalized vowels; I mostly chose vowels from that inventory for the Sith language. The distribution of mostly mid and high vowels was chosen with no particular logic, other than that they were largely borrowed from the Breton inventory.

10.3.3.2 Orthography

Prior to this class, I had taken a historical linguistics class, so there was some material from that class that I was able to bring to the table when creating the orthography. Since I knew the origins of the species, this gave me the opportunity to go back and do research on ancient human communities, how they represented their languages visually, the tools that were realistically available to them, and how those tools might have influenced their orthographies. It also expanded my own learning about the importance of semantic memory and its connection to orthography. Both topics are something that I would have probably never taken the time to learn, if not for this course.

For all varieties of the language, the written systems are a cross between a featural and non-featural linear alphabetic system, and all varieties use the same symbols. The symbols are all angular, as the main tools of writing were stone and the arid ground of the planet. The nuances of curvature to the symbols only came during a brief three-hundred-year period, where the planet was less dry and the soil was softer. Each symbol represents one phoneme, but there are instantiations where the two phonemes of a consonant nasal pair are represented as one symbol, with some redundancy. The vowels are typographically smaller than consonants. The height of the vowel in writing is greater when there is a consonant nasal pair before it (as a typographical representation of the length of the vowel and its nasalization). The symbols of the voiced phonemes have low stems and the unvoiced have high stems; this is because the early speakers noticed a difference between voiced and voiceless sounds, and later adopted this into the written language. The written system is left to right and has no real punctuation except spacing between words. Lastly, the type design of the language is similar to that of a musical staff. The top line for nasalized vowels, the mid line for oral vowels, and the bottom line for vowel/consonant pairs, as shown in Figure 10.8.

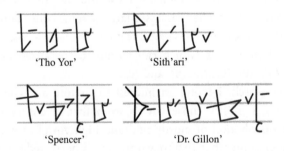

Figure 10.8 Example written words in Tho Yor

10.3.3.3 Clausal order and language type
Tho Yor has a verb-subject-object (VSO) word order (6).

(6)   x:ufiᶀðiɮ-x:ɴõ:-kuỹ   x:ŋɛ̃:-ðøjøɮ   bœjuɮ
       PRES.hurt-TRANS-3SG.ERG   DEM-language   brain
       'This language hurts my brain.'

The reasoning behind this was simply that I wanted the language to have a focus on the verb. The ancient Sith had a strong innate connection to the Force, and a VSO word order represented to me a manifestation of that in the language. It is polysynthetic, and arguments can be dropped. For example, the subject 'we' is only marked as a suffix on the verb in (7).

(7)   budʋðĩðiɮ-x:ɲõ:-kuỹ   x:ŋɛ̃:-bisɐn
       FUT.kill-TRANS-1PL.ERG   DEM-Jedi
       'We will kill the Jedi.'

The reasoning behind the choice of polysynthesis is my favorite part about this language. I went through a lot of research material, and one day I discovered a single comic from the early 1990s that showed a single panel. In this panel, a Sith was speaking, and the text was written in ancient Sith. I instinctively knew it was a polysynthetic language by looking at it, but I had never actually understood how polysynthesis operated on a syntactic level. It was moments like this that led to the best part of the class, because they allowed me to explore, with guided assistance from CG, something separate from what my peers were addressing. It was almost like a mini-independent study within the course. So, with an enormous amount of help from CG, I dived into the inner complexities of polysynthetic languages and their formation. Their high morpheme-to-word ratios and the intimate nature I saw in polysynthetic languages through their use of polypersonal agreement was fascinating to me. So, a single piece of naming language in a comic became the base of my language.

10.3.3.4 Number system

As the course progressed, there were these superb moments where CG would give us optional challenges for those who wanted to push their linguistic knowledge. Numbering systems were something that I had never heard of in my linguistics coursework. CG gave those interested some information to assist and as always strove for us to think outside the box. I was excited and realized that I needed to come up with some way of counting. Not only were the ancient Sith innately connected to the Force, but so were the animals on the planet. All Sith, therefore, had a deep respect for the animals on the planet.

Some were taken as pets, but most were left alone. One creature they revered was called a *Silooth*, a beetle the size of an elephant, with six spider-like claws. I used this as the inspiration for creating a base-6 counting system. It felt natural to have the name for the creature also represent the number 'six'; the distinction between them comes in the syntax (noun vs. numeral). A partial representation of the number system is shown in (8).

(8) kɐ-xœd   'one' (lit. 'one-claw')
     xɐ-xœd   'two' ('two-claw')
     ɢɐ-xœd   'three' ('three-claw')
     tɐ-xœd   'four' ('four-claw')
     fɐ-xœd   'five' ('five-claw')
     sʔmxœd   'six; Silooth'
     sʔmxœd-kɐ   'seven' ('Silooth-one')
     xɐ-sʔmxœd   'twelve' ('two-Silooth')
     xɐ-sʔmxœd-ka   'thirteen' ('two-Silooth-one')
     ɢɐ-sʔmxœd   'eighteen' ('three-Silooth')
     sʔmxœd-sʔmxœd   'thirty-six' ('Silooth-Silooth')
     sʔmxœd-sʔmxœd-   'one thousand two hundred ninety-seven'
        sʔmxœd-sʔmxœd-kɐ   ('Silooth-Silooth-Silooth-Silooth-one')

10.4 Outcomes

There were two expected outcomes for this course: (i) the production of a new conlang, with a well-described structure and enough vocabulary to have short conversations in, and (ii) a better understanding of language and linguistics. These were indeed met. However, there were other outcomes, including a spark in creativity, an interest in pursuing research, and the ability to take the languages outside of the classroom into the wider public, that were also met, which we discuss in this section.

10.4.1 Linguistic knowledge

This course allowed students to delve deeper into any aspect of language they wanted to explore. Thus, each student had a different experience and a different set of linguistic features that they took from this course. Because the course was semi-self-directed (CG provided a topic and information about that topic—the kinds of relevant features they might want to use—but otherwise, let the students explore whatever they liked), students had to make decisions about what they wanted to learn about in order to flesh out their language. For example, ED had to think about lexical semantics in creating words for his synthetic humans, RM had to think about how the physical shape of the Feral Goblins' mouths would constrain their ability to use certain sounds, and SM had to learn about polysynthesis for his Sith language. The class didn't actively teach students how to be researchers, but it did force the students to build those skills—skills that are useful for future classes and projects.

It also gave students an overview of the scope of linguistics and how large the field really is. This course touched on speech science, phonetics, phonology, the development of orthographies, morphology, morphophonology, morphosyntax, syntax, lexical and truth-conditional semantics, pragmatics, anthropology, and storytelling.

10.4.2 Creativity

Linguists are creative by nature, but students often do not get a chance to use that creativity in other classes. This course tapped into the natural creativity of the students and provided an outlet to use it while also learning linguistic theory. It also brought in pop culture (*Star Trek, Avatar, Game of Thrones*, etc.), allowing students to connect to the material in a new and different way. This course allowed students to tap into their internal geekdom, and it helped them connect their interest in language to their other, geekier, interests.

Developing a language allows for a great deal of creativity. Students are able to decide on their own sound system, morphology, syntax, etc. for a world of their own imagination, and the options for what they can use in their language are endless. There are a couple of minor requirements for creating a language, however. First, students need to have at least some parameters for their language. Second, students need to decide how these different systems interact with one another, which they often discover as they create their language. Constructing a language requires research, such as looking into various languages, features, typologies, etc., and there is also plenty of tinkering with the different systems of the language (e.g. phonology, morphology, and syntax) in order to make the language fit in the imagined culture, or to incorporate a feature they discovered and found interesting. What makes constructing a language feel considerably less like doing research is that it is an original creation. However, the research done for a constructed language generally allows the students to make deeper discoveries about language and linguistics, which in turn can lead to the discovery of more specific linguistic interests, including actual academic research within linguistics.

To construct a language, students minimally must learn about some subfields of linguistics, as discussed in Section 10.4.1. It is possible to create a language that functions similarly to students' first or second languages or languages they have some knowledge of. However, the world's languages display a great deal of linguistic variation, and some of this variation can be incorporated into their languages. It is useful to know how languages vary; students can use knowledge of that variation to create or improve their language. By learning more about different subfields and more about how other languages behave, students might find that one or two of the linguistic subfields are more enjoyable to play around with. Similarly, creating an orthography for a language might prompt students to consider how and why orthographies develop, as well as the impacts that an orthography might have on a language (e.g. cultural traditions or impacts on variation or stability over time). Constructing a language allows students to get acquainted with other linguistic interests that they might not encounter in their undergraduate classes, and it also allows them to conduct research beyond the basic ways that individual systems within a language can function. More specific interests that students might find appealing include language change, relationships between culture and language, relationships between languages beyond culture, and the interfaces between different subfields of linguistics. Many unexpected research topics can arise when constructing a language, and they often differ from person to person, depending on each student's constructed language and the topics the students need to research for it.

This class produced many creative examples of languages, including three magic languages; an underground railroad language; three other alien languages, in addition to the Sith language described in Section 10.3.3 (Martians, dolphin-like aliens on Europa, and aliens from a made-up location); the language of the dead; three mermaid(-like) languages; a vampire language; Dufi (a truncation of Duty-Free); a Siberian universal language; an escape language; two military languages; four medieval(-like) languages; two creoles (English-Mandarin and Korean-English); a subarctic language; Atlantean; a children's language; and a love language. There were many highlights. The written language for the underground railroad language, which involved different quilting patterns for each syllable within a square, was particularly creative. Dufi, which was the result of seventeen people being stuck in a duty free (Du-fi) store at the Dubai airport, had a writing system that was constrained by the use of the cash registers. The language of the dead used lots of fricatives, in an attempt to model the sounds that dead people might be capable of making. Most of the students made an effort to ensure their language made sense within their story, the anatomy of the speakers, etc. We were impressed with the breadth of language types as well as the creativity of each individual student.

10.4.3 Interest in research

Constructed languages are created for an imagined world, and there is no limit on the kinds of beings you can create a language for, what the culture of the intended speakers is like, or the time or location that the language is created for. These decisions are up to the creator of the language, and this imagined world is kept in consideration throughout the language construction process. As mentioned earlier, CG suggested that constructed languages made for humans should follow some patterns that human languages follow, and that alien or non-human languages probably should not. Thus, some linguistic knowledge about the typology of human languages is necessary, whether you are following those rules or breaking them. A constructed language must be specific to the imagined world, and so, more research is required. Exactly what needs to be researched depends on the imagined world. Perhaps the setting is near a place where an existing language is spoken, and there is a language family you want your language to be a part of, so you research that language family. Perhaps the world is a post-apocalyptic world, where the oceans have dried from global warming and fish have adapted to live on land and developed anatomy to be able to speak a language, so you research human language patterns in order to make your language utterly different, and you also research how vocal tracts might be affected by not-yet-disappeared gills. Many things could be researched to tailor a constructed language to a certain imagined world, and this research for the constructed language then shapes what one learns about linguistics and its subfields—whether it be about diachronic language change, the anatomy that allows humans to produce the sounds of language, social factors that influence language, etc.

The setting of the imagined world can influence research into relevant linguistic topics. For example, if a constructed language is created for a world in a different time period—perhaps it is set in what we now know as Africa, but prior to humanity, or in the middle of year 3028 in what used to be New York City—investigating language change can help to create a more realistic-seeming language. Students can look at actual languages spoken in an area, in both past and present time, and research the changes they have undergone, such as vowel shifts or a reduction of a case system. Then, similar changes can be incorporated into the constructed language, either by imagining how the changes would advance for a future language, or by reversing the patterns for an older language. In this case, research on diachronic language change—including phonological, syntactic, and semantic change—could help students create a more realistic invented language, if realism is the goal. Students might also discover different types of diachronic change, which might spark an interest in historical linguistics. Or, they could become intrigued by a particular language's development and the factors that influenced change, sparking an interest in that language. Their research could also lead them to discovering something about a dead language, perhaps sparking an interest in dead languages or preserving endangered and dying languages.

Students' research could lead them to Greenberg's (1963) "universals," such as word order correlations found cross-linguistically, which are unrelated to the locations or cultures of the speakers of the languages. Languages with certain word orders, OV or VO, tend to have fixed word orders in other phrasal constituents as well (e.g. English has VO word order and P-NP order, while Lezgian [Dageztan] has OV word order and NP-P order). There is no connection between these universals and culture, but rather, the universals seem to shed light on the cognitive structures of human language. Thus, deciding whether or not to align with these universals in a constructed language is an important decision if one wants to make the language seem appropriate for their imagined world, because the decision can make the language seem either like a human language or like a non-human language. Constructing a language requires the student to constantly consider an imagined world so that the language can be tailored to that culture, setting, and speakers. Natural languages differ in many ways, in some ways depending on culture and setting, and in numerous ways not. Students who encounter this problem probably have questions about the cognitive structure of language that they would like to answer. Or perhaps they would like to document as many languages as possible in order to compare the similarities or differences to other documented languages. These are just some examples of how research for a language can lead a person to larger research that could be even more interesting—and more relevant to the field as a whole.

*   *   *

RM: My constructed language led me to research specific areas. My constructed language was created for a novel that was based on Celtic mythology.

The language was created for feral goblins that existed before humanity and were isolated from humans and human languages. I created the language so that it could plausibly have influenced Irish, which was passed to humans by an evil goddess in the novel. In creating the language, I researched the structure of Irish. I investigated language change as well, and tried to imagine the changes in reverse, to create a language that was a precursor to Irish. I incorporated Irish word order, and I researched other VSO languages and word order universals more generally.

Irish and Irish English have a form of the perfect aspect that is created by a preposition meaning 'after' followed by a verbal noun, called an after-perfect. (In Irish English, the structure of the Irish remains, but the words are English.) The discovery of the after-perfect during research for my constructed language led me to investigating it for Yale's Grammatical Diversity Project webpage (https://ygdp.yale.edu/phenomena/after-perfects) as part of my graduate studies. The after-perfect did not make it into my constructed language, but the questions it sparked back then remained, motivating further research.

When constructing my language, I spent a great deal of time reading about relative clauses, relative pronouns, relative particles, and complementizers. My current research project at Yale investigates the structure of relative clauses, genitive relative clauses, relative pronouns, and genitive relative pronouns. Thus, I began my current research project during this conlang class, although my questions have since narrowed.

Finally, on a more general level, constructing a language allowed me to explore different subfields in more detail, which sparked my interest in syntax. What I enjoyed most about the construction process was the challenge of figuring out and tinkering with syntactic structures that were different from any of the languages I knew. The joy I got from researching syntax convinced me to continue research in graduate school with a focus on syntax. Not everything I discovered while creating my language made it into my language, but my discoveries provoked questions that motivated my later research in graduate school.

* * *

Constructing a language allows students to focus on their own linguistic interests, while still learning enough about different aspects of language and subfields of linguistics to create a language. Research in each of the subfields can propel students into academic research in linguistics. In researching various aspects of language, students are able to discover interests in linguistics, pushing them to think creatively about the aspects they find most interesting. This research can lead to research that is relevant to the field as a whole, such as language change, the cognitive structure of language, or the anatomy that allows humans to create the sounds we use to speak.

10.4.4 Culminating experiences

In this section, each of the former students in this course discusses an experience that arose from participating in this course. There were two major events that involved students from this course: LibCon and Phoenix Comicon.

10.4.4.1 LibCon

LibCon is a small local comic convention in Chandler, Arizona, geared toward teenagers. CG was asked by a librarian at the Chandler public library to create a panel for LibCon on Alien Languages. CG decided to ask some of the students to join her as a way to enliven the discussion, to bring linguistics into the community and out of the classroom, and to provide those students with public speaking experience. She asked the four students who were working on alien conlangs in the class to join her. Two of the students were willing and able to join.

The panel thus consisted of CG, SM, and another student from the class (who created a language for dolphin-like aliens on Europa). Prior to the panel, the three presenters designed a presentation that was geared toward its teenaged audience. CG created an introductory section about other forms of animal communication and fictional examples of alien communication. CG also presented background information about xenolinguistics and the mindset people must be in when they begin to create their own language. Since the panel was held during the middle of the course, the other two sections were the students giving background to the rough concepts to their languages. The remaining time was set aside for questions from the audience. In what follows, SM provides a reflection on his experience to the panel.

*   *   *

SM: I did not really know what to expect from LibCon, but it was great to see a community event geared toward creating a space for youth to express themselves in such a nerdy way. Before the panel with CG, I presented for a small group about Star Wars facts at LibCon as well. I dived into the rich text that created a diverse universe all its own. When the time came to do the panel presentations on conlangs with CG, I was excited to see that there were people there who were interested in our panel's topic. My slides focused on two aspects, the first being the representation of language in the Star War universe currently, which was an integral part to the creation of my language. I then discussed the main focal points of my language. First, I wanted to ensure that I did not violate any previous discussion of the Sith'ari culture, language, or representation in the books. Second, I explained how the three main classes lead to the creation of three variations of Tho Yor. At the end, it was awesome to have the audience ask questions from us. As a hopeful linguist, I could see how panels like this could inspire future linguists and it made a lasting impression on me.

Having the opportunity to present at LibCon also showed me that there are people who are interested in conlangs. I was opened to a whole other community within linguistics that really could mix many passions into one. Since presenting at LibCon, I have begun investigating other conlanging communities. I also created a website called glossopoeist.com, which I continue to work on. My end goal for the site is to have it be something like the conlang course: a place where language lovers can come and learn about conlangs. Hopefully people will use the site as a springboard to start their own conlanging journey.

* * *

LibCon is a small convention, so our panel had perhaps ten attendees. However, we received great feedback from the audience members. They were all young (12–18), and one of the audience members told us that he was now planning on taking linguistics in university (as well as business, his original plan).

10.4.4.2 Phoenix Comicon

Phoenix Comicon has science programming that sometimes includes linguistics panels. In 2016, CG offered to create a panel on conlangs for the science program, which was accepted. She then asked the top four students in the course (based on grades) to join her (this included SM, who was unable to make it), thinking that the panel should not get overly large. Only two of the students (ED and RM) were able to attend.

The Comicon panel thus consisted of ED, RM, and CG, along with an ASU graduate student working on machine recognition of sign language. Beforehand, the four of us collaborated on a large presentation—CG created an introductory activity, and RM and ED included whatever bits of their languages they most wanted to show off to the world. ED added slides about his language's writing system and derivational morphology, and RM added slides about the sound system of her language. In what follows, ED and RM each provide a first-person reflection of their experiences.

*   *   *

ED: The first surprise of the afternoon was that the event was attended. Furthermore, it was *well*-attended. The room was filled almost to capacity. We started the panel with CG's activity. The audience was shown an amusing gif and a set of sounds, and asked to use the latter to describe the former. It immediately hooked the audience, who took no small amount of delight in demonstrating the words and sentences they had created.

My portion of the panel involved my language's writing system and derivational morphology. I had built some questions into my presentation in order to make it more interactive, but I hardly needed the help—audience members were quick to answer and rather enthusiastically asked questions of their own. For example, to make sure we were on the same page, I asked the audience for examples of an abjad writing system and was rewarded with an entire small discussion about different types of writing systems. Similarly, the derivational morphology section felt more like a dialogue than a diatribe, which I quite appreciated—people were interested in the examples I brought and had questions about how to make more.

I had never, before that day, been in the same room as that many nerds who shared my interest in conlangs. All panel members were bombarded with questions (and disquisitions disguised as questions), both about our languages and about language in general. It was a meaningful experience, not just because we got a chance to engage in discourse with so many like-minded people, but also because we had something to *bring* to that discourse. It was exciting to field so many questions about something that interests me so much, and deeply satisfying to be able to answer them. "Why are all of your vowels lax? That's not very common," asked a nitpicky attendant. "Just to be a contrarian," I got to reply, suddenly incredibly grateful that someone had noticed.

*   *   *

RM: As I watched numbers and numbers of constructed language enthusiasts and Comicon fans pile into the room, my initial thoughts were a bit apprehensive. When we began with the activity, I was unsure if we could get all of the (80? 100?) people in the audience to participate. However, with clear instructions for the activity and an amusing animation on screen, there was no need to worry. The audience became immediately involved, sharing their small creations from the activity, and they seemed immersed in the panel from then on.

For my section of the presentation, I decided to share some of the aspects of my language that I found the most fun to develop, because they required a lot of thought about the speakers of the language—specifically, their anatomy. I first explained the creatures for which my language was created: Feral Goblins. With an image of an alien creature displayed (Disney's Stitch), I discussed the shape of the Feral Goblins' mouths. I explained my thought process for how I chose sounds for the language, those that I thought would be easier for the goblins to produce. With huge tongues, small lips and teeth, and shallow, wide mouths, I imagined they might have an easier time producing coronal and alveolar consonants, and unrounded and front vowels. Next, I explained their hands and discussed their writing system. The goblins only have three fingers, and they typically carve their writing, so their writing system was modeled after a runic system. I thought symbols with straight lines would be easier for the goblins to write since they only had three fingers to stabilize a writing utensil, and their writing was typically carved. I was delighted to share the reasoning behind every decision I made about the language.

Focusing on these aspects allowed me to share some of my favorite kinds of decisions about conlanging. Exploring how vocal anatomy works, as a beginner in the field, and then thinking about how tinkering with this anatomy would affect the voice and sounds produced, were some of my favorite discoveries and deliberations in the creation process. When I developed these aspects, specifically the sound system, I realized I had not ever put so much thought into the ways in which humans are able to produce so many sounds to communicate. Vocal anatomy and phonetics became really intriguing. Another reason I chose these aspects was because I think one of the most creative components in constructing a language is considering what features of language would be the most natural as having developed from its speakers. These aspects both opened my mind to an intriguing area of linguistics and allowed me to express my creativity. In illustrating some of my own creative decisions, I hoped to influence others to construct a language, which would lead them to their own exciting discoveries.

Overall, the panel seemed to run really smoothly. The audience members were clearly engaged throughout the presentation, and they asked plenty of questions at the end, ranging from questions about language creation in general, our specific languages, constructed language ideas of audience members, and more. The question arose of where other conventions or discussions about constructed languages can be found, and multiple audience members seemed enthused to become a part of the community. I was grateful to see so many people intrigued by the same thing I was so intrigued by. I left the panel hopeful that we had influenced more people to embark on the journey of constructing a language, which is in fact a journey of discovering the field of linguistics and unexpected elements of our complex system of language— masked in creativity, amusement, and gratification.

*   *   *

This panel was much larger than the LibCon panel. There were approximately 100 people in the audience. Many people came up to us afterward to express their excitement. One teenage girl told us that she was going to take linguistics in university after attending this panel (in a different state). One man kept in contact with CG asking for advice on his conlang. It was a very successful panel.

10.5 Conclusion

This class was extremely successful in a number of different ways. It allowed students to see the connections between different parts of language (and linguistics) in ways that are unlikely in a more traditional linguistics course. It also allowed them to use their creativity, unlike most other university courses. It sparked interest in undertaking real linguistic research. And finally, it gave some students (and CG) the opportunity to take their knowledge out of the classroom and into the wider public, as well as an opportunity to showcase linguistics. We were able to introduce linguistics (and conlangs) to approximately 110 people. At least two audience members—one at each panel—told us that they were inspired to take linguistics as a result of our presentations. Teaching conlangs—and then bringing students outside of the classroom to talk about their creations—can be a way to disseminate knowledge about our field in a new and fun way.

11

The interdisciplinarity of conlangs

Moving beyond linguistics

Nathan Sanders and Christine Schreyer

11.1 Introduction

Certain constructed languages (conlangs) designed for fictional worlds (such as Elvish in Tolkien's Middle-earth universe, Klingon in the *Star Trek* franchise, and the *Game of Thrones* languages Dothraki and Valyrian) achieve popularity in large part because of their linguistic verisimilitude, which depends in part on a grounding in other areas of knowledge besides linguistics. These interdisciplinary underpinnings provide an opportunity to use conlangs as a way to make explicit and memorable connections with other fields of study when teaching linguistics. In this chapter, we discuss how interdisciplinarity and the concept of world-building have worked alongside linguistics in the courses we have taught where students were required to construct their own languages. We provide case studies from our courses to discuss how conlangs, and by extension, their constructed speakers, cultures, and histories, provide opportunities to underscore the links between linguistics and biology, physics, anthropology, and other fields.

In the first two case studies, Sanders describes how his students have used the peculiarities of nonhuman anatomy and radically different environmental conditions to provide physical rationales for the phoneme inventories in their conlangs. Schreyer then provides examples of how her students developed new vocabulary for Kryptonian (the conlang she developed for the 2013 film *Man of Steel*), based on their knowledge of the language, to show their understanding of the relevant culture, how culture impacts vocabulary, and why they cannot create a language in a vacuum, but rather, need to consider who the speakers are before they are able to get very far in their creative process. By using language construction in the classroom, the connections between

Nathan Sanders and Christine Schreyer, *The interdisciplinarity of conlangs: Moving beyond linguistics* In: *Language Invention in Linguistics Pedagogy*. First edition. Edited by: Jeffrey Punske, Nathan Sanders, and Amy V. Fountain, Oxford University Press (2020). © Nathan Sanders and Christine Schreyer.
DOI: 10.1093/oso/9780198829874.003.0011

language and the body, the external physical environment, and associated culture can be reinforced in ways that engage students' creativity. Consequently, this can enhance their personal investment in the learning experience and solidify their understanding of the material.

11.1.1 The benefits of interdisciplinary teaching

For the purposes of this paper, we view interdisciplinarity as the merging of content and theoretical perspectives from different, especially divergent, fields of study. While interdisciplinarity is often viewed from the perspective of strengthening scholarly research, it also has both pedagogical and cognitive benefits to students (Newell 1994, Lattuca et al. 2004, Jones 2009). For example, scholars have argued that interdisciplinarity can:

(a) forge connections to students' prior knowledge and experience;
(b) assist students in developing complex understandings in particular subject areas;
(c) promote the development of sophisticated views of knowledge and learning;
(d) influence thinking skills;
(e) build students' capacity to recognize, evaluate, and use differing (multiple) perspectives;
(f) engage student interest and increase motivation; and
(g) enact constructivist and active learning strategies

(Lattuca et al. 2004: 44)

Lattuca and colleagues also stress the need for continued research into interdisciplinary courses and the benefits they might provide to students, suggesting that "the combination of interdisciplinary topics and intentional pedagogy may promote learning better than either in isolation" (2004: 44). In this chapter, we add to this literature and provide details from our own teaching practices, which included intentional active learning opportunities that were also interdisciplinary in nature. From our experiences, we agree with Jones that "[s]tudents and their teachers will advance in critical thinking, communication, creativity, pedagogy, and essential academia with the use interdisciplinary techniques" (2009: 81). We further argue that interdisciplinary pedagogy is particularly effective in teaching linguistics and that conlangs are an ideal tool for exploring interdisciplinarity with linguistics.

11.1.2 The interdisciplinarity of linguistics

Linguistics is inherently interdisciplinary. For example, there are many related, yet divergent, fields of linguistics, from theoretical to applied to experimental. Students within linguistics are also often required to take introductory courses covering a range of subfields (phonology, syntax, sociolinguistics, etc.) before they specialize within a particular branch. Similarly, anthropology within North America is often known as a four-field discipline, including cultural anthropology, biological or physical anthropology, archaeology, and linguistic anthropology. In fact, others also include applied anthropology as a new fifth field, while others continue to argue that all anthropology is applied in nature (Rylko-Bauer et al. 2006).

Furthermore, language is used in nearly every human endeavor and daily interaction, so it intersects with essentially everything humans do and is a core part of human identity. Because the human body has the anatomy it does, there is an obvious connection between linguistics and biology; language is constrained by the particular properties of human biomechanics: the vocal tract is roughly tube-shaped with a single bulky tongue, highly flexible lips, a larynx, etc., which all together allow for a particular range of possible and impossible speech articulations, while the shape of sign language depends on how the arms, hands, and torso can move. Similarly, human language is conveyed through the physical world, which imposes its own limitations on what language can do. For example, spoken language travels through air, which determines the speed at which it travels and the frequencies at which it resonates. Thus, there are very real connections between linguistics and the physical sciences.

Language is also intimately tied to culture. Languages are primarily used by human beings to communicate with one another, and that interpersonal communication takes place in multiple larger contexts: the relationship between the interlocutors; their different and shared social identities; the cultural allusions, icons, literature, and traditions they are familiar with; etc. Language is shaped as much by human cultural considerations as by our anatomy and physical environment, so linguistics has inherent connections to these other domains of knowledge. Language simply cannot be fully understood without understanding the external factors that shape it. Thus, interdisciplinary methods are well-suited to teaching linguistics.

11.1.3 Teaching linguistics with conlangs

Along these lines then, conlangs are an ideal way to explore the interdisciplinarity of linguistics for a variety of reasons. Most importantly, conlangs allow for controlled change of the variables that shape language. Humans beings have a given biology and a set of existing cultures, and what exists is all that is available for direct study. By constructing languages for imaginary beings in imaginary cultures, we can explore the linguistic consequences of nonhuman biology and alternative social structures, solidifying our understanding of the relationship between language and our bodies, our humanity, and the world around us.

In addition, conlanging provides students with an opportunity to use creative methodology and artistic expression not normally available or appropriate in linguistics courses, allowing for a multidimensional approach to learning that can help solidify the course content (Sanders 2016: e201ff). Further, conlangs are popular, and students' "enthusiasm and personal attachment can easily be channeled from conlangs to linguistics, enlarging our audience, enriching students' classroom experience, and solidifying their commitment to the material" (Sanders 2016: e195).

Because of the enhanced learning environment and other benefits, we have each included language creation projects in our courses. Sanders has taught an upper-level course in multiple linguistics departments on linguistic typology that uses conlanging as a primary course-long activity (see Sanders 2016: e199–201 for a fuller description). In his course, students are tasked with creating a full conlang, from a phonemic inventory to a sufficiently complex morphosyntactic system and lexicon with the capacity to translate a few significant texts, plus a professional-style grammar. The conlang project is embedded in a larger discussion of linguistic typology, and the students are expected to use typological facts to help guide their decision-making process in building their conlangs. Though they are guided by the typology of natural languages (natlangs), they are given a fair amount of flexibility, and many of them take advantage of that to create conlangs that require knowledge about biology and physics beyond what is relevant to ordinary natlangs. In Sections 2 and 3, Sanders describes two case studies showing how conlangs can be used to explore the relationships between language and the physical sciences.

The conlang projects that Schreyer has assigned in her courses are from two different courses in anthropology: a first-year introduction to linguistic anthropology and a fourth-year course on pidgins, creoles, and created languages. As in Sanders's course, students in Schreyer's first-year course are required to build a language throughout the semester as they learn about the various aspects of language. For example, when they learn about phonology, they are required to choose the phonemes of their language, and when they learn about non-verbal communication, they are required to develop gestures for their language. Schreyer and her students reported on what they learned in this first-year assignment; particularly, they argue "that creating languages allow [sic] students to more fully understand the concept of 'cultural relativity' or the idea that each culture is unique and that we should not judge a culture based on how it compares to our own way of looking at the world" (2013: 1).

Similarly, students in Schreyer's fourth-year course are required to reflect on culture for their language-creation assignment. In this case, however, students reflect not on a cultural group they have made up, but rather on one that exists in popular culture. In the most recent two offerings of this course (2014 and 2016), students were tasked with developing words that they thought should be included in the Kryptonian language corpus; they were given the option of developing words based on the culture of the Kryptonian people, as portrayed in the film, or of developing words relevant for the expansion of the language for daily human use. Almost all students chose to develop words for aspects of Kryptonian culture. In Section 4, Schreyer expands on two predominant themes from the students' word creation (language and society, and language and birth) to illustrate how building these words allowed the students to develop an appreciation of cultural relativity (as previously suggested in Schreyer et al. 2013).

11.2 Case study #1 (Sanders): Biology and avian conlangs

When students are given complete freedom to create their own full conlangs (as in the course described in Sanders 2016: e199–201), many of them design conlangs for aliens and other nonhuman creatures.[1] A common archetype that students often gravitate to is some sort of bird-like creature.[2] Because of their radically different mouths and throats, avian creatures pose interesting biological issues that would affect the structure of any language they might speak. Creating a naturalistic conlang for avian speakers thus requires delving into

---

[1] Interestingly, in Schreyer's first-year course, anthropology students rarely choose to design languages for aliens and nonhuman creatures, but instead focus on creating languages for a range of imagined human cultural groups. This perhaps speaks to their interests as anthropology students, as anthropology can be defined as "the study of all people, at all times, and in all places" (Ottenheimer and Pine 2018: 2). That is, as anthropology courses focus on humans, the conlangs in Schreyer's anthropology courses also focused on humans, while students in Sanders's linguistics course seemed less concerned with restricting themselves to humans as speakers of their conlangs.

[2] I do not know why this is a common choice for my students. A few students have designed conlangs for some other archetypes (felines, reptiles, etc.), but birds are easily the second most popular creatures after humanoids, with at least one student per offering of the course designing an avian creature of some sort.

anatomical differences between birds and humans. The clear majority of my students who decide to work with nonhuman beings are eager to learn about the relevant differences and incorporate at least some of that knowledge into their conlangs, though a few do end up shying away from it, either ignoring the anatomical differences completely or shifting back to human speakers. In this section, I describe some of the anatomical issues that students have considered when constructing an avian conlang.

11.2.1 Bills and labial sounds

Perhaps the most obvious difference between human and avian vocal tracts is a bird's rigid bill (Lovette and Fitzpatrick 2016; the issues discussed here would also be relevant to other creatures with a similar rostrum, such as turtles and crustaceans, as well as imaginary beings made of hard materials like rock, wood, or metal). Human lips are very flexible, with multiple possible labial configurations (rounding, spreading, protrusion, compression, etc.), while bird bills cannot change their shape so drastically. Thus, there are many kinds of labial speech sounds found in human natlangs that would not be possible in a biologically naturalistic avian conlang.

For example, without the availability of lip rounding, avian conlangs should not have truly round vowels. Thus, a typical avian five-vowel inventory might look more like (1a), with only unrounded vowels, rather than the more traditional human inventory in (1b), where back vowels are round. Students who have designed conlangs for avians and other creatures with immobile outer mouth parts typically find this the easiest constraint to impose and easily choose vowel systems with only unrounded vowels, like (1a).[3]

(1)   a. /i e a ʌ ɯ/
      b. /i e a o u/

Similarly, avian conlangs should have no rounded consonants like /kʷ/ or /w/ and should not use rounding to enhance front-back contrasts (as happens with English /ʃ/ to further distinguish it from /s/). Thus, we would expect not only that rounded consonants would be absent in naturalistic avian conlangs, but

---

[3] Some birds, such as parrots and hill mynahs, are able to simulate the acoustics of round vowels with other articulations (Catchpole and Slater 1995: 63), which itself would be an interesting property for a student to explore in a conlang.

also that front-back contrasts should be rarer, since there would be fewer available ways to enhance them.

Additionally, small imperfections in the edge of the bill would prevent birds from making a full stop closure to allow air pressure to build up for a proper plosive release. These imperfections may also prevent the formation of a consistent fricative opening. Thus, labial obstruents like /p/ and /f/ are expected to be nonexistent in avian conlangs. However, percussive sounds made by snapping the bill together would still be possible, and such sounds could serve as a suitable replacement for labial stops in the phonological system (so they might, for example, pattern with other stops as a natural class). Students often enjoy this aspect of their avian conlangs, as it provides an easy and intuitive way to introduce a bilabial "click" in the guise of a percussive sound (which would not itself be phonemic in a human language).

11.2.2 The syrinx versus the larynx

Instead of a larynx, most birds have a syrinx in their throat. One of the key differences between the two structures is that the larynx sits at the top of the trachea, while the syrinx sits much lower at the bottom, where it splits into the bronchi (the two pathways leading to the lungs). In addition, sound in the syrinx is implemented differently from how it is in the larynx, primarily through vibration of tympaniform membranes along the walls of the syrinx (as opposed to vibration of the human vocal folds, which stretch across the larynx).

In a songbird's syrinx specifically (schematized in Figure 11.1), there are two tympaniform membranes in each bronchus (the tympaniformis lateralis in the external syrinx wall and the tympaniformis medialis in the internal syrinx wall), which can be vibrated separately and at different frequencies from those

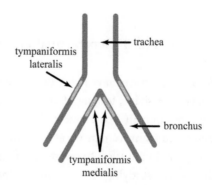

Figure 11.1 General structure of a songbird syrinx

in the other bronchus (Riede and Goller 2010). This means that different pitches can be articulated in quick succession, using the membranes in one bronchus alone, then the other, without having to smoothly transition between pitches in the same membrane as humans do. Some songbirds, such as brown thrushes and grey catbirds, can even vibrate the two sets of membranes at different frequencies simultaneously (Suthers 1990). This opens up the possibility for a wider range of tone patterns than are available for human languages.

For example, a single avian syllable could carry a high level tone followed immediately by a low level tone (/áà/) without requiring a falling contour. More complex tone alternations (high-low-high, etc.) would also be possible, and for certain avian conlangs, it would even be possible to produce two tones simultaneously (/a̋/). These two possibilities could theoretically be combined, allowing for highly complex tone patterns within a single syllable, such as a quick succession of a simultaneous high-low, then high-mid, then low-mid (/a̋a᷇a᷆/). Additionally, any membrane can transition smoothly between different pitches, just as the human vocal folds can, so not only would it be possible to have multiple level tones on the same syllable (sequential or simultaneous), contour tones would also still be available just as they are for human natlangs. This would allow avian conlangs to have such tonal contrasts as /áà/ (high then low) versus /a̋/ (simultaneous high-low) versus /â/ (falling), or even more complex possibilities. Students are typically intrigued by these possibilities, but they do not generally follow through on making such complex tone systems for their avian conlangs, opting for more human-like tone patterns. However, I did have one student who decided to follow the model of some other bird species, like condors, that do not have a developed syrinx or any other structure capable of similar vibration (Snyder and Snyder 2005), so their conlang had more limited phonation than in human natlangs, with no tone or even voicing.

11.2.3 General anatomical concerns for conlangs

Avian vocal tracts have many other anatomical differences from human vocal tracts (size, shape, tongue, etc.), and of course, birds are not the only creatures with nonhuman vocal tracts that a conlang might be created for. Every difference from human vocal anatomy opens up a rich area for the student to explore in the effort to create a more naturalistic conlang. Students may find themselves studying the anatomical intricacies of cricket chirps or dolphin clicks, or even looking into the various ways that animals can communicate without sound, such as bioluminescence or electrocommunication. These are topics not ordinarily discussed to any significant degree in a typical linguistics classroom, but they could appeal to a student creating a naturalistic nonhuman conlang. The resulting study would enrich their understanding of the connection between biology and language.

11.3 Case study #2 (Sanders): Physics and underwater conlangs

Even if a student is designing a conlang for creatures with human-like anatomy, some still choose to have those creatures live in an environment that could affect how sound travels, such as underwater for mermaids and other similar aquatic creatures. Because sound travels through water differently, this will affect what kinds of speech sounds should be more or less common in comparison to those of air-based natlangs. As with nonhuman biology, students who design languages for other mediums typically embrace at least some of the challenges of learning and incorporating the required information to make their conlangs naturalistic.

11.3.1 The speed of sound and formants

Sound travels through water about four times faster than in air (Baltasar et al. 2011). This difference in speed has important consequences for the sound of speech. In particular, the resonant frequencies of cavities in the vocal tract are proportional to the speed of sound; for example, the nth resonant frequency of the entire mouth when articulating [ə] can be approximated with the formula $(2n − 1)s/4L$, where L is the vocal tract length from lips to glottis and s is the speed of sound (Johnson 2012). With water's higher speed of sound, the resonant frequencies will be higher. These resonant frequencies correspond to formants in vowels and sonorant consonants, which effectively means that the formants for an underwater conlang will be shifted upward in comparison to those of air-based natlangs.

For vowels, the two most important formants to consider are the two lowest, F1 and F2. There is a close link between F1 and vowel height, with high vowels having a lower F1 and low vowels having a higher F1. Since F1 is higher under water, we would expect underwater vowels to sound as if they were articulated

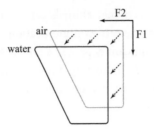

Figure 11.2 Shifted underwater vowel space

lower. Similarly, there is a relationship between F2 and vowel backness, with back vowels having a lower F2 and front vowels having a higher F2. Again, formants are higher under water, so underwater vowels should sound fronter. Thus, the vowel space for an underwater conlang is expected to be shifted lower and fronter in comparison to the vowel space for natlangs spoken in air (Figure 11.2).

11.3.2 Density and dampening

Part of the reason why water transmits sound faster than air is because of its higher density, which has another effect on sound quality. With the molecules packed more closely together in water than in air, a sound wave loses energy faster because it passes through more molecules and transfers that energy to them. This effect is even greater for a high-frequency sound wave, since it has a shorter wavelength, so it goes through an entire wave cycle over a shorter distance.

The overall effect of this dampening is that higher frequencies will be dispreferred in an underwater conlang, because they will be softer, and thus, harder to tell apart (this is similar to why languages typically have a relatively small number of nasal stops, because of the dampening effect of the sinuses). Fricatives generally make crucial use of higher frequencies than other sounds do, so we might expect an underwater conlang to use fewer fricative contrasts than we typically find in air-based natlangs. This will also have an impact on the vowel space, which is already shifted into higher frequencies (as discussed in Section 11.3.1). This can effectively be viewed as an underwater conlang's vowel space being compressed into the low-front region of an air-based vowel system (Figure 11.3), so that a typical underwater conlang might have a vowel system that would seem like /e ɵ a/ to land dwellers, as in the first mermaid conlang a student ever designed in my course.

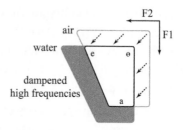

Figure 11.3 Compressed
underwater vowel space

In addition, this dampening effect applies to all frequencies, so, although higher frequencies are more affected, all sounds are going to be harder to hear, regardless of the frequencies they use. Thus, we might expect an underwater conlang to have fewer contrasts within all natural classes, with speech sounds that are already acoustically weak (laryngeals, nonstrident obstruents, nasals, etc.) being particularly dispreferred.

To compensate for the relatively sparse phoneme inventory, it seems reasonable that underwater conlangs might be more likely to have phonemic tone (readily available for any sonorant, not just vowels), and they may even make use of three-way length contrasts, which are rare in air-based natlangs.

11.4 Case Study #3 (Schreyer): Language and cultural relativity

As noted in Section 11.1, students in Schreyer's course learned to embrace cultural relativity, a concept that they have been exposed to since first-year anthropology courses, through working within the cultural framework of Kryptonian culture. The Kryptonian Word Creation assignment comes from the fourth-year Anthropology course—Pidgins, Creoles, and Created Languages. The study of contact languages makes up the beginning two-thirds of the course, while the final third is dedicated to constructed languages. In 2014's and 2016's iterations of the class, students were provided two assignment choices related to constructed languages—the Kryptonian Word Creation project or an Esperanto position paper. In 2014, eleven of twenty-eight students chose to create Kryptonian words, and in 2016, eight of fourteen students chose this option. The assignment guidelines are as follows:

> For this assignment, you will be using what you have learnt from my discussion of the Kryptonian language [including phonological rules], as well as from the first section of the movie *Man of Steel* (watch the sections

filmed on Krypton and in Kryptonian space ships) in order to develop ideas for words that *YOU THINK should* be included in the Kryptonian language corpus. These words should be either based on the culture of the Kryptonian people, as portrayed in the Man of Steel film, or relevant to the expansion of the language for daily human use.

Taking into account the phonology of the language and some of the word formation processes (see the document Kryptonian Language Details), create *four* words in the Kryptonian language that you would like to see included in a potential future Kryptonian dictionary and provide the English translation for them.   (Schreyer ANTH 474 assignment guidelines, 2016)

The students were then tasked with writing a 5–7-page critical analysis of their work including "why [they] chose to create these words and how relevant they are to the Kryptonian culture or to humans who wish to learn Kryptonian" (Schreyer ANTH 474 assignment guidelines, 2016). The students were also asked to reflect on the issue of "ownership" of language and how likely it would be for Warner Bros. (the owners of the intellectual property of the Kryptonian language created for Man of Steel) to accept their words as part of the "official canon" of Superman.

11.4.1 Language, society, and governance

In the 2013 film *Man of Steel*, viewers are initially introduced to Kryptonian society through a scene which depicts members of the Kryptonian council sitting in council chairs and listening to Jor-El (Superman's father) describing how their society is about to implode. The council chairs are covered in Kryptonian writing (especially on the grey surfaces in Figure 11.4) and include phrases from Kryptonian history (see Warner Brothers 2013). The scene illustrates how Kryptonian society proceeds with governance.

Using their knowledge from the film, the students in Schreyer's class developed the words in (2) in regard to society and governance.[4]

---

[4] All Kryptonian words appear here in the International Phonetic Alphabet, with periods indicating syllable breaks. Schreyer and graphic designer Kristen Franson developed the Kryptonian orthography for the movie, but the font is not publicly available, which is why the students wrote their words phonetically. As well, this allowed them to illustrate their understanding of Kryptonian phonology and allophonic rules.

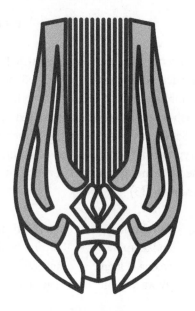

Figure 11.4 Schematic diagram of a
council chair from *Man of Steel* (2013)

(2)   hu.kɑŋ   'the act of taking part in a political debate'
       kɪɪ.ɛm.tæl.na   'a collaborative decision-making process made by the
                       ruling council'
       kɪɛ.pæg.ɦɔɹ.ta 'headdresses worn by Kryptonian council members'
                       (specifically, the prongs that spike upward in a
                       crown-like fashion)
       ŋɔɹ.ʤɑ̃ò   'chair of honor' (lit.), a respectful term used to address
                       the chair of one's house (the member of a house who is
                       on the council); it can also refer to the actual physical
                       chair in the council chambers (Figure 11.4)

Two students chose to create words related to the act of speaking as a part
of governance, participating in a political debate and a collaborative decision-
making process, which illustrates that students saw these aspects of Kryptonian
society as something worthy of word creation. The other two examples here are
related to the physical world, the prongs of the headdresses worn by council and
the chairs of council. The example *ŋɔɹ.ʤɑ̃ò* 'chair of honor', which can represent
a person as well as the physical chair, indicates that this student had internalized
concepts of governance from English (such as chair of a committee) and
reapplied them to this particular world. However, in this society, there are
multiple chairs rather than a singular chair, and these students embraced a
more diverse notion of governance than their own, illustrating that they had
incorporated a degree of cultural relativity into their word creation.

11.4.2 Language and birth

In *Man of Steel*, Jor-El and his wife Lara have conceived their son naturally, a practice which has not occurred on Krypton for centuries. Their world is crumbling and, in order to save their son, they send him in a spaceship to Earth where he is found and raised by human parents as Clark Kent. Students in Schreyer's course were also much intrigued by the idea of natural birth in Kryptonian society, and as a result, felt that this concept needed a name; therefore, many students developed words for this topic, which now has many synonyms (3).[5]

(3)   waŋ.ɦo.ɹa.læm.aɹ   'natural birth'
      bo.kæl.ɪp   'natural birth'
      wʊ.ŋa.la.kæn   'natural reproduction'
      jɪv.wɛ.gɛŋ.zut   'natural conception' (but also a synonym for 'heresy')

One of the most interesting aspects of this particular assignment is that while individual students independently decided to focus on the concept of natural birth for their word creation, they chose a wide range of linguistic features to represent this concept (including diverse phonemes and syllable structures). Another interesting aspect of this particular set of words is the difference between birth and reproduction or conception, which all have related yet different meanings in English. Finally, the last word above also indicates embedded layers of meaning in their word, using polysemy, to build the idea of heresy on top of the definition of natural conception. This illustrates that the student was aware not only that words often have polysemic relationships, but also how polysemy might work in an alternate culture.

By far, the concept of natural versus pre-planned birth in Kryptonian society was an area of interest for these Linguistic Anthropology students, who successfully utilized cultural concepts portrayed to them in the film and various other multimedia tools (behind-the-scenes videos and books about the design of Krypton) to develop words to meet the needs of this particular society. Other words that were also associated with birth include those in (4).

---

[5] It should be noted that individual students did not create synonyms, but as many students developed words for this concept, these words became synonyms in the language.

(4)   kɪ.læn.fɪks   'incubation period of a Kryptonian embryo'
      ma.zu.ba.kɹu.lɑk   'artificial life sac'
      kɹa.hɛɹo   'bloodlines'
      kwɛj.mɑl   'of blood or bloodline'
      ko.ʤɪv   'person's predetermined purpose/future, according
                           to the Codex'[6]

11.4.3 Student reflections

Within their assignments, students were required to reflect on their word-creation process and whether the Kryptonian "language authorities" (in this case Schreyer and Warner Brothers Entertainment) would accept their words as "authentic" Kryptonian words. The majority of students felt that while they enjoyed the process of language creation, it was unlikely that their words would be accepted, since they knew little about the wider details of the language (the full list of Kryptonian words and details of its grammar have not been publicly released by Warner Brothers Entertainment). For example, one student wrote:

> Since I am unsure about the morphological typology of Kryptonian, my adjectives may end up seeming incongruous when compared to the ones Schreyer has created. When creating the words, I felt like I had a great deal of creative license due to my ignorance, but this may be of questionable value if my words do not end up being functional.   (student ANTH 474, 2014)

While another included the following in their assignment:

> One reservation I have about my ability to do this is that I was unable to view the 300 words already in existence. Having this information available to me would have allowed me to look for patterns amongst words and might have assisted in my decision making regarding which words and sounds to include. However, this may also have limited my creativity and I feel confident that the words I did create were not influenced by anything other than my imagination, which may prove to be beneficial.
>
> (student ANTH 474, 2016)

---

[6] Within the movie *Man of Steel*, the Codex holds the DNA of all Kryptonians and is used to determine the role individuals will play in Kryptonian society.

The students were hesitant about embracing the role of language creator for a language that had already begun, but also enjoyed the creative freedom that this assignment allowed them. This is interesting in itself, since new words are developed all the time in many different languages, but often these creations are spontaneous (such as the development of the selfie) and not planned inventions. The emphasis on creativity here also demonstrates how students were embracing new concepts and ideas from different cultures and seeing the artistic nature of the practice of language creation. For example, one student in their reflection commented on the wider appreciation they now had for both conlangs and natural languages:

> However, regardless of whether or not my words would be accepted by Schreyer and Warner Brothers, the process of creating Kryptonian words has allowed me *to appreciate the art of conlanging* to a further extent. Personally, I now have a greater appreciation for how language is formed after attempting to create a few words of my own in a foreign language. An incredible amount of factors influence the creation of a language, and I have realized *how formulaic yet limitlessly creative language creation can be.*
> (student ANTH 474, 2016, emphasis added)

Overall, through the inclusion of language-creation assignments in Schreyer's courses, students have learned more about the concepts of cultural relativity, world-building, and the role of artlangs (artistic languages) in popular culture, as well as about the basic structures of language.

11.5 Conclusion

In this chapter, we have discussed the benefits of bringing interdisciplinarity intentionally into our linguistics teaching, as well as the importance of introducing students to believable world-building. Sanders's students sought out real-world knowledge of avian anatomy and underwater physics to develop conlangs as spoken in imagined worlds with imaginary nonhuman beings. Schreyer's students used their knowledge of anthropology, and cultural relativity in particular, to view a preconstructed world from popular culture and apply the concepts they had learned to linguistics and their Kryptonian word creation.

As described above, in both courses, we used intentional pedagogy, defined by scholars as teaching that is thoughtful, informed, and deliberate, to provide students with hands-on learning opportunities that not only required them to use prior knowledge, but also challenged them to apply what they were learning about linguistics in our courses. In addition, students in our courses have a growing knowledge of conlangs from popular culture and were more likely to be invested in the course assignments owing to their ability to personalize the material. Students reacted very positively to these conlang assignments, seeking out additional resources and knowledge when needed, as well as using high levels of creativity, which are not normally required in more analytic linguistics courses; indeed, many students in these courses have explicitly reported afterward that these more creative assignments allowed them greater flexibility in their approaches to learning and motivated them to take the initiative to expand their knowledge beyond the assigned course material. As one anonymous student reviewer wrote in Schreyer's 2016 course evaluations, "this [course] opened a lot of doors for me and help me to critically think about historical, economic, social, education and other aspects involved in languages. I enjoyed learning the processes put into created languages." As instructors, we also benefited from watching students in multiple years utilize and manipulate the knowledge provided to them in our courses. In conclusion, as we have noted above, linguistics is an inherently interdisciplinary subject, and if instructors are able to embrace that interdisciplinarity head-on and pair it with their own intentional pedagogy, both they and their students will benefit in the long term.

Acknowledgments

Sanders would like to thank his students in various iterations of his typology and conlang course at Williams College and Swarthmore College, who have gleefully pushed the boundaries of what a language can do. Schreyer would like to thank her ANTH 474 Pidgins, Creoles, and Created Languages students who took the time to develop new Kryptonian words and allowed her to share their work here. Thanks also to Khadija Jagani for her editing help.

12

Teaching Proto-Indo-European
as a constructed language

Brenna Reinhart Byrd and Andrew Miles Byrd

12.1 Introduction

This chapter attempts to conflate the authors' research areas in Indo-European
Studies (IES), language pedagogy, and general linguistics into a unique method
for teaching IES and historical linguistics simultaneously. The advances that
the authors have been able to make in their own teaching practices have come
through the application of pedagogies from other disciplines that have been
learned in collaboration with other colleagues and with each other, as well as
through multiple workshops and training in curriculum design and multimodal learning.[1] When discussing linguistics pedagogy, there is no standard
handbook of teaching linguistics that is used in the training of new instructors
(in comparison to the plethora of introductory textbooks devoted to teaching
writing or languages, for example). Useful articles on specific tools to improve
the teaching of linguistics can be found in various journals, such as Squires and
Queen's 2011 article on using mass-media clips for teaching American Speech
patterns, yet there is not a single practical guide for instructors to use that
discusses overarching theories of teaching and learning. Additionally, it is
extremely rare, if not unheard of entirely, for graduate students in
Linguistics departments to complete any formal training in teaching methods
or educational psychology beyond a couple weeks of basic lesson planning and
microteaching. Therefore, the advances in transformative learning that have
been made in educational psychology have taken longer to reach linguistics, as

[1] Brenna would like to thank the American Association of Teachers of German (AATG) for
selecting her to participate in a three-day workshop on curriculum redesign in 2014, and the
University of Kentucky Presentation U for selecting her to participate in a mentored faculty fellows
program 2015–17 on multimodal learning. Both of these opportunities, as well as continued mentoring
by Molly Reynolds at Presentation U, contributed greatly to her understanding and implementation of
pedagogies that promote transformative learning.

Brenna Reinhart Byrd and Andrew Miles Byrd, *Teaching Proto-Indo-European as a constructed language* In: *Language
Invention in Linguistics Pedagogy*. First edition. Edited by: Jeffrey Punske, Nathan Sanders, and Amy V. Fountain,
Oxford University Press (2020). © Brenna Reinhart Byrd and Andrew Miles Byrd.
DOI: 10.1093/oso/9780198829874.003.0012

well as many other disciplines at the university level (For a summary of the core principles of transformative learning, see Slavich & Zimbardo 2012). Additionally, faculty are not routinely offered opportunities to learn new teaching methods, nor are there usually any professional incentives for faculty to radically change the way subject material has been taught for decades. This means that many faculty still heavily rely on behaviorist models of learning, using lectures for class time and exams which test the ability to repeat back what the faculty covered in the lecture (Fosnot & Perry 2005). The focus of many courses at the university level is on the delivery of facts, and the students are responsible for memorizing these facts, as evidenced by the types of assessments used in class. Yet research indicates that not only is the lecture format not as effective for long-term retention as student-centered, collaborative-style learning, the recent generation of students is also less interested in reading through long texts or listening to lengthy lectures, preferring a more interactive learning experience (Michael 2006; Twenge 2009).

IES is perhaps the most conservative subfield of linguistics, being one of the founding subjects of the discipline and still attracting mostly scholars of classical languages. While other types of linguistics classes may offer some active learning strategies[2] in the form of analysis of data sets for patterns, rules, or strategies that explain the alternations and exceptions at hand, this is not the case for IES. In general, within subdisciplines such as phonology, morphology, and syntax, an example set of data is presented to the students and discussed, leading to the formation of strategies for pattern recognition, discussion of correct formatting and notation, and the incorporation of the ramifications of the data on current conceptions of linguistic theory. At this point, students are introduced to additional data or a different problem set, which the student is expected to analyze using the strategies taught to them thus far.

In IES, however, it is extraordinarily rare that only a single change or a single type of change has occurred in the evolution of the words from Proto-Indo-European (PIE) to their cognates in an attested daughter language. This makes handling actual data much less manageable for students—and therefore much more overwhelming. In addition, multiple rules do not usually coexist in

---

[2] We use the definition of active learning from *The Greenwood Dictionary of Education* (Collins & O'Brien 2011: 6): "The process of having students engage in some activity that forces them to reflect upon ideas and how they are using those ideas. Requiring students to regularly assess their own degree of understanding and skill at handling concepts or problems in a particular discipline. The attainment of knowledge by participating or contributing. The process of keeping students mentally, and often physically, active in their learning through activities that involve them in gathering information, thinking, and problem solving."

a single synchronic grammar, which requires a chronology for the changes in question: in order for the derivation to work, rule 1 must precede rule 2, etc. For instance, let us say we are deriving words from PIE into Old English (OE), such as the most basic words of kinship: 'mother', 'father', 'sister', 'brother'. It is simple enough to lecture that PIE *meh₂tér > OE modor, PIE *ph₂tér > OE fæder, PIE *swésōr > OE sweostor, and PIE *bʰréh₂tēr > OE broþor, but nearly impossible for students to discover the processes required without explicit instruction, as each derivation requires multiple changes, with each change ordered in a particular way. Thus, PIE *méh₂tēr is realized as *mah₂tér already in PIE, as *mātér in a very early post-PIE period, as *māþér in Proto-Germanic, then *mōdér, then *mōdēr, and finally in OE, modor, with the change of *-e- to -o- in the final syllable (Ringe 2006: 12). To further complicate matters for students, in order to understand the data set in question, one typically has to have a fairly comprehensive background in the subject matter. Thus, in order to fully grasp the linguistic history of English, one needs to have studied at least some Old English, and preferably other ancient Germanic languages as well, such as Gothic and Old High German. It is therefore uncommon to see any type of active learning in an IES course unless students are already experts in multiple ancient languages, making truly *introductory* IES courses less engaging and less likely to attract new students to the field.[3]

It is against this background that we propose a way of teaching IES that allows for students with no background in either linguistics or ancient languages to become intimately familiar with both the PIE language and PIE culture, as well as the nature of language change, all within a single introductory course. By using a constructed language (conlang) version of PIE in the classroom and teaching it as if it were a living language, we propose that instructors will be able to teach the foundations of IES as well as the basics of historical linguistics to a wider range of students from a more diverse background (for a definition of conlangs and their use within teaching linguistics, see Sanders 2016: 192). In addition, the application of the principles of transformative learning (Slavich & Zimbardo 2012) will hopefully improve students' ability to perform analysis and boost student interest and motivation in the course material and the field as a whole.

---

[3] Many courses, although called, for instance, "Introduction to IES" still require a significant amount of work with either linguistics or language study before the applicant is allowed to take them. For example, Uppsala University requires a minimum of thirty hours of language study and graduate student level status before a student can take the Introduction to Indo-European Linguistics course. These courses are rarely offered as undergraduate courses without substantial prerequisites.

Our method for teaching Indo-European (IE) linguistics by using PIE as a conlang was not invented overnight, but rather gradually evolved out of multiple experiences that both authors had leading up to our work on the video game *Far Cry Primal*, for which we created two working versions of PIE and trained the actors both virtually and on set to speak these languages in a believably authentic manner. In this chapter, we will detail the journey taken to arrive at the conclusion of teaching PIE in this way, in an effort to be transparent and perhaps also to embolden others to take risks with their own instruction that could lead them to exciting and unpredictable results. We also want to stress the importance of seeking interdisciplinary collaborations whenever possible, as we have found this to be a continued source of inspiration for new ways to think about things we may take for granted in our own fields. The combination of Brenna's background in language teaching and pedagogy and Andrew's in linguistics and IES has resulted in numerous fruitful collaborations, one of which is the format of the Introduction to Indo-European Studies course that Andrew has taught at the University of Kentucky, which we discuss in this chapter.

12.2 The traditional approach to teaching Indo-European Studies

For nearly a century, the study of PIE and the evolution of the IE languages had been synonymous with linguistics as a whole, with IE linguistics dominating the field up until the early twentieth century. Ferdinand de Saussure, the founder of structuralism (and many say, of modern linguistics) was himself a student of IE, a synchronic reactionary within a group of scholars that was preoccupied primarily with diachrony, and a scholar widely hailed as one of the great Indo-Europeanists for positing the PIE laryngeal theory, among much else (Fortson 2010; for a comprehensive early history of IE linguistics, see Pedersen 1924). The advent of structuralism and the rise of synchronic analysis in general led to a decline in interest in diachrony, leading to a significant decrease across North America and Europe in both professorships and students in the field of IES; in fact, since the authors finished graduate school in 2010, only one tenure-track job in North America has been publicized specifically for an IE linguist. It is therefore not hyperbole to note that the field of IE linguistics is not as healthy as it once was. Awareness of the field is most likely also in decline, given that fewer students today are studying ancient languages, which is usually a prerequisite for studying IE. For instance, according to a recent study,[4] there has been a marked decrease in the study of Latin in the United States over the twentieth century. In the mid-1930s, the number of Latin students was at its peak at 899,000; in 1962, this number fell to 702,000, with a precipitous drop by 79 percent in 1976 to 150,000, rising slightly to 188,833 in 1994. Much of this decline in Latin education may be attributed to a change in college requirements as well as an attitudinal shift in what constitutes an "educated" individual. In any case, the field of IE has lost the relevance on the international stage that it once held, and many programs have been in decline or have been closed entirely in the past fifty years.

Yet, despite the dwindling number of students in the Classics, introductory courses to IE linguistics have not deviated much from a traditional classroom format. Courses tend to revolve around the lecture, with supplementary readings including seminal articles and books on topics that are difficult to convey in a concise manner in an introductory textbook. Typically, instructors will assign an IE handbook to accompany class lectures, such as Szemerényi 1999, Clackson 2007, Fortson 2010, Meier-Brügger 2010, or Beekes 2011. Courses invariably include a survey of the most archaic IE languages, such as Latin, Ancient Greek, Sanskrit, and Hittite, which either follow an explicit overview of the PIE grammar or provide the basis for the discussion of particular grammatical reconstructions. Thus, instructors may decide to teach about the possible evolution of the thematic conjugation[5] from an earlier *h_2e-conjugation[6] within an overview of PIE itself, or they may choose to do so in the context of the $ḫi$-conjugation of Hittite. Other typical approaches are to briefly introduce IES within a course on historical linguistics or an ancient IE language, such as Gothic or Sanskrit. While aspects of IES may be introduced in these courses, such as the comparative method or specific sound changes like Grimm's Law, we are not including these courses in our discussion in this chapter, as their learning goals are limited in the expectations of the student's knowledge of the field by the end of the course.

When Andrew first taught IE linguistics at the University of Kentucky (UK) in Spring 2012, the course had not been taught at UK in over fifty years. Given

---

[4] http://education.stateuniversity.com/pages/2160/Latin-in-Schools-Teaching.html (accessed June 1, 2018).

[5] There were two basic types of verbs in PIE: those which utilized a thematic vowel *$-e/o-$ after the root, such as *b^her-e-ti 'carries' (continued by Latin fer-i-t 'carries', Greek p^her-e-i, Sanskrit bhar-a-ti) and those which did not, which are called athematic verbs, such as *h_1es-ti 'is' (continued by Latin es-t, Greek es-ti, and Sanskrit as-ti).

[6] This controversial theory, meticulously set forth in Jasanoff (2003), puts forth the idea that the Hittite $ḫi$-conjugation is an archaism, and that certain PIE roots were not inflected in the present and aorist systems with the expected endings *$-m(i)$, *$-s(i)$, *$-t(i)$, etc., but rather *$-h_2e$, *$-th_2e$, *$-e$.

that this was also the first time he had taught this particular course, he decided to teach it in a way that could be best described as traditional to the field: most classes were lecture-based, and the learning goals were to be able to repeat the information covered in the course and to apply this information to reconstruction sets on a take-home final exam. He used Benjamin Fortson IV's textbook *Indo-European Language and Culture* (2010, first published in 2004), which contains a broad overview of the language, culture, and historical context of each branch of Indo-European, as well as exercises on internal and comparative reconstruction methods. Fortson's 2010 book is an incredibly valuable reference guide for both students and scholars alike, broad in its scope and comprehensive on nearly all topics. However, given its breadth and depth, the book can be a bit intimidating as an introductory textbook for those without any prior knowledge of ancient IE languages or linguistics.

Fortson presents the field as is typical in an introductory course to IES, by beginning with a history of the field and its methodologies (such as the comparative method, internal reconstruction, and the importance of philology). He then gives an overview of what most scholars believe to be true of PIE culture, looking into questions of the IE homeland, the types of plants and animals which lived among these people, the gods they believed in, and the cultural practices they held. At this point, Fortson produces a concise look of the reconstructed PIE grammar (phonology, morphology, nominal morphology, verbal morphology, and syntax), followed by specific histories of each language branch (as well as *Restsprachen*, IE languages which contain small corpora and which are not classified in any of the main ten sub-branches, such as Messapic, Venetic, and Phrygian).

In the past, IE introductory handbooks solely provided textual overviews of the fundamental concepts in IES. One benefit of using Fortson 2010 is that for the first time in the history of the field, exercises are found at the end of each chapter, which the instructor may use for assignments throughout the course, such as the following exercise from Chapter 15 on the history of the Germanic branch:

(1) Sample exercise assessing knowledge of Germanic Sound Laws (Fortson 2010: 379)

Give the PIE sound from which the boldfaced sounds in the English words below are likely to have descended:

a. *leech*	c. *seep*	e. *stare*	g. *hollow*
b. *quoth*	d. *have*	f. *root*	h. *bloom*

In examining the exercise, the student should have a working knowledge of both Grimm's and Verner's Laws,[7] as well as knowledge of specific phonological changes that have occurred in the history of English (such as palatalization).[8] While the exercises are useful, the reader should note that the majority of them are quite different from most linguistics assignments. The students are not given data with which they may deduce the changes that have occurred based on strategies they have been taught or some particular theory that they are aware of; rather, the exercise above asks the student to first memorize a specific sound change and its relationship (chronology) to other sound changes, and then apply that knowledge to the reconstructed history of a particular word. The sound change is decontextualized—the students do not discuss the naturalness of the change and are not given the opportunity to discover where the sound change in question applied. The result is that this type of exercise is less engaging because it does not adhere to principles of active learning: students do not need to analyze or problem-solve, but instead, to borrow a phrase from mathematics, they take a couple of rules and "plug and chug."

Typically, assessments in IE courses include testing knowledge through exams or papers, the former on specific topics in IE linguistics, such as ablaut or the tense-aspect system, the latter on a specific topic of a student's choosing. In Andrew's 2012 course, assessments consisted of exams that tested student understanding of core concepts and the memorization of specific changes in phonology and morphology within the daughter IE languages. For instance, in the take-home final exam, students were asked to analyze certain correspondence sets, for which they had to reconstruct a common root for PIE and to discuss any phonological or morphological changes that have occurred in that form's history. Two such examples are given below:

(2)   Sample final exam questions from A. Byrd's 2012 IES course
    1. Skt. *ániti* 'breathes', Gk. *ánemos* 'wind', Lat. *anima* 'breath'
    2. Hitt. *ta-a-ye-ez-zi* 'steals', OLat. *stātōd* 'let him steal', Gk. *tētáomai* 'I deprive of'

---

[7] Grimm's Law is typically described as a chain shift of three phonological changes, in which the PIE voiceless stops, voiced stops, and voiced murmured stops become Proto-Germanic voiceless fricatives, voiceless stops, and voiced stops, respectively. Verner's Law describes the shift of voiceless fricatives in Proto-Germanic to voiced fricatives. For discussion with examples, see Fortson 2010: 339–41.

[8] Students' answers should be as follows: (a) *$\acute{g}$/$\acute{g}$, (b) *g^w, (c) *b, (d) *p, (e) *t, (f) *d, (g) *k/$\acute{k}$, (h) *b^h.

To be able to analyze these questions, the students needed to have a working understanding[9] of the sound laws from PIE to the individual daughter languages, as well as any analogical or morphological changes that have occurred in the relevant language or sub-branch, or even in PIE itself. To give an example of the former, to arrive at the reconstruction of *h_2enh_1- for the first problem, students needed to know that *h_2 "colored" a following */e/ vowel to *a, and that only *h_1 could be realized as -i- in Sanskrit, as -e- in Ancient Greek, and as -i- in Latin (through vowel reduction of *-a-). To give an example of the latter, while Hittite *tāyezzi* (< *ta-a-ye-ez-zi*) 'steals' may derive directly from PIE *$teh_2yéti$ through expected sound changes, the initial s- in Latin was a secondary addition of "s-mobile" (Fortson 2010: 76–7), and the unexpected mediopassive ending in Greek -*mai* was analogically refashioned in a number of ways (for which, see Fortson 2010: 259). Each of these facts was explicitly taught to the students through lecture during the course. In essence, the course required them to demonstrate that they internalized this information by applying it in novel situations.

The students who stuck with the course were successful in that they were able to perform well on the assessments described above. But many did not stick with the course—failing to see the relevance of this type of knowledge in their own studies, be they linguistics majors or otherwise. The course initially consisted of a relatively small group of thirteen students, and only one student had a background in an ancient IE language (Latin). Many of them had studied Spanish, German, or French, though some had no background in linguistics or a non-English IE language at all. As was just mentioned, the traditional way of teaching IES assumes some background in either classical languages or linguistics, and in order to cover even the basic problems in reconstructing PIE, a course can only spend a couple days at most on each subset of linguistics, such as phonology and sound change. Anyone who has taught an introductory course in linguistics at the undergraduate level knows just how difficult some of the basic concepts, such as the phoneme, can be for a student who has never before thought about the way language works. It therefore comes as no surprise that the combination of an introduction to linguistics with an introduction to IES in one semester could be overwhelming for students. Consequently, three students immediately dropped the course after the first day of class, and two dropped mid-semester, despite Andrew's working with these students outside of class on a regular basis. Andrew consulted with each student who dropped the course, and the reason for

---

[9] Not through memorization, however, as this was a take-home test.

dropping was consistent: the material was too hard. What we understand from this repeated statement is that it is wrong to assume that students either know or are able to learn quickly the core concepts of linguistics and language study, and yet, as previously mentioned, this was a necessary assumption for instructors to make in order to make any headway in an IES course (as it is traditionally taught), especially in only one semester.

Even those who did perform well on the assessments found the course a strange bypass in their linguistics trajectory—the "cocktail party knowledge" course of their degree. It is for this reason that the traditional approach to teaching IE linguistics is problematic—for many students, the introduction of a grammatical category, such as the aorist, is not grounded in any previous knowledge and is untethered to any conception of language or linguistics that they hold. Moreover, the traditional approach creates an uneven playing field for students—their background in large part determines their success in the course. Many students interested in the prehistory of English are surprised to discover that they will need a background in Latin and Ancient Greek to be able to follow the discussions in an introductory IES course. Additionally, in order for the course to continue to be taught, we needed to maintain enrollment at ten students at the very minimum. The course therefore needed some drastic changes if it was to be offered on a regular basis.

12.3 Teaching Indo-European Studies at UK, second time around

After the authors had taught the introductory IES course in Spring 2012, an opportunity presented itself that changed the way they thought about IES as a field. In the September/October 2013 issue of *Archaeology Magazine*, Eric Powell wrote an article detailing the work of archaeologists David Anthony and Dorcas Brown on the interpretation of the remains of a large number of dogs and wolves at a site in Krasnosamarskoe, Russia, nearly all of which had been butchered in the wintertime.[10] Consulting scholarship in IES, Anthony and Brown made a striking discovery: the sacrifice of dogs may be reconstructed as a PIE ritual, a wintertime initiation ceremony in which young men are brought into a **koryos*, a "roving youthful war band." The magazine decided to include recordings of PIE with the article, in order for the public

---

[10] https://www.archaeology.org/issues/102-1309/features/1205-timber-grave-culture-krasnosamarskoe-bronze-age (accessed June 1, 2018).

to obtain a better understanding of what PIE was. Powell asked Andrew to edit and record a sample of himself reading aloud two fables reconstructed in PIE, which were posted online at the end of September 2013. As of the date of writing this chapter (June 1, 2018), the two recordings have received well over one million listens on Soundcloud, the more popular of the two being his rendition of the fable "The Sheep and the Horses" by August Schleicher (with substantial updates by H. Craig Melchert). The fable goes as follows:

h₂áu̯ei̯ h₁i̯osméi̯ h₂ul̥h₁náh₂ né h₁ést, só h₁éku̯oms derḱt. só gʷr̥hₓúm u̯óǵʰom u̯eǵʰed; só méǵh₂m̥ bʰórom; só dʰǵʰémonm̥ h₂óḱu bʰered. h₂óu̯is h₁ékʷoi̯bʰi̯os u̯eu̯ked: "dʰǵʰémonm̥ spéḱi̯oh₂ h₁éku̯oms-kʷe h₂áǵeti, ḱḗr moi̯ aǵʰnutor". h₁éku̯ōs tu u̯eu̯kond: "ḱludʰí, h₂ou̯ei̯! tód spéḱi̯omes, n̥sméi̯ aǵʰnutór ḱḗr: dʰǵʰémō, pótis, sē h₂áu̯i̯es h₂ul̥h₁náh₂ gʷʰérmom u̯éstrom u̯ept, h₂áu̯ibʰi̯os tu h₂ul̥h₁náh₂ né h₁esti. tód ḱeḱlu̯u̯ós h₂óu̯is h₂aǵróm bʰuged.

A sheep that had no wool saw horses, one of them pulling a heavy wagon, one carrying a big load, and one carrying a man quickly. The sheep said to the horses: "My heart pains me, seeing a man driving horses." The horses said: "Listen, sheep, our hearts pain us when we see this: a man, the master, makes the wool of the sheep into a warm garment for himself. And the sheep has no wool." Having heard this, the sheep fled into the plain.

The popularity of these recordings, combined with Brenna's interest in proficiency-based language instruction, sparked numerous conversations between the two authors on whether PIE could be taught as if it were a living language. Both authors vividly remember an exercise in Donka Minkova's Old English class at UCLA in 2004 where we were asked to translate popular song lyrics into Old English, with some hilarious and engaging results. We wondered, could such an exercise be as successful in PIE?

This conversation resurfaced when Andrew taught the introductory course to IES for a second time in the spring of 2014. Once again, the course was structured around Fortson's textbook, but this time, in the middle of the term, students would be asked to use their newly acquired knowledge of PIE grammar to translate something from English into PIE. The obvious choice for a translation exercise was a fable, much like the one that Schleicher himself had created. We decided it would be best to ask students to create a fable in English based on a set of core vocabulary that can be reconstructed, which the students would then translate into PIE. The assignment, however, became complicated by the translation task—how do we get students to the skill level of Schleicher himself in less than a semester?

It is at this point that we decided to introduce PIE to the students not as a collection of reconstructed grammatical and lexical facts, but rather as a living language. Traditionally, PIE is the "end product," such that the students are introduced to the reconstruction of a particular word, form, morpheme, or feature in the proto-language through the comparisons of attested forms in the daughter languages. Our approach would be the opposite: students would instead be given a glossary of forms in PIE which they would modify for the translation according to the reconstructed synchronic rules of the language, and only after this exercise delve into the history of the daughter branches.

The first half of the IES course taught in 2014 was quite similar to the first half of the one taught in 2012 (Section 12.2), beginning with an introduction to the methodologies of the field, the reconstructed culture of the Indo-Europeans, and an overview of the different components of the PIE grammar. Around roughly the midpoint of the semester, the students were asked to produce a fable in English in the style and length of "The Sheep and the Horses" using PIE words found in the word index of Fortson 2010. This exercise included the following stipulations: (1) the theme of the fable must be grounded in the cultural themes discussed in Fortson (such as reciprocity, everlasting fame, the names and roles of the gods, etc.);[11] (2) it should make use of the following words: (a) 'bear' (b) 'woman' (c) 'honey' (d) 'smoke' (e) 'put' (f) 'snake' (g) 'house' (h) 'sweet' (i) 'eye' (j) 'see' (k) 'nose' (l) 'sense' (m) 'mouth' (n) 'tongue' (o) 'taste'; and (3) any other words must come from the word index at the back of Fortson 2010. The items on the list of required words were chosen for two reasons. First, they are all securely reconstructable for PIE. Second, these words showcase a large variety of morphological categories—among the nominals there are *o-, *eh₂-, *i-, *u-, and consonant stems; and among the verbs the student must use a variety of

---

[11] The usefulness of this part of the exercise is that it allows the students to be creative while focusing their attention on the culture and society that we can reconstruct for the Indo-Europeans. Of course, language is not just a grammar; it is entwined in the culture in which it is used. Therefore, when we treat PIE as a complete, living language, we must understand it as deriving from a particular historical time and place, with a specific culture and belief system. Scholars in fact know quite a bit about how and where the Proto-Indo-Europeans lived and how they perceived the world. For instance, it is striking that scholars are not able to reconstruct different words for the concepts "give" and "take"; while there are multiple roots reconstructable (*deh₃-, *nem-, etc.), each seems to encode both meanings of "give, take" (Fortson 2010: 22), presenting to us a culture that was fixated upon reciprocity, a belief that permeated all levels of society. This type of cultural knowledge was integrated within the exercise in order to make the active use of PIE more engaging and to lead to a deeper understanding of the culture as a whole.

different inflections, including active and mediopassive verbs, stative perfects, root aorists, etc.

The students then submitted their fables and the whole class voted anonymously for the one they felt had the best narrative and best fit the genre of fable. The fable that won was then chosen as the subject of their group translation exercise from English to PIE. Allowing students to create a fable, and then vote on their favorite, provided two separate ways for students to control the content and direction of the learning material, thus combining cooperative and competitive group learning styles to increase intrinsic motivation (for more on the benefits of combining competition and cooperation in the classroom, see Tauer & Harackiewicz 2004). Giving students agency over their learning is a key ingredient in increasing both motivation and also what some refer to as *deep learning*, that is, an understanding of the material that transcends superficial short-term memorization (Fosnot & Perry 2005; Mundy & Consoli 2013). Once the fable had been chosen for the translation task, Andrew simplified the language to remove anything that would be too difficult for the students to construct with the knowledge of PIE they had learned up to this point. The students were given the simplified fable with a full vocabulary list, including important information such as conjugation forms, etc. (see Appendix 1). The students brought their translations into class, and the class as a whole discussed the translations line by line—together, as a class, we discussed the best way in which an Indo-European would have recounted this fable. The course then continued on per the 2012 class syllabus and investigated the histories of the individual language branches.

Overall, the addition of a fable translation exercise was received very well by the students. In the course evaluations, students remarked how much it helped their engagement with the course—it is perhaps for this reason that no students dropped the course in this semester owing to its difficulty, unlike the previous offering. In addition, it provided another way to assess the students' knowledge of categories within PIE, looking at for example their understanding of the different functions of cases, how ablaut works, and when and when not to use perfective and imperfective verbal forms. However, as exciting as this exercise was, the basic structure of the course was the same as that of the 2012 IES course. As before, some students struggled, especially those without a significant background in linguistics and/or the study of highly inflected languages. It is our belief that to make the course more accessible and more comprehensible to those without a linguistics and/or language background, further integration of PIE as a conlang will be necessary (see discussion in Section 12.5).

12.4 PIE in action: Making *Far Cry Primal*

The next collaborative project that we worked on further put the usefulness of teaching PIE as a conlang to the test. Following the success of these fables produced for *Archaeology Magazine*, we were approached by a major video game company, Ubisoft Entertainment SA, to design two languages, Wenja and Izila, for an upcoming project entitled *Far Cry Primal* (henceforth *FCP*), a first-person shooter set at the beginning of the Mesolithic Period. Their idea was quite radical—the characters would speak languages based on PIE throughout the entire game, in order to create a more immersive experience for the player. We were tasked with creating a functioning version of PIE that the actors could not only pronounce, but could also memorize and understand as they spoke it, in order to give effective and believable performances on set.

The creative team at Ubisoft wanted two conlangs that were close enough to PIE to be believable, in order to give players a *feeling* of authenticity that could not be created without the use of a prehistoric language. The perceived authenticity of a fictional world is often vital to its popularity, and the marketing team on the project assured us that the average gamer today would not accept a prehistoric setting whose inhabitants spoke a modern language (and this theory was proved to be correct in the initial market testing of the game). The believability of the fantasy world is a force so strong that it can often outweigh actual academic evidence to the contrary. One example from this game was the inclusion of a large saber-toothed cat, which the main character could tame and ride into battle. All archaeological evidence shows that this animal was extinct by the time of the setting for the game; however, owing to popular fictional narratives that feature not only saber-toothed cats but also dinosaurs coexisting with humans, the inclusion of Smilodon in the game was accepted as authentic *enough* by most of the game's consumers. For the same reason, a prehistoric-*sounding* language was important for the game developers. The actual accuracy of the languages according to research in Indo-European was less important to the developers, and the fact that consumers could virtually not know the difference was of small enough importance for the language designers to take certain liberties.

In the end, we had to constantly negotiate the rules of the languages with both our team of linguists as well as with the writers, directors, actors, and development team at Ubisoft. We learned through trial and error to strike a balance between historical accuracy according to current research, the preexisting beliefs of the consumer, the difficulty of language learning for the actors, and the usability of the language in the game setting. While our goal was always to make the languages as true to PIE as possible, at times its structure conflicted with the gameplay or with the vision of the *FCP* creative team at Ubisoft. For instance, it was not unusual for PIE words to be much longer than words in English, resulting in overlong cutscenes and in-game interactions, and so the team of linguists[12] was asked to shorten certain common words in both Wenja and Izila, for instance *walkwa* 'wolf' > *wal*.[13] At other times, original features of the PIE language were perceived as being too complicated or even too modern by the *FCP* creative team at Ubisoft, and it is for this reason that Wenja changed from being a pitch-accent language like Swedish, to one that is quantity-insensitive, where trochees are assigned from the left edge of the word.[14] In the end, the team was able to create two full conlangs based on PIE, with lexicons of over 2,400 words combined and two fully functioning grammars, generated through the translation and recording of nearly 40,000 words of dialogue.[15]

We were also tasked with training and coaching actors on set to perform in the languages within motion-captured scenes.[16] The actors were taught the two conlang versions of PIE, Wenja and Izila, using a combination of the Audiolingual Method (ALM),[17] the Total Physical Response (TPR) method,[18]

---

[12] Owing to the enormity of the task, we requested additional help from former colleagues in the creation and translation stages of the project: Chiara Bozzone (LMU Munich), Jessica DeLisi (The Milken School), and Ryan Sandell (LMU Munich).

[13] The word *walkwa* was re-lexicalized to mean 'wolf-pack' in Wenja.

[14] Note that this change was partially based in our modern conception of PIE prosody, as many now (following Kiparsky 2010) believe the first syllable of a word received stress in the absence of an underlying accent.

[15] For a short behind-the-scenes documentary, see https://www.youtube.com/watch?v=dBiAtokSOzc (accessed June 1, 2018). For an example of Wenja, the primary language of the game, see https://www.youtube.com/watch?v=ZEs5tBVjhJM (accessed June 1, 2018), in which Sayla, the village's gatherer and Takkar, the player character, first interact. For an example of Izila, designed to be a slightly simplified version of the PIE typically reconstructed by scholars (e.g. as presented by Fortson 2010), the reader may watch https://youtu.be/JexrTnlPMBY?t=938 (accessed June 1, 2018), which shows the first confrontation between Queen Batari, the main antagonist in the game, and Takkar.

[16] For those not familiar with video games and the production of CGI, many companies today make use of a process called motion capture, where the physical movements of the actors are captured in detail as they act through a scene, right down to facial expressions and mouth movements. This made it incredibly important that the actors would be speaking the language as they moved through the scenes, so that the digitally rendered characters' lips would synchronize with the recorded lines.

[17] The Audio Lingual Method, where the instructor leads the students through the memorization and acting out of a scripted interaction, was most popular in the United States in the 1960s (Byram 2004). While its reliance on script memorization falls short of the full communicative goals of modern-language classrooms today, it is quite useful for actors preparing for rehearsed performances.

[18] Total Physical Response, another language-teaching method first developed in the 1960s, is most commonly used in introductory language classes (Cain 2004). In this method, the instructor demonstrates concrete actions through pantomime while repeating a sentence in the target language describing the action. The instructor then motions to the students to repeat this action themselves (all while staying in the target language).

and the Direct Method,[19] staying completely in the target language during each of the lessons. All three of these language teaching methods require both the instructor as well as the learners to stay in the target language the entire time, putting the focus on *practicing* the language and learning the grammar *implicitly* instead of talking about the language and grammar *explicitly*. These three methods also put a large emphasis on the repetition of entire sentences as accurately as possible and usually involve the memorization of interactive scripts. Since the goals for the actors of *FCP* were to repeat their lines perfectly, and not to improvise or communicate with actual native speakers of PIE, these methods were deemed the most appropriate. These group lessons were followed by individual coaching on the pronunciation of the lines and meaning of the words and grammar so that actors could make choices about what syllables or words to emphasize based on how they wanted to play a scene. The surprising result of this type of intense teaching of PIE (or modified versions of PIE, as was the case with Wenja and Izila) was that many of the actors were able to spontaneously create new utterances through analogy as well as to understand the grammar well enough to find mistakes in the script even before we noticed them. This intense use of PIE as a spoken language gave the actors a deeper understanding of the language than anticipated, one which is rarely achieved within the lecture-based setting of a traditional introductory course to IES.

After the release of *FCP*, the authors published a blog at http://speakingprimal.com. The website has been the "go-to" resource for fans of the game, who are interested in learning more about Wenja and Izila. The authors have posted grammar and pronunciation lessons, discussions of specific etymologies and how the authors derived the two languages from PIE, and have even included lessons like "How to Flirt in Wenja" (*Ku tiyi shambipachitra? Ti-fakwisu apashkanti buha-buham.* "Do you have a map? I'm getting lost in your eyes.")[20] The website has been quite successful, with over 220,000 visits since going live. Some extra-dedicated fans have made their own compositions in Wenja, such as a discussion of other caveman

---

[19] The Direct Method (sometimes referred to as the Berlitz Method as it was widely used by Charles Berlitz in his language schools) is another language-teaching method which relies on inductive grammar teaching and total immersion in the target language. Developed in the late nineteenth century, it was the precursor to ALM and TPR, but in practice tends to emphasize more the acquisition of vocabulary associated with pictures and testing student knowledge through simple yes/no or either/or questions (Weihua 2004; Brown 2007: 21–4). This method, like ALM, puts a high degree of importance on correct pronunciation of complete sentences, and is different in this way from the Communicative Approach that became widespread in the 1990s.

[20] http://speakingprimal.com/how-to-speak-wenja-kwati-samkwayha-lija-how-to-flirt-with-someone/ (accessed June 1, 2018).

media in Wenja,[21] a poem about the fictional land of Oros from the game,[22] and even a music video.[23]

12.5 Future class design and transformative learning

Such compositions in Wenja make a key point about the use of PIE as a conlang—when we allow people to be creative in their learning of PIE, it is easier to generate excitement about and engagement with the language and the field in general. It is for this reason that we believe a course that is structured around teaching PIE as a living language that adheres to principles of student-centered, active, and collaborative learning is the optimal approach to creating a truly introductory course in IES and to increasing interest in the field. We are currently designing such a course and Andrew, with Brenna's help, will be teaching it in the Fall 2019 semester.

In this course, PIE is the *first* language the class is introduced to, not the last. By creating a conlang version of PIE, complete with conversational inter-actions in the language, students can learn PIE as if it were a living language without needing prior knowledge of Greek, Latin, or Sanskrit. As students gain a working knowledge of PIE, they can compare PIE forms to cognates in ancient languages, helping them better understand the linguistic processes that each daughter language has undergone. No longer an abstract exercise, the derivations from PIE into the daughter languages become tangible and real.

The course will derive its structure through backwards lesson design plan-ning from two main learning objectives:

- Students will have a basic working knowledge of the PIE conlang such that they will be able to:
  a) carry on a brief (2–3 min) interpersonal conversation in PIE and
  b) write a short fable in PIE with the help of their notes on the grammar and vocabulary of PIE covered in class
- Students will be able to identify at least seven major branches of Indo-European and at least one attested language from each branch, and, through comparisons with PIE, deduce the most significant linguistic innovations of each branch

---

[21] http://speakingprimal.com/guest-post-by-dansurka/ (accessed June 1, 2018).
[22] http://speakingprimal.com/urusis-sangwa-konradiha/ (accessed June 1, 2018).
[23] https://www.youtube.com/watch?v=ADT6EUlFmiU (accessed June 1, 2018).

These larger learning objectives can be broken down into smaller manageable tasks for each unit, and three to five smaller goals for each day. For example, personal introductions are commonly found in ancient inscriptions and texts, and usually include the name of the person and their father. The first week of the course will then focus on introductions, with the following learning objectives:

- I can introduce myself, including my name and the name of my parent(s) in PIE
- I can ask someone else their name in PIE
- I can introduce someone else and use the appropriate gendered pronoun in PIE
- I can identify the meaning of at least four family words in PIE
- I can figure out at least two sound changes from PIE into Ancient Greek by comparing cognates in both
- I can use this knowledge of sound change to reconstruct the PIE for a few words in Ancient Greek
- I can identify the linguistic environmental factors that affect how these sounds change
- I can identify the place of articulation of the sounds affected by this change and recognize that place of articulation can affect both how sounds change and how sounds impact and are impacted by nearby sounds

Each day will be broken up into a communicative lesson, followed by linguistic discussion, exploration, and problem-solving, by comparing PIE to sentences or snippets of texts in a daughter language. The communicative lesson will consist of short immersion lessons in PIE, similar to the work that the actors did on the set of *FCP*. Students will learn 1–2-sentence dialogues on sharing interpersonal information, using various language learning methods such as ALM, TPR, etc. Vocabulary is taught through the Direct Method, using images to depict new vocabulary, and they would have some Communicative Method tasks, where they would have to ask for personal information from their neighbors. The immersion part of the lessons would serve a few important functions: first, they would set the stage for thinking about PIE as a living language; second, they would build rapport in the classroom through personal interactions, which would reduce student anxiety and increase their confidence in the classroom; and third, they would be able to observe the language in action before analyzing it and breaking it down into individual working parts. In this way, some basic grammatical structures would first be learned inductively, that is, through exposure to the language in context rather than explicit teaching (Krashen 1985; Shrum & Glisan 2010). After the communicative lesson, students would work through short exercises in reconstruction to increase familiarity with the comparative method. Again, in order to maintain an active learning style, students would not be simply given the paradigm to memorize but rather would be encouraged to recognize patterns from the daughter languages. To reduce student anxiety and to increase the likelihood that they would be successful in this exercise, most of the reconstruction would be provided for them, and students would work together to fill in gaps in words which they can predict if they find the appropriate pattern in the data. By simplifying the exercise to a point where students would be able to use analogy to reconstruct proto-forms, we can bypass covering the multiple complicated steps that most likely occurred between PIE and the daughter languages.

Classes will end with a review of the learning objectives, students being asked to demonstrate that they can do each task. Finishing with learning objectives gives students a sense of progress and leaves them with a sense of accomplishment for the day. This feeling of accomplishment and the sense that one can learn something well, which is called *self-efficacy* in the educational psychology and second-language-acquisition research, is directly tied to how well students actually perform (Zimmerman et al. 1992). It is therefore important for the success of the class that students not only learn, but that they *feel* that they are learning. Additionally, if students are allowed to work in smaller groups to discuss how to complete exercises, they can build rapport, which will further reduce their anxiety and build motivation for them to succeed in the class. Tasks completed in small groups lead students to feel that they are working together to accomplish a common goal, resulting in a greater desire to continue the course and to contribute to class discussions (Dörnyei & Malderez 1997). A sample lesson plan for a 75-minute class period is included in Appendix 2.

12.6 Conclusion

While the proposed method of teaching is a significant departure from how IES has traditionally been taught, we believe that the changes laid out above would be welcomed by students at the introductory level, especially in secondary and post-secondary institutions where there are few opportunities to study ancient languages. Our experiences in teaching Wenja and Izila to the actors of *Far Cry Primal* as well as teaching PIE through the creation of a fable in the classroom setting strongly suggest that using a PIE conlang can lead to better student understanding and retention of the basic structure of PIE and the fundamental changes that have occurred in the daughter languages. Moreover, as the incorporation of principles of transformative learning combined with an immersive language experience can lead to higher student motivation and interest, we believe that students will leave the course feeling more rewarded and more motivated to continue study in the field. This fall (2019), Andrew will teach an undergraduate IES course again, using the PIE conlang as the primary teaching tool. We plan to assess this model's effectiveness and hope to publish an update on its use in the near future. We of course invite all interested to teach IES in this manner, and we will gladly share teaching materials and welcome any feedback. Finally, we would like to note that this model of teaching is not restricted to teaching about IES or PIE. We see this as an effective teaching paradigm for any type of historical linguistics course that goes into detail about a particular language family.

APPENDIX 1

(There) was (a) woman. She was (the) wife of (the) king. To her (there) was everlasting fame for (her) sweet honey. A bear smelled (the) honey and went to her house and tasted it. The woman saw (the) bear and thought: "To him are sweet eyes." She put honey onto (a) tree for (the) bear at dawn. The drunken king went to the house, saw honey on the bear's nose, tongue, and mouth, and was furious. He made (a) fire with much smoke, and (the) bear went away. The drunken king did not see, but (a) big snake came and took (the) queen. (The) bear returned and killed (the) snake. He carried (the) queen to her house. The queen gave her heart to (the) bear, and (the) bear became (a) man.

1.	"to be"	*$h_1$esti
2.	"woman"	*g^wénh₂, *g^wnéh₂s (animate noun)
3.	"he, she, it" (NOM.SG)	*só, *séh₂, *tód
4.	"he, she, it" (DAT.SG)	*tósmei̯, *tósi̯eh₂ei̯, *tósmei̯
5.	"he, she, it" (GEN.SG)	*tósi̯o, *tósi̯eh₂s, *tósi̯o
6.	"wife"	*pótnih₂, *potnii̯éh₂s (animate noun)
7.	"king"	*h₃réḱs, *h₃réḱs (animate noun)
8.	"for"	(use dative)
9.	"sweet"	*su̯éh₂du- (u-stem adjective)
10.	"honey"	*méd^{h}u, *məd^{h}éu̯s (neuter noun)
11.	"everlasting"	*n̥d^{h}g^{wh}itó- (o-stem adjective)
12.	"fame"	*ḱléu̯os, *ḱléu̯eses (neuter s-stem)
13.	"bear"	*h₂ŕ̥tḱos, *h₂ŕ̥tḱosi̯o (animate noun)
14.	"to smell"	*h₃edi̯eti
15.	"to go"	*h₁ei̯ti
16.	"house"	*dóms, *déms (animate noun)
17.	"to taste"	*ǵeǵou̯se
18.	"to see"	*derḱt

19. "to think"   *memone
20. "eye"   *h₃ókʷs, *h₃ékʷs (animate noun)
21. "to put, make"   *dʰeh₁t
22. "tree"   *dóru, *dérus (neuter noun)
23. "dawn"   *h₂éusōs, *h₂usés (animate noun)
24. "drunken"   *madtó- (o-stem adjective)
25. "nose"   *nás, *nasés (animate noun)
26. "tongue"   *dn̥ǵʰuéh₂, *dn̥ǵʰuéh₂s (animate noun)
27. "mouth"   *h₁óh₁s, *h₁eh₁sés (neuter noun)
28. "to be angry"   *mn̥ietor
29. "fire"   *péh₂ur̥, *pəh₂uéns (neuter noun)
30. "much"   *pélh₁us, *pl̥h₁ués (u-stem adjective)
31. "smoke"   *dʰuh₂mós (animate noun)
32. "to go away"   *ápo . . . h₁eiti
33. "not"   *né
34. "big"   *méǵh₂onts, *məǵh₂n̥tés (nt-stem adjective)
35. "snake"   *h₁ógʷʰis, *h₁égʷʰis (animate noun)
36. "queen"   *h₃réǵnih₂, *h₃réǵniiéh₂s (animate noun)
37. "took"   *selh₁t
38. "to return"   *ápo . . . gʷemt
39. "to kill"   *gʷʰent
40. "give"   *deh₃t
41. "heart"   *ḱḗr, *ḱr̥dés (neuter noun)
42. "become"   *bʰuh₂t
43. "man"   *h₂nḗr, *h₂n̥rés (animate noun)

APPENDIX 2 Sample Lesson Plan

5 min.	**Learning objectives:** • Introduce myself in PIE in at least one of two possible ways • Ask someone what their name is in PIE • Introduce someone else in PIE **Warm-up:** Looking at the following examples of how to say "My name is . . . " in different IE languages, what do you think the word for "name" is in each? Ancient Greek: Ὄνομα μοι . . . (Ónoma moi . . .) Latin: Nomen mihi est . . . Sanskrit: अहम् . . . (aham . . .)मम नाम . . . (mama nāma . . .) Persian: است . . . من نام (naam e man . . . ast)
15 min.	**Communicative practice of PIE as a conlang** (including a review of the previous lessons, if applicable). **Introductions:** Andrew points to self: "Andrew h₁esmi." Andrew points to self, repeats "**Andrew** h₁esmi." Then points to student. "Kʷís h₁esi?"

	Student gives their name. Andrew repeats student's name X to the class: "X $h_1$esti!" In doing so, Andrew also PIE-ifies their name. (Andrew = H_1éndrus) Andrew continues on to the next student (Y). "**H_1éndrus** $h_1$esmi. K^wís $h_1$esi?" and then introduces new student to the class: "Y $h_1$esti!"
	
	 After a few students have answered, the following dialogue is presented on the board:
	
	     Student X: " _____ $h_1$esmi. K^wís $h_1$esi?"
	     Student Y: " _____ $h_1$esmi."
	
	 Students are encouraged to introduce themselves to one another. Andrew calls on one student and points to their neighbor, asking "$K^w$is $h_1$esti?" Students are encouraged to respond with the full sentence.
	
	 For linguistic support, the following dialogue is put on the board alongside an image that makes it obvious two people are talking about a third person:
	
	     "K^wís $h_1$esti?"
	     "Jennifer $h_1$esti."
	
	 After a couple students have been called on, Andrew points to self: "H_1nóh₃mn̥ moy H_1éndrus $h_1$esti."
	
	 (Andrew writes "H_1nóh₃mn̥ moy H_1éndrus $h_1$esti." = "H_1éndrus $h_1$esmi." on board)
	
	 Andrew asks a couple more students "H_1nóh₃mn̥ toy k^wid $h_1$esti?" to see if they can produce the longer form as well.

5 min.	**Transition by drawing attention to one linguistic aspect of the communicative exercise above.** Andrew puts the following up on the board and asks students to identify which word they think means "name." H_1nóh₃mn̥ moy H_1éndrus $h_1$esti. H_1nóh₃mn̥ toy k^wíd $h_1$esti?
10 min.	**Comparison of a single grammatical construction or sound in PIE with the same forms in an attested daughter language** (allowing students through guided tasks to notice similarities or differences and make inferences about the changes that they see in the data presented) Andrew puts the following on the board: <table><tr><td>PIE</td><td>Ancient Greek</td></tr><tr><td>H_1éndrus $h_1$esmi.</td><td>Ἔνδρυς εἰμι. (Endrus eimi.)</td></tr><tr><td>H_1nóh₃mn̥ moy H_1éndrus $h_1$esti.</td><td>Ὄνομα μοι Ἔνδρυς ἐστι. (Onoma moy Endrus esti.)</td></tr><tr><td>K^wís $h_1$esi?</td><td>Τίς εἶ; (Tís eî?)</td></tr><tr><td>H_1nóh₃mn̥ toy k^wíd $h_1$esti?</td><td>Ὄνομα τοι τί ἐστι; (Ónoma toy tí esti?)</td></tr></table>

	Students are asked to discuss in groups the differences between PIE and Ancient Greek and come up with at least three sound changes. Students then as a class are asked specifically to describe what happens to the PIE /kʷ/ in Ancient Greek.
10 min.	**Additional data is presented from attested daughter language to allow students to make generalizations and form rules to describe the changes they see.** More data that shows the PIE /kʷ/ sound in Ancient Greek; students will need in groups to come up with the rules for when /kʷ/ becomes /p/, /t/, or /k/ based on the environment. Example: wékʷos 'voice' > épos; kʷís > tís 'who'; gʷowkʷólos > boukólos 'cowherd' Students will also be given data for /gʷ/ and /gʷʰ/ and will come up with similar rules. Example: gʷóws > boũs 'cow', gʷʰónos > pʰónos 'murder', etc.
5 min.	**Assess student comprehension thus far by having them apply the rules they have deduced to new data, reconstructing back to PIE.** Students will be given new words in Ancient Greek with the sounds /p/, /t/, and /k/ that they must reconstruct back to PIE.
5 min.	**Lead students to deduce from the descriptive rules the underlying reasons behind the rules (natural classes, assimilation, semantic broadening, etc.).** Students will be led to describe the placement of the sounds in the mouth and which features /kʷ/, /gʷ/, and /gʷʰ/ share, as well as how the vowels that affect the environmental changes are similar or dissimilar.
5 min.	**Short discussion of these rules or reasons behind the rules in broader linguistic scope to make connections between IES and modern Linguistics.** Examples of assimilation to nearby vowels in the history of English, such as palatalization in *church, child, yard, witch*, etc.
10 min.	**Concluding task that combines all of the new information learned that day** Students are given a short text in Ancient Greek that includes an introduction. Some of the text has already been reconstructed back into PIE, but students must figure out the rest. They have five minutes to work individually, and then the last five minutes to compare with their neighbors and come to a conclusion.
5 min.	**Review of learning objectives and transition to the next lesson.**

13

Learning about language through language invention

"I was really proud of the language I created"

*Skye J. Anderson, Shannon T. Bischoff, Jeffrey Punske,
and Amy V. Fountain*

13.1 Introduction

This chapter discusses the use of a language invention project in introductory undergraduate courses outside the Linguistics major. We describe the rationale and origins of the project, first implemented at the University of Arizona and later adapted for use in distinct contexts at Purdue University Fort Wayne and most recently at Southern Illinois University. We contend that language invention can be effective in introducing linguistics to diverse student populations in a range of institutional contexts and course sizes. We further argue that, through the language invention project, students cultivate knowledge and skills that translate well beyond the linguistics classroom—and that such a project can generate strong attachment of students to the study of linguistics even if they do not pursue subsequent courses in the discipline.

13.1.1 Rationale

Linguistics has long had an awareness problem. Most people never study linguistics, and many are unfamiliar with what linguistics is (Stollznow 2017). Furthermore, most students come to college with little or no practice in bringing their tacit understanding of the basic structures of language to the surface (Curzan 2013). Not all universities offer linguistics courses outside of the major or minor; furthermore traditional methods for teaching introductory

Skye J. Anderson, Shannon T. Bischoff, Jeffrey Punske, and Amy V. Fountain, *Learning about language through language invention: "I was really proud of the language I created"* In: *Language Invention in Linguistics Pedagogy*. First edition.
Edited by: Jeffrey Punske, Nathan Sanders, and Amy V. Fountain, Oxford University Press (2020).
© Skye J. Anderson, Shannon T. Bischoff, Jeffrey Punske, and Amy V. Fountain.
DOI: 10.1093/oso/9780198829874.003.0013

linguistics aren't always well suited for a generalist audience (Kuiper 2011a). Nevertheless, linguists know that language, and the study of language, are fundamental to our understanding of humans, societies, and cultures at every level. As early as the turn of the millennium linguistics departments in the United States were beginning to develop ways for the incoming undergraduate student to learn some linguistics, even if they had no intention of pursuing the major (Spring et al. 2000).

Linguistics has important advantages over better-known academic disciplines for both students and Universities. Culturally, at least in the US, linguistics has a nerd-cachet that can attract students to our courses and the major. Since the 1960s, invented languages—most prominently Klingon—have caught the imagination of young fans of science fiction. Portrayals of linguists in popular media, including the film *Arrival*, discussed in Coon (this volume, Chapter 4), garner the attention of students and the public alike. The raised profile of language invention and conlanging has been put to use in the linguistic classroom elsewhere (see especially Sanders 2016). This is a positive change.

Academically, linguistics is clearly situated in the science, technology, engineering, and math (STEM) fields and in the humanities and fine arts. In this regard, we have the potential to reach students in all disciplines. Furthermore, including linguistics courses as part of general education curricula allows students to develop key skills that are broadly useful across the curriculum. Doing linguistics builds analytic skills, including pattern identification and explication, abstract and representational thinking, and careful description of complex phenomena. Doing linguistics also cultivates scholarly skills such as writing and developing research methods. These observations have led to an increased focus among linguists on innovating instructional practices that connect the non-specialist undergraduate student with the study of linguistics (Berardi-Wiltshire and Petrucci 2015; Babcock et al. 2015; Van Herk 2017; Anderson 2016).

Linguistics courses have long used instructional practices that today would be referred to as "problem-based learning" (Hmelo-Silver 2004), "collaborative learning" (Cabrera et al. 2002), "engaged learning" (Smith et al. 2005), and "active learning" (Freeman et al. 2014). This approach (see for example Kuiper 2011a, Curzan 2013, Lillehaugen et al. 2014) has served linguistics students well, and similar practices are increasingly being recognized across the curriculum as powerful engines of student learning and retention, particularly for students from traditionally underserved populations (Cabrera et al. 2002; Smith et al. 2005; Freeman et al. 2014).

More broadly, linguistic study allows us to debunk a variety of commonly held but deeply destructive beliefs about language—for example, that linguistic varieties associated with powerful social groups are inherently more complex and expressive than those associated with lower-status groups, or that some languages are beautiful and valuable, while others are ugly and harmful, or that languages are merely sets of words that ought to be mutually mappable in a one-to-one fashion, so that the "lack" of a word for some concept in one language indexes a conceptual or cognitive deficit for speakers of that language (Lippi-Green 2012 discusses great examples of such misunderstandings). The subject of Linguistics is in a unique position to cultivate an appreciation of diverse populations and cultural practices, both locally and globally. In treating actual language behavior as an inherently valid object of study, linguistic training develops in students an appreciation for the intricacy of their own linguistic varieties and those of others—including varieties associated with stigmatized populations. Linguistics curricula that introduce students to the actual range of variation of living languages, and the historical development of languages, inevitably encourage students to develop a clearer understanding of the diversity of human experience. As such, linguistics courses have the potential to reshape our campus climates and improve Universities' ability to facilitate upward mobility of our students (Wolfram 2017).

13.1.2 Project origins

None of the preceding arguments are new, and such reasoning led to the inclusion of a linguistics course in the University of Arizona's General Education Curriculum as a Tier One (freshman) offering in the Social Sciences beginning in 1998 (Spring et al. 2000). The courses in this category were designed to be interdisciplinary and outside of any student's major or minor requirements. They tended to have large or very large enrollments. From 1998 through 2005, the course was taught under a number of guises— from offerings that could be characterized as a "light" version of a typical introductory course for majors to offerings that were more sociolinguistic in focus, to those that asked students to develop, run, and report on mini-research projects. After co-author Fountain offered the course using those models, she inventoried perceived strengths and weaknesses of the offerings. While the course was relatively popular, it did not seem to advance students' understanding of the fundamental building blocks of language, and students' written work seemed to be vulnerable to many of the endemic problems in "standard" academic writing—lack of interest, relatively high rates of academic integrity violations, and failure to demonstrate mastery of course concepts.

In the hopes of avoiding these shortcomings, generating increased enrollment and excitement about the field, and more effectively addressing students' misapprehensions about language, we developed an offering of this course built around an invented language project. It was scaled to be practicable in a course with 400–500 students meeting twice a week in lecture and once a week in small (typically 30–35-students) discussion sections. Subsequently, we have refined the project and transported it to a variety of colleges and universities in the United States. In this chapter, we review our experiences and strategies and evaluate the effectiveness of using language invention in introductory courses for non-majors as well as for students with an interest in linguistics.

13.2 The project

While details of the project have varied across offerings, the overall structure has not. Our courses were offered on a semester (sixteen-week) calendar. Courses at University of Arizona and Purdue University Fort Wayne were offered at an introductory level, but were not limited in enrollment to freshmen.

Students complete the project in four steps, with a fifth submission that revises the complete report.[1] At each step after the first, students revise the material they've previously submitted, and draft new material. Assessment of revised material focuses on improvement and mastery, while assessment of draft material emphasizes demonstrated effort and completeness. The project ultimately requires each student to provide a table of ten core vocabulary items, a consonant and vowel inventory with representative minimal pairs, a brief phonotactic grammar, three inflectional paradigms, examples of simple sentences, question formation, and a pragmatic practice associated with joking, teasing, swearing, irony, or sarcasm. In our version of the project, students do not invent an orthography—they use the International Phonetic Alphabet (IPA) and three-line glossing for presentation of linguistic forms.[2]

---

[1] A more complete description of the project, including instructions and grading rubrics, can be found at https://sites.google.com/a/email.arizona.edu/lsa2017-invented-languages/.

[2] This approach has the unfortunate consequence of preventing students from inventing signed languages.

In the first step students draft a narrative in which they encounter a language undocumented by linguists; as inspiration, students receive recent news reports of such "discoveries" (for example Hotz 2010, Bakalar 2013). Students then visit Ethnologue[3] via a university subscription, locate their newly discovered language in a geographic region, and identify at least one neighboring (real) language. Students then review a list of core vocabulary items (a Swadesh list; for our purposes we recommend the list provided in Bowern 2007), and select ten concepts from the list as the inspiration for their first invented words. They then imagine an elicitation session in which they use their selected concepts as prompts—and create a word for each concept. Students receive an abbreviated version of the IPA and write their imaginary words phonetically. They also discuss how their imagined words are not simply translations of the English word on the Swadesh list—but instead how their words demonstrate an "organization of knowledge" in their new language that differs from that found in English.

At the second submission, students revise their first submission and add a section on phonemic inventories and one on phonotactics. During this time, course readings and lectures focus on phonetics and phonology, and students are asked to make generalizations about the sound system of their invented language based on their first ten words. Students build a consonant and vowel inventory from the sounds they used in their first words, and supplement each inventory with additional sounds. They add to their languages' vocabularies by creating new words that function as minimal pairs for a set of phonemic distinctions evident in their inventories. They review the patterns found in the way they interleaved consonants and vowels in their invented words, and generalize those to a set of syllabification rules. Students are directed to find and review an article from the *Journal of the International Phonetic Association*'s "Illustrations of the IPA" series to use as a model for presentation of the sound system of an unfamiliar language. Students also utilize key readings from the World Atlas of Language Structures Online (henceforth "WALS"[4]). At this point, students demonstrate proficiency in using the IPA and in describing articulatory phonetics and basic phonological concepts. When the second step is submitted, the new material is graded as a draft, but the previously submitted material is graded as a revision. Revised work earns credit for improvement and proficiency (but not for completion per se).

---

[3] http://ethnologue.com. As of 2020, the project directs students to Glottolog (https://glottolog.org) rather than Ethnologue.

[4] http://wals.info.

At the third submission, students revise their previously submitted work and add sections on inflectional morphology and sentence formation. During the time that this material is being drafted, course readings and lectures focus on basic morphology, core inflectional categories, and basic syntax—focusing on the concepts of compositionality, constituency, and simple sentence structures. Students are asked to identify the morphosyntactic type of their imaginary language as analytic, agglutinative, synthetic, or polysynthetic—and they begin presenting their example words and sentences using three-line glossing. Students present their inflectional morphology in the form of illustrative paradigms, and they create three example sentences: a simple transitive sentence, a simple intransitive sentence, and a sentence with an adpositional modifier. In building their paradigms and sentences, students use relevant chapters of WALS for guidance. We also provide students with a link to the Leipzig Glossing Conventions[5] for examples of three-line glossed words and sentences in unfamiliar languages.

The fourth submission is the last step in which students draft new material. The two new sections at this step are question formation and pragmatics of expressive speech. Students transform their simple sentences into at least one polar question, using an intonation strategy, a question particle, or a pattern of syntactic movement; and a content question in which they substitute a constituent with an invented interrogative phrase and decide whether their language leaves that phrase in situ, or moves it to sentence-initial position. Students review the relevant WALS chapters in order to see models for discussion of question-formation strategies, and to get a sense of how common the different strategies are in real languages. For their discussions of "expressive speech," students are asked to choose a genre from this inventory: joking, teasing, swearing, word taboo, irony, or sarcasm. They then search the scholarly literature in linguistics and anthropology to find an example of a real speech community's practice, and devise a system in their imaginary language that provides a reasonable comparison or contrast with the system described in the scholarly work. In class, students read and learn about two overarching theories of pragmatics (Austin and Searle's Speech Act Theory and Grice's Conversational Maxims), and they are asked to discuss their system using either of those theoretical orientations.

After students have received feedback on all parts of their work, they revise the entire project and submit it as their final "Field Report." The Field Report is graded as a revision and constitutes the largest point-value item in the course,

---

[5] https://www.eva.mpg.de/lingua/resources/glossing-rules.php.

giving students the opportunity to demonstrate mastery of the underlying course concepts on a high-stakes item that they have received significant feedback on and help with throughout the semester. Students also present brief oral reports to their peers, in a "conference talk" session near the end of term.

By the end of the semester, students have developed a multiply revised written assignment of at least ten pages, exclusive of references.[6]

13.3 Institutional contexts

We now discuss the range of contexts in which this project has been applied and the outcomes of the project for student learning. Our data come from a variety of class sizes, course goals, undergraduate cohorts, and implementations of the project across three public universities over the last twelve years. We identify patterns of effective implementations of the project by analyzing data collected inside and outside of these courses, assessing students' mastery of core concepts in linguistics, their beliefs and attitudes about language, and their perception of the utility of language invention for their own learning.

13.3.1 University of Arizona

The University of Arizona is a large[7] research-intensive, land-grant institution located in Tucson, Arizona. The project just described has been used in a variety of offerings of a freshman-level general education course unhelpfully titled "Mind, self and language: Language" since 2006.[8] Offerings have ranged from very large in-person lecture classes with weekly discussions, to small in-person classes, to fully online formats. Fully online offerings have served two distinct student populations: main campus students who take some courses online, and students enrolled in a separately enrolling online campus called "Arizona Online."[9]

---

[6] Where our classes have benefited from Graduate Teaching Assistant (GTA) support, a 0.25FTE has typically been assigned a maximum of 35–40 students. Where the courses are taught without benefit of GTAs, workload is a significant limiting factor for use of the project.

[7] In 2016–17, the most recent year for which statistics were available, UA's undergraduate enrollment was 34,072.

[8] The course title was amended in 2015 to "Language in the World."

[9] Arizona Online students matriculate separately, enroll on a per-credit basis, and take all coursework online; they are more likely than main campus students to be older (our oldest student so far celebrated his 92nd birthday while inventing his language), to be returning veterans or active military, and/or to have children or full-time employment.

Because the UA is a PhD-granting institution, and because our course has large enrollment, we benefit from the participation of Graduate Teaching Assistants in instruction. Often, this course marks the first teaching experience for new graduate students in Linguistics at the University of Arizona. During the period described in this paper, more than sixty graduate students have participated on the instructional team. The project has evolved based not only on undergraduate students' needs and feedback, but it has also benefited tremendously from the insights of these graduate students. From the point of view of instructional resources, the invented language project has proven to be adaptable to the differing levels of experience of the graduate teaching assistants who have participated, and a felicitous way for new graduate students to stretch and practice their own approaches to the study of linguistics.

Based on accessibility of reliable data from our registration system, we report aggregate grades data from Fall 2013 through Spring 2018, but include enrollment counts and enrollment by class standing from Fall 2010 through Spring 2018 below. Overall, the data show that the project has scaled successfully from very small to very large classes, and across in-person and online modalities and distinctive student populations (Honors, Arizona Online). The summary in (1) shows the range of class sizes in which we've used this project.

(1)   Range of class sizes 2010–18
    a. Total number of degree-seeking students: 4,320
    b. Largest enrollment: 419 (Spring 2010, in-person, non-Honors)
    c. Smallest enrollment: 11 (Spring 2016, online, Arizona Online)

Though our course is designed for freshmen, students can enroll at any point in their careers. The summary in (2) shows the number and percentages of students in this course based on class standing.[10]

(2)   Summary of students' class standings 2010–18
    a. Freshman: 2,660 (61.6%)
    b. Sophomore: 1,066 (24.7%)
    c. Junior: 379 (8.8%)
    d. Senior: 215 (5.0%)

[10] The data for the entire range (2010–present) were filtered to remove students with no class standing specified (twenty-seven in total) as well as students who were listed as non-degree-seeking (thirteen in total).

Our course cannot be counted toward a major or minor requirement—it fulfills only a general education requirement. The summary in (3) shows that the course primarily serves students who had not declared a major in Linguistics at the time of enrollment.

(3)   Representation of Linguistics majors in enrollments 2013–18
   a. Total enrollment during this time: 2594
   b. Linguistics is listed as a first, second or third major: 73 (2.8%)
   c. Linguistics is listed as the first major: 70 (2.7%)

We turn next to the context of the project as it has been implemented at Purdue University Fort Wayne.

13.3.2 Purdue University Fort Wayne

In this section we report on use of this project at Purdue University Fort Wayne.[11] Purdue Fort Wayne is a large masters-granting institution according to the Carnegie Classification, with an enrollment of just over 12,000 in AY 2017–18, and serving a majority of first-generation university students.

The invented language project has been implemented in a freshman-level general education course titled "Introduction to the Study of Language" and is required of students in the university's "Teaching English as a New Language" program. The course is generally offered in three sections, each taught by one of three full-time tenured faculty members. Only co-author Bischoff has used the project in this context, and has done so since Spring of 2012. Enrollments range from sixteen to forty students during Spring and Fall semesters, and from seven to fifteen students in Summer sessions. The data were provided by the Office of Institutional Research and cover the period beginning in Fall 2011 and continuing through Summer 2018. It is important to note that the project was introduced in the Spring of 2012. Enrollments at Purdue Fort Wayne are summarized in (4).

---

[11] Prior to July 2016, Purdue Fort Wayne was known as Indiana University Purdue University Fort Wayne.

(4) Range of class sizes 2011–18
   a. Total number of degree-seeking students: 927 (includes course with project and without)
   b. Largest enrollment: 40 (with project)
   c. Smallest enrollment: 7 (with project)

The course is intended for freshmen, but students may enroll at various stages in their academic careers, as seen in (5). Enrollment at Purdue Fort Wayne has included two graduate students and four high-school dual-credit students.

(5) Summary of students' class standings 2011–18
   a. Freshman: 267 (28.8%)
   b. Sophomore: 252 (27.2%)
   c. Junior: 212 (22.9%)
   d. Senior: 179 (19.3%)
   e. High School Dual-Credit: 4 (.4%)
   f. Non-Degree (undergraduate): 11 (1.2%)
   g. Graduate: 2 (0.2%)

Students from each of the Colleges and Schools from across the campus are represented in the course. However, the largest number come from Arts and Sciences (55.8%) and Education and Public Policy (27.2%).

(6) Enrollment by college 2011–18
   a. Arts and Sciences: 517 (55.8%)
   b. Business: 9 (1.0%)
   c. Continuing Studies: 44 (4.7%)
   d. Education and Public Policy: 252 (27.2%)
   e. Engineering Technology and Computer Science: 9 (1.0%)
   f. Health and Human Services: 9 (1.0%)
   g. Unit of Affiliated Programs 76 (8.2%)
   h. Visual and Performing Arts 11 (1.2%)
   i. Total 927 (100.0%)

13.3.3 Southern Illinois University

We note that, while our previously described offerings involve lower-division courses and non-majors, the project is being scaled for a more advanced population at Southern Illinois University-Carbondale (SIU). SIU is a PhD-granting institution with a student population of approximately 18,000. The use of the project at SIU has been the most limited in both time and scope. The primary object of this section is to discuss how a project like this may be scaled into a freestanding course on language invention.

Unlike the courses discussed in this chapter but like many others described in this volume, this course comprised a specialized class on language invention: "LING 302: From Esperanto to Dothraki: The Linguistic Reality of Language Invention." At the time of writing, the course has been offered once, in Spring 2017. It was available to all undergraduates but did not fulfill general education requirements. Students who enrolled took it either as a major elective (if majoring or minoring in Linguistics) or a general elective (if not).

There were twenty-two students enrolled in the course. Thirteen of those were majoring in Linguistics (59%) with the remaining nine (41%) of various campus majors. Most had some previous experience with linguistics, primarily through the Anthropology department, but for four (18%), this was their first course in the discipline.

As noted, the project was implemented in a fundamentally different way in the SIU context from the way it was in the others discussed in this chapter. As such, it required some degree of adaptation, illustrating the scalability of such a project in different contexts. A key challenge for the SIU context stems from the fact that many of the SIU students had considerable background in linguistics while a significant proportion had a limited exposure or no exposure at all.

Scaling the project to support these distinct cohorts was accomplished in several ways. The core of the project remained identical to that developed at the University of Arizona, but with an expanded array of optional and advanced categories that students with more confidence and exposure to Linguistics could pursue. For example, the section on grammatical relations and sentence formation included options for more advanced number systems and ergativity. Such minor, optional expansions were made throughout the project, allowing students with advanced knowledge of linguistic content to feel challenged by the project, while keeping the options simple and understandable for students with limited exposure to the field. Thus projects like this may be useful beyond introductory classes including tailored specialized classes open to all students like the one at SIU or other sorts of elective courses.

13.4 Outcomes: Evidence of student learning

In this section, we provide evidence from the University of Arizona and Purdue University Fort Wayne that teaching with language invention is successful for most students.[12] We operationalize success in two ways: first, we show that the language invention project does not generate higher than normal rates of withdrawal, drops, or failing grades—in fact, we see lower such rates than we might expect for courses with similar profiles. Second, we show that overall course-grade distributions are strong for students across class standing and areas of academic specialization. While high grades distributions could be seen as an indicator of lenient evaluation rather than student success, several factors contradict that analysis. First, we note that at the University of Arizona grades are normed across multiple graduate teaching assistants rather than controlled by a single instructor. Second, because of the length and complexity of the invented language project, students who successfully complete the course have done so by developing a complex writing assignment requiring four or more rounds of revision and requiring at least ten pages, often more. Third, because a project of passing quality will necessarily include student-generated language examples using the International Phonetic Alphabet and morpheme-by-morpheme glossing, we can attest that students who earn a passing grade have necessarily mastered complex technical skills at a rate we do not generally find in analogous courses without the project.

13.4.1 Rates of withdraw, drop, or fail

The summary in (7) shows the incidence of students enrolled in relevant courses at the University of Arizona who did not finish the semester with a passing grade.[13] The categories of most concern for those interested in teaching with invented language include students who finish but do not pass, combined with those who withdraw from the class. When course withdrawals are combined with failing marks, the rate of unsuccessful completion is 16.5%,

---

[12] Data from SIU are not included because the project has not yet been implemented across multiple offerings on that campus.

[13] Note that offerings included online courses. Overall, online courses tend to have slightly to moderately higher withdraw-drop-fail rates than in-person courses (Angelino et al. 2007). Online courses targeted at non-traditional student populations, such as the Arizona Online campus offerings, may tend to have higher rates of this sort as well.

which is slightly lower than the typical withdraw-drop-fail rate, which was about 20% for courses in this category over this timeframe at our institution.[14]

(7)   University of Arizona students not earning a passing grade 2013–18
   a. total number of students not earning a passing grade: 499 (19%)
   b. finished the course with a failing grade: 275 (10.6%)
   c. withdrew from the course: 152 (5.9%)
   d. withdrew from the University, were registered for audit, or did not receive an official grade: 69 (3.6%)

The summary in (8) shows similar patterns for courses offered at Purdue Fort Wayne. The majority of students enrolled in the course finish with a passing grade.[15] However, a small percentage withdraw from the course (8.3%); while an even smaller number receive a failing grade (4.6%). The overall rate of withdraw-drop-fail at Purdue Fort Wayne is lower than that at Arizona, and the rate for this course is not higher than those of other courses targeted at the same student population.

(8)   Purdue University Fort Wayne students not earning a passing grade 2013–18
   a. total number of students not earning a passing grade: 125 (13.5%)
   b. finished the course with a failing grade: 43 (4.6%)
   c. withdrew from the course: 77 (8.3%)
   d. withdrew from the University, were registered for audit, or did not receive an official grade: 5 (0.5%)

13.4.2 Grades distributions across student populations

For students who complete the course with a passing grade at the University of Arizona, Figure 13.1 shows that we find similar grades distributions regardless of modality of instruction (in-person main campus, main campus online, and Arizona Online). In all populations, a plurality of students are highly successful.

Furthermore, Figure 13.2 shows that grades distributions do not vary much across class standing at Arizona; crucially, freshmen are nearly as successful

---

[14] Institutional efforts at improving retention rates may be moving this number downward, and the trend in our course has been that this rate has generally decreased over time.
[15] These numbers include both sections that used the project and sections that did not.

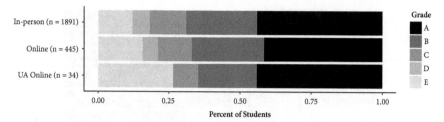

Figure 13.1 Distribution of grades by mode of instruction

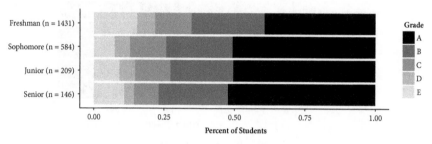

Figure 13.2 Distribution of grades by class standing

as upperclassmen, and in all categories the most common outcome is a grade of A.

To explore variability in Arizona students' success based on academic interests, Figure 13.3 presents the distribution of grades by the academic college of students' first major. This is not a straightforwardly interpretable listing, because academic departments at the University of Arizona are not necessarily housed in the college reflecting their scholarly tradition,[16] but the data indicate that students with a wide variety of academic interests are overwhelmingly successful in language invention at the introductory level.

At Purdue Fort Wayne during the Fall 2011, Spring 2012, and Fall 2012 terms, a formal assessment was conducted to assess the impact of the project on student performance. Student scores on the second exam of the course, chosen because it occurs ten weeks into the sixteen-week semester, after students have completed a significant portion of the coursework and project, were compared across the three semesters. The only difference in material and instruction was the use of the project in the Spring 2012 and Fall 2012

---

[16] For example, the English, History, and Philosophy departments are housed in the College of Social and Behavioral Sciences rather than the College of Humanities, while the Psychology Department is housed in the College of Science rather than the College of Social and Behavioral Sciences.

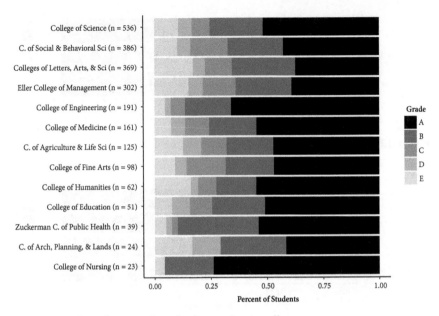

Figure 13.3 Distribution of grades by academic college

Key for Figure 13.3: "C" = College; "Colleges of Letters, Arts & Sci" = Colleges of Letters, Arts and Sciences, which is a unit that houses several interdisciplinary undergraduate programs, and is home to most students who have not yet declared a major. "C. of Agriculture & Life Sci" = College of Agriculture and Life Sciences, a unit that houses programs in Animal Sciences, Nutritional Sciences, but not traditional Biological Science majors. "C. of Arch, Planning & Lands" = College of Architecture, Planning and Landscape Architecture.

Table 13.1 Exam 2 results before and after introduction of project

	Spring 2011	Spring 2012	Fall 2012
Project	No	Yes	Yes
N	36	30	28
Mean	62.6% (F)	82.6% (B−)	89.5% (B+)
Median	77.3% (C)	86.5% (B)	93% (A−)

offerings but not in the Fall 2011 offering. The results appear in Table 13.1 and show that there was a sizeable improvement in student scores after the introduction of the project. We suspect that extra time with the IPA developing the phonetic inventory, syllable structure, and lexicon of the invented language plays a significant role in the shift in exam scores. A considerable portion of the exam involves providing the phonetic inventory for English and producing the relevant consonant and vowels charts. In addition, the exam requires students to define the syllable and provide examples of various syllable types. Together these make up more than 40% of the exam score. Naturally, we recognize correlation does not indicate causation, but we do take these results to suggest that use of a language invention project is potentially helpful to students.

13.4.3 Student perceptions of their learning

Using the invented-language project necessitates devoting a significant amount of course time and resources directly to the mechanics of language invention. While this structures instruction on basic linguistic units fairly straightforwardly, it can leave less space in the course to directly confront other important topics (language in society, language development, language endangerment, linguistic diversity, etc.) compared to a more traditional introductory class.[17] Furthermore, because the project is an unusual type of assignment—one that most students will never see again—we explore students' evaluations of the utility of the project for developing their general scholarly skills, and the relevance and durability of those skills in their subsequent academic work.

We find evidence that language invention is at least somewhat effective in improving students' understanding of key ideas in linguistics beyond the mechanics needed for creating a language, and that many students believe that the process of language invention has been helpful to them in their subsequent academic work. Furthermore, a number of students report strong positive attitudes toward the project and about their invented language itself even years after their enrollment.

The data in this section come from several sources. First, we analyze results of two obligatory in-class surveys named "pre-test" and "post-test" and both administered to all students in all University of Arizona offerings. This dataset includes responses from 2,594 students enrolled in the course between Fall 2013 and Spring 2018. The surveys are worth a nominal number of points, and students are prevented from accessing subsequent assignments until they complete them. The pre-test survey is administered at the start of term and the post-test immediately before the final exam. These surveys are identical to

---

[17] To blunt this to some extent at Purdue University Fort Wayne, students are assigned an outside reading, *Don't Sleep There are Snakes* by Daniel Everett (2008), and provided three separate occasions to discuss the readings in class in order to relate them to what is being learned in discussion. Students complete brief written summaries in which they are encouraged to relate the readings to the remaining course content.

each other for the most part, although some items were altered during the time frame of investigation. The surveys have items in two main blocks: "beliefs and knowledge about language" and "self-assessment." The first category includes questions reflecting students' knowledge about language and linguistics, as well as items inquiring about students' opinions about language-related matters. The second category asks students to respond to questions about preferred learning modalities and confidence at various academic tasks. Within each block, items were sampled from a question library (so each student saw a subset of all items), and the order of presentation within the block was randomized.

Second, we investigated long-term effects of the course by conducting a web-based survey (which we will refer to as the "follow-up survey") to students who were enrolled between Fall 2013 and Spring 2017 in a class that used the invented-language project at the University of Arizona or that at Purdue University Fort Wayne.[18] Email invitations were sent via students' official university email addresses and included approximately 2,200 successful contacts.[19] Survey participation was anonymous, and there was no incentive for participation—as a result, response rates were predictably low ($N = 195$, <1%). The follow-up survey contained many of the same items as the pre-test/ post-test surveys, as well as a set of items asking after some demographic information and students' reflections on the utility of the project for them. Like the pre-test/post-test surveys, these blocks sampled items from a larger library, and the order of presentation of items within each block was random-ized. Unlike the pre-test/post-test surveys, the order of presentation of the blocks was also randomized. Responses strongly suggest considerable positive bias in survey respondents—overwhelmingly, those who responded were those who remembered and enjoyed the project anywhere from one semester to five years post-enrollment.

In the data that follow, we present findings from the pre-test/post-test surveys, as well as from the follow-up survey. Importantly, the pre-test/post-test survey results were the only ones subjected to significance testing. We used Pearson's Chi-squared test with Yates' continuity correction on contingency tables of counts of responses to each question/answer pair in the pre- and post-tests to test the null hypothesis that the distribution of responses is the same between the two surveys.[20] Here we will discuss only comparisons that

---

[18] SIU is was not included because the project had not yet been offered in multiple courses.

[19] By "successful contacts," we mean email invitations that did not come back as no longer in use or misdirected.

[20] Because considering multiple comparisons inflates the probability of Type I error, we adjusted our critical p-value using the fairly conservative Bonferroni method in which $p_{adjusted} = \alpha/m$, where α is the

Table 13.2 Student characteristics

	Yes	No	Other	Total
Traditional	153	14	4	171
First-Gen	43	122	6	171
Online	20	149	0	169
Honors	57	106	6	169

achieved significance. We present follow-up survey response distributions for informal comparison only.[21]

Our results do not speak to the question of whether language invention in particular is the engine of any change we see, and we cannot compare these results to introductory linguistics classes for general education students that use other approaches. Instead, we demonstrate that language invention is at least not inconsistent with student learning in these areas for these student populations.

13.4.3.1 Follow-up survey respondents' characteristics

The respondents to the follow-up survey are not necessarily representative of the student population, so we describe relevant characteristics of this subgroup here. Students' responses about their status and course modality are listed in Table 13.2.[22]

Table 13.3 summarizes respondents' identifications of the areas of their academic major(s). To accommodate students with double and triple majors, respondents were allowed to select multiple options.

The following sections discuss results from pre-test/post-test survey comparisons.

13.4.3.2 Beliefs about language and languages

Students often come to linguistics believing that English is exceptional in its richness and complexity. This belief is often extended to include other languages, particularly those of Western Europe, but not necessarily minoritized or Indigenous languages, or those found outside of Europe. Introductory linguistics classes aim to help students understand the richness and expressive

---

desired probability of a Type I error for the entire set of comparisons and m is the number of comparisons made. As we made thirteen comparisons and desired the traditional $\alpha = 0.05$, our critical p-value was $0.05/13 = 0.00385$.

[21] Low response rates and vastly different sample sizes render any systematic comparison of pre-test/post-test data with follow-up survey data invalid.

[22] Rows will not add to 195 because these items were optional.

Table 13.3 Student-reported areas of major(s)

Area	Count	%
Social and Behavioral Sciences	60	30%
Natural Sciences	33	17%
Engineering	22	11%
Humanities	21	11%
Other	20	10%
Business or Management	12	6%
Fine Arts	11	5%
Education	6	5%
Public Health	4	2%
Nursing	4	2%
Pharmacy	4	2%
Optical Sciences	1	.5%
Total	198	101.5%

power inherent in all human language and to realize that such characteristics are not reserved for linguistic varieties with cultural prestige. This misconception is often evident early in the language-invention project when students create a cultural context for their invented language, with students often applying descriptors such as "simple" or "primitive" to their own invented languages and peoples. The many rounds of subsequent feedback and revision provide an opportunity for the instructional team to engage with this issue. Figures 13.4, 13.5, and 13.6 show students' responses to statements making (false) assertions about the relative complexity or advancement of different languages, and the related claim that some ideas are only expressible in a particular language, or that the language we speak limits our ability to understand the world. All show that post-test responses are significantly less friendly to such claims.

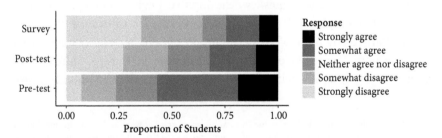

Figure 13.4 Responses to the prompt *Some languages are more advanced than others*

The distribution of answers between pre-test and post-test changed significantly ($\chi^2(4) = 110.44$, $p < 0.0001$).

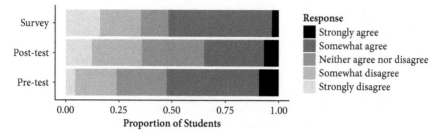

Figure 13.5 Responses to the prompt *Our ability to understand the world is constrained by the categories given us by the particular language(s) we speak*
The distribution of answers between pre-test and post-test changed significantly ($\chi^2(4) = 46.82$, $p < 0.0001$).

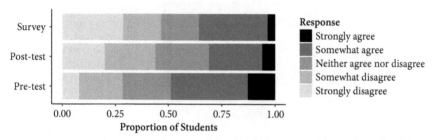

Figure 13.6 Responses to the prompt *English is more complicated than most languages*
Distribution of answers between pre-test and post-test changed significantly ($\chi^2(4) = 56.93, p < 0.0001$).

In terms of relationships between languages, introductory study of linguistics should generate an appreciation for differences between languages in terms of how information is packaged into individual lexical items, and language invention seems to help in this regard. For example, students were initially friendlier to the idea that language creation might involve word-by-word mapping from English than they were by the end of term, as shown in Figure 13.7. This may be related TO improved understanding of how linguistic organization can vary across languages, e.g. what is expressed in a single word in one language may be encoded phrasally or as a bound morpheme in others. Alternatively, students may have gained an insight into the work that is done by grammatical structures—not merely words.

Figure 13.8 shows a shift in students' opinions about a genuinely contestable claim regarding the possibility of 'perfect' translation. Students were significantly more likely to respond "neither agree nor disagree" to this statement at

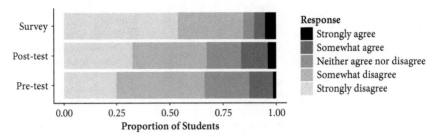

Figure 13.7 Responses to the prompt *Inventing a language mostly involves translating English words into made-up words*

The distribution of answers between pre-test and post-test changed significantly ($\chi^2(4) = 18.36, p < 0.002$).

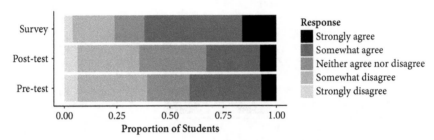

Figure 13.8 Responses to the prompt *Truly accurate translation between languages is impossible*

The distribution of answers between pre-test and post-test changed significantly ($\chi^2(4) = 23.34, p < 0.0002$).

the end of the term than they were at the beginning. We think that it is useful to consider the value of linguistics courses in undermining spurious certainty about language, and we see this move as positive.

13.4.3.3 Learning linguistic concepts
Language invention requires students to analyze linguistic expressions at a micro-level, and we find that students report improved confidence in their ability to recognize and manipulate various structures. For example, Figures 13.9–13.11 show students' confidence in their ability to recognize morphosyntactic structures increased from pre- to post-test.

13.4.3.4 Self-assessment of scholarly skills
The project requires students to invest significant effort in word-processing, including using non-standard characters, manipulating line and paragraph spacing, aligning text, and using footnotes and automatic page-numbering.

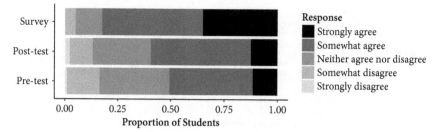

Figure 13.9 Responses to the prompt *I can usually break complicated new words into their component parts, and figure out what they mean*

The distribution of answers between pre-test and post-test changed significantly ($\chi^2(4) = 19.82, p < 0.001$).

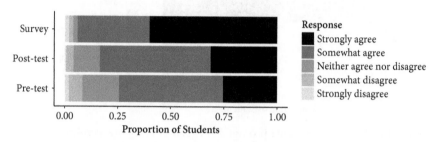

Figure 13.10 Responses to the prompt *I can readily identify words in sentences by their parts of speech (i.e. 'noun', 'verb', 'adjective', etc.)*

Distribution of answers between pre-test and post-test changed significantly ($\chi^2(4) = 21.28, p < 0.0003$).

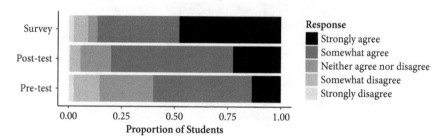

Figure 13.11 Responses to the prompt *I know how to identify the main parts of a sentence (i.e. 'subject', 'direct object', 'predicate')*

The distribution of answers between pre-test and post-test changed significantly ($\chi^2(4) = 75.68, p < 0.0001$).

Additionally, we ask students to track their feedback on drafts and to summarize their responses to that feedback, which builds general organizational and writing skills. We find some evidence that students experience growth in such transferrable academic skills as a result of their work in language invention.

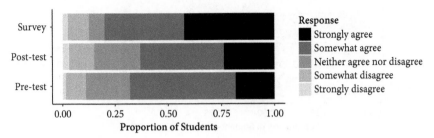

Figure 13.12 Responses to the prompt *I am a well-organized student*
The distribution of answers between pre-test and post-test changed significantly
($\chi^2(4) = 19.67, p < 0.001$).

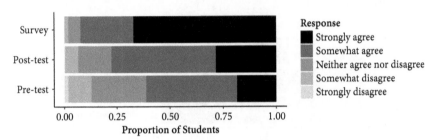

Figure 13.13 Responses to the prompt *I am good at using my word-processing program to format documents in different ways*
The distribution of answers between the pre-test and post-test changed significantly
($\chi^2(4) = 53.74, p < 0.0001$).

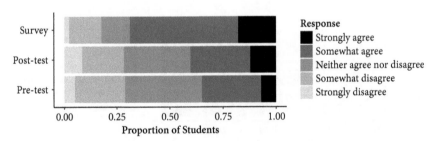

Figure 13.14 Responses to the prompt *I like working on big, multi-part projects*
The distribution of answers between pre-test and post-test changed significantly
($\chi^2(4) = 22.00, p < 0.0003$).

Figure 13.12 shows a slight decrease in students' self-assessments as "well-organized" at the end compared to the beginning of the term. Figure 13.13 shows that students see improvement in their ability to work with the formatting requirements inherent in the project. Figure 13.14 shows polarization of students' attitudes toward long, complex projects, with fewer students ambivalent about the idea by the post-test. The latter results hopefully reflect a positive reality check for students who are unaccustomed to managing complex projects.

13.4.4 Lasting effects

Finally, we report students' reflections in the follow-up survey about the project. We share them as evidence that the project is meaningful and memorable to at least some students, and could therefore contribute to long-lasting connections between students and the study of linguistics.

The comments presented in (9) are representative of some of the more positive reactions expressed by survey-takers. Respondents reflected on their emotional connections with the project, both at the time and later on, and a number of them noted their belief that doing the project had relatively durable positive effects for them.

(9)   Students' reflections on language invention
   a. "Inventing a language was something I dreamed of as a little kid."
   b. "It was one of my favorite projects I've ever done. With other classes, the papers I write mean nothing after the due date. With this one, there was always room for improvement, and I had something I was really proud of in the end."
   c. "I believe that the course has immensely helped me communicate more accurately with both spoken and signed languages. Creating my own language enabled me to more fully comprehend language. I believe that while it is a bit more work, as a writer this class propelled my comprehension tenfold."
   d. "Having to apply course concepts to invent a language, rather than just seeing them applied in existing languages helped deepen my understanding of the material."
   e. "I learned more about language in that one class than in 15 years of studying foreign languages. I think the project played a major role in keeping the class engaging, and in making the lessons relevant."

When asked to assess the effectiveness of the project, participants answered as noted in Figure 13.15. Respondents were most positive about the effectiveness of the project in helping them better understand language. Over 80% of respondents agreed or strongly agreed that the project was also effective in helping them develop their scholarly skills and organize complex projects.

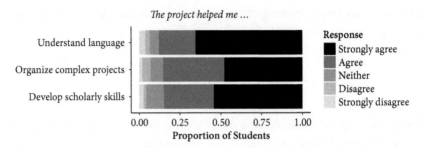

Figure 13.15 Responses about the effectiveness of the project

13.4.4.1 Reflecting on length and complexity

As noted, language invention—at least as we implement it—requires more writing of students than most other freshman-level general education courses, as well as management of a relatively complex, multistage project. Follow-up survey respondents confirm that the project was longer and more complex than they had expected, but they largely found this to be a positive aspect of the class. Representative comments on this topic are presented in (10).

(10) Students' reflections on the effects of the length and complexity of the project:
   a. "That linguistics class was one of the first I took at the university and I really felt like the project whipped me into shape."
   b. "My final field report ended up being about 40 pages long, which was the longest assignment I had ever written at the time. I remember feeling very proud of myself as well as the language that I had created, and all of the work that I put into it during that semester. I would say that a project like this will help me immensely in the upcoming year, as I complete my senior capstone and honors thesis before I graduate! I will definitely use the pacing of the invented language project as a model for how I would like to approach my research going into other large-scale projects."

A large majority of respondents reported that the project was longer than a typical class assignment (73% agreement) and almost half (44%) reported that it was more difficult than a typical class project. Nevertheless, most (70 and 72% respectively) disagreed or strongly disagreed with the statements "the project was too long," and "the project was too complicated," as reported in Figure 13.16. Students' comments often addressed this tension, noting that the

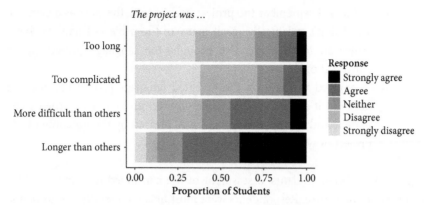

Figure 13.16 Responses about the complexity and length of the project

project was memorable in part because it was relatively involved—but that at least in retrospect they recognized value in the challenge it posed.

The length and complexity of the project are not without problems for some students, however. A few survey respondents provided comments that reflect frustration and disconnection with the project. The following are representative of these.

(11)   Examples of negative student comments:
    a. "Creating my own language was frustrating and futile. I went out of my way to warn people against taking LING150 and I know others did so as well."
    b. "Worst class ever."

13.4.4.2 Students' reflections on the longer-term relevance of the project

Many of the students who completed the follow-up survey expressed continued connection to the project and class, even one to four years after their enrollment. Representative comments are presented in (12).

(12)   Students' reflections on the lasting relevance of the project itself:
    a. "Though I'm not amazing at it, I can still read IPA pretty well. I think it's a useful skill. The class was easily one of my favorites. The project was a brilliant way to teach students how language works."
    b. "This class was the reason I pursued a minor in Linguistics. I still value the lessons I learned in this class, and continue to use the skills I gained."

    c. "At least I remember the project itself! I took the class as a Gen-Ed, and I don't specifically recall many of the projects I had for them. However, to this day, I've brought the language project up in conversation."

    d. "I enjoyed working on the invented language project because not only did it allow me to challenge my creativity but I learned to be patient and let my ideas flow. I was pleased by the outcome of my project, it was worth any obstacles along the way."

Figure 13.17 shows students' assessment of the continued relevance of skills acquired in the course. Respondents were most likely to identify the academic skills they acquired through the project as being of continued relevance, with more than 70% agreeing or strongly agreeing with the relevant statement. Perhaps not surprisingly, the least likely skillset to be identified as still useful was the linguistic skills, but even these were still relevant to more than 60% of respondents. The technical skills required by the project (for example, document formatting, use of special characters and layout features, etc.) were seen as durable by a similar proportion of respondents.

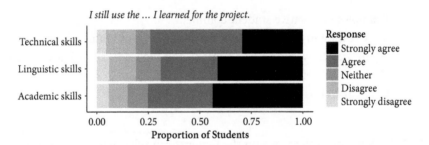

Figure 13.17 Responses about continued relevance of the project

13.4.4.3 Students' pride in their work
One survey item that stood out in analysis was the statement "I was really proud of the language I created." As illustrated in Figure 13.18, approximately 77% of responding students agreed or strongly agreed with that statement, and only 11% disagreed or strongly disagreed. Uneven response rates don't allow us to significance-test for effects of student characteristics (Figure 13.19) or students' majors (Figure 13.20, which includes only major categories for which

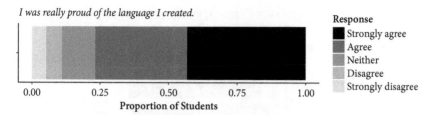

Figure 13.18 Responses to the statement "I was really proud of the language I created" across all respondents

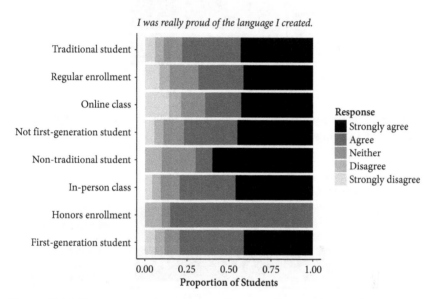

Figure 13.19 Responses to the statement "I was really proud of the language I created" by student characteristic

more than five students responded), but there is no subset of respondents of whom fewer than 60% expressed pride in the output of their work.

Finally, respondents reflected on their experiences with the project. Approximately 84% reported enjoying the process of language creation, and 65% said that they shared the project they created with friends or family, as noted in Figure 13.21. We suspect that this reflects a level of enthusiasm that students might not experience for a more traditional class project. The potential for language invention to generate interest outside of the classroom may be one of the benefits of using this kind of project.

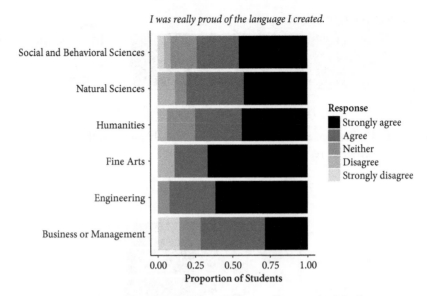

Figure 13.20 Responses to the statement "I was really proud of the language I created" by student's program area

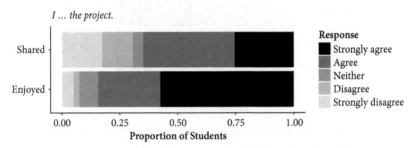

Figure 13.21 Responses to the statements "I enjoyed creating my own language" and "I shared my language with friends or family"

13.5 Conclusions

We've reported on the use of language invention in introductory linguistics classes at three institutions, with a very different time depth at each school. The University of Arizona's linguistics department developed the first offerings of the courses we report on, and the project has been implemented there for more than 4,000 students over a decade. The project was transported more recently to Purdue University Fort Wayne, where it has been modified to serve the needs of a different student cohort. Most recently, the project is being implemented at Southern Illinois University. Where the project has been established, we have convergent evidence that it is a useful way to introduce students to linguistics, even if they choose not to continue in the field.

One of the motivations to use language invention in our course was to see whether doing so would increase the number of students who major or minor in linguistics. While we can't be sure that this move was a contributor to the growth of our undergraduate programs, the University of Arizona program did undergo significant growth—nearly doubling—during these years. In the case of the linguistics minor program and the Teaching English as a New Language Program at Purdue University Fort Wayne, the growth was more than double. Anecdotally, students do sometimes report that the invented language project caused them to consider a major in linguistics.

(13) Students' reports of the influence on the project on later academic decisions:
  a. "When I was enrolled in this class I was undecided in my major but after completing the project and the course, I changed my major to Linguistics with a minor in Anthropology and it opened a lot of doors for me. I did sociolinguistic research as well as linguistic anthropology research with a professor of Anthropology at U of A. I also did a preceptorship with her in 1 of her linguistic anthropology courses and 2 of her anthropology courses on race. This class completely shaped the rest of my undergrad career at U of A. Furthermore, my degrees have allowed me to work in diverse fields after gradation including interpretation/translation as well as human rights work."
  b. "It led to me minoring in linguistics and eventually declaring a double degree in Linguistics and SLHS [Speech, Language and Hearing Sciences] and I will complete an honors thesis with Linguistics over the next 2 semesters."

While we see utility for language invention in growing our program, there are also risks in using a project like this for introductory students outside of the major. Language invention requires significant writing and is technically challenging. While our course has excellent success rates compared to its competitors, we know that it suffers in some environments from student perceptions of excessive workload compared to courses that have fewer or simpler assignments. At both Arizona and Purdue we have anecdotal evidence from students and advisers that the perception of our course as 'hard' makes it less appealing to some entering freshmen than other courses that fulfill the same requirement.[23] Impressionistically, however, the frequency of negative comments from students about the invented language project is lower than we find in other courses fulfilling similar requirements.

Language invention is a promising way to engage with and effectively teach introductory linguistics students, majors and non-majors alike, about the workings of natural human language. A language invention project can be effectively scaled for use in both very small and very large courses across various teaching platforms. The highly customizable nature of the project makes it versatile and flexible enough to use with diverse student populations and with different institutional and course goals, and the range of technical tasks involved in language invention make the skills students acquire transferrable to non-linguistic disciplines. Finally, this type of non-traditional project can generate long-lasting connections between students and linguistics.

Acknowledgments

Thanks to our reviewers and colleagues who contributed to this volume. Thanks also to staff in the University Information Technology offices and Institutional Research at University of Arizona and Purdue University Fort Wayne. Most importantly, thanks to the students and Graduate Teaching Assistants who have participated in the courses reported on here. Any errors are our own.

---

[23] This reputation may also be part of the reason for the course's success with students who are likely to declare a linguistics major later on.

14

Extraterrestrial message construction

Guidelines for the use of xenolinguistics in the classroom

Sheri Wells-Jensen and Kimberly Spallinger

14.1 Introduction

First, it was the moon. Then, it was Mars.

For countless generations, we humans have been casting our hopes into the night sky, searching for other worlds like our world which might nurture other beings like us. The first notions of how to communicate across the distances between these worlds were audacious in spirit and very large in scope. In the 19th century, there was a plan to carve a giant proof of the Pythagorean theorem into stretches of Siberian tundra. Nikola Tesla suggested flashing a series of lights to catch the Martian eye and later advocated listening with more complex equipment. Another scheme called for miles of ditches to be dug through the Sahara, filled with oil, and set afire, like an interplanetary super-sized neon sign (Oberhaus 2019).

The idea motivating these proposed communications was that we and our alien neighbors would have some things in common: concepts of basic geometry, the understanding that precisely drawn shapes do not occur naturally, some analog of visual perception, and some interest in gazing into the night sky in the first place. They would see our displays and deduce that intelligent life existed on Earth. None of these quixotic plans to send a message ever came to fruition, alas, but we still watched, scouring the Lunar and Martian surfaces with increasingly powerful telescopes, hoping to detect some sign of their civilization, or better, some deliberate signal from their culture to ours.

In 1924, when Mars made its closest approach to Earth in over a century, many felt sure that the advanced civilization living there would seize the astronomical opportunity to contact Earth by radio. Both civilian and military receivers poised themselves to hear the message, and for a few anxious

Sheri Wells-Jensen and Kimberly Spallinger, *Extraterrestrial message construction: Guidelines for the use of xenolinguistics in the classroom* In: *Language Invention in Linguistics Pedagogy*. First edition. Edited by: Jeffrey Punske, Nathan Sanders, and Amy V. Fountain, Oxford University Press (2020). © Sheri Wells-Jensen and Kimberly Spallinger.
DOI: 10.1093/oso/9780198829874.003.0014

moments, a few thought perhaps they had done just that (consult White 2003 for a summary of events during late August 1924).

Cocconi and Morrison (1959) kicked off the era of modern SETI (Search for Extraterrestrial Intelligence) with the publication of an article in *Nature* suggesting specific guidelines for receiving messages from other planets, including, they hoped, Mars.

Radio was chosen because it is clear that for the foreseeable future, the tremendous distances between the stars make a face to "face" encounter with ET extraordinarily unlikely.

In 1960, following Cocconi and Morrison's suggestions, Frank Drake employed the radio telescope in Green Bank, West Virginia, to listen to two nearby stars, hoping to detect something clearly artificial. The attempt, dubbed Project Ozma, was the first of many similar endeavors. The first known instance of active SETI by radio, i.e. sending an intentional message rather than listening for one, was a brief radio signal broadcast from the Arecibo Radio Telescope in 1974 (Oberhaus 2019). Since then, dozens of serious and not-so-serious broadcasts have been made, including various kinds of codes, pictures, and even a Doritos commercial. (For a listing of messages sent, consult Quast 2018, and for a compelling discussion of whether or not it is advisable or ethical to send such messages, see Johnson 2017, Shostak 2015, 2017, SETI.ORG, and METI.ORG.)

This chapter will discuss how the creation and analysis of signals intended for extraterrestrial scientists can be usefully employed in teaching basic linguistic concepts to students on Earth. Linguistics instructors are continually searching for ways to engage students in introductory courses, and we have found that the data set reproduced here, which we have used with slight modifications in both graduate and undergraduate linguistics courses, enables students to expand their perception of language and gain a better understanding of the cross-disciplinary possibilities that the study of linguistics provides.

14.2 Some introductory student discussion topics: Why signals are difficult

14.2.1 The importance of context

Even when two human conversational partners have no language in common, it is possible to reach some basic understandings quickly. Let's take, for example, a speaker of Spanish and a speaker of Chinese. Meeting perhaps by chance at a small café, our potential conversational partners employ reassuring smiles, gestures, and vocal intonation to affirm a friendly intent and a desire to begin to communicate. This is accomplished in seconds. A quick try at an exchange of greetings confirms that the two do not share a language. To begin, the Chinese speaker might hold up a cup and say *béizi*, and the Spanish speaker could reply with *taza*, if the two intend to try to learn two languages at once. Alternatively, one might attempt to copy the other's pronunciation, and they will assume roles of teacher and learner. The Chinese speaker might then proceed to spoon (*xiǎo*) and knife (*dáozi*). Despite their differences, these two particular dinner partners share an enormous amount of cultural and cognitive content:

- an intent to communicate;
- the same basic body plan, so they both understand acts of lifting and drinking;
- a compatible theory of mind, and knowledge of how to direct the attention of a conversational partner;
- basic emotions and the ability to demonstrate non-aggressiveness, humor, confusion, and frustration;
- a linguistic system from which they can deduce that the other's language can be learned;
- some idea of how languages are taught;
- an understanding that indicating an object is, in this context, most likely a request for a noun naming that object;
- a cultural understanding that these objects are appropriately placed in this context, and that, although the *dáozi* could be a weapon in some contexts, it is not intended as a weapon here;
- notions such as actions and descriptors and the associated ability to infer when a pantomime calls for an action rather than a noun;
- the (often unconscious) concept of some complexity within grammars and what might be present there, so that indicators such as plurality, deictics, and case exist, but typically are not addressed until some groundwork has been laid;
- immediate access to the same physical surroundings, offering a potentially limitless source of new words and phrases to be learned;
- the ability to manipulate that same environment in real time; and
- the conversational implicatures that allow repetitions potentially to be understood as correction (from the teacher) and attempts to learn (from the learner).

Given all these advantages, the two might be able to build the necessary mutual understanding to hold a simple conversation (see Everett 2016 and Pinker 1994 for two different approaches to the issue of shared cultural norms). However, this scenario has almost nothing in common with an interstellar message where there is no way to confirm shared cognitive constructs and no access to shared context of any kind. All that exists is the message itself, with no readily available referents.

Thus, having students discuss what would be required for communication with extraterrestrial intelligence is an excellent way to highlight some of the assumptions that make communication possible. We generally employ demonstrations of monolingual language teaching or field methods and techniques as a way of beginning this conversation.

We have also used activities that encourage students to explore their intuitive knowledge about language. One that has worked well is an adaptation of a simulation from *New Ways in Teaching Culture* (Fantini 1997) in which small groups of students separately create naming languages and send ambassadors to other groups to try to communicate. Afterward, they discuss what it means to know a language and what assumptions they made both about what it means to know a language and how they could tell if messages were received.

14.2.2 Pictures

When first introduced to the possibility of extraterrestrial message construction, students often suggest that the message should consist of pictures. However, Oberhaus (2019) reminds us that how things are drawn is culturally mediated, e.g. conventional two-dimensional representations of three-dimensional objects. Further, Kershenbaum (2019) also reminds us that intelligent ETs might not share our sensory apparatus, rendering images useless. Photographs or moving images have the additional disadvantage that the recipient would have to construct very specific pieces of technology to access them; once obtained, they still might not be comprehensible. Therefore, it is implausible that sending movies into space will solve the communication problem.

14.2.3 Why use math and science(|)

After students have considered these possibilities, they can then be introduced to the use of math and science messages in construction. Hogben (1963) and

Freudenthal (1959) are among the many proponents of sending messages that begin with mathematics. They separately constructed a series of sequenced statements (or lines of code), which began with simple arithmetic and led eventually to assertions about the physical sciences and humankind.

The argument is that any civilization capable of detecting our signal would have to have built some type of advanced radio. So although we can make no hypotheses about what their body plan or cultural rules might be like, we know they built that radio, and this implies a certain competence with basic math and physics. Their systems of counting or their understanding of these theories might differ from ours, but they were able to build functioning technology that is compatible with our own. So that's a starting place in common.

Because the use of xenolinguistics (extraterrestrial message construction) in a classroom setting is primarily pedagogical and specifically linguistic, the system introduced in Section 14.3 is a good deal simpler than either of these extant systems (consult Shklovski and Sagan 1966 and Vakoch 2011 for further discussion of message construction).

14.3 The message

We present the data for analysis here, for the benefit of those who might choose to work the problem set themselves before proceeding to the discussion.

14.3.1 Instructions

In the data in (1)–(12), numbers indicate their usual interpretation as numbers. Items in caps are the arbitrarily assigned "words" whose meaning you must interpret.

Thus, in (1a), '5' and '2' mean 'five' and 'two', respectively, while *SAG* and *BLAR* are words whose meaning must be deduced based on what is plausible in the given context. Assume that groupings of lines here are separated by longer pauses when this message is sent. Think of it as perhaps a pause between thoughts.

(A set of options for matching, provided in Section 14.6, can be used, but more advanced and interesting discussions can occur if students must fill in their own answers. Limiting choices might be advisable, though, if the particular group of students expresses any degree of wariness about mathematics.) To assist those who wish to work the problem on their own, the list of choices for matching appears just above the conclusion section. The answers to the problem are in Section 14.8.

(1)   a. 5 SAG 2 BLAR 7
      b. 9 SAG 4 BLAR 13
      c. 6 SAG 7 BLAR 13
      d. 1 SAG 1 BLAR 2

(2)   a. 8 VLIP 3 BLAR 5
      b. 43 VLIP 40 BLAR 3

(3)   a. 6 SI 4 BLAR 24
      b. 65 SI 3 BLAR 195

(4)   a. 8 VLIP 8 BLAR TOF
      b. 64 SI TOF BLAR TOF

(5)   a. 45 KA 2 BLAR 22 NIM 5
      b. 19 KA 4 BLAR 4 11 NIM 75

(6)   a. 5 BOOM BLAR 25
      b. 10 NIM 3 BOOM BLAR 106 NIM TOF 9

(7)   a. 19 SAG 2 VLIP 14 SI 6 BLAR 42
      b. 2 BOOM BOOM BOOM BOOM BLAR 32

(8)   a. 10 KA 3 BLAR 3 NIM 3 DU
      b. 10 KA 7 BLAR 1 NIM 42857 DU
      c. 3 NIM 1415926 DU FI BLAR GOM

(9)   a. 4 SAG 1 I BLAR 19
      b. 2 SAG 5 I BLAR 6
      c. 5 BOOM I BLAR 29
      d. TOF I BLAR 17

(10) e. 1 8 5 10 9 HU 10
      f. 100 84 6 1 222 19 HU 222
      g. 4 85 19 HU 85
      h. 6 1 4 5 HU 6

(11)   GOM SI LU BOOM BLAR WIF

(12)   HU WIF BLAR DU

First, fill in the blanks in (13) or use the options for matching in Section 14.6. There are several possibilities on the list for matching as distractions, and none are used more than once. After this, translate line (12) as best you can.

(13)   BLAR _____   HU _____   SAG _____
       BOOM _____   I _____   SI _____
       DU _____   KA _____   TOF _____
       FI _____   LU _____   VLIP _____
       GOM _____   NIM _____   WIF _____

14.4 Pedagogical use of the message

Any linguistic concept that can be taught with natural language data or with invented language data can be illustrated using this kind of interstellar message construction.

The class will, of course, need to be supported by a reputable introductory linguistics text; we remain steadfastly agnostic here about which of the myriad available possibilities would be best. It might also be suitable to have on hand a few brief, cogent references on aspects of basic physics. In this regard, we recommend Bynum (2012) and Sagan (1987). We also recommend that, whenever practical, concepts taught using this or similar constructed message data be reinforced by providing examples from one or more natural languages. Obviously, instructors will want to adapt the problem to play to the strengths and needs of different groups of students, perhaps increasing the amount of repetition, increasing or decreasing the difficulty of the arithmetic, or making other changes.

14.4.1 Phonetics, phonology, and encoding

Depending on the level of scientific sophistication of the students, it would be possible to begin by discussing how a message would be encoded. Freudenthal (1960) uses binary numbers, for example, but a simpler (if less elegant) system might use non-arbitrary indexing for numbers (one short pulse equals 1, two pulses 2, five pulses for 5, etc.), and arbitrary groups of pulses of other lengths for the words. If desirable, a kind of phonetics could be designed, built from features such as pulse duration and frequency modulation.

A set of "phonemes" could be established, complete with allophonic variation. However, if the students are not already reasonably well-versed in the necessary knowledge about electromagnetism, this would probably prove unnecessarily frustrating. In any case, it might be prudent to return to this question after the other sections. (For a reasonably accessible account of the science for doing this, consult Walmsle 2015 and Bova 1983). For other students, it might be preferable to skip this step almost entirely.

14.4.2 Morphosyntactic and word order analysis

The first thing that can be taught using these data is the general technique of language data analysis. In (1), students have to determine a meaning for both *SAG* and *BLAR* by examining the relationships between the numbers given. Most students will probably swiftly identify that *SAG* means something like 'plus' and *BLAR* means something like 'equals'. In this case, that is the intent. If, however, a focus of the assignment is to teach word-order variation or to demonstrate ways in which languages can be unlike English, the data can be arranged so that the problems read right to left. This means that the first line of the data (1a) might be glossed as either '5 plus 2 equals 7' or, if operations move from right to left, '7 minus 2 equals 5'.

It is only at line (2a) that one can be sure which is intended. Building on this initial analysis, students move through the lines of the message just as they would through lines of traditional language data.

14.4.3 Polysemy

If students are not given fixed choices for the meanings of the operators in the lines of data but instead asked to produce meanings of their own, this can generate a discussion of polysemy.

For example, *SAG* might be initially given any of the following meanings, any of which could be accurate if only the lines in (1) are considered: 'plus', 'and', 'together with'. *BLAR* could be given any of these initial meanings: 'equals', 'becomes', 'is', 'true'. It is possible to devise a set of lines where the difference between 'and' and 'plus' would be clear, as in (14):

(14)   3 SAG 5 SAG 7 SAG 11 SAG 13 BLAR ZOOP

If *SAG* means 'plus', then *ZOOP* would be '39'. However, if *SAG* means 'and' and *BLAR* means 'is/are', then *ZOOP* could mean a great many things, such as 'odd', 'increasing', or 'prime', depending on subsequent clarification.

This might also be a good time to talk about polysemy across languages: how, for example, English *back* has both 'behind' and 'rear surface of the body roughly from shoulders to hips' as polysemous meanings, while Spanish *espalda* has only the second.

14.4.4 Information packaging

In (2) and (3), the students learn the forms for 'minus' and 'multiplied by'. It is at this point that one could discuss the packaging of information across languages. 'Minus' by default follows the syntactic rules for 'plus', but when working with multiplication, English chooses from two different syntactic forms: *six times seven* and *six multiplied by seven*.

14.4.5 The arbitrariness of language

In (4), a word for 'zero' is introduced. This is necessary given the rudimentary way the message encodes numbers, as each number is non-arbitrarily represented by a set of pulses (Section 14.4.1). It is impossible in this scenario to distinguish silence indicating 'zero' from silence indicating the space between words. Even if the phonetics section is passed over, the choice to encode zero as an arbitrary word rather than a non-arbitrary number could warrant discussion. This is an excellent time to talk more about the arbitrariness of language: indexes versus icons versus arbitrary representations (see Everett 2017 and Samuels & Punske 2019 for discussions of indexing).

14.4.6 Recursion

In (5), the decimal point is introduced, and in (6), the concept 'squared' is lexicalized. Also, in (6b), we find the first instances of existing words being combined to produce new words. The sentences in (7) are also examples of recursion, demonstrating productivity within a language. The examples of recursion provide an opportunity to discuss given versus new information and how languages choose to encode these.

14.4.7 Gricean implicatures

Just as the first four lines were grouped to set up the word order and nature of the message, pairs of lines have been used to establish a rhythm throughout. The lines in (8) are the first triple set of lines, which provides an opportunity to talk about Gricean conversational maxims. Why would this grouping be different? Does the sudden increase in the number of lines imply that the sender believes this sequence to contain information that is difficult? Important? Odd in some way? Why would the maxim of quantity be flouted here?

These lines are both an opportunity to establish *FAM* 'pi' and an explication of a carefully drawn semantic difference between *DU* and *FI*. In line (8a), *DU* could mean a variety of things: 'endless', 'repeat', 'one thing always repeating', 'always the same'. (8b) narrows that definition by showing that *DU* can refer to a pattern of numbers in addition to a single repeating number. (8c) introduces the concept 'pi' by giving a satisfyingly long string of digits after the decimal point. Or, at least, a string the *sender* considers long enough to be indicative of pi, telling the ET something about how we think. Students can then discuss, perhaps using semantic features, which quality of the never-ending, never-repeating string of digits is covered by *DU* and which by *FI*, and decide if their determination is satisfactory or if more examples are needed.

14.4.8 Negation

The lines in (9) introduce negation. Once again, the possibility that this is a more difficult concept is signaled by the number of lines given to its definition. This would be an opportune moment to look across languages for a typological analysis of possible negation systems (Dryer and Haspelmath 2013).

14.4.9 Extending definitions beyond mathematics

The lines in (10) show a slightly different syntactic structure and provide the first real example of a word that can easily be thought of as outside of the immediate mathematics territory, and line (11) offers a geometric definition that should be recognizable. The formula, like the number pi, should be shared information across species and thus possible to understand. It has been our experience that 90 percent of students do, in fact, recognize this formula (although many inaccurately assume that *LU* means 'diameter' rather than 'radius').

14.4.10 Translation

Line (12), the last line of the message, is an opportunity for students to try translation and to talk about different theories of translation. It has been our experience that answers range very widely from the reasonably literal 'the big circle is endless' to the more whimsical 'our Earth is eternal' to the somewhat weird 'big spinners never stop'.

14.5 Other activities

Just as with other language problems, students can:

- use the syntax and the forms already provided to write new lines of the message, perhaps making each of the initial pairs of lines into triplets;
- define new forms: roughly from simplest to more difficult, here are some suggestions: division, square root, exponent, first, last, smallest, prime, even, odd, infinity, disk, parentheses, question marker, if-then, until, past-present-future; and
- exchange their work to see if it can be decoded.

Students with a grounding in the hard sciences can employ numbers such as the atomic weights of specific elements, periods of pulsars, and physical properties of Earth to convey more tangible and complex concepts. Those with even more extensive training in astronomy can work with data from pulsars detectable from Earth to attempt to transmit information about our location and the time the message was sent.

14.6 List of choices for matching with distractors

big / biggest, changing continually, circle, decimal point, diameter of an object, divided by, Earth, equals, few, hypotenuse, infinite / goes on forever the same way, many, minus, mathematics, multiplied by, negation, noun, pi, plus, prime number, radius of an object, small, smallest, sphere, square, squared, star, triangle, verb, zero.

14.7 Conclusion

Working with interstellar message construction provides a unique opportunity for different groups of students to learn and utilize basic concepts in linguistics. Students who do not think of themselves as "language people" may find working with numbers to be an easier step into the field than traditional language data sets. Students who have a strong foundation in mathematics might benefit from discussions of the human-centric component in mathematics, as put forward by Lakoff and Nuñez (2000). The data could also be expanded indefinitely to supplement course textbook materials. Alternatively, it might be used as a stand-alone survey of linguistic concepts.

14.8 Answer to the problem

(15) BLAR 'equals'   HU 'bigger; biggest'   SAG 'plus'
      BOOM 'squared'   I 'negation'   SI 'times; multiplied by'
      DU 'repeats forever'   KA 'divided by'   TOF 'zero'
      FI 'always changing'   LU 'radius'   VLIP 'minus'
      GOM 'pi'   NIM 'decimal point'   WIF 'circle'

15

Artistry in language invention

Conlang pedagogy and the instructor as authority

David J. Peterson

15.1 The modern conlang class

The very first time I told a linguistics professor I was creating my own language he laughed at me. That was in 2001 at UC Berkeley. Nearly two decades later, things have changed quite a bit—capped off by my teaching a class on language creation in the linguistics department at UC Berkeley in the summer of 2017. The class is by no means an isolated phenomenon: dedicated language creation classes have been cropping up for at least a decade (Fish 2005, Barker et al. 2017). It's not much of a secret why: language creation is a creative, linguistics-adjacent activity that has received increased popular attention since the release of *Avatar* in 2009. Dipping into my old major, it's something akin to having creative writing classes in an English department. Having a course on language creation is a great way to draw otherwise uninterested or unaware undergraduates to the linguistics major—even if the course is gated (*Conlanging* 2017).

While increased enrollment is an obvious benefit to a linguistics department, what we haven't necessarily seen is increased involvement from the conlang community itself. Though individuals have been creating languages for nearly a millennium (see Sanders in this volume, Chapter 2), a community, in the sense of a group of individuals with a common interest who interact semi-frequently, didn't exist until the founding of the Conlang Listserv in the early 1990s (Peterson 2015). As more individuals came to the Internet, more conlangers found the Conlang Listserv, and the community grew. As it grew, the community's shared sense of artistry grew and expanded as well. What began as an individual endeavor had grown into a movement, with a shared terminology, classification system, and sense of aesthetics. Though no one had set out to do so, a set of best practices had emerged simply through contact

David J. Peterson, *Artistry in language invention: Conlang pedagogy and the instructor as authority* In: *Language Invention in Linguistics Pedagogy*. First edition. Edited by: Jeffrey Punske, Nathan Sanders, and Amy V. Fountain, Oxford University Press (2020). © David J. Peterson.
DOI: 10.1093/oso/9780198829874.003.0015

and communication. The activity of a few isolated individuals had become an art form.

As will happen with communities, conlangers became protective of their culture: the very practice of language creation. Some viewed language creation as an entirely private endeavor, and lamented "outsiders" even knowing about it (Brown 2016). Others threw up their hands and accepted that this was the way of things if the hobby was to become an art form and gain some kind of an outside audience. Still, many of those in the "in group," so to speak, had an active desire to at least have a hand in how language creation was discussed and shared in the outside world. This, indeed, was one of the founding principles of the Language Creation Society (2007).

As someone who was one of the original community members, I regarded the rise of the conlang class with ambivalence. With a few notable exceptions (among them classes by Matt Pearson and Sheri Wells-Jensen), conlang classes at universities were being taught by linguists (or not—cf. Fish 2005) with little to no practical conlanging experience. This isn't much of an issue if the point of a conlang class is merely to increase undergraduate interest in the linguistics major *and* such classes have little to no impact on the state of conlanging. While the former is debatable, the latter, I will argue, is not.

15.2 Conlanging as art

There are as many definitions of art as there are artists. While there may be no generic, succinct definition that will satisfy all possible art forms, I believe there is sufficient evidence that conlanging qualifies as an art form.[1] Creating a language, in its purest form, is the intentional combination of form in whatever medium one desires (e.g. phones, intonation, hand shape, body position, words, crucial ordering, etc.) and meaning. The decisions involved in creating a language crucially determine the character of the result, and need be informed by nothing more than the artist's will. While it's still debated even in the conlang community precisely how a conlang ought to be presented (cf. Brown 2013 and subsequent discussion), it's possible to appreciate every level of the art of language creation, not simply a performance of the finished product (as in dialogue in a film or a poem written in a conlang). A better way of capturing this nuance is that many language creators appreciate the

---

[1] For some discussion on this topic, see Peterson (2002), Bangs (2002), and Peterson (2015).

execution of a given grammatical function or paradigm whether or not they've ever heard the language spoken aloud or seen it used for translation.

As an anecdotal example of what I mean by execution, allow me to share my reaction to the instantiation of a tripartite marking system I encountered many years ago. For background, a tripartite marking system, as the conlanger will understand it,[2] is a system whereby the agent of a transitive verb (A), the patient of a transitive verb (P), and the subject of an intransitive verb (S) are each marked separately. A simple instantiation of this kind of system is shown in (1).

(1)   a. keli   'cat (S)'
      b. keli-s   'cat (A)'
      c. keli-n   'cat (P)'

To use the system in (1), one simply uses one of each of these forms in the precise place it's supposed to be used, without exception. It requires about as much time and effort to create as it takes to type, if not less. It's the rough equivalent of taking two slices of bread, a slice of tomato, a leaf of lettuce, and two slices of bacon out of the refrigerator, placing them each onto a platter, next to one another, and calling the result a BLT.

For a more nuanced example of a tripartite marking system, I shall introduce David Bell's ámman îar (2010), a project begun many years ago which Bell continued to work on for the rest of his life. In ámman îar, there is an overarching animacy system, whereby certain types of arguments are considered to be more animate than others. The system can be summarized as follows.

the animacy system of David Bell's ámman îar from most to least animate

1st person pronouns > 2nd person pronouns > demonstrative > nouns
3rd person and
pronouns

This is a fairly standard animacy system, and one wouldn't be surprised to find it in a natural language that was sensitive to argument animacy. Bell's ámman îar also has a case-marking system, so that both nominals and pronouns

---

[2] This distinction is nontrivial. There are many identical terms used commonly in the conlang community and in linguistics whose definitions are dissimilar. For an example, see the proliferation of the term *trigger language* and its use in the conlang community as compared to actual languages with so-called Austronesian alignment (Peterson 2006).

Table 15.1 The core cases of David Bell's ámman îar

semantic function	1st- and 2nd-person pronouns	3rd-person and demonstrative pronouns	nouns
A	–	-e	-e
S	–	–	–
P	-in	-in	–

co-occur with suffixes when instantiating certain syntactic roles. How those suffixes are used depends entirely on the animacy of the argument. The full system for core cases is summarized in Table 15.1.

In Table 15.1, we have three separate marking strategies based on animacy and three different realizations: two suffixes (/-in/ and /-e/) and the bare root. The "meaning" of the suffixes is not fixed. Rather, an interpretation is derived based on the exponence and the animacy of the noun. Thus, it's perfectly possible in ámman îar to have a transitive sentence with no marking whatsoever (e.g. a first-person pronominal agent and a nominal patient); a transitive sentence with full marking (e.g. a nominal agent and a first-person pronominal patient); a transitive sentence with standard accusative marking (e.g. a first-person pronominal agent and a third-person pronominal patient); and a transitive sentence with standard ergative marking (e.g. a third-person pronominal agent and a nominal patient). An example of each of these types is shown in (2).[3]

(2) a. ner eleθen i dais erdemiraen.   (bare A and P)
        I AUX DEF tiger kissed
        'I kissed the tiger.'

     b. i dais-e eleθen ner-in erdemiraen.   (marked A and P)
        DEF tiger-ERG/NOM AUX I-ACC kissed
        'The tiger kissed me.'

     c. ner elethen al-in erdemiraen.   (bare A and marked P)
        I AUX he-ACC kissed
        'I kissed him.'

     d. al-e elethen i dais erdemiraen.   (marked A and bare P)
        he-ERG AUX DEF tiger kissed
        'He kissed the tiger.'

---

[3] Some morphological detail has been left out of these examples for the sake of explanatory simplicity.

The off-the-cuff tripartite system in (1) is presented as a simple fact about the world: the creator came upon a new language and found it thus. One can react positively or negatively to it, but the reaction can never move beyond pure subjectivity: whether one appreciates that the conlanger decided on a tripartite system or not; whether one appreciates the use of suffixes for marking or not; whether one appreciates the phonological forms of the suffixes or not; etc.

The tripartite system of ámman îar, by contrast, has been achieved by dint of effort while working within a series of constraints which the conlanger himself created. The language is intended to be naturalistic (to the best of the conlanger's ability), and so the work can be evaluated more or less objectively. What one sees, then, is a tripartite system that fell out naturally from the implementation of a naturalistic animacy system. The system struck me as beautiful because it is both intricate *and*, by my estimation, something that could occur in a natural language.

One could just as easily imagine a very poor system with the same setup where the nine cells in Table 15.1 are filled with nine different forms of exponence. Such a thing would never occur in a natural language, and would miss the sheer elegance of Bell's system, which takes advantage of two common traits found throughout human languages: first, nominal arguments are often treated differently depending on how animate they are, as defined by a language's users; and second, marking most frequently co-occurs with arguments when they are doing something out of the ordinary. Inanimate objects are commonly patients (unmarked), and rarely agents (marked with /-e/); animate objects are commonly agents (unmarked), and rarely patients (marked with /-in/). The last piece of the puzzle is that third-person pronouns are commonly associated with either animate arguments or inanimate arguments—hence the split.

Without so much as working through a single example from Bell's language, I was stunned by this system—and all I needed to do to appreciate it was to glance first at his animacy system and then at Table 15.1. That was enough for me to fully appreciate the genius of the system, and to acknowledge what Bell had accomplished.

If conlanging is an art form, then it must be taken seriously, by both the conlanger and the evaluator. Specifically, the level of effort a conlanger puts into their work is the level of effort the evaluator should put into evaluating their work. Each has a responsibility. If a conlanger is presenting a serious work, they have the responsibility to do the following:

- state the specific goals of their work;
- state the limitations of their work; and
- demonstrate how their conlang achieves the goals they laid out for it, within the stated limitations.

A serious evaluator, then, has the following responsibilities:

- evaluate the goals, and determine their worth (a subjective measure);
- determine whether the limitations placed on the work are reasonable and sufficient; and
- evaluate how successful the conlanger was in achieving the goals they set for their conlang, given the limitations.

Having clearly delineated goals for a conlang is a prerequisite for serious evaluation. Absent these goals, there is no appropriate non-subjective evaluation. Furthermore, the goals need to be achievable (or, to use an analogy from linguistics, a hypothesis needs to be falsifiable), otherwise evaluation is impossible. It might be interesting to suggest that there is an invisible, intangible, and instrumentally undetectable elf that sits on our tongues and makes sure the language we speak is syntactically well-formed, but the suggestion can't be tested, and so there's really no stake in claiming that it's either true or false. Similarly, if the goal of a conlang is to be exactly what the conlanger likes, then it can't be seriously evaluated by anyone other than the conlanger themselves.

While there are some goals that are fairly well-established within the community (such as the goal of naturalism, where the goal is to create a language that, to the best of our abilities and understanding, behaves precisely as a natural language would, given the circumstances of its users and their environment), they need not be tied to our understanding of human language. For example, the goals of John Quijada's Ithkuil (2011) can be summarized as follows:

- to *explicitly* express every element, both semantic and grammatical, that a human language encodes both explicitly and implicitly;
- to be completely unambiguous; and
- to be concise.

The language that attempts to achieve these goals simultaneously will, of course, be nothing like a natural human language—after all, no human language attempts to satisfy even *one* of these goals, let alone all three. Despite that fact, the explicitness of these goals allows the conlang to be evaluated as a serious work of art. The result may not sound "pretty", but such a subjective evaluation has no real merit, given the stated goals of the language. Another conlanger may one day decide to use the same three goals and add a fourth: to have the language sound "pretty".[4] For such a language, an evaluation of its phonaesthetics would be appropriate, even though it would not be for Ithkuil.

Potentially, any goal can be sufficiently rigorous to produce a conlang that can be subject to serious evaluation: the goal just needs to be fully defined by the conlanger. For example, a conlang that's good for music is too vague. What type of music? Is it just the lyrics? If it's the lyrics, what then is the goal? Part of what makes poetry such an amazing accomplishment is that the form is difficult to achieve given the constraints of the language (for example, haikus are relatively simple to write in English, given how semantically dense our syllables are compared to Japanese). If the conlang made lyric writing or rhyming or matching the stress/intonation of the language to the tone of the song a simple matter, would the resultant lyrics be better art, or would they be lesser art, given how simple they were to write, thus undermining the original goal? If, instead, the goal was to create a language that was simple enough to fit to a meter and to rhyme specifically so that a singer could get a song out without having to stress over poetic form (something they may have no natural talent for), that would be interesting.

Returning to the subject of a conlang class, if one accepts the role of the conlanger and evaluator in the artistic pursuit of conlanging (as opposed to pursuing it as a hobby or recreation), what ought the role of the instructor in a conlang class to be? As I see it, the instructor has three roles, which correspond to the three roles of the conlanger and evaluator:

- Teach the conlanger the importance of setting specific goals for their work, teasing out precisely how the specificity of these goals will define the character and quality of the evaluation of their work. Also explore how to determine whether a goal is worthwhile or not by determining if it's both achievable and sufficiently rigorous.[5]
- Teach the conlanger exactly how a conlang will be limited (e.g. by constraints such as time and our understanding of how language initially emerged, or by the fact that we can't necessarily create the types of aliens who will use our alien language, etc.), and how they ought to cordon off their work, so to speak, in taking those limitations into account.
- Teach the conlanger how to evaluate a conlang based on its goals and limitations.

---

[4] To some specific audience, one would hope, as such evaluations can only be subjective.
[5] One doesn't want to end up with a situation where the goal was to create a language where every possible meaning is compressed into a single syllable.

These are the three most important student learning outcomes of any conlang class. The individual strategies for determining phonotactic constraints, creating morphology, generating vocabulary, etc., will be useful for students in class, and for those who continue to create languages afterward, but when it comes to the state of the art, the presentation and evaluation of a conlang is paramount.

At present we live in a world where conlanging has commercial value. It's hard to imagine that cat going back into the bag at this point, which means that anyone who creates a language or learns to create a language has to accept that there is the possibility, however remote, that they may one day be paid to do so. Many skip right over the notion of possibility and land on expectation. In fact, there are a good number who learn about language creation for the first time from the work I have done on one show or another and proceed to skip right over conlanging, instead asking me directly how they can get a job like mine, despite the fact that they've never created a language before in their life, and, crucially, have no intention of doing so unless they're being paid to do it. On the one hand, I sympathize, given that if there are paying jobs in conlanging, then there should be some realistic pathway to obtaining such a job, in an ideal world. On the other hand, creating a language for a novel or TV show or movie—being the next Marc Okrand—has been the unattainable dream of conlangers since Tolkien. As someone who came out of that community, it's difficult for me to jump right over the conlangers who've struggled with the art for ten or more years and try to help someone who never once dreamed of creating a language to get a job creating languages for money in Hollywood.

Where conlanging goes from here is still unclear. Nevertheless, since conlang education is now an immutable fact of life, I believe it should acknowledge the fact that it plays a role in how conlanging itself is regarded both by the public and in the marketplace. Whether or not a conlang class produces new lifelong conlangers, it should produce critical conlang consumers. We need consumers who understand that there is a difference between a language that has been created to adhere to specific goals and a language that has been created haphazardly. The bar for mere functionality is too low to clear, given that it can be satisfied by a simple relexification of an already existing language. At this point I think we've moved beyond the era of a television show putting together gibberish and passing it off as a full conlang, but if a staff writer can relex German and produce a new language, why would they ever hire someone who knows what they're doing to create a new conlang? Presumably they would do so if the audience could tell the difference, and demanded better—and this is what a student with an elementary education in conlanging should be able to do.

15.3 An experimental conlang course

In the fall of 2014, I was approached by Dr. Andrew Garrett[6] from the UC Berkeley linguistics department to teach a course on language creation for the upcoming summer term. The course could be whatever I wanted. In effect, the only constraint was that the linguistics department wanted to work "Game of Thrones" into the course title somehow. On my end, I had the rather serious constraint of living 400 miles away and, essentially, commuting, so I decided to make the course run for six weeks, with four two-hour class sessions per week. In terms of instruction, then, I had to figure out how best to achieve the three student learning outcomes listed above with an extremely abbreviated timeline.

Ultimately, I made the following decisions:

(i) The term project would be to create a naturalistic conlang within the *Song of Ice and Fire* universe.[7] George R. R. Martin hints at the existence of many languages in his books, but the only ones we see, for the most part, are Dothraki and Valyrian. Students would have an opportunity to flesh out his world a little more as they learned to create languages.[8]

(ii) The language-construction process itself would involve creating the proto-stage of the language and evolving its phonology, grammar, lexicon, and orthography to the "modern" era (modern, in this case, being the time of action for the series *Game of Thrones*, which is modeled after our late Middle Ages).

(iii) Students would present their work periodically both to gain feedback from other students and so that they could get a glimpse of others' progress.

---

[6] It's important for me to note here that Dr. Garrett was *not* the linguist who laughed at me when I told them I was creating a language years before.

[7] Initially, I intended that each student take a different language, but I ended up allowing several students to do alternate takes on the same language.

[8] Furthermore, this would license including "Game of Thrones" in the course title, which became "Linguistics 183: The Linguistics of Game of Thrones and the Art of Language Invention."

(iv) Biweekly assignments would assess students' comprehension of and facility with the specific conlang strategies presented in class, and also serve as a step-by-step roadmap to the creation of their language.

(v) Only students who had taken, at the very least, a course on introductory linguistics would be admitted.

Naturally most conlang courses will have some variation on (iii) and (iv) (and the necessity of item (v) will soon become evident), so I'll focus on what I see as the key differences in (i) and (ii). The first is the requirement that students create a *naturalistic* language—i.e. one which attempts to be as close to a natural language as possible, such that, minus the setting and fantasy-inspired vocabulary, a linguist would be unable to distinguish it from a natural language they simply hadn't come across before.

I decided to restrict student choice for three reasons. The first is quite practical: with a six-week course, there was no time for students to be deciding if they were going to create a naturalistic artlang or an alien auxlang or a language made out of mixing the various soil types of the Bay Area, or what have you. It was choice enough for them to pick a language *within* the *Game of Thrones* universe.

Second, a constraint can be quite freeing and can inspire creativity. Assigning a class a poem may inspire some students, but will fill many with dread, as they drown in a sea of possibility. Assigning the same class a sonnet may disappoint some, but can give hope to those unaccustomed to writing poetry, for at least now they can focus on *what* to write without having to worry about *how*.

Finally, if conlanging is an art form, then, like any other art form, it should have styles—and, indeed, it does. The styles are innumerable, and we haven't even scratched the surface, as this art form is still in its infancy. Much like painting or sketching, though, it's my belief that it can only benefit the conlanger to work through a naturalistic conlang—and the earlier the better. It's difficult to break the rules of human language if one doesn't know what the rules are. Even if what future conlangers there were in my class would go on to do more abstract work, I believed that working through a full-fledged naturalistic language would allow them to better understand how to create something truly abstract and nonhuman later on.

As we move on to (ii), it's worth digging deeper into the concept of naturalism. Within the language-creation community, the terms we've used were never defined by a single authority as much as they emerged through use and opposition. For example, within the auxiliary language construction community, naturalism is often applied to languages that are modeled after or incorporate elements from natural languages (thus Esperanto would be naturalistic while Solresol would not be). Within the artlang community, the de facto notion of naturalism was defined in opposition to engineered or philosophical languages as well as auxlangs. Basically, if one was trying more or less to create a language spoken by realistic beings, the goal was naturalism—again, more or less. Beyond that, though, there were far fewer distinctions than exist today.

Some language creators, inspired by J. R. R. Tolkien (among them David Bell, whose work was presented in Section 15.2), incorporated sound changes into their work, to give their languages a bit of historical depth, but this was atypical outside of a posteriori conlanging (e.g. serious alternative linguistic history projects such as Ill Bethisad). More common was an imprecise method whereby the conlanger would "kind of" make the conlang "look" naturalistic by somewhat haphazardly employing suppletive forms in the language or alternate exponence based on semantic or morphophonoloical characteristics of the base or phonological variation that might hint at a proto-form of some kind which the conlanger hadn't actually created. Essentially, the attempt was to get the *effect* of a natural language without doing the evolutionary legwork associated with *producing* that effect. We'll call this approach *faux naturalism*.

Within more serious naturalistic endeavors, two modern trends have emerged. The first we'll call *statistical* or *weak naturalism*. The idea behind weak naturalism is that of the world's 6,000+ languages, a certain percentage will behave one way, while the rest will behave another way, with respect to any given linguistic feature. Table 15.2, for example, shows a breakdown of the ordering of subject, object, and verb from a sample of the world's languages (Dryer 2013a):

Table 15.2 A crosslinguistic sample of subject, object, and verb ordering

ordering	# of languages	% of total
SOV	565	41.03
SVO	488	35.44
VSO	95	6.90
VOS	25	1.82
OVS	11	0.80
OSV	4	0.29
no dominant order	189	13.73
total	1377	100

The idea behind weak naturalism is that with respect to this feature of word order, the percentage in the third column in Table 15.2 should be how likely a conlang is to have that particular dominant word order. To the extent that one can determine such distributions for *all possible* features in a language, a naturalistic conlang will be one that follows the dice rolls, so to speak (cf. Pearson's contribution to this volume, Chapter 7). Naturally, implicational universals will affect the weightings (so, for example, if one rolls VSO word order, one will have a better chance of rolling prepositions as opposed to postpositions than one would should one roll SOV), but with a sufficiently advanced algorithm, one could gin up a conlang in a matter of seconds—right down to the phonology and probably even some basic word choices, if one folds in onomatopoeia and phonological iconicity.

Weak naturalism can be useful for remixing elements of natural languages, but it's hard to say what skills one gains from it—or how one would use it to evaluate a single conlang. Provided that $n \geq 1$ for any given feature, any language with features that fall *somewhere* on the spectrum should be theoretically possible, even if a given combination is statistically improbable. Thus, for almost any language, the answer to the question "Is it naturalistic?" is a simple "Yes." It might be unlikely, but all the "proof" one needs is a readout of the virtual dice rolls.

Crucially, weak naturalism has nothing to say about features that have never occurred or been discovered in a natural language. Such things aren't hard to imagine: if we delve back into human history, there were many, *many* points where we discovered features in a natural language that had never been seen in a language before. All weak naturalism can say is whether or not it's happened before. While it might be sufficient for producing a naturalistic conlang that can be supposed to exist in our world, or in a world like ours with human speakers, it teaches the conlanger nothing about how a language might naturally evolve in different circumstances. For example, if there was a planet with humans much like ours with no sight, how might the language differ? If the default was for a human to have six fingers, surely base-12 would be more common, but how else might the language be different? And what if the conlanger were to design a totally new alien with an entirely different set of senses? Presumably several thousand of these alien languages would need to exist to allow one to successfully create a new one.

Additionally, it's possible to satisfy the dictates of weak naturalism with a flat or synchronic structure. In other words, a set of words like those in (3) would be naturalistic enough, according to weak naturalism.

(3) kala   kalabaluriakum   kalax   'cat (SG/DU/PL)'
     bit   bitpaluriakum   bitx   'dog (SG/DU/PL)'
     sor   sorbaluriakum   gripugagu 'man (SG/DU/PL)'

There's nothing wrong with having a language that has singular, dual, and plural forms. Of those languages, there's nothing wrong with the dual and plural co-occurring with suffixes. There's also nothing wrong with having a suppletive form for the plural of 'man' (i.e. a very common lexeme that often has irregular forms in one of its paradigm slots, as in English). One can even detect a bit of phonology in (3), with the voiced /b/ of the suffix /-baluriakum/ becoming [p] next to a voiceless consonant. Nevertheless, it's hard to imagine a linguist believing these data came from a natural language—ultimately the goal of any naturalistic conlang.

The features can be refined further and further (e.g. perhaps there's a maximum length for affixes), but if we flip this around and look at it from the evaluator's standpoint, under the framework of weak naturalism, how can one evaluate this? How could one express that the very similar set of words in (4) is much more likely to occur in a natural language?

(4) kala   kalan   kalax   'cat (SG/DU/PL)'
     bit   bitɨn   bitʰ   'dog (SG/DU/PL)'
     sor   sorn   søx   'man (SG/DU/PL)'

Given the general multifariousness of language, I find myself less than comfortable claiming a given alternation or a paradigm or an entire conlang passes the test of naturalism unless I can see how the language creator got there. The same is true of any natural language displaying any feature one considers bizarre. The history of the thing tends to bear it out.

This is where I'll introduce an alternative form of naturalism I call *evolutionary* or *strong naturalism*. Strong naturalism rejects entirely any reference to linguistic universals, implicational or otherwise. Rather, the choice of any given ordering or alternation or paradigmatic function will be borne out in its history.

As a small example, consider the choice between prepositions or postpositions (presumably before a stage where borrowing of adpositions might happen). This is a choice that's strongly correlated with word order, as illustrated in Table 15.3 (Dryer 2013b):

Table 15.3 The relationship between object-verb order and adposition-noun phrase order

ordering	# of languages	% of total
OV + postpositional	472	41.33
OV + prepositional	14	1.23
VO + postpositional	42	3.68
VO + prepositional	456	39.93
no strong correlation	158	13.84
total	1142	100

Correlations such as the one in Table 15.3 were part of what led to our notion of headedness: that the most important part of a phrase will tend to be in the same spot for a given language. And, indeed, if you combine the rows where the head of the verb phrase and the head of the adpositional phrase are in the same spot (rows 1 and 4), you get 81.26% of the sample. None of these facts, though, tells us *why* this should be the case—let alone why it should ever *not* be the case, outside of borrowing.

If we look at how adpositions evolve in language after language we actually are furnished an answer to both questions. First, though adpositions are a separate part of speech in just about every language where they are present, they were not always so. Many adpositions ultimately derive from one of two sources: nouns or verbs. Some more recent prepositions of English whose original sources are known are given in (5).[9]

(5)   a. derived from nouns: aboard, beside, like, outside
       b. derived from verbs: come, during, past, save

While it may be unusual for a student new to linguistics or conlanging to imagine using a verb by itself as a preposition, native English speakers have no

---

[9] Certain of these are morphologically complex, but the key piece of them is either nominal or verbal (e.g. the "head," if you'll allow, of the original complex preposition *beside* is *side*, and is the piece that the dependent would be governed by).

trouble with a sentence like *we'll run out of food come winter*. Once the conlanger understands this, it's easy to figure out where the preposition would be with respect to the noun: it's where the verb is. If the verb is always at the end of the sentence, it will become a postposition; if it comes before the object, it will be a preposition—unless something specific happens to push it in a different direction.[10] The same goes for nouns, except it will be how the nouns are placed in apposition when the underlying complex expression is serving as the complement or object of a verb phrase—again, unless something specific pushes it in a different direction.

Similarly, case assignment in case languages with adpositions is often determined (at least initially) by the semantics of the original expression that gave rise to the adposition. In (6), for example, is an adposition from Veps with an etymological interlinear (Grünthal 2010).[11]

(6)   išt-ta   kuzo-n   ǵürü-u
      sit-INF   spruce-GEN   root-ADESS
      'sit under a spruce tree'

Here the word for 'root' has come to be used for the concept of 'under'. Its position with respect to the noun phrase it governs has been determined by the ordering of standard genitival constructions in the language, and the case of the governed noun has been determined by the relationship between the two original nouns (i.e. 'of the spruce (its) root').

From a conlanging standpoint, following the dictates of strong naturalism is a step-by-step guide to creating a naturalistic conlang. For the evaluator, rather than needing to refer to typological universals to assess the naturalism of a conlang, one simply has to look at the conlanger's work. Does the language have both prepositions and postpositions? No problem. How did each set evolve? If there's a story, then there's something to evaluate. Furthermore, the method is itself an argument for the naturalism of the conlang. In other words, if a conlanger follows a plausible, naturalistic progression to get from state x to state $x + n$, then the result will be naturalistic *whether or not any such combination of features has ever existed in the real world*. In such a case, where the conlang exhibits a heretofore unheard-of grammatical structure that was evolved via a strong naturalistic progression, all one can say is that it's

---

[10] Looking at English, for example, the unergativity of *come* and common VS order (e.g. *said the carpenter*) is possibly what led to *come winter* and not *winter come*.

[11] I've followed the nomenclature of the source in presenting these data. ADESS refers to the adessive case, and ǵ is the palatalized sound /gʲ/.

mere happenstance that such a structure has not yet been found in a natural language.

The drawbacks to strong naturalism are both liberating and deflating at the same time. The major drawback is that we know little about the historical development of the languages of the world, let alone how language emerged for the very first time. While volumes and volumes have been written about Proto Indo-European, the language itself only goes back to about 4500 BCE, as near as we can tell. Humans have had languages for tens of *thousands* of years. The most speculative of our evidence-based reconstructions still barely scratch the surface of the history of human languages. Furthermore, barring the invention of time travel, it seems unlikely we will ever know more about the origin of human language. Using the tools of linguistic evolution to create a naturalistic language immediately gives rise to a "turtle-stacking" problem. If the way to get a naturalistic language is to evolve it from some other source, where does *that* source come from? If it's another naturalistic conlang, then what naturalistic conlang is *that* conlang in turn derived from? And so on. The best advice one can provide to a naturalistic conlanger is that since we know so little about the pre-history of our languages, there is simply a point at which the conlanger must decide to draw the curtain, so to speak. At time *x*, the conlanger creates a language (either via faux naturalism or weak naturalism or some other means) and declares that before that time period nothing is known. The drawbacks to doing this are the same as those stated above, but if one uses that state— or any state, really—and applies the principles of strong naturalism moving forward, the result will become increasingly naturalistic as one goes along.

Another major drawback of strong naturalism is the field of linguistics itself still knows, collectively, very little about the mechanisms of language change— especially when compared to, for example, what we know about phonetics, or even synchronic syntax. Grammatical change in particular still requires much exploration. This means the conlanger won't have as much of a roadmap moving forward, but also means they're able to take more liberties. It means that both the conlanger and the evaluator will be asking themselves the same question in evaluating a conlang—for example, is it plausible that a noun referring to the top of something could turn into a preposition meaning 'above', which in turn becomes an indefinite future-tense auxiliary? If it hasn't happened before in a language, it's up to the conlanger to explain why they think the mapping is plausible, and it's up to the evaluator to judge their logic.

Importantly, taking the strong naturalism approach gives the evaluator *something* to base their evaluation on other than subjective reactions, intuition, or appeals to linguistic authority. As an instructor such a metric should be valuable, as ultimately they will need to assign the student a grade of some kind (at most educational institutions), and they will need to defend their decision. Strong naturalism provides a framework for doing so.

In all, this was the theory behind my class. By providing students with a fictional framework for creating a naturalistic conlang they were able to focus on the nuts and bolts of language creation. Additionally, the subject matter allowed us to explore a topic rarely touched on in mainstream linguistics courses: orthography. Students used IPA for all their work until the fifth week of class, at which point we turned our attention to orthographic systems. We explored the history of orthography in our world and how orthographies evolved naturally, and students emulated this process of natural orthographic evolution to produce a unique orthography for their own languages. By the sixth week of class, each of the students had the beginnings of a naturalistic conlang with its own orthography and an attached culture. In effect, they did what I had done working on *Game of Thrones*—with an accelerated timeline that was quite reminiscent of working in Hollywood.

15.4 A sample evolution assignment

To demonstrate how precisely strong naturalism can be used on a basic level, I'll present a problem set I used in our course. Problem sets such as the one I share here were inspired by problem sets in mathematics. Consider the equation in (7).

(7) $3x + 2 = 8$

The problem is simple enough. However, in a math class, if the student provides the answer (8), they'll get, at best, half credit—often no credit. A proper solution looks something like (9).

(8) $x = 2$

(9) $3x + 2 = 8$
       $3x + 2 - 2 = 8 - 2$
       $3x + 0 = 6$
       $3x = 6$
       $3x \div 3 = 6 \div 3$
       $(1)x = 2$
       $x = 2$

In common parlance, the student must show their work. The conlang problem set I present here was designed to allow the student to do the exact same thing, only using human language rather than numbers and operators.

To begin, students were given the data in (10).[12]

(10)

hut	'hand'	fud	'husband'	tel	'leg'
dap	'house'	meg	'club'	mih	'cave'
gal	'rock'	sib	'stomach'	hig	'daughter'
bok	'girl'	set	'summit'	fas	'son'
sil	'man'	sup	'spring'	nuh	'mother'
taf	'woman'	tug	'face'	pen	'father'
hik	'boy'	min	'thing'	kep	'sister'
pas	'fox'	fig	'branch'	gub	'brother'
lam	'cow'	maf	'pile'	mem	'back'
kah	'wife'	sag	'sky'	nak	'chest'

The makeup of the list of nouns in (10) is monosyllabic CVC word forms with a fairly flexible structure (i.e. there's no reason to believe that any consonant would be restricted in its distribution) and meanings that are more or less basic.[13] Taking these nouns as their starting point, students were asked to do the tasks in (11).

(11)   a. Create a case system with four distinct case forms from this data. List the cases with their names and forms below, along with an example of one of the nouns in (10) inflected in all four forms. State the sound changes you used along with your answer.

b. Create a gender system with at least three genders. Give two examples of each gender below, showing singular and plural for each. State the sound changes you used along with your answer.

c. Imagine you had a two-gender system (animate and inanimate). How might the two genders have entirely different ablative, genitive, partitive, or allative singular case forms? (Choose one of those cases and show how it'd have two different singular case forms.)

---

[12] I did clarify for students the specific meanings of certain of these words which are polysemous in English (e.g. 'club' and 'back').

[13] Which is to say, the meanings assigned to these word forms appear in a large number of languages as basic roots. There are certainly natural languages where some of these words won't be basic, but it's not outlandish to suggest that all of these might be basic in some language.

   d. Working with your answer from (a), create something different. You can either (i) create two more cases to add to your original set, or (ii) change the inflection from adpositions to affixes, or vice versa, or (iii) change the inflection from prefixes to suffixes, or vice versa.

   e. Working with your answer from (b), create something different. You can either (i) create two more genders to add to your original set, or (ii) create different genders (again, at least three), or (iii) change the inflection from adpositions to affixes, or vice-versa, or (iv) change the inflection from prefixes to suffixes, or vice versa.

At this stage in the course,[14] students had learned about a variety of specific sound changes, and also the physical and acoustic sources of sound change (so they could create sound changes they hadn't previously encountered that were licit). They had also learned about certain phenomena that occur independently of grammaticalization, such as reduplication and affective/iconic lengthening and/or stress shift.[15] They had also learned about compounding and headedness and how they interact. In addition, they were familiar with Bybee's theory of grammaticalization and its progression. Specifically, they were familiar with the concepts of the continuum of semantic and phonetic reduction, such that grammatical items exhibit further semantic *and* phonetic reduction when compared to similar non-grammatical items (Bybee et al. 1994).[16] And, of course, this assignment followed a general introduction to the lexical sources of noun-case morphology, plural morphology, and gender morphology. Again, though it was compressed given the time frame, students were equipped to tackle this assignment, modulo their individual understanding of the material and familiarity with the processes relevant to conlanging.

If one takes a look at (11a), one can see that there are any possible number of four-case systems that might be derived using the vocabulary presented. In (12), a partial list of some cases is given along with their potential sources.[17]

---

[14] I'll note here that the only required text for the course was my book *The Art of Language Invention* (2015). Recommended texts were Bybee et al.'s *The Evolution of Grammar* (1994); Campbell's *Historical Linguistics* (2013); Heine and Kuteva's *World Lexicon of Grammaticalization* (2002); and Lakoff and Johnson's *Metaphors We Live By* (2008). In effect, it was a course on historical linguistics.

[15] Part of the reason for including a list of monosyllabic words was to allow the students to design their own stress system, should they wish to incorporate stress as a part of their solution.

[16] To summarize Bybee et al. (1994), as the relative age of a grammatical marker (or gram) increases, both its semantic load and its phonetic form are reduced in tandem.

[17] Much of the material in this table is taken or extrapolated from Heine and Kuteva (2002).

(12)   a. nominative, absolutive, etc.: —
  b. accusative: from *hut* 'hand', *nuk* 'chest', or the dative
  c. dative, allative: from *hut* 'hand', *dap* 'house', *set* 'summit', or the illative
  d. locative: *dap* 'house', *mih* 'cave', *set* 'summit', or *sib* 'stomach'
  e. ablative: *sup* 'spring', *dap* 'house', *mih* 'cave'
  f. ergative: *hut* 'hand', *mem* 'back', or the instrumental
  g. inessive, illative: *sib* 'stomach' or *mih* 'cave'
  h. instrumental: *hut* 'hand', *meg* 'club', *gal* 'rock', or *fig* 'branch'
  i. genitive: *hut* 'hand' or the ablative or locative
  j. vocative: *sil* 'man', *taf* 'woman', *gub* 'brother', *kep* 'sister', or affective lengthening.

In effect, the task is deciding what role the unmarked case will fulfill, and then deciding what system makes sense, given the material available and the specific lexical items selected. For example, a relatively simple system would have the base co-occur with subjects and objects in a nominative–accusative system; an ablative that derives from *sup* 'spring' (a spring is a source; metaphorical extension) that could also fulfill genitival functions; an allative/illative that derives from *set* 'summit' (a summit is the goal of a mountain climber; metaphorical extension) that could also fulfill dative functions; and an instrumental/comitative that derives from *hut* 'hand' (one uses one's hand to hold an instrument or another's hand; metonymy). Despite the limited exponence, the system is fairly robust, and would be capable of covering a lot of semantic territory without resorting to the use of adpositions or other prolix expressions.

Deciding on the case system is the first step. Figuring out how to instantiate it is the second. Before working with the material itself, the student must decide on the headedness of their language, to determine how noun sequences in apposition will be interpreted—that is, whether *hut sil* or *sil hut* would be taken to mean 'the man's hand'. Once this is decided, the student decides whether the grammatical elements will become affixes (as well as the relative time depth), or if they will become adpositions. Then it's a matter of applying sound changes.

In the following, I present two potential solutions for (11a) using the four-case system already outlined with sample discussion. The data for the first solution are in Table 15.4.

Table 15.4 One potential solution to (11a)

case	exponence	examples	glosses
nominative	–	pǒ, mà	'girl', 'pile'
ablative	sú	sú pǒ, sú mà	'from the girl', 'from the pile'
allative	ʃé	ʃé pǒ, ʃé mà	'to the girl', 'to the pile'
instrumental	hú	hú pǒ, hú mà	'with the girl', 'with the pile'

In Table 15.4, the data from (10) have become tonal. The sound changes in (13)–(19) occurred in order. First, voiced obstruents devoice in word-final position (13).

(13) a. Word-Final Devoicing: C[–cont, –nasal] > [–voice] / ___#
      b. *meg 'club' > mek

Then final obstruents neutralize, with stops becoming [ʔ] at the end of a word and fricatives becoming [h] at the end of a word (14).

(14) a. Word-Final Obstruent Simplification: C[–cont] > ʔ / ___#, C[+cont]
          > h / ___#
      b. *meg 'club' > *mek > meʔ
          *taf 'woman' > *taf > tah

Then voiceless onsets give high tone coloring to a following vowel, while voiced onsets give low tone coloring to a following vowel (15).

(15) a. Tone Coloring I: V > V́ / C[–voice]___, V > V̀ / C[+voice] ___
      b. *meg 'club' > *mek > *meʔ > mè̀ʔ
          *sup 'spring' > *sup > *suʔ > súʔ

Then voiced obstruents devoice across the language (16), leaving only tone to distinguish syllables that were previously distinguished only by voice.

(16) a. Devoicing: C[–nasal] > [–voice]
      b. *bok 'girl' > *bok > *boʔ > *bò̀ʔ > pòʔ

Then vowels before word-final stops take on a slight high tone, and vowels before word-final fricatives take on a slight low tone (17), which may result in contour tones.

(17)   a. Tone Coloring II: V > V́ / __C[-cont], V > V̀ / __C[+cont]
     b. *bok 'girl' > *bok > *boʔ > *bòʔ > *pòʔ > pǒʔ
       *sup 'spring' > *sup > *suʔ > *súʔ > *súʔ > súʔ
       *taf 'woman' > *taf > *tah > *táh > *táh > tâh
       *maf 'pile' > *maf > *mah > *màh > *màh > màh

Then all obstruents were lost in word-final position (18).

(18)   a. Loss of Word-Final Obstruents: C[-nasal] > Ø / __#
     b. *bok 'girl' > *bok > *boʔ > *bòʔ > *pòʔ > *pǒʔ > pǒ
       *sup 'spring' > *sup > *suʔ > *súʔ > *súʔ > *súʔ > sú
       *taf 'woman' > *taf > *tah > *táh > *táh > *tâh > tâ
       *maf 'pile' > *maf > *mah > *màh > *màh > *màh > mà

Finally, coronal consonants became palatoalveolar consonants before [i] and [e] (19).

(19)   a. Palatalization: C[+cor] > [-ant] / __V[-back, -low]
     b. *set 'summit' > *set > *seʔ > *séʔ > *séʔ > *séʔ > *sé > ʃé
       *tel 'leg' > *tel > *tel > *tél > *tél > *tél > *tél > tʃél

The second solution takes the data set in a different direction. The data are presented in Table 15.5.

In Table 15.5, the data from (10) have become fusional. The sound changes in (20)–(26) occurred in order. First, in fixed grammatical expressions, grams lose their word status and become suffixes to the words they modify (20).

Table 15.5 Another potential solution to (11a)

case	exponence	examples	glosses
nominative	-a, -u, -i	bogu, mava	'girl', 'pile'
ablative	-su	boksu, massu	'from the girl', 'from the pile'
allative	-si	boksi, massi	'to the girl', 'to the pile'
instrumental	-hu	boxu, mahhu	'with the girl', 'with the pile'

(20)   a. Affixation: WORD + GRAMMATICAL WORD > WORD + SUFFIX

     b. *bok sup 'girl's source' > boksup
        *maf sup 'pile's source' > mafsup
        *maf set 'pile's summit' > mafset

Then words ending with a consonant pick up a copy vowel so that all words now end with a vowel (21).

(21)   a. Word-Final Epenthesis: $\emptyset > V_x / V_xC$ ___#

     b. *maf 'pile' > *maf > mafa
        *maf sup 'pile's source' > *mafsup > mafsupu
        *maf set 'pile's summit' > *mafset > mafsete

Then voiceless consonants voice in between vowels (22).

(22)   a. Intervocalic Voicing: C > [+voice] / V___V

     b. *maf 'pile' > *maf > *mafa > mava
        *maf sup 'pile's source' > *mafsup > *mafsupu > mafsuvu
        *maf set 'pile's summit' > *mafset > *mafsete > mafsede

Then an obstruent becomes a copy of the consonant following it, provided its [cont] feature matches. Additionally, stop+/h/ consonant clusters coalesce and become fricatives in the place of articulation of the stop (23).

(23)   a. Cluster Simplification: $C[\alpha cont] > C_x /$ ___$C_x[\alpha cont]$, Ch > C[+cont]

     b. *bok hut 'girl's hand' > *bokhut > *bokhutu > *bokhudu > boxudu
        *maf set 'pile's summit' > *mafset > *mafsete > *mafsede > massede

Then mid vowels raise at the end of a word (24).

(24)   a. Word-Final Vowel Raising: V[–low] > [+high] / ___#

     b. *maf 'pile' > *maf > *mafa > *mava > *mava > mava
        *bok 'girl' > *bok > *boko > *bogo > *bogo > bogu
        *tel 'leg' > *tel > *tele > *tele > *tele > teli

Then consonants disappear in between vowels in grams (25).[18]

---

[18] Perhaps with an in-between stage as a voiced fricative or approximant.

(25)   a. Phonological Reduction of Grams: $C > \emptyset \; / \; V\_\_V$

   b. *bok hut 'girl's hand' > . . . > *boxudu > boxuu
       *maf set 'pile's summit' > . . . > *massedi > massei

Finally, consecutive vowels coalesce (26). The results of this coalescence will be numerous, but relevant for this problem set is that a [−high] vowel followed by a [+high] vowel is absorbed by the [+high] vowel.

(26)   a. Vowel Coalescence: $V_xV_x > V_x$

   b. *bok sup 'girl's source' > . . . > *boksubu > *boksuu > boksu
       *bok hut 'girl's hand' > . . . > *boxudu > *boxuu > boxu
       *maf set 'pile's summit' > . . . > *massedi > *massei > massi

For a full treatment, one might want to know what, if anything, happens to stress in this language, but the amount of detail here is sufficient for this problem set.

What I've shown here are two possible solutions to one part of the problem set using the same case system. The potential solutions are limitless—enough to inspire creativity without leaving students with a blank page. The process detailed here would apply to the other parts of the problem but in different areas. In response to (11b), there's plenty of lexical material to create a masculine, feminine, and other-gender system, but other types of genders could also be derived (e.g. handheld items using *gal* 'rock'; humans using any of the human words; a location gender using any of the location terms; a part gender, using a branch or a body part; a diminutive or augmentative gender, etc.). For plurals, the word *maf* 'pile' is available, perhaps *hut* 'hand' with the meaning 'handful', as are the options of not pluralizing for one gender and/or reduplication.

In response to (11c), students could separate the lexical sources of the cases into animate and inanimate. Thus, *set* 'summit' could serve as an allative source for the inanimate class, while *nak* 'chest' or *tug* 'face' could serve as the allative for the animate class. There's enough material there to make a similar decision for any of the cases listed in the prompt.

In response to both (11d) and (11e), one would employ the strategies listed here, just using different lexical material, perhaps, or different sound changes to produce a different outcome.

While there is a nontrivial element of speculation associated with strong naturalism, the process is precisely what a conlanger goes through in creating a naturalistic conlang, even if only unconsciously. With years of practice, much of this thinking occurs automatically, but it's precisely this type of thinking that needs to be taught. Furthermore, knowing the process will allow students to better understand naturalistic conlang construction in general—as well as the work of veteran conlangers who may have missed a step here or there.

In terms of linguistic instruction, there are three areas of potential further exploration once the assignment is finished. The first is crucial rule ordering. For example, (27) presents a different rule ordering for the second presented solution for (11a) (simplified for the sake of exposition).

(27)   a. Affixation: WORD + GRAMMATICAL WORD > WORD + SUFFIX
        b. Intervocalic Voicing: $C > [+voice] / V\_\_V$
        c. Cluster Simplification: $C[\alpha cont] > C_x / \_\_C_x[\alpha cont]$, $Ch > C[+cont]$
        d. Phonological Reduction of Grams: $C > \emptyset / V\_\_V$
        e. Vowel Coalescence: $V_xV_x > V_x$
        f. Word-Final Epenthesis: $\emptyset > V_x / V_xC\_\_\#$
        g. Word-Final Vowel Raising: $V[-low] > [+high] / \_\_\#$

In (27), we have a bit of an ordering mix-up. The intent of the solution is to deal with the grammatical affixes first, and then deal with the nominative class suffixes. As written, though, these sound changes don't work, as, in effect, intervocalic voicing would need to be reapplied after word-final epenthesis. As written, the nominative of 'girl' would be *boku*, not the intended *bogu*. Furthermore, the word-final consonants of the grammatical suffixes would no longer be in intervocalic position, and so wouldn't voice. It could be worked out, but it would need to be a different series of events from those listed in (27). Basically, the student knew what they wanted and knew how to get it, but didn't actually tease out what would happen if they followed their rules in order.

Another problem that may occur is the student not thinking through the full set of consequences of their sound changes. For example, say a student wanted to achieve the minimally effortful result in Table 15.6:

Table 15.6 A third potential solution to (11a)

case	exponence	examples	glosses
nominative	–	bok, maf	'girl', 'pile'
ablative	-su	boksu, mafsu	'from the girl', 'from the pile'
allative	-se	bokse, mafsi	'to the girl', 'to the pile'
instrumental	-hu	bokhu, mafhu	'with the girl', 'with the pile'

A student might consider that all they had to do was simply have two rules ordered as in (28):

(28)   a. Affixation: WORD + GRAMMATICAL WORD > WORD + SUFFIX
       b. Word-Final Stop Deletion: C[−cont, −nasal] > Ø / ___#

At a glance, the rules in (28) *should* produce the results we see in Table 15.6. Unfortunately, they do a bit more work than the student most likely intends. The results of these rules with several relevant forms are given in (29).

(29)   a. *bok 'girl' > *bok > bo
       b. *bok sup 'girl's source' > *boksup > boksu
       c. *bok set 'girl's summit' > *bokset > bokse
       d. *bok hut 'girl's hand' > *bokhut > bokhu
       e. *maf "pile' > *maf > maf
       f. *maf sup 'pile's source' > *mafsup > mafsu
       g. *maf set 'pile's summit' > *mafset > mafse
       h. *maf hut 'pile's hand' > *mafhut > mafhu

Of course, a student may actually intend for the results in (29) to be their answer, but their data in Table 15.6 would need to agree with the results of their sound changes shown in (29). A solution like the one provided here would be an opportunity for further discussion regarding the consequences of sound change and how they can be used to achieve a conlanger's intended result.

Finally, an incorrect solution may prompt a discussion of exactly what is likely. It's speculation, but nevertheless linguists do have a fairly good sense of what is likely and what isn't. For example, a student presented with the unintended consequences shown in (29) might try to amend their rules as in (30).

(30)   a. Affixation: WORD + GRAMMATICAL WORD > WORD + SUFFIX
       b. Polysyllabic Word-Final Coronal/Labial Stop Deletion:
          {C[−cont, −nasal, +cor] / C[−cont, −nasal, +lab]} > Ø / σ . . . ___#

The rules in (30) achieve the exact result the student intends (i.e. the data in Table 15.6), but (30b) is such a narrow rule that it simply taxes the credulity of any linguist. Importantly, it misses some key generalizations about language and fails to utilize some of the information students will have received in class by this time. Specifically, a student should already know by this point that grams experience greater phonological reduction than other elements. They might utilize this knowledge to target their sound change. Furthermore, they should realize that labial and coronal stops rarely pattern together to the exclusion of velar stops. Finally, it would be odd for a language to be sensitive to the number of syllables in a word only to determine whether one of a very small number of sounds at the end of a word is deleted—or at least with no other supporting material.

Key in this exercise is that students show their thinking on paper. Whether the answer is plausible or implausible, demonstrating the student's thinking will allow the instructor or other classmates to engage with that student's work—to ask why a given sound change was chosen, whether the sound change is independently motivated or plausible, and/or whether it actually achieves what the student was trying to achieve. It's precisely this level of engagement that will prove invaluable both to a conlanger and to a student of linguistics.

15.5 A word of caution regarding theory

When engaging with conlangers, it is absolutely vital to understand how linguistic theory impacts language creation at the most basic levels. There is a lot of unspoken wisdom required to employ the tools of linguistic theory accurately that is often taken for granted because the data are fixed. In conlanging, the data are *not* fixed, and applying linguistic theory uncritically can produce undesirable results.

Take the bizarre rule in (30b). Any linguist can look at that rule and know that, at least in the context presented, it's totally unrealistic. Consider, though, that the "theory" behind this rule is almost exclusively what is shown in (31):

(31)   A > B / C__D

There's nothing about (31) that prevents a rule such as (32) from existing.

(32)   V[+high] > ɹV[+back, +round]l / d__#

The rule in (32) would take a potential word *bædi* and return *bædɹul*. The notion that such a rule could exist in a natural language is beyond absurd,[19] but there's nothing in the machinery of the theory to prevent it.

---

[19] And, for that very reason, perhaps worth including in a parody language.

When teaching a conlanging class specifically, it's crucial for the teacher to carefully consider the effect of implementing theory in their class. Theory can be useful, as it helps the conlanger to think about language at a meta level, but there are pitfalls to believing that linguistic theories can be used as language-construction tools. In the following, I discuss some specific theoretical conceits with commentary regarding their potentially destructive uses.

15.5.1 Phonemes

Phonemes are accepted by most linguists,[20] but when employing them, recall how the phoneme-allophone structure works. In English, for example, we can say that the phoneme /p/ has allophones of [p] and [pʰ], with [pʰ] occurring as the first consonant in stressed syllables, and [p] occurring elsewhere. There's nothing in the theory to suggest that a phoneme /p/ couldn't have allophones of [p] when occurring word-finally after [ʟ], [ʕ] when occurring word-finally otherwise, [ɻ] word-internally, and [j] at the beginning of a word. Provided the sounds are in complementary distribution, the theory allows it. A linguist's intuition must inform whether phones ought to be grouped together as a single phoneme regardless of whether they are in complementary distribution. (Note: with the strong naturalism method of language construction, such things can mostly be avoided, as phonemes will emerge naturally as the result of sound change.)

15.5.2 Optimality Theory

While OT can be useful in designing non-lexical stress systems and level-tone languages, its specific explanatory power in terms of determining which sound changes occur, for example, or determining the surface form of an affix is questionable. That is, it's not clear what it would offer over a verbal description. OT's insights regarding broad language trends can be useful, but the machinery may end up producing odd results, given the universal ranking of constraints.[21]

---

[20] For a take by one who doesn't, see Port 2008.

[21] That is that constraint ranking applies throughout the language, which can lead to unintended results down the line. Naturally, this is the intended consequence of the theory, but it's more important for the conlanger to follow the historical progression of their language than the constraint ranking they devised to achieve some specific result.

15.5.3 Morphemes

Morphemes are a particularly dangerous theoretical concept, as most linguists can't imagine how language can function without them. It remains true, though, that morphemes are purely a theoretical construct, and their status is by no means settled (cf. Stewart 2016). A conlanger who understands and subscribes to morphemic theory ends up producing only one type of conlang: an agglutinative conlang. Every possible meaning, semantic or otherwise, must have exactly one phonological correspondence, and then conlanging itself is simply an exercise in deciding how to line them up. Morphemic theory is quite powerful, in that, aided by zero morphs, there's no possible language it can't describe. By way of analogy, morphemic theory is like a cheese grater, and language is like cheese. No matter what the type of cheese, the grater will grate it. Starting with a pile of grated cheese, though, no one can construct a block of cheese—especially not if the only tool they're handed is a cheese grater. It's crucial for the conlanger to understand that no piece of exponence is required to have one and only one meaning, and that meaningless exponence can exist—and, further, that sometimes grammatical meaning derives from phrasal constructions.

15.5.4 Syntactic theory

Syntactic theory has no place in conlang instruction. Syntactic theory is descriptive and synchronic. Descriptive theory is of no real use to a language creator; it's for the evaluator to use once the language is done. And while it's useful to know what a live speaker will do with language data, as the conlanger is modeling a diachronic process, synchronic knowledge is useful insofar as it's employed iteratively. Even so, considering how the conlang works in the head of *one* speaker can sidetrack a conlanger creating a language that's spoken by millions over centuries. The useful insight from theoretical syntax is to have the conlanger constantly ask themselves: At this state, how will older speakers believe their language works? Middle-aged speakers? Teenaged speakers? Children? That, and the variety of choices one has for linear precedence, are about as much as theoretical syntax can offer without unnecessarily curtailing creativity. Consider that most theories of syntax handle the "usual" well, and have complex machinery to explain the "edge cases." A conlanger thoroughly grounded in a specific syntactic theory will produce a conlang that perfectly adheres to the syntactic theory—even if it makes no sense given the historical evolution of their language.

In short, tools of analysis are not necessarily tools of construction, and each has their place. The job of a linguist *is* analysis (and description). It's understandable that analytical tools would suggest themselves to a linguist who teaches a conlang course—after all, they are at hand. But I urge the linguist who teaches a conlang course to consider the cost. It's trivial to produce a conlang that can be perfectly analyzed by a given analytical tool, but it's nearly impossible to make such a conlang naturalistic.

15.6 Concluding remarks

My intent here is not to discourage linguists who are teaching or would teach conlang courses at the university level. Indeed, the course I have described here is not necessarily presented as a model, so much as an example of an advanced conlanging course that engages seriously with the artistic aspect of language creation. The value is not in producing great artists, but in producing those who can judge the value of a conlang by some metric other than how much money its creator was paid to make it.

Conlanging is a very young art, and its use as a pedagogical tool is younger still. It's vital to understand both that the two, conlanging and pedagogy, are not independent of one another, and also that just as conlanging as an art has room to grow, so does conlang pedagogy. I would challenge linguists to seriously engage with questions of art when creating a conlang course. The reason is that the linguistic benefits of incorporating conlang pedagogy are obvious, and are more or less gotten for free. Engaging in conlanging of any kind immediately and crucially requires many of the tools and insights linguists wish to engender in their students anyway.

Furthermore, I urge the teacher of a conlang course to remember that they are not striking out on their own in terms of teaching conlang artistry. Yes, there are other courses, but better still, there are conlangers who have been honing their craft for years, and who could serve as a resource for any potential conlang course. In my own course I was able to bring in John Quijada, the creator of Ithkuil, to give a lecture on the application of George Lakoff's theory of conceptual metaphor to language creation, and Trent Pehrson, creator of Idrani and its amazing scripts (2018), to teach a lecture on glyph design. Then in class, we studied key pieces of the conlangs of those within the community whose work is well-known (e.g. David Bell, Sylvia Sotomayor, Jan van Steenbergen, Sally Caves, Denis Moskowitz, Andrew Smith, Doug Ball, Matt Pearson, and many others). By the end, students were able to evaluate this work critically, which is crucial.

We are awash in conlang expertise, and yet it seems conlang courses at the university level rarely take advantage of that fact. There are experienced language creators all over the world, and most would be honored and ecstatic to share their experience, if asked. More often a conlanger will learn that a course on language creation was taught very near to their home some months or years later, and they're left to wonder whether what expertise they have is of any value at all—if perhaps the years they've devoted to the art are worth less than the work of an inexperienced professor throwing together a course whose primary purpose is to get students interested in "real" linguistics. It falls to those of us with a foot in both camps to build a bridge, so that the art of language invention and the science of language study have a better, more productive relationship moving forward.

Acknowledgments

Thank you to Sheri Wells-Jensen for her notes on how to improve this chapter.

References

Adams, Michael (ed.) (2011a). *From Elvish to Klingon: Exploring Invented Languages.* Oxford: Oxford University Press.

Adams, Michael (2011b). 'The spectrum of invention.' in Michael Adams (ed.), *From Elvish to Klingon: Exploring Invented Languages.* Oxford: Oxford University Press, 1–16.

Adams, Richard (1972). *Watership Down.* London: Rex Collings Ltd.

Adger, David (2010). 'Gaelic syntax', in Moray Watson and Michelle Macleod (eds), *The Edinburgh Companion to the Gaelic Language.* Edinburgh: Edinburgh University Press, 304–51.

Adger, David and Coppe van Urk (2020). 'Three conlang projects at three educational levels', in Jeffrey Punske, Nathan Sanders, and Amy V. Fountain (eds), *Language Invention for Linguistics Pedagogy.* Oxford: Oxford University Press, Chapter 5, 49–68.

Adger, David, Daniel Harbour, and Laurel Watkins (2009). *Mirrors and Microparameters: Phrase Structure beyond Free Word Order.* Cambridge: Cambridge University Press.

Aissen, Judith, Nora C. England, and Roberto Zavala Maldonado (eds) (2017). *The Mayan languages.* London and New York: Routledge.

Alster, Bendt (1997). *Proverbs of Ancient Sumer: The World's Earliest Proverb Collections.* Potomac, MD: CDL Press.

Anderson, Catherine (2016). 'Learning to think like linguists: A think-aloud study of novice phonology students', *Language* 92(4): 274–91.

Anderson, Skye, Shannon Bischoff, Amy Fountain, and Jeffrey Punske (2017). 'An invented language project for the introductory linguistics classroom', *Fiat Lingua.* Online. http://fiatlingua.org/2017/06/, accessed June 7, 2018.

Andrews, Avery (2007). 'The major functions of the noun phrase', in Timothy Shopen (ed.), *Language Typology and Syntactic Description* (2nd edition), vol. I: Clause Structure. Cambridge: Cambridge University Press, 132–222.

Angelino, Lorraine M., Frankie Keels Williams, and Deborah Natvig (2007). 'Strategies to engage online students and reduce attrition rates', *The Journal of Educators Online* 4(2): 1–14.

B. E. (1698). *A new dictionary of the terms ancient and modern of the canting crew, in its several tribes, of gypsies, beggers, thieves, cheats, &c., with an addition of some proverbs, phrases, figurative speeches, &c. Useful for all sorts of people, (especially foreigners) to secure their money and preserve their lives; besides very diverting and entertaining, being wholly new.* London: W. Hawes, P. Gilbourne, and W. Davis.

Babcock, Rebecca Day, Elizabeth Bilbrey McMellon, and Sailaja Athyala (2015). 'Teaching online courses in linguistics', *Digital Scholarship in the Humanities* 30(4): 481–94.

Bakalar, Nicholas (2013). 'A village invents a language all its own', *New York Times.* Online. https://www.nytimes.com/2013/07/16/science/linguist-finds-a-language-in-its-infancy.html, accessed August 18, 2019.

Baker, Mark C. (1996). *The Polysynthesis Parameter.* Oxford: Oxford University Press.

Baker, Mark C. (2001). *The Atoms of Language: The Mind's Hidden Rules of Grammar.* New York: Basic Books.

Baltasar, Eduardo Hidalgo, Merced Taravillo, Valentín G. Baonza, Pedro D. Sanz, and Bérengère Guignon (2011). 'Speed of sound in liquid water from (253.15 to 348.15) K and pressures from (0.1 to 700) MPa', *Journal of Chemical & Engineering Data* 56: 4800–7.

Bangs, Jesse S. (2002). Lighting some flames: Towards conlang artistry. Online. Electronic mailing list message. https://listserv.brown.edu/archives/cgi-bin/wa?A2=ind0203B&L=CONLANG&P=R13933, accessed September 10, 2018.

Barker, Muhammad Abd-al-Rahman, William Shipley, and John Moore (2017). 'A useful grammar of Colyáni and text with commentary', *Fiat Lingua*. Online. http://fiatlingua.org/wp-content/uploads/2017/07/fl-000047-00.pdf, accessed September 10, 2018.

Bausani, Alessandro (1970). *Geheim- und Universalsprachen. Entwicklung und Typologie*. Sprache und Literatur 57. Stuttgart: Kohlhammer.

Beck, Cave (1657). *The universal character by which all the nations in the world may understand one anothers conceptions, reading out of one common writing their own mother tongues. An invention of general use, the practice whereof may be attained in two hours space, observing the grammatical directions. Which character is so contrived, that it may be spoken as well as written*. London: Thomas Maxey for William Weekley.

Beekes, Robert (2011). *Comparative Indo-European linguistics: An introduction. Second edition, revised and corrected by Michiel de Vaan*. Amsterdam/Philadelphia, PA: John Benjamins.

Bell, David (2010). *The pages of the Gray Wizard*. Online. http://graywizard.conlang.org/, accessed September 10, 2018.

Bendera, Jon (in progress). *MaddConn*.

Berardi-Wiltshire, Arianna and Peter Petrucci (2015). 'Bringing linguistics to life: An anchored approach to teaching linguistics to non-linguists', *Te Reo* 58: 59–75.

Bergen, Benjamin K. (2001). 'Nativization processes in L1 Esperanto', *Journal of Child Language* 28: 575–95.

Blevins, Juliette (1995). 'The syllable in phonological theory', in John Goldsmith (ed.), *The Handbook of Phonological Theory*. Oxford: Blackwell, 206–44.

Bliss, Charles Kasiel (1949). *International semantography: A non-alphabetical symbol writing readable in all languages. A practical tool for general international communication, especially in science, industry, commerce, traffic, etc. and for semantical education, based on the principles of ideographic writing and chemical symbolism*. Sydney: Institute of Semantography.

Bomfim, Anari Braz (2012). *Patxohã, "língua de guerreiro": Um estudo sobre o processo de retomada da língua pataxó*. Masters thesis. Salvador, Brazil: Universidade Federal da Bahia.

Bomfim, Anari Braz (2017). 'Patxohã: A retomada da língua do povo Pataxó', *Revista Linguística / Revista do Programa de Pós-Graduação em Linguística da Universidade Federal do Rio de Janeiro* 13: 303–27.

Boud, David (2001). 'Introduction: Making the move to peer learning', in David Boud, Ruth Cohen, and Jane Sampson (eds), *Peer Learning in Higher Education: Learning from and with Each Other*. New York: Routledge, 1–18.

Bova, Ben (1983). *The beauty of light*. New York: John Wiley & Sons.

Bowern, Claire (2007). *Linguistic Fieldwork: A Practical Guide*. London: Palgrave Macmillan.

Braakman, Jacob (1888). *Systeem voor eene internationale reis- of handelstaal, onder den naam van el mundolinco, dat is: de wereldtaal. Ontworpen en spraakkunstig voor het Nederlandsche volk bewerkt*. Hillegom: Bureau van Mundolinco.

Brocardo, Antonio [published anonymously] (1545). *Nuovo modo de intendere la lingua zerga. Cioè parlare forbescho. Novellamente posto in luce per ordine di alfabeto. Opera non men piacevole, che utilissima.* Ferrara: Giovanmaria di Michieli & Antonio Maria di Sivieri.

Brown, H. Douglas (2007). *Teaching by Principles: An Interactive Approach to Language Pedagogy.* White Plains, NY: Pearson Education.

Brown, James Cooke (1960). 'Loglan', *Scientific American* 202: 53–63.

Brown, Jeffrey (2013). How to describe a conlang. Online. Electronic mailing list message, https://listserv.brown.edu/archives/cgi-bin/wa?A2=ind1301a&L=CONLANG&P=15902, accessed September 10, 2018.

Brown, Padraic (2016). Re: Lighting some flames: Towards conlang artistry. Online. Electronic mailing list message. https://listserv.brown.edu/cgi-bin/wa?A2=ind1605E& L=CONLANG&P=R1984, accessed September 10, 2018.

Bucks County Courier Times (1974). 'New language is created for series', *Tune-In! TV Magazine* 22 September 1974: 1.

Burgess, Anthony (1962). *A Clockwork Orange.* London: William Heinemann Ltd.

Burroughs, Edgar Rice (1917). *A Princess of Mars.* New York: Grosset & Dunlap.

Bybee, Joan, Revere Perkins, and William Pagliuca (1994). *The Evolution of Grammar: Tense, Aspect, and Modality in the Languages of the World.* Chicago, IL: University of Chicago Press.

Bynum, William (2012). *A Little History of Science.* New Haven, CT: Yale University Press.

Byram, Michael (2013). 'Audiolingual method', in Michael Byram and Adelheid Hu (eds), *Routledge Encyclopedia of Language Teaching and Learning.* London and New York: Routledge, 65–7.

Byrd, Andrew Miles (2018). 'The phonology of Proto-Indo-European', in Jared S. Klein, Brian Joseph, Matthias Fritz, and Mark Wenthe (eds), *Handbook of Comparative and Historical Indo-European Linguistics.* Vol. 3. Berlin: de Gruyter, 2056–79.

Cabrera, Alberto, Jennifer Crissman, Elena Bernal, Amaury Nora, Patrick Terenzini, and Ernest Pascarella (2002). 'Collaborative learning: Its impact on college students' development and diversity', *Journal of College Student Development* 43(1): 20–34.

Cain, Robin (2013). 'Total Physical Response', in Michael Byram and Adelheid Hu (eds), *Routledge Encyclopedia of Language Teaching and Learning.* London and New York: Routledge, 731–3.

Carey, John (1990). 'The ancestry of Fénius Farsaid', *Celtica* 21: 104–12.

Carpenter, Angela (2020). 'Teaching invented languages: A capstone course for the undergraduate major', in Jeffrey Punske, Nathan Sanders, and Amy V. Fountain (eds), *Language Invention for Linguistics Pedagogy.* Oxford: Oxford University Press, 107–24.

Catchpole, Clive K. and Peter J. B. Slater (1995). *Bird Song: Biological Themes and Variations.* Cambridge: Cambridge University Press.

Chiang, Ted (1999). 'Story of your life', in David G. Hartwell (ed.), *Year's Best SF 4.* New York: Harper Collins, 119–81.

Chomsky, Noam (1993). 'A minimalist program for linguistic theory', *MIT occasional papers in linguistics* 1. Cambridge, MA: Distributed by MIT Working Papers in Linguistics.

Chomsky, Noam and Morris Halle (1968). *The Sound Pattern of English.* Cambridge, MA: MIT Press.

Christiansen, Morten, Chris Collins, and Shimon Edelman (2009). *Language Universals.* Oxford: Oxford University Press.

Clackson, James (2007). *Indo-European Linguistics: An Introduction*. Cambridge: Cambridge University Press.

Claire, Bowern (2007). *Linguistic Field Work: A Practical Guide*. London: Palgrave MacMillan.

Clemens, Lauren and Jessica Coon (2018). 'Deriving verb-initial word order in Mayan', *Language* 94(2): 237–80.

Cocconi, Guiseppe and Philip Morrison (1959). 'Searching for interstellar communications', *Nature* 184: 844–6.

Collins, John Williams and Nancy P. O'Brien (2011). *The Greenwood dictionary of education*. Santa Barbara, CA: Greenwood. Online. http://ebooks.abc-clio.com/?isbn=9780313379314. (Password protected.)

Comrie, Bernard (1978). 'Ergativity', in Winfred Lehmann (ed.), *Syntactic Typology*. Austin, TX: University of Texas Press, 329–94.

Comrie, Bernard (1989). *Linguistic Universals and Linguistic Typology: Syntax and Morphology*, 2nd edition. Chicago, IL: University of Chicago Press.

Comrie, Bernard and Norval Smith (1977). 'Lingua descriptive studies: Questionnaire', *Lingua* 42: 1–72.

Conklin, Harold C. (1956). 'Tagalog speech disguise', *Language* 32: 136–9.

Conlanging: The Art of Crafting Tongues (2017). Britton Watkins, director. Film.

Conley, Tim and Stephen Cain (2006). *Encyclopedia of Fictional and Fantastic Languages*. Westport, CT: Greenwood Press.

Cook, Margaret, Alison Littlefair, and Greg Brooks (2007). Responses to Wyse and Styles' article, 'Synthetic phonics and the teaching of reading: The debate surrounding England's "Rose Report"', *Literacy* 41: 169–70.

Coon, Jessica, Diane Massam, and Lisa Travis (eds) (2017). *The Oxford Handbook of Ergativity*. Oxford: Oxford University Press.

Corbett, Greville (2000). *Number*. Cambridge: Cambridge University Press.

Corey, James S. A. [Daniel Abraham and Ty Franck] (2011). *Leviathan Wakes*. London: Orbit Books.

Corsetti, Renato (1996). 'A mother tongue spoken mainly by fathers', *Language Problems and Language Planning* 20: 263–73.

Cowan, John Woldemar (1997). *The Complete Lojban Language*. Fairfax, VA: Logical Language Group, Inc.

Croft, William (2002). *Typology and Universals* (2nd edition). Cambridge: Cambridge University Press.

Curzan, Ann (2013). 'Linguistics matters: Resistance and relevance in teacher education'. *Language* 89: 1–10.

Dalgarno, George (1661). *Ars Signorum, vulgo Character Universalis et Lingua Philosophica. Qa poterunt, homines diversissimorum idiomatum, spatio duarum septimanarum, omnia animi sua sensa (in rebus familiaribus) non minus intelligibiliter, sive scribendo, sive loquendo, mutuo communicare, qam linguis propriis vernaculis. Præterea, hinc etiam poterunt juvenes, philosophiæ principia, & veram logicæ praxin, citius & facilius multo imbibere, qam ex vulgaribus philosophorum scriptis*. London: John Hayes.

Danesi, Marcel (2004). *A basic course in anthropological linguistics*. Studies in Linguistic and Cultural Anthropology 2. Toronto: Canadian Scholars Press.

Derbyshire, Desmond C. (1977). 'Word order universals and the existence of OVS languages', *Linguistic Inquiry* 8: 590–9.

Dixon, R. M. W. (1979). 'Ergativity', *Language* 55(1): 59–138.

Dixon, R. M. W. (1994). *Ergativity*. Cambridge: Cambridge University Press.

Dörnyei, Zoltán and Angi Malderez (1997). 'Group dynamics and foreign language teaching', *System* 25(1): 66–81.

Douet, Jean (1627). *Proposition présentée au roy, d'une escriture universelle, admirable pour ses effects, tres-utile et nécessaire à tous les hommes de la terre.* Paris: Jacques Dugaast.

Dreyfuss, Emily (2017). 'That cool language on *The Expanse* mashes up 6 languages', *Wired.* 5 April 2017. Online. https://www.wired.com/2017/04/the-expanse-belter-language, accessed August 18, 2018.

Dryer, Matthew S. (1992). 'The Greenbergian word order correlations', *Language* 68: 81–138.

Dryer, Matthew S. (2007). 'Word order', in Timothy Shopen (ed.), *Language Typology and Syntactic Description* (2nd edition), vol. I: Clause Structure. Cambridge: Cambridge University Press, 61–130.

Dryer, Matthew S. (2013a). 'Order of subject, object and verb', *The World Atlas of Language Structures Online.* Online. Leipzig: Max Planck Institute for Evolutionary Anthropology. https://wals.info/chapter/81, accessed September 10, 2018.

Dryer, Matthew S. (2013b). 'Relationship between the order of object and verb and the order of adposition and noun phrase', *The World Atlas of Language Structures Online.* Online. Leipzig: Max Planck Institute for Evolutionary Anthropology. https://wals.info/chapter/95, accessed September 10, 2018.

Dryer, Matthew S. and Martin Haspelmath (eds) (2013). *The World Atlas of Language Structures Online.* Online. Leipzig: Max Planck Institute for Evolutionary Anthropology. http://wals.info, accessed September 10, 2018.

Eco, Umberto (1993). *La ricerca della lingua perfetta nella cultura europea.* Rome: Laterza.

Eco, Umberto (1995). *Ricerca della lingua perfetta nella cultura europea. The Search for the Perfect Language.* Translated by James Fentress. Cambridge, MA: Blackwell.

Ekman, Fredrik (2012). 'An interview with Paul Frommer', *Fiat Lingua.* Online. http://fiatlingua.org/2012/03/, accessed August 17, 2018.

Elgin, Suzette Haden (1984). *Native Tongue.* New York: DAW Books.

Elgin, Suzette Haden (1988). *A First Dictionary and Grammar of Láadan: Second Edition.* Madison, WI: SF3.

Emre, Side (2017). *Ibrahim-i Gulshani and the Khalwati-Gulshani order: Power brokers in Ottoman Egypt.* Studies on Sufism 1. Leiden, The Netherlands: Brill.

England, Nora C. (2007). 'The influence of Mayan-speaking linguists on the state of Mayan linguistics', in Peter K. Austin and Andrew Simpson (eds), *Endangered Languages.* Linguistische Berichte Sonderheft 14. Hamburg: Helmut Buske Verlag, 93–111.

Erickson, Hal (1998). *Sid and Marty Krofft: A critical study of Saturday morning children's television, 1969–1993.* Jefferson, NC: McFarland & Company.

Erman, Adolf (2012). *Ancient Egyptian Literature.* London / New York: Routledge.

ETCSL [The ETCSL Project] (2003–7). *The Electronic Text Corpus of Sumerian Literature.* Oxford: Faculty of Oriental Studies, Oxford University. Online. http://etcsl.orinst.ox.ac.uk/, accessed August 16, 2018.

Everett, Daniel (2008). *Don't Sleep There are Snakes: Life and Language in the Amazonian Jungle.* New York: Vintage Departures.

Everett, Daniel (2016). *Dark Matter of the Mind: The Culturally Articulated Unconscious.* Chicago, IL: University of Chicago Press.

Everett, Daniel (2017). *How Language Began: The Story of Humanity's Greatest Invention.* New York: Liveright Publishing.

Fant, Clyde E. and Mitchell G. Reddish (2008). *Lost Treasures of the Bible: Understanding the Bible through Archaeological Artifacts in World Museums.* Grand Rapids, MI: Williams B. Eerdmans Publishing.

Fantini, Alvino E. (1997). *New Ways in Teaching Culture*. Alexandria, VA: TESOL Publications.

Fellman, Jack (1973). *The Revival of Classical Tongue: Eliezer Ben Yehuda and the Modern Hebrew Language*. Berlin: De Gruyter.

Fimi, Dimitra and Andrew Higgins (2017). 'Invented Languages', in Mark J. P. Wolf (ed.), *The Routledge Companion to Imaginary Worlds*. New York: Routledge, 21–9.

Fish, Stanley (2005). 'Devoid of content', *The New York Times*. Online. https://www.nytimes.com/2005/05/31/opinion/devoid-of-content.html., accessed September 10, 2018.

Flemming, Edward (2005). 'Speech perception and phonological contrast', in David Pisoni and Robert Remez (eds), *The Handbook of Speech Perception*. John Wiley & Sons, 156–81.

Forster, Peter G. (1982). *The Esperanto Movement*. The Hague: Mouton.

Fortson, Benjamin W. IV (2010). *Indo-European Language and Culture*. Malden, MA and Oxford, UK: Wiley-Blackwell.

Fosnot, Catherine Twomey and Randall Stewart Perry (2005). 'Constructivism: A Psychological Theory of Learning', in Catherine Twomey Fosnot (ed.), *Constructivism: Theory, Perspectives, and Practice*. New York: Teachers College Press, 8–38.

François, Alexandre (2005). 'A typological overview of Mwotlap, an Oceanic language of Vanuatu', *Linguistic Typology* 9: 115–46.

Frank, Austin F. and T. Florian Jaeger (2008). 'Speaking rationally: Uniform information density as an optimal strategy for language production', *Proceedings of the Annual Meeting of the Cognitive Science Society* 30: 939–44.

Freeman, Scott, Sarah L. Eddy, Miles McDonough, Michelle K. Smith, Nnadozie Okoroafor, Hannah Jordt, and Mary Pat Wenderoth (2014). 'Active learning increases student performance in science, engineering, and mathematics', *Proceedings of the National Academy of Sciences* 111(23): 8410–15.

Freudenthal, Hans (1960). *Lincos: Design of a Language for Cosmic Intercourse*. Amsterdam: North-Holland.

Garrett, Danny (2016). 'Language creation in early learning', *Fiat Lingua*. Online. http://fiatlingua.org/2016/10/, accessed June 7, 2018.

Garvía, Roberto (2015). *Esperanto and its Rivals: The Struggle for an International Language*. Philadelphia, PA: University of Pennsylvania Press.

Gelb, Ignace J., Benno Landsberger, and A. Leo Oppenheim (1962). *The Assyrian Dictionary of the Oriental Institute of the University of Chicago*. Vol. 16. Chicago, IL: The Oriental Institute.

Gibbon, Dafydd, Moses Ekpenyong, and Eno-Abasi Urua (2010). 'Medefaidrin: Resources documenting the birth and death language life-cycle', in Nicoletta Calzolari, Khalid Choukri, Bente Maegaard, Joseph Mariani, Jan Odijk, Stelios Piperidis, Mike Rosner, and Danile Tapias (eds), *Proceedings of the Seventh Conference on International Language Resources and Evaluation (LREC'10)*. Valetta, Malta: European Languages Resources Association, 2702–8.

Gibson, Edward, Steven T. Piantadosi, Kimberly Brink, Leon Bergen, Eunice Lim, and Rebecca Saxe (2013). 'A noisy-channel account of crosslinguistic word-order variation', *Psychological Science* 24: 1079–88.

Gleitman, Lila, and Anna Papafragou (2005). 'Language and thought', in Keith J. Holyoak and Robert G. Morrison (eds), *The Cambridge Handbook of Thinking and Rasoning*. Cambridge: Cambridge University Press, 633–62.

Gobbo, Federico (2013). 'Learning linguistics by doing: The secret virtues of language constructed in the classroom', *Journal of Universal Language* 14: 113–35.

Godwin, Francis (1638). *The man in the moone: Or a discourse of a voyage thither by Domingo Gonsales the speedy messenger.* London: John Norton.

Gordon, Edmund I. (1954). 'The Sumerian proverb collections: A preliminary report', *Journal of the American Oriental Society* 74: 82–5.

Greenberg, Joseph H. (1963). 'Some universals of grammar with particular reference to the order of meaningful elements', in Joseph H. Greenberg (ed.), *Universals of Human Language.* Cambridge, MA: MIT Press, 73–113.

Grice, H. Paul (1975). 'Logic and Conversation', in Peter Cole and Jerry Morgan (eds), *Syntax and Semantics 3. Speech Acts.* New York: Academic Press, 41–58.

Grünthal, Riho (2010). *Finnic Adpositions and Cases in Change.* Helsinki: Société Finno-Ougrienne. Online. https://www.sgr.fi/sust/sust244/sust244.pdf, accessed August 31, 2018.

Hale, Kenneth (1966). 'Kinship reflections in syntax: Some Australian cases', *Word* 22: 318–24.

Hale, Kenneth (1992). 'Language endangerment and the human value of linguistic diversity', *Language* 68(1): 35–42.

Hale, Kenneth and David Nash (1997). 'Damin and Lardil phonotactics', in Darrell Tryon and Michael Walsh (eds), *Boundary Rider: Essays in Honour of Geoffrey O'Grady.* Canberra: Pacific Linguistics, Research School of Pacific and Asian Studies, Australian National University, 247–59.

Hale, Ken, Michael Krauss, Lucille J. Watahomigie, Akira Y. Yamamoto, Colette Craig, LaVerne Masayesva Jeanne, and Nora C. England (1992). 'Endangered languages', *Language* 68(1): 1–42.

Hamel, Anton G. van (1915). 'On *Lebor Gabála*', *Zeitschrift für celtische Philologie* 10(1): 95–197.

Harley, Heidi and Elizabeth Ritter (2002). A feature-geometric analysis of person and number. *Language* 78: 482–526.

Hawkins, John (1983). *Word Order Universals.* New York: Academic Press.

Hawkins, John (1990). 'A parsing theory of word order universals', *Linguistic Inquiry* 21: 223–61.

Hawkins, John (2004). *Efficiency and Complexity in Grammars.* Oxford: Oxford University Press.

Hawkins, John (2014). *Cross-Linguistic Variation and Efficiency.* Oxford: Oxford University Press.

Heine, Bernd and Tania Kuteva (2002). *World Lexicon of Grammaticalization.* Cambridge: Cambridge University Press.

Herbert, Frank (1965). *Dune.* Philadelphia, PA: Chilton Books.

Higley, Sarah L. (2007). *Hildegard of Bingen's Unknown Language: An Edition, Translation, and Discussion.* New York and Hampshire, England: Palgrave MacMillan.

Hinton, Leanne and Kenneth Hale (eds) (2001). *The Green Book of Language Revitalization in Practice.* San Diego, CA: Academic Press.

Hinton, Leanne, Leena Huss, and Gerald Roche (2018). 'Introduction: Language revitalization as a growing field of study and practice', in Leanne Hinton, Leena Huss, and Gerald Roche (eds), *The Routledge Handbook of Language Revitalization.* New York: Routledge, xxi–xxx.

Hmelo-Silver, Cindy E. (2004). 'Problem-Based Learning: What and How do Students Learn?', *Educational Psychology Review* 16(3): 235–66.

Hogben, Lancelot (1963). *Science in Authority.* New York: W. W. Norton.

Hotz, Robert Lee (2010). 'Rare find: a New Language', *Wall Street Journal.* Online. https://www.wsj.com/articles/SB10001424052748703843804575534122591921594, accessed August 18, 2018.

Hütlin, Matthias (1509). *Liber vagatorum: Der betler orden*. Augsburg: Johann Froschauer.

Jakobson, Roman, C. Gunnar M. Fant, and Morris Halle (1954). *Preliminaries to Speech Analysis: The Distinctive Features and Their Correlates*. Cambridge, MA: MIT Press.

Jasanoff, Jay (2003). *Hittite and the Indo-European Verb*. Oxford: Oxford University Press.

Jespersen, Otto (1928). *An International Language*. London: George Allen & Unwin.

Johnson, Keith (2012). *Acoustic and Auditory Phonetics*. Third edition. Malden, MA: Wiley-Blackwell.

Johnson, Steven (2017). 'Greetings, ET, please don't murder us', *New York Times Magazine*. June 28, 2017.

Jones, Casey (2009). 'Interdisciplinary Approach - Advantages, Disadvantages, and the Future Benefits of Interdisciplinary Studies', *ESSAI* 7: 76–81.

Keenan, Edward (1985). 'Relative clauses', in Timothy Shopen (ed.), *Language Typology and Syntactic Description* (second edition), vol. I: Clause Structure. Cambridge: Cambridge University Press, 141–70.

Keevak, Michael (2004). *The Pretended Asian: George Psalmanazar's Eighteenth-Century Formosan Hoax*. Detroit, MI: Wayne State University Press.

Kelly, John (2001). 'Atlantis linguist creates his own undersea speak', *Sun Sentinel*. June 26. Online. http://articles.sun-sentinel.com/2001-06-26/lifestyle/0106250263_1_indo-%20european-language-atlantis, accessed September 11, 2018.

Kelly, Piers (2012). *The word made flesh: An ethnographic history of Eskayan, a utopian language and script in the southern Philippines*. Doctoral dissertation. Canberra: The Australian National University.

Kershenbaum, Eric (2020). 'Many ways to say things: What the diversity of animal communication on Earth can tell us about the nature of alien language', in Douglas Vakoch and Jeffrey Punske (eds), *Xenolinguistics: Toward a Science of Extraterrestrial Language*. In prep.

King, Susan (2005). 'Ku spoken, but only here', *Los Angeles Times*. April 27. Online. http://articles.latimes.com/2005/apr/27/entertainment/et-kingku27, accessed August 18, 2018.

Kiparsky, Paul (2010). 'Compositional vs. paradigmatic approaches to accent and ablaut', in Stephanie W. Jamison, H. Craig Melchert, and Brent Vine (eds), *Proceedings of the 21st Annual UCLA Indo-European Conference*. Bremen: Hempen, 137–81.

Knowlson, James (1975). *Universal Language Schemes in England and France, 1600–1800*. Toronto: University of Toronto Press.

Koç, Mustafa (2005). *Bâleybelen, Muhyî-i Gülşenî: İlk yapma dil*. İstanbul: Klasik.

Kramer, Samuel Noah (1968). 'The "Babel of Tongues": A Sumerian version'. *Journal of the American Oriental Society* 88: 108–11.

Kramsch, Claire (1998). *Language and Culture*. Oxford: Oxford University Press.

Krashen, Stephen D. (1985). *The Input Hypothesis*. London: Longman.

Kuiper, Koenraad (2011a). 'LING101', in Koenraad Kuiper (ed.), *Teaching Linguistics: Reflections on Practice*. London: Equinox, 182–8.

Kuiper, Koenraad (2011b). *Teaching Linguistics: Reflections on Practice*. Sheffield: Equinox.

Labbé, Philippe (1663). *Grammatica linguæ universalis missionum et commerciorum, simplicissimæ, brevissimæ, facillimæ, ut eius ope ac beneficio multa dicantur & audiantur paucis, multa scribantur & legantur paucis, terra fiat labij unius, fideique christianę ac sacrarum expeditionum propagatio promoveatur in dies. Accessere lexiciatque tyrocinij specimina*. Third edition. Paris: Jacques Roger.

Lakoff, George and Rafael Nuñez (2000). *Where Mathematics Comes From: How the Embodied Mind Brings Mathematics into Being*. New York: Basic Books.

Lambert, Wilfred G. (1960). *Babylonian Wisdom Literature*. Oxford: Clarendon Press.

Language Creation Society (2007). *Articles of Incorporation of Language Creation Society: A Public Benefit Corporation*. Online. https://docs.google.com/document/d/1bJAlyIGJWzdDlT9NfYgIo1i-mhca81W4XcH89Xdpygs/preview, accessed September 10, 2018.

Large, J. Andrew (1985). *The Artificial Language Movement*. Oxford: Blackwell.

Lattuca, Lisa R., Louis. J. Voigt, and Kimberly Q. Fath (2004). 'Does interdisciplinarity promote learning?: Theoretical support and researchable questions', *Review of Higher Education* 28: 23–48.

Laycock, Donald C. (1972). 'Towards a typology of play-languages, or ludlings.' *Linguistic Communications* 6: 61–113.

Laycock, Donald C. (1978). *The Complete Enochian Dictionary: A Dictionary of the Angelic Language as Revealed to Dr. John Dee and Edward Kelley*. London: Askin.

LeVine, Steve (2016). 'A Silicon Valley linguist invented a new sci-fi language and it's catching on here on Earth', *Quartz*. 6 May 2016. Online. https://qz.com/675453/a-silicon-valley-linguist-invented-a-new-sci-fi-language-and-its-catching-on-here-on-earth, accessed August 18, 2018.

Levinson, Steven (1997a). 'Language and cognition: The cognitive consequences of spatial cognition in Guugu Yimithirr', *Journal of Linguistic Anthropology* 7: 98–131.

Levinson, Steven (1997b). 'From outer to inner space: linguistic categories and nonlinguistic thinking', in Jan Nuyts and Eric Pederson (eds), *Language and Conceptualization*. Cambridge: Cambridge University Press, 13–45.

Lillehaugen, Brook Danielle, Gabriela Echavarría Moats, Daniel Gillen, Elizabeth Peters, and Rebecca Schwartz (2014). 'A tactile IPA magnet-board system: A tool for blind and visually impaired students in phonetics and phonology classrooms', *Language* 90(4): 274–83.

Lindblom, Björn and Olle Engstrand (1989). 'In what sense is speech quantal', *Journal of Phonetics* 17: 107–21.

Lippi-Green, Rosina (2012). *English with an accent: Language, ideology and discrimination in the United States*. New York: Routledge.

Lodwick, Francis (1647). *A common writing: Whereby two, although not understanding one the others language, yet by the helpe thereof, may communicate their minds one to another*. London.

Lodwick, Francis (1652). *The ground-work, or foundation laid, (or so intended) for the framing of a new perfect language: And an universall or common writing. And presented to the consideration of the learned, by a well-willer to learning*. London.

Long, Alison (2018). 'How I invented a new language for *The City and the City*', *The Conversation*. April 4, 2018. Online. https://theconversation.com/how-i-invented-a-new-language-for-the-city-and-the-city-94189, accessed August 17, 2018.

Lovette, Irby J. and John W. Fitzpatrick (eds) (2016). *Handbook of Bird Biology* (third edition). Chichester: John Wiley & Sons.

Macaulay, Monica (2004). 'Training linguistics students for the realities of fieldwork', *Anthropological Linguistics* 46(2): 194–209.

MacKillop, James (2005). *Myths and Legends of the Celts*. London: Penguin Books.

Maddieson, Ian (1984). *Patterns of Sounds*. Cambridge: Cambridge University Press.

Malotki, Ekkehart (1983). *Hopi Time: A Linguistic Analysis of Temporal Concepts in the Hopi Language*. Berlin: De Gruyter.

Mansell, Warwick (2017). 'Battle on the adverbials front: Grammar advisers raise worries about SATS tests and teaching', *The Guardian*. May 9, 2017.

Martin, George R. R. (1996). *A Game of Thrones*. New York: Bantam Spectra.

Martin, Laura (1986). '"Eskimo words for snow": A case study in the genesis and decay of an anthropological example', *American Anthropologist* 88(2): 418–23.

Massam, Diane (2001). 'Pseudo noun incorporation in Niuean', *Natural Language and Linguistic Theory* 19: 153–97.

Maximilian, Prinz zu Wied-Neuwied (1820–1821). *Reise nach Brasilien in den Jahren 1815 bis 1817.* 2 vols. Frankfurt: Heinrich Ludwig Brönner.

McWhorter, John H. (2014). *The Language Hoax: Why the World Looks the Same in any Language.* Oxford: Oxford University Press.

Meier-Brügger, Michael (2010). *Indo-Germanische Sprachwissenschaft.* Ninth edition. Berlin & New York: de Gruyter.

Mesgarani, Nima, Connie Cheung, Keith Johnson, and Edward F. Chang (2014). 'Phonetic feature encoding in human superior temporal gyrus', *Science* 343: 1006–10.

Michael, Joel (2006). 'Where's the evidence that active learning works?', *Advances in Physiology Education* 30(4): 159–67.

Miéville, China (2009). *The City & the City.* London: Macmillan.

Moravcsik, Edith (2013). *Introducing Language Typology.* Cambridge: Cambridge University Press.

More, Thomas (1516). *De optimo reipublicæ statu, deque nova insula Utopia, libellus vere aureus, nec minus salutaris quam festivus clarissimi disertissimique viri Thomæ Mori inclutæ civitatis Londinensis civis & vicecomitis.* Louvain: Thierry Martens.

Mundy, Darren P. and Robert Consoli (2013). 'Here be dragons: Experiments with the concept of "Choose Your Own Adventure" in the lecture room', *Innovations in Education and Teaching International* 50(2): 214–23.

Nemet-Nejat, Karen (2014). 'Akkadian wisdom literature', in Mark W. Chavalas (ed.), *Women in the Ancient Near East: A Sourcebook.* London: Routledge, 75–100.

Newell, William (1994). 'Designing interdisciplinary courses', *Interdisciplinary Studies Today* 58: 35–51.

Newmeyer, Frederick (2005). *Possible and Probable Languages: A Generative Perspective on Linguistic Typology.* Oxford: Oxford University Press.

Nichols, Johanna (1986). 'Head-marking and dependent-marking grammar', *Language* 62: 56–119.

Oberhaus, Daniel (2019). *Extraterrestrial Languages.* Boston MA: MIT Press.

Okrand, Marc (1985/1992). *The Klingon Dictionary.* New York: Pocket Books.

Okrand, Marc (1997). *Klingon for the Galactic Traveler.* New York: Pocket Books.

Okrand, Marc, Michael Adams, Judith Hendriks-Hermans, and Sjaak Kroom (2011). 'Wild and whirling words: The invention and use of Klingon', in Michael Adams (ed.), *From Elvish to Klingon: Exploring Invented Languages.* Oxford: Oxford University Press, 111–34.

Okrent, Arika (2010). *In the Land of Invented Languages: Adventures in Linguistic Creativity, Madness, and Genius.* New York: Spiegel & Grau.

Oliver, Frederick Spencer (1894). *A Dweller on Two Planets: Or, the Dividing of the Way.* Los Angeles, CA: Baumgardt.

Oostendorp, Marc van (2019). 'Language contact and constructed languages', in Jeroen Darquennes, Joe Salmons, and Wim Vandenbussche (eds), *Language Contact: An International Handbook.* Handbücher zur Sprach-und Kommunikationswissenschaft / Handbook of Linguistics and Communication Science 45/1. Berlin: de Gruyter, 124–35.

Orwell, George (1949). *1984.* London: Secker & Warburg.

Ottenheimer, Harriet Joseph and Judith M. S. Pine (2018). *The Anthropology of Language: An Introduction to Linguistic Anthropology*. Fourth edition. Boston, MA: Cengage Learning.

Palmer, F. R. (1994). *Grammatical Roles and Relations*. Cambridge: Cambridge University Press.

Payne, Thomas (1997). *Describing Morphosyntax: A Guide for Field Linguists*. Cambridge: Cambridge University Press.

Pearson, Matt (2017). 'Using language invention to teach typology and cross-linguistic universals', *Fiat Lingua*. Online. http://fiatlingua.org/2017/04/, accessed June 7, 2018.

Pearson, Matt (2020). 'Using language invention to teach typology and cross-linguistic universals', in Jeffrey Punske, Nathan Sanders, and Amy V. Fountain (eds), *Language Invention for Linguistics Pedagogy*. Oxford: Oxford University Press, 86–106.

Pehrson, Trent M. (2018). *Welcome to the only official description of the Idrani language*. Online. http://idrani.perastar.com/, accessed September 10, 2018.

Pellegrino, François, Christophe Coupé, and Egidio Marsico (2011). 'A cross-language perspective on speech information rate', *Language* 87: 539–58.

Peterson, David J. (2002). Re: Calling all conlangers! Online. Electronic mailing list message https://listserv.brown.edu/archives/cgi-bin/wa?A2=ind0201C&L=CONLANG&P=R13751 &K=2, accessed September 13, 2018.

Peterson, David J. (2006). A rebuttal of the notion of a trigger language. Online. https://en.wikibooks.org/wiki/Talk:Conlang/Advanced/Grammar/Alignment/Trigger, accessed September 10, 2018.

Peterson, David J. (2014). *Living Language Dothraki: A Conversational Language Course Based on the Hit Original HBO Series Game of Thrones*. New York: Living Language.

Peterson, David J. (2015). *The Art of Language Invention: From Horse-Lords to Dark Elves, the Words Behind World-Building*. New York: Penguin Books.

Peterson, David J. (2018). 'Slides for Linguistics 183: The Linguistics of Game of Thrones and the Art of Language Invention', *Fiat Lingua*. Online. http://fiatlingua.org/2018/09/, accessed September 10, 2018.

Peterson, David J. (2020). 'Artistry in Language Invention: Conlang Pedagogy and the Instructor as Authority', in Jeffrey Punske, Nathan Sanders, and Amy V. Fountain (eds), *Language Invention for Linguistics Pedagogy*. Oxford: Oxford University Press. 251–81.

Piñeros, Carlos Eduardo (1988). *Prosodic morphology in Spanish*. Doctoral dissertation. Columbus, OH: The Ohio State University.

Pinker, Steven (1994). *The Language Instinct: How the Mind Creates Language*. New York: Harper Collins.

Pinker, Steven (2011). *The Better Angels of Our Nature: Why Violence Has Declined*. London: Penguin Books.

Pirro, Jean (1868). *Essai d'une langue universelle*. Bar-le-Duc: Le Guérin.

Port, Robert F. (2008). 'All is prosody: Phones and phonemes are the ghosts of letters'. Online. https://www.cs.indiana.edu/~port/HDphonol/Port.Prosody2008.keynote.pdf, accessed September 11, 2018.

Prisco, Jacopo (2018). 'How do you design a language from scratch? Ask a Klingon,' *CNN*, July 3, 2018. Online. https://www.cnn.com/style/article/star-trek-klingon-marc-okrand/index.html, accessed September 15, 2018.

Psalmanazar, George (1704). *An Historical and Geographical Description of Formosa, an Island Subject to the Emperor of Japan*. London: Dan. Brown, G. Strahan, W. Davis, Fran. Coggan, and Bernard Lintott.

Psalmanazar, George (1764). *Memoirs of ****. Commonly known as George Psalmanazar; A Reputed Native of Formosa*. London: R. Davis, J. Newbery, L. Davis, and C. Reymers.

Pullum, Geoffrey K. (1991). *The Great Eskimo Vocabulary Hoax and Other Irreverent Essays on the Study of Language*. Chicago, IL: University of Chicago Press.

Quast, Paul (2018). 'Celestial heritage arising from the Cold War era 1957–1991 (working catalog)'. Manuscript, University of Edinburgh.

Quijada, John (2011). 'Introduction', *Ithkuil: A philosophical design for a hypothetical language*. Online. http://ithkuil.net/00_intro.html, accessed September 10, 2018.

Rabelais, François (c. 1532). *Pantagruel. Les horribles et espouvantables faictz et prouesses du tresrenomme Pantagruel Roy des Dipsodes, filz du grant geant Gargantua. Composez nouvellement par maistre Alcofrybas Nasier*. Lyon: Claude Nourry.

Rhiemeier, Jörg (2007/2010). *A brief history of conlanging*. Online. http://www.joerg-rhiemeier.de/Conlang/history.html, accessed August 16, 2018.

Riede, Tobias and Franz Goller (2010). 'Peripheral mechanisms for vocal production in birds—differences and similarities to human speech and singing', *Brain and Language* 115: 69–80.

Ringe, Don (2006). *From Proto-Indo-European to Proto-Germanic*. Oxford and New York: Oxford University Press.

Rizzolo, Olivier (2006). 'Utrovački and Šatrovački: Description and theoretical perspectives of two Serbo-Croatian language games', in Richard Compton, Magda Goledzinowska, and Ulyana Savchenko (eds), *Formal Approaches to Slavic Linguistics: The Toronto meeting, 2006* [Michigan Slavic Materials 52]. Ann Arbor, MI: Michigan Slavic Publications, 264–81.

Roget, Peter Mark (1853). *Thesaurus of English Words and Phrases, Classified and Arranged so as to Facilitate the Expression of Ideas and Assist in Literary Composition*. Second edition. London: Longman, Brown, Green, and Longmans.

Rose, Gilbert (2013). 'La téléphonie de Jean-François Sudre', in *Communications de l'année académique 2012–2013*. Mémoires de l'Académie Nationale de Metz 2013. Metz: Académie Nationale de Metz, 159–66.

Rosen, Michael (2015). 'Dear Ms Morgan: In grammar there isn't always one right answer', *The Guardian*. November 3, 2015.

Rosenfelder, Mark (2010). *The Language Construction Kit*. Chicago, IL: Yonagu Books.

Rylko-Bauer, Barbara, Merrill Singer, and John van Willigen (2006). 'Reclaiming Applied Anthropology: Its Past, Present, and Future', *American Anthropologist* 108: 178–90.

Sagan, Carl (1987). *Cosmos*. New York: Random House.

Samuels, Bridget and Jeffrey Punske (2020). 'Where does Universal Grammar fit in the universe? Human cognition as a strong, minimalist thesis', in Douglas Vakoch and Jeffrey Punske (eds), *Xenolinguistics: Toward a Science of Extraterrestrial Language*. In prep.

Sánchez, Liliana (2010). *The Morphology and Syntax of Topic and Focus: Minimalist Inquiries in the Quechua Periphery*. Linguistik Aktuell/Linguistics Today 169. Amsterdam: John Benjamins.

Sanders, Nathan (2016). 'Constructed languages in the classroom', *Language* 92: e192–e204.

Sanders, Nathan (2020). 'A primer on constructed languages', in Jeffrey Punske, Nathan Sanders, and Amy V. Fountain (eds). *Language Invention for Linguistics Pedagogy*. Oxford: Oxford University Press, 6–26.

Sanders, Nathan and Christine Schreyer (2020). 'Moving beyond linguistics: The interdisciplinarity of conlangs', in Jeffrey Punske, Nathan Sanders, and Amy V. Fountain (eds), *Language Invention for Linguistics Pedagogy*. Oxford: Oxford University Press, Chapter 11, 169–85.

Schachter, Paul and Timothy Shopen (2007). 'Part-of-speech systems', in Timothy Shopen (ed.), *Language Typology and Syntactic Description* (second edition), vol. I: Clause Structure. Cambridge: Cambridge University Press, 1–60.

Schipfer, Joseph (1839). *Versuch einer Grammatik für eine Allgemeine Communications- oder Weltsprache*. Wiesbaden: Riedel.

Schleyer, Johann Martin (1880). *Volapük. Die Weltsprache. Entwurf einer Universalsprache für alle Gebildete der ganzen Erde*. Sigmaringen: C. Tappen.

Schreyer, Christine (2011). 'Media, information technology, and language planning: What can endangered language communities learn from created language communities?', *Current Issues in Language Planning* 12(3): 403–25.

Schreyer, Christine, Clarke Ballantine, Vanessa Bella, Joanne Gabias, Brittany Ganzini, Robyn Giffen, Pamela Higgins, Justin Kroeker, David Lacho, Stacy Madill, Louisa McGlinchey, Sasha McLachlan, Shelley Nguy, Tara Wolkolsky, and Vanessa Zubot (2013). 'The culture of conlanging: What can we learn about culture from created languages?', *Fiat Lingua* FL-000017-00. Online. http://fiatlingua.org/2013/08/, accessed June 7, 2018.

Shklovsi, I. S. and Carl Sagan (1966). *Intelligent Life in the Universe*. San Francisco, CA: Holden-Day.

Shopen, Timothy (ed.) (1985). *Language Typology and Syntactic Description*. Cambridge: Cambridge University Press.

Shopen, Timothy (ed.) (2007). *Language Typology and Syntactic Description* (second edition). Cambridge: Cambridge University Press.

Shostak, Seth (2015). 'Should we keep a low profile in space?', *The New York Times* March 29, 2015, SR: 3.

Shostak, Seth (2017). 'Humankind just beamed a signal at space aliens. Was that a bad idea?', *SETI.org* Online. https://www.seti.org/humankind-just-beamed-signal-space-aliens-was-bad-idea, accessed 30 July 2019.

Shrum, Judith L. and Eileen W. Glisan (2010). *Teacher's Handbook, Contextualized Language Instruction*. Boston, MA: Heinle Cengage Learning.

Slavich, George M. and Philip G. Zimbardo (2012). 'Transformational teaching: Theoretical underpinnings, basic principles, and core methods', *Educational Psychology Review* 24: 569–608.

Slobin, Dan I. (1980). 'The repeated path between transparency and opacity in language', in Ursula Bellugi and Michael Studdert-Kennedy (eds), *Signed and Spoken Language: Biological Constraints on Linguistic Form*. Deerfield Beach, CA: Verlag Chimie, 229–43.

Smith, Karl A., Sheri D. Sheppard, David W. Johnson, and Roger T. Johnson (2005). 'Pedagogies of engagement: Classroom-based practices', *Journal of Engineering Education* 94(1): 87–101.

Snyder, Noel F. R. and Helen A. Snyder (2005). *Introduction to the California Condor*. California Natural History Guides 81. Berkeley, CA: University of California Press.

Song, Jae Jung (2018). *Linguistic Typology*. Oxford: Oxford University Press.

Sotomayor, Sylvia (1980–2019). *An Introduction to Kēlen*. Online. http://www.terjemar.net/kelen/kelen.php, accessed April 21, 2019.

Spolsky, Bernard and Robert L. Cooper (1991). *The Languages of Jerusalem*. Oxford: Oxford University Press.

Spring, Cari, Rae Moses, Michael Flynn, Susan Steele, Brian D. Joseph, and Charlotte Webb (2000). 'The successful introductory course: Bridging the gap for the nonmajor', *Language* 76(1): 110–22.

Squires, Lauren and Robin Queen (2011). 'Media clips collection: Creation and application for the linguistics classroom', *American Speech* 86(2): 220–34.

Stewart, Thomas W. (2016). *Contemporary Morphological Theories: A User's Guide.* Edinburgh: University of Edinburgh Press.

Stokes, Patricia D. (2005). *Creativity from Constraints: The Psychology of Breakthrough.* New York: Springer Publishing Company.

Stollznow, Karen (2017). ' "How many languages do you speak?" Perceptions and misconceptions about linguistics and linguists', *Lingua* 205: 15–28.

Stria, Ida (2016). *Inventing Languages, Inventing Words: Towards a Linguistic Worldview for Artificial Languages* [Dysertacje Wydziału Neofilologii UAM w Poznaniu 29]. Poznań: Wydziału Neofilologii UAM w Poznaniu.

Sudre, François (1866). *Langue musicale universelle.* Tours: Mazereau.

Suthers, Roderick A. (1990). 'Contributions to birdsong from the left and right sides of the intact syrinx', *Nature* 347: 473–7.

Swift, Jonathan (1726). *Travels into several remote nations of the world. In four parts. By Lemuel Gulliver, first a surgeon, and then a captain of several ships.* London: Benjamin Motte.

Szemerényi, Oswald (1999). *Introduction to Indo-European Linguistics.* Oxford & New York: Oxford University Press.

Tauer, John M. and Judith M. Harackiewicz (2004). 'The effects of cooperation and competition on intrinsic motivation and performance', *Journal of Personality and Social Psychology* 86(6): 849–61.

Tolkien, J. R. R. (1937). *The Hobbit.* London: George Allen & Unwin.

Tolkien, J. R. R. (1954). *The Fellowship of the Ring.* London: George Allen & Unwin.

Tolkien, J. R. R (1977). *The Silmarillion.* London: George Allen & Unwin.

Tolkien, J. R. R. (1981). *The letters of J. R. R. Tolkien.* Humphrey Carpenter & Christopher Tolkien (eds), Boston, MA: Houghton Mifflin.

Tolkien, J. R. R. (1997). 'A secret vice', in Christopher Tolkien (ed.), *The Monsters and the Citics, and Other Essays.* London: HarperCollins, 198–223.

Travis, Lisa (1989). 'Parameters of phrase structure', in Mark Baltin and Anthony Kroch (eds), *Alternative Conceptions of Phrase Structure.* Chicago, IL: University of Chicago Press, 263–79.

Trubetzkoy, Nikolai S. (1939). *Grundzüge der Phonologie.* Travaux de Cercle Linguistique de Prague 7. English Translation 1969: *Principles of Phonology.* Berkeley, CA: University of California Press.

Twenge, Jean M. (2009). 'Generational changes and their impact in the classroom: Teaching Generation Me', *Medical Education* 43(5): 398–405.

UNESCO Ad Hoc Expert Group on Endangered Languages (2003). *Language Vitality and Endangerment.* Online. http://www.unesco.org/new/fileadmin/MULTIMEDIA/ HQ/CLT/pdf/Language_vitality_and_endangerment_EN.pdf, accessed June 4, 2018.

Urquhart, Thomas (1652). *Ekskybalauron: or, The Discovery of a most exquisite Jewel, more precious then Diamonds inchased in Gold, the like whereof was never seen in any age; found in the kennel of Worcester-streets, the day after the Fight, and six before the Autumnal Æquinox, anno 1651. Serving in this place, to frontal a Vindication of the honour of Scotland, from that infamy, whereinto the Rigid Presbyterian party of that*

Nation, out of their Coveteousness and ambition, most dissembledly hath involved it. London: James Cottrel and Richard Baddely.

Urquhart, Thomas (1653). *Logopandecteision, or, an introduction to the universal language digested into these six several books, Neaudethaumata, Chrestasbeia, Cleronomaporia, Chryseomystes, Nelcadicastes, & Philoponauxesis.* London: Giles Calvert and Richard Tomlius.

Vakoch, Douglas (2011). *Communication with Extraterrestrial Intelligence.* Oxford: Oxford University Press.

Van Herk, Gerard (2017). 'The very big class project: Collaborative language research in large undergraduate classes', *American Speech* 83(2): 222–56.

van Urk, Coppe (2019). 'Object licensing in Fijian and the role of adjacency', *Natural Language and Linguistic Theory* 37: 1–52.

van Urk, Coppe and Norvin Richards (2015). 'Two components of long distance extraction: successive cyclicity in Dinka', *Linguistic Inquiry* 46: 113–55.

Velupillai, Viveka (2012). *An Introduction to Linguistic Typology.* Amsterdam: John Benjamins.

Versteegh, Kees (1993). 'Esperanto as a first language: Language acquisition with a restricted input', *Linguistics* 31: 539–55.

Villon, François (1489). *Jargon et jobellin dudit Villon.* Paris: Pierre Levet.

Wallace, Daniel (2013). *Star Wars: Book of Sith.* San Francisco, CA: Chronicle Books.

Walmsle, Ian (2015). *Light: A Very Short Introduction.* Oxford: Oxford University Press.

Walsh, Michael (2018). '"Language is like food . . . ": Links between language revitalization and health and well-being', in Leanne Hinton, Leena Huss, and Gerald Roche (eds), *The Routledge Handbook of Language Revitalization.* New York: Routledge, 5–12.

Warner Bros (2013). 'The language of Krypton', in *Man of Steel: Krypton by Design.* iBooks: Warner Bros. Digital Distribution.

Weihua, Yu (2013). 'Direct Method', in Michael Byram and Adelheid Hu (eds), *Routledge Encyclopedia of Language Teaching and Learning.* London and New York: Routledge, 200–2.

Weltman, Jerry (2015). *Language Processing and the Artificial Mind: Teaching Code Literacy in the Humanities.* Masters thesis. Baton Rouge: Louisiana State University.

Whaley, Lindsay J. (1997). *Introduction to Typology: The Unity and Diversity of Language.* Thousand Oaks, CA: SAGE Publications.

White, Thomas H. (2003). 'Extraterrestrial DX. Circa 1924: Will We Talk to Mars in August?' *SearchLites* 9(3): 3–4.

Whorf, Benjamin Lee (1936/2000). 'An American Indian model of the universe', in J. B. Carroll, (ed.), *Language, Thought and Reality: Selected Writings of Benjamin Lee Whorf.* Cambridge, MA: MIT Press, 57–64.

Whorf, Benjamin Lee (1940/2000). 'Science and linguistics', in J. B. Carroll (ed.), *Language, Thought and Reality: Selected Writings of Benjamin Lee Whorf.* Cambridge, MA: MIT Press, 207–19.

Wierzbicka, Anna (1985). 'Different cultures, different languages, different speech acts', *Journal of Pragmatics* 9: 145–78.

Wierzbicka, Anna (1986). 'Does language reflect culture? Evidence from Australian English', *Language in Society* 15: 349–73.

Wilkins, John (1668). *An Essay towards a Real Character and a Philosophical Language.* London: The Royal Society.

Williams, Mark (2016). *Ireland's Immortals: A History of the Gods of Irish Myth.* Princeton, NJ: Princeton University Press.

Wolfram, Walt (2017). 'Linguistic Accommodation: Critical Strategies in Public Engagement', *Linguistic Society of America Annual Meeting Plenary Address*. Austin, Texas.

Woods, Christopher (2013). 'Grammar and context: Enki & Ninhursag ll. 1–3 and a rare Sumerian construction', in David S. Vanderhooft and Abraham Winitzer (eds), *Literature as Politics, Politics as Literature*. Winona Lake, IN: Eisenbrauns, 503–26.

Yeats, William Butler (1899). 'The Hosting of the Sidhe', in *The Wind Among the Reeds*. London: Elkin Mathews, 1–2.

Zamenhof, L. L (1887). *Д-р Эсперанто Международный язык. Предисловие и полный учебник*. Warsaw: Ch. Kelter.

Zimmer, Ben (2009). Skxawng! *The New York Times Magazine*. December 9, MM20.

Zimmer, Ben (2016). 'The languages of "Star Wars: The Force Awakens": How the makers of the film crafted alien dialogue for the film's interplanetary ensemble', *The Wall Street Journal*. January 15. Online. https://www.wsj.com/articles/the-languages-of-star-wars-the-force-awakens-1452892741, accessed June 7, 2018.

Zimmerman, Barry J., Albert Bandura, and Manuel Martinez-Pons (1992). 'Self-motivation for academic attainment: The role of self-efficacy beliefs and personal goal setting', *American Educational Research Journal* 29(3): 663–76.

Index